D1488543

New York University Studies in Near Eastern Civilization
Number XIX

Peter Chelkowski and Jill N. Claster, General Editors

Number I: F. E. Peters, *Aristotle and the Arabs*
Number II: Jacob M. Landau, *Jews in Nineteenth-Century Egypt*
Number III: Lois Anita Giffen, *Theory of Profane Love Among the Arabs: The Development of the Genre*
Number IV: Lewis V. Thomas, *A Study of Naima,* Norman Itkowitz, editor
Number V: Carl Max Kortepeter, *Ottoman Imperialism During the Reformation: Europe and the Caucasus*
Number VI: Linda Fish Compton, *Andalušian Lyrical Poetry and Old Spanish Love Songs: The Muwashshah and Its Kharja*
Number VII: Peter J. Chelkowski, *Taʿziyeh: Ritual and Drama in Iran*
Number VIII: Arthur N. Young, *Saudi Arabia: The Making of a Financial Giant*
Number IX: Donald Quataert, *Social Disintegration and Popular Resistance in the Ottoman Empire, 1881–1908: Reactions to European Economic Penetration*
Number X: Tawfiq Al-Hakim, *The Return of Consciousness,* Bayly Winder, translator
Number XI: F. E. Peters, *Jerusalem and Mecca: The Typology of the Holy City in the Near East*
Number XII: Bruce Masters, *The Origins of Western Economic Dominance in the Middle East: Mercantilism and the Islamic Economy in Aleppo, 1600–1750*
Number XIII: Julian Baldick, *Mystical Islam: An Introduction to Sufism*
Number XIV: Martin Camaj, *Selected Poetry,* Leonard Fox, translator
Number XV: Aharon Layish, *Divorce in the Libyan Family: A Study Based on the Sijills of the Sharīʿa Courts of Ajdābiyya and Kufra*
Number XVI: Mona N. Mikhail, *Studies in the Short Fiction of Mahfouz and Idris*
Number XVII: Shmuel Moreh, *Live Theater and Dramatic Literature in the Medieval Arab World*
Number XVIII: Ronald C. Jennings, *Christians and Muslims in Ottoman Cyprus and the Mediterranean World, 1571–1640*

New York University Studies in Near Eastern Civilization

The participation of the New York University Press in the University's commitment to Near Eastern Studies provides the American and international public with a greater diversity of exposure to professional perceptions of the Near East. Focusing on those various peoples, religions, arts, and cultures of the Near East who throughout the centuries have profoundly influenced and given form to mankind's most fundamental concepts, and whose economic and political spheres have been wide reaching, this series, New York University Studies in Near Eastern Civilization, seeks, solicits, and publishes significant research in this ever vital area. The concept embraces many facets of the Near East, welcomes varied and even disparate interpretations as well as concentration on specific historical periods, including the whole spectrum of social scientific approaches. It is, moreover, particularly sensitive to work in two aspects of the area as a whole that reflect the Unviersity's expertise and concern, and that have perhaps received less attention than their excellence merits. These are literature and art. Again with the intention of widening the impact of New York University Press publications, the series welcomes translations of significant Near Eastern Literature, as an integral part of its attempt to deepen and enrich the experience of Near Eastern thought, prose, and poetry, for an audience unacquainted with the original languages.

Peter Chelkowski
Jill Claster
General Editors

A History of Arabic Astronomy

Planetary Theories during the Golden Age of Islam

George Saliba

NEW YORK UNIVERSITY PRESS
New York and London

NEW YORK UNIVERSITY PRESS
New York and London

Copyright © 1994 by New York University
All rights reserved

Library of Congress Cataloging-in-Publication Data
Saliba, George.
A history of Arabic astronomy : planetary theories during the golden age of Islam / George Saliba.
p. cm.—(New York University studies in Near Eastern civilization)
Includes bibliographical references and index.
ISBN 0-8147-7962-X
1. Astronomy, Arab. 2. Planetary theory—History. I. Title. II. Series.
QB23.S25 1994
520′.917′49270902—dc20 93-31745
CIP

New York University Press books are printed on acid-free paper, and their binding materials are chosen for strength and durability.

Manufactured in the United States of America

10 9 8 7 6 5 4 3 2 1

QB
23
.S25
1994

Contents

III. Observations and Observatories

IV. Theory and Observation

V. Arabic Astronomy and Copernicus

Preface

This book presents a series of articles, written over a period of two decades, all devoted to the study of the various aspects of non-Ptolemaic astronomy in medieval Islam. The texts, which formed the subject of these studies, were all written in Arabic and represent a small sample whose chronological domain extends from the eleventh to the fifteenth centuries. The articles themselves were originally intended to form a survey of such non-Ptolemaic theories in medieval Islam. They were originally published in various journals, some of which are not easily accessible to the present-day reader. Since they were published over a period of years, it became necessary to update some of the results reached in those articles in light of the more recent findings. A new essay was written for that purpose, as it was also intended to introduce these articles and to place them within the general framework of Islamic astronomy, by analyzing their contents and by raising questions regarding the place of such theories within medieval Islamic society at large.

The main thesis, for which this collection of articles can be used as evidence, is the one claiming that the period often called a period of decline in Islamic intellectual history was, scientifically speaking from the point of veiw of astronomy, a very productive period in which astronomical theories of the highest order were produced. Some of the techniques and mathematical theorems developed during this period and discussed in these articles were identical to those that were employed by Copernicus in developing his own non-Ptolemaic astronomy.

Most importantly, these articles shed a more needed light on the conditions under which such theories were developed in medieval Islam. They demonstrate very clearly the distinction that was drawn between astronomical and astrological activities. Contrary to common perceptions about medieval Islam, these articles also demonstrate the accommodation that was obviously reached between religion and astronomy in particular, and the degree to which such astronomical planetary theories were supported, and at times even financed, by the religious community itself. This is in contradistinction to the systematic attacks the same religious community leveled against astrology.

In order to reduce the cost of reproducing these articles photomechanically, we have made no attempt to correct the various typos and oversights that existed in the original publications. After reviewing them rather carefully, I have judged them to be of minor significance, and believe they can be easily corrected by an attentive reader. We have made some attempt, however, to improve the quality of the pictures and diagrams by redrawing some and rephotographing others.

Since the articles were originally published in several journals, the original format and pagination has been slightly altered to fit the standard format of the book. Readers wishing to refer to the pages of the original publications, however, may still do so by calculating the corresponding page number from the present book pagination. This can be done in all cases except for article 2, "Astrology/Astronomy, Islamic," which was originally in double columns and was reset to conform to the present book format. Pages of all other articles were simply reproduced in facsimile here with some adjustments to the photographs and the diagrams, but not to the textual contents of the page. The original pages can therefore be recalculated by using the following page equivalences:

1. *Arab Studies Quarterly* 4 (1982): 211–25, now pages 51–65.
2. *Dictionary of the Middle Ages* 1 (1982): 616–24, now pages 66–81.
3. *Journal for the History of Arabic Science* 4 (1980): 376–403, now pages 85–112.
4. *Isis* 70 (1979): 571–76, now pages 113–18.
5. *Journal for the History of Arabic Science* 3 (1979): 3–18, now pages 119–34.
6. *Journal for the History of Astronomy* 20 (1989): 157–64, now pages 135–42.

7. *Archives Internationales d'Histoire des Sciences* 37 (1987): 3–20, now pages 143–60.
8. *Isis* 74 (1983): 388–401, now pages 163–76.
9. *Journal for the History of Astronomy* 16 (1985): 113–22, now pages 177–86.
10. *Zeitschrift für Geschichte der Arabisch-Islamischen Wissenschaften* 2 (1985): 47–67, now pages 187–207.
11. *Centaurus* 29 (1986): 249–71, now pages 208–30.
12. *Journal for the History of Astronomy* 18 (1987): 35–43, now pages 233–41.
13. *Revue de Synthèse* 108 (1987): 361–73, now pages 245–57.
14. *Arabic Sciences and Philosophy* 1 (1991): 67–99, now pages 258–90.
15. *Zeitschrift für Geschichte der Arabisch-Islamischen Wissenschaften* 1 (1984): 73–87, now pages 291–305.

I thank the editors of the above journals and publications to whom these copyrights belong for allowing me to reproduce the material cited.

The curators of the Oriental collections, Dr. Colin Wakefield of the Bodleian Library (Oxford) and Dr. Jan Just Witkam of the Universiteitsbibliotheek of Rijks Universiteit (Leiden), as well as C. A. Mescall, head of the photographic services administration at the British Library, have all been very gracious in supplying photographs from their collections and in granting permission for the material to be reproduced here. Doris Nicholson of the Bodleian has been extremely helpful even when my communications were sometimes confusing. I owe her a special gratitude.

Introduction

This book is not a comprehensive history of Arabic astronomy. It is an attempt to focus attention on a very important episode of the history of the planetary theories that have been studied so far and were devised between the eleventh and fifteenth centuries. Planetary theories in this context refer to the various constructions of geometric models that represented the motion of the celestial spheres and planets that were different from the ones represented by the models produced by Ptolemy and designed to describe the same phenomena. Most important, this new model-building activity and the new planetary theories were not supposed to suffer from the same contradictions that had plagued the Ptolemaic models.

Because the production of these alternative models was a direct result of the dissatisfaction with the Ptolemaic models and with the whole structure of Ptolemaic astronomy, I consider this episode in the history of Arabic astronomy to have been the most creative one. It was through this type of activity that one could document the pervasive criticism of Greek astronomy that finally led to its demise during the Renaissance. I want to express a note of caution to the reader about the emphasis I place on the achievements in this area during the five centuries covered in this book. This emphasis reflects my own prejudices, in that I chose to investigate this specific domain of Arabic astronomy and not another. This does not mean that other areas of astronomy could not be similarly studied and that they would not produce equally promising results.

This book therefore makes no attempt to cover other important areas of

Arabic astronomy. For example, the area of computational astronomy, which is usually treated in the astronomical handbooks called *azyāj* (sing. *zīj*), is not covered here.[1] Similarly, I make no attempt to include the area of what one could call "sacred" astronomy, which covers problems related mostly to religious matters and is usually treated in the *mīqāt* (timekeeping) literature that was created during this period and engaged the most active astronomers of the time. Quantitatively, *mīqāt* literature became the most abundant and dominated the astronomical intellectual progress of the period. I will not treat the topic of astronomical instruments in any fashion, even though the field saw the most brilliant developments in Islamic instrument making during those centuries.[2] I will not study the institutions of astronomy, namely the most impressive observatories, which were also developed during this period into veritable professional centers, for these were already studied by Aydın Sayılı.[3]

The articles reprinted in this book form a part of a much larger research project. Although they were intended to survey only one field of astronomy, that is, the field of planetary theories, I hoped that they would also shed light on other aspects of the general history of Arabic science in order to give us a wider picture of Arabic science overall.

From that perspective, my original intent was for these articles to shed light on four fundamental questions related to the development of Arabic science in medieval Islamic times. First, I wanted to determine to what extent the so-called age of decline in Islamic intellectual history, usually defined as beginning around the end of the twelfth century, was applicable to the field of astronomy. I wanted to investigate the pervasiveness of this claim by first determining whether it included the field of astronomy, and then, by concentrating on astronomy, I wanted to establish a profile of the causes that led to that decline if it indeed took place.

Second, I wanted to investigate the relationship between astronomy and the religious sciences in order to determine if astronomy experienced the same kind of treatment as philosophy,[4] which was claimed to have been the cause of the intellectual decline in medieval Islam. I thought that by concentrating on the period of decline, and by surveying the astronomical activities over a period of a few centuries, I would certainly be able to note the general decline of astronomical activities if this decline did indeed take place, and if astronomy did indeed face the same fate as philosophy.

Third, I wanted to determine the geographical range of astronomical activities, and to determine if there was any reason to think that the Mongol invasion and the destruction of Baghdad in 1258 A.D. left any impact on astronomical activities. The reason why I pursued that line of research has to do with the need to investigate the veracity of the commonly repeated claim that the decline in Islamic intellectual progress can be attributed to the devastation of Baghdad, the Abbasid center, at the hands of the Mongols in 1258. My reasoning went as follows: if the Mongol invasion did indeed bring the intellectual activities in Baghdad to a halt, then we should expect the same Mongol invasion to leave similar effects in other areas. The fact that the Mamluk areas in Syria and Egypt did not come under direct Mongol rule and did not suffer the same devastation as Baghdad should allow us to test this hypothesis at least in one field, namely astronomy. I would have believed the claim to be true if I had found that astronomical activities continued to flourish in Syria and Egypt but declined in the eastern lands that fell under the Mongols.

Finally, I wanted to investigate the temporal and geographical boundaries of that decline. I wanted to know how long it took for this decline to become widespread, when it really started, and how long it lasted. Also I wanted to know if there had been any geographical areas that escaped this decline, and if so, what conditions prevailed in those areas.

Such questions could have been answered in several ways. One may spend several years reading the relevant astronomical works, devise some organizing scheme to synthesize them, and hope that one day the results of this research will become manageable enough for an analytical integrated answer to emerge.

Another alternative was to collect all the data, in this instance the manuscripts of all the astronomical works that were written during this age of decline, produce critical editions of these works, translate them, write commentaries to make them accessible to the larger community of scholars, and then hope that enough of these texts would become available to produce a synthesis and answer the remaining questions.

A third possibility was to continue the practice already started by E. S. Kennedy and his collaborators in the late fifties and early sixties,[5] namely to survey the manuscripts and publish descriptions of their contents, and only occasionally quote the contents of the texts in translation. If a large-enough number of these works could be analyzed this way, then one could reach some conclusions regarding the questions raised above.

Finally, there was the approach I adopted here. I first had to determine the kinds of texts that I deemed illustrative enough of the kind of astronomical activities that were taking place during this period. Then I had to select from these texts those which best illustrated the kinds of problems that captured the concerns of the astronomers of the period. Having established a group of significant texts, I edited them whenever possible, translated them, and supplied a commentary that would explain their contents and place them within the larger context of astronomical activities. In this fashion, I thought I would bring the reader a step closer to appreciating the importance of the questions raised above. I also thought it necessary to supply concrete textual evidence that would help in the assessment of the quality of the intellectual achievements of that period.

In practical terms, none of these approaches can be judged as inherently superior to the others. Each approach has advantages as well as disadvantages. Moreover, all suffer from some practical hurdles that cannot easily be overcome. Ideally, all the available texts should be critically edited, translated, and commented upon, which would then enable us to address unanswered questions. But because of the hundreds of texts and manuscripts involved, I deemed this approach impractical at this time. It will take generations of historians of Arabic astronomy to accomplish this task.

The alternative adopted here required that a group of representative texts be assembled and studied as extensively as possible, that the novelties they bring into the field be isolated, and that they are then organized so they can be used as supporting textual evidence for the kinds of conclusions we seek. The articles presented here should therefore be seen as the first attempt to shed some light on the history of Arabic science after the eleventh century, by use of data gleaned from the field of astronomy. This introduction is the first attempt to synthesize the results obtained to date.

I am aware that the articles included here were published over a period of several years, and that they reflect my changing perceptions of what is important. There is also some inevitable duplication. More important, when read together, the articles reflect the changes in my own thinking about the importance and the context of the results.

To give only one example, the reader will note that I had originally accepted the popular opinion about the motivation behind model-building, which was done specifically in protest to Ptolemaic astronomy. The prevalent opinion was that this activity was motivated mainly by philosophical considerations,[6] and hence should not be seen as a reflection of a genuine scientific spirit, however that spirit may be defined. When I later considered the works of Ibn al-Shāṭir of Damascus (d. 1375), especially his objections to the

Ptolemaic solar model,[7] I began to realize the importance of observational data with respect to model-building, as well as the intricate interplay between theory and observation. It was then that I began to see the model-building activity as part of a very complex larger scientific conceptual scheme in which philosophical considerations were only one component. I began to see this activity as part of a proper examination of the nature of science, where the emphasis was put on the need for consistency between the various scientific fields and on the need to present scientific results as part of a coherent whole, where the axioms and the results derived therefrom remain consistently interdependent. One should read all the articles collected here before being able to come to grips with the kind of evidence used to support such conclusions. I will return to this point below.

Format of the Book

There remains the question of the format of the book. Why approach these results in a series of articles, and not in a coherent integrated unit like a book that consists of an introduction, a conclusion, and several chapters in between? The answer has something to do with the nature of the subject matter being used here.

The planetary theories that are studied here are usually treated in a specific type of astronomical texts, known as *hay'a* texts. The term *hay'a* itself has no equivalent in the Greek tradition and is difficult to translate. It can best be described as a conceptually organizing term that refers to the type of astronomical texts in which the form (i.e., *hay'a* = form, configuration, etc.) and behavior of the celestial spheres were usually discussed. *ʿIlm al-hay'a* (Science of *hay'a*), on the other hand, was understood during the period with which we are concerned as part of a larger discipline called *ʿilm al-nujūm* (Science of the Stars). But astronomers who wrote such *hay'a* texts wanted their work to be considered distinct from that of the astrologers, which was usually included under the same more general term *ʿilm al-nujūm*. The social, religious, and intellectual reasons for this distinction are touched upon in some of the general background articles collected in this book. We will also return to the question regarding the rise of *ʿilm al-hay'a* later in this introduction.

These *hay'a* texts had their origin in the synthesizing attempts, which were begun as early as the ninth century. Astronomers writing on the subject wished to combine two Greek traditions represented by two works of Ptolemy, namely, the tradition of the *Almagest,* which has a mathematical description of the motions of the celestial spheres, based on actual observations, and the tradition of the *Planetary Hypotheses,* where the same, and more qualitative, description is applied to the celestial spheres as real physical bodies. Once these two traditions were brought together in the *hay'a* texts under a single tradition, writers of the *hay'a* texts were forced to consider a new set of problems that looked like contradictions to them. In the *Almagest,* Ptolemy had constructed mathematical models that accounted rather well for the observational data he assembled. And throughout the *Almagest,* he never lost sight of the physical reality of the planetary configurations described by the models, although he did not often dwell on it. In the *Planetary Hypotheses,* on the other hand, Ptolemy spoke of the same planetary configurations as having an undeniable physical reality. As we shall see again and again, problems would arise if one tried to apply the strict sense of the physical reality known from the *Planetary Hypotheses* onto the mathematical models depicted in the *Almagest.*

Naturally, as the *hay'a* tradition began to mature,[8] these problems and the sophisticated concepts they generated began to emerge. By the eleventh century a series of analytical texts began to be written in which the authors attempted to identify these problems, thereby casting doubt on the inherited Ptolemaic edifice of astronomy.[9] Such works were commonly grouped under the category of *shukūk* (doubts). They are only marginally discussed in some of the articles assembled here because they contained only criticisms of Ptolemaic astronomy and offered no alternative mathematical models, which form the general theme of this collection.

The texts with which we are concerned here, and which were expressly written for the purpose of reforming Ptolemaic astronomy by offering new mathematical models that were consistent from both the mathematical and the physical points of view, usually went a step beyond the doubts expressed against Ptolemy. They offered new alternatives, and were all clearly perceived as belonging to the continually developing *hay'a* tradition where such alternatives were the main concern.

We should remember that there are tens of such *hay'a* texts that have been identified so far. And if we count the commentaries on each of them, which often contain new original material, that number can be increased to the hundreds. Because none of these *hay'a* texts have yet been critically edited, translated, and explained,[10] a coherent analytical book analyzing and integrating their contents cannot yet be written. The articles collected here therefore deal with illustrative sections of what is obviously a much larger body of literature represented by these texts. Whenever possible, and when the policies of the respective journals permitted it, the relevant sections have included editions of the original Arabic texts, translations, and general historical and technical commentaries. The collection of these various sections of texts should at least provide an overview of this creative activity and give some sense of the language and the context in which the activity took place. This also explains why a few Arabic sections are reprinted here, since they form part of that textual evidence.

The sample illustrative evidence presented in these articles should be understood as a first step in a much larger plan that would ultimately include the editions and analyses of all the relevant texts. With the textual examples presented here, we can tell that such evidence does exist, such research is possible, and that such results promise to be fruitful.

Methodology and the Range of This Book

The reader will note that the range of activities covered in these articles is mainly limited to the works produced in the eastern domain of medieval Islam between the eleventh and the fifteenth centuries. It so happens that the most famous observatory of medieval Islam, namely that which was built at Maragha in northwest Iran in 1259 during the reign of the Ilkhanid dynasty, fell within this period. Naturally, the work of the astronomers associated with the Maragha observatory, sometimes referred to as the Maragha School production,[11] constituted the central portion of that range. This does not mean that similar activities were not taking place in the western part of medieval Islam or that no such activities were taking place beyond the fifteenth century in the east. In fact, we shall soon see that there are a few scattered hints that reveal the existence of similar works that were being written in the western part of Islam as early as the eleventh century, and others definitely beyond the fifteenth century in the east. What we have here is only a reflection of my research interests during the last few years. More will certainly come in the future.

From another perspective, assembling the evidence in the manner I have done here serves another general purpose and has been my main motivation in producing this book. That is, since the articles all deal with astronomical activities taking place after the eleventh century, they constitute by their very nature a statement about the type of scientific production during that period that was commonly known as a period of decline in Islamic intellectual history. In that regard, these articles shed some light on the kinds of questions regarding the development of Arabic science that we asked above. As we shall see below, the evidence surveyed in this collection of articles will also shed light on the whole concept of periodization, and will cast doubt on the validity of the so-called period of decline in specific. In fact, one of the articles included in this collection, *Synthèse* (1987), deals with this very point. But more will be said in the sequel.

On the basis of the same evidence, the subtitle of the book intentionally designates this period as the Golden Age of Islam. This may be disturbing to students of Islamic intellectual history who are used to dismissing the works produced during this period as insignificant. What the evidence presented here now suggests is that if we can find such original work in astronomical planetary theories, and such mathematical sophistication and maturity in the presentation of results, shouldn't we consider other disciplines as well, and try to find out if such vigorous scientific activity can be substantiated in other fields? In fact, at various points in these articles I suggest that such research would promise to be extremely rewarding.

Moreover, once the traditional periodization is abandoned, shouldn't we seek to explore the extent to which a new periodization can be restructured? Can't we begin to refine our results, and speak of decline and renaissance in certain fields, and not in others? Couldn't we then investigate the variations in the actual output among the various scientific fields in order to find out more about the social formative forces that allowed certain disciplines to decline and others to flourish? The evidence presented here only encourages us to seek answers to such questions, and supplies concrete textual evidence from at least one field, namely, the astronomical field of planetary theories.

The Structure of This Collection of Articles

There still remains a need to introduce the structural relationship that connects this collection of articles. My central thesis here is to argue for the existence of a very sophisticated group of astronomical texts, written between the eleventh and the fifteenth centuries, all dealing with planetary theories. Samples of these texts are analyzed in five separate articles, here grouped under the subtitle, "Development of Planetary Theories." The sample is not intended to be exhaustive, rather it is supposed to be just that—a sample. It demonstrates, however, the genres of writings in which such theories can be found. The works of the astronomers partially studied in these five articles include those of Abū ʿUbayd al-Jūzjānī (d. c. 1070), the student of Avicenna, and the two distinguished astronomers, Mu'ayyad al-Dīn al-ʿUrḍī (d. 1266), and Naṣīr al-Dīn al-Ṭūsī (d. 1274). These genres include among other things the straightforward objections to Ptolemaic astronomy, which were accompanied by an attempt to resolve the contradictions therein. They may also include a general overhaul of Ptolemaic astronomy—as one would find in a typical *hay'a* text. And finally, they may include the subgenre of astronomical commentaries, a field that has not yet been well studied but promises to reveal very interesting results, as was already shown here in the case of Ṭūsī's commentary on the *Almagest*.

Two introductory essays are included for the specific purpose of placing the planetary theories in the larger framework of Arabic science. In these essays I deal with some very general questions relating to the early history of Arabic science, its development, and its functioning within the larger Islamic society. Several of these questions merit full studies in order to pursue the results only hinted at in these articles, and I hope that the results will trigger such studies. But most important, these general essays allow the reader to appreciate the motivation behind the development of the planetary theories. On the other hand, by attempting to place this astronomical activity within the general framework of Arabic science, the general essays sharpen the focus for the need to write the history of Arabic astronomy as part of the general history of Arabic science, and not as part of the general history of astronomy alone.

The next four articles, grouped under the subtitle "Observations and Observatories," are devoted to the investigation of the relationship between observations and model building in particular. But they also raise questions of great interest to other fields of research, such as the relationship between observations and actual ephemerids or *zīj* production. This investigation is concluded by the article entitled "Theory and Observation."

The reason why this line of research was undertaken in the first place has to do with the general assessments regarding the motivation behind the model building activity and the role played by these planetary theories in the general history of astronomy that were beginning to appear in the secondary literature at the time when these articles were written. As we have seen above, the commonly held opinion, which was beginning to emerge then, was that these activities were not at all motivated by the actual observations and were only philosophically driven. Some have used terms to describe the activities of the

Maragha astronomers to imply that the activities were some sort of philosophical tinkering with Ptolemaic astronomy and had no bearing on the reality of the observable physical phenomena.[12]

In order to investigate the relationship between theory and observation, I thought that sample texts devoted to that activity specifically should be included in this collection. Knowing that other more elaborate texts touching the core of the subject, such as the book *Taᶜlīq al-Arṣād* by Ibn al-Shāṭir of Damascus (d. 1375), were no longer available for investigation and are presumed to be lost, I thought that the next best thing to do was to study some of the available texts that touch upon the same issue, although in a marginal fashion. The works of Yaḥyā ibn abī al-Shukr al-Maghribī (d. 1283) and Mu'ayyad al-Dīn al-ᶜUrḍī (d. 1266) received the lion's share of this attention. The reader should note from this group of articles the concern expressed by these medieval astronomers for the methodology of observation. In the case of ᶜUrḍī we note that he had abandoned the Ptolemaic technique for solar observations as known from the *Almagest,* and he also abandoned the *fuṣūl* method, which was developed by early ninth-century astronomers who were dealing with the shortcomings of the same Ptolemaic method; instead he opted for a third method that allowed for the simplification of the techniques and increased the reliability of the results.

Maghribī, on the other hand, seems to have undertaken a full-scale project aimed at reevaluating the whole Ptolemaic enterprise. From the fragment of the notebook that is studied in two of these articles, the reader can verify the extent to which Maghribī was interested in reinvestigating the parameters of Ptolemaic astronomy.

Although Maghribī's program may have had more to do with the need to update astronomical handbooks *(zījes)* (he did this by producing his *zīj* incorporating the new parameters he had found through his new observations) than with the needs of the planetary theorists, it is hard to determine whether the planetary theorists could not have made use of such research anyway. If the case of Ibn al-Shāṭir, whose work on the apparent diameters of the sun and the moon is studied in the next article, is any indication, one can see how a simple parameter determination such as the apparent diameter of the sun did indeed lead to the reconstruction of the Ptolemaic solar model.

More important, the documentation of such observational activities is only begun here, and the preliminary results have already demonstrated that the study of such documents can be extremely useful for the ongoing research on planetary theories. Yet the study of these documents is important in its own right, because, as the article devoted to Maghribī's observational notebook shows, other results relating to the technology used for these observational activities is inherently interesting enough to be investigated on its own.

Other questions relating to other fields of astronomy also benefit from this research, as in the case of determining which of the *zījes* that were produced at the Maragha Observatory did indeed benefit from the fresh observations conducted there. By establishing the connection between the observational program to determine new parameters and how they are used in new *zīj* compositions, as was done by Maghribī, one can also shed light on the historical question relating to the numerous *zījes* produced throughout medieval Islamic times which were actually based on fresh observations.

This relationship between the new observations and the production of *zījes* becomes more significant in light of the remark made by ʿUrḍī, one of the planetary theorists who did not produce his own *zīj* nor had his own observational program, when he accuses *zīj* authors of deliberately changing the parameters of their *zījes* to give the impression that the *zījes* were based on new observations.

The climax of this activity of observational astronomy was undoubtedly reached by Ibn al-Shāṭir of Damascus, not only because he was conscious of the relationship between observations and model building, as he has demonstrated in his new solar model and his book *Taʿlīq al-Arṣād,* which was devoted to the subject, but because he was also aware of the need to answer the philosophical questions that were being raised in connection with the inherited Ptolemaic astronomy. In a different connection, I demonstrated how Ibn al-Shāṭir's new models for all the planets were also subject to the same philosophical scrutiny that was applied to the Ptolemaic models. The classical objection to the use of eccentrics by Ptolemy, for example—which is in a way a philosophical objection more than an observational one—was also answered by Ibn al-Shāṭir by adopting models that contained no eccentrics whatsoever.

I consider this intricate relationship among the observational activities, the philosophical objections, the actual celestial motions, and the need to represent these motions with sound geometric models that can still account for the observational phenomena to be the height of maturity as far as the astronomical sciences were concerned. When coupled with the all-encompassing Aristotelian cosmology regarding the place of the earth in the cosmos and the unavailability of a gravitational theory that could replace it, one can see why the work of someone like Ibn al-Shāṭir could be said to have achieved all that is possible within the constraints of the prevailing scientific doctrines. This is not a trivial result, because one can still wonder why Copernicus used the same models as Ibn al-Shāṭir and then transformed them to fit a heliocentric universe with no gravitational force to hold it together. Philosophically speaking, Ibn al-Shāṭir had a much more integrated system than Copernicus.

As we shall argue again, this level of sophistication in astronomical research was not known in the previous centuries, and its very sophistication and originality should force us to reconsider the general characterization of this period as a period of decline. It should also stimulate research in other fields in order to ascertain whether a similar sophistication can be established. To take only one instance, I would find it hard to believe that astronomers who were capable of using already existing geometric theorems, and adding some of their own, were not in direct contact with first-rate mathematicians who could supply mathematical results with equal sophistication.

Methodologically, the last three articles, grouped under the subtitle "Arabic Astronomy and Copernicus," attempt to open two new lines of research in Arabic astronomy. On the one hand, they offer a sample of the kind of results that could be achieved by pursuing the line of investigation explored here regarding the relationship between the mathematical theorems devised and employed by the Maragha astronomers and the same theorems employed by Copernicus (1473–1543) some two to three centuries later. The example given in the last article touches upon the use of the ʿUrḍī lemma in ʿUrḍī's *hay'a* text, and its identical use later by Copernicus in an attempt to overcome the same difficulty in the Ptolemaic model for the upper planets. Others have investigated the use of another theorem, now called the Ṭūsī Couple, by both Naṣīr al-Dīn al-Ṭūsī and by Copernicus, which is discussed here only tangentially in onc of the remaining two articles.[13] Some have gone as far as to suggest that Copernicus, in his use of the Ṭūsī Couple, used the same alphabetic letters to designate the same geometric points as Ṭūsī did three hundred years earlier.[14]

Naturally, this line of research has now led historians of Copernican and Renaissance astronomy to raise the same questions in regard to the same problems encountered while investigating the Copernican models. ʿUrḍī's lemma, for example, appears to have been the center of investigation by Maestlin (1550–1631) in his correspondence with Kepler (1571–1630).[15] Byzantine astronomy has also been reexamined in an attempt to determine how Copernicus may have gained access to the results of the earlier Muslim astronomers.[16] More about this connection will be said later.

The second line of research signaled by these results has to do with the history of Arabic astronomy itself, irrespective of its relationship to that of Copernicus. In the second article in this group I attempt to plot a program of research specifically designed to answer questions relating to the development of these planetary theories, the results uncovered so far, and the routes that future research could possibly take. This article supplies evidence that the activity of model building went on beyond the fifteenth century (the upper limit of this collection of articles), and that future research may uncover the true dimensions of this activity after examining a variety of texts that still must be consulted. The significance of this research lies in the fact that it will help us determine the role played by astronomy within Islamic society.

More significantly, if one can show that the model building activity continued to be pursued even after contact with Europe and after the transfer of Copernican astronomy to the east had been completed, then one may be able to examine that phenomenon alone independently of its relationship to the Copernican theory. In other words, we may be able to produce a better assessment of the role played by these planetary models in the scientific outlook of Islamic society even during a period of intellectual "decline."

Planetary Theories and the Problem of Periodization

The evidence presented in these articles establishes beyond doubt that the activities of model building which seem to have started around the eleventh century did indeed continue to develop and to take different forms and shapes until at least the early part of the fifteenth century. In fact, other evidence that is currently being studied pushes this period of creativity well into the sixteenth century, if not beyond.

Having established that the upper limit of this period is yet to be determined, one finds that the starting point is equally elusive. We have conveniently taken the eleventh century as a starting point for three main reasons. First, the eleventh century was chosen because it was the century during which Ibn al-Haytham had composed his seminal work, *al-Shukūk ʿAlā Baṭlamyūs,* which was published in the early 1970s.[17] Second, although we know of earlier works that may have raised doubts against Ptolemy, Ibn al-Haytham's work remains to be the most extensive and most sophisticated of all works that have come to light so far. Third, recent investigations, mostly published in the articles selected here, have already demonstrated the abundance of such eleventh-century works. The names of Abū ʿUbayd al-Jūzjānī

(c. 1070), Bīrūnī (d. c. 1050), and the anonymous Spanish astronomer referred to in the article, "The Astronomical Tradition of Maragha: A Historical Survey and Prospects for Future Research," all attest to the productivity of this century. But one should not forget that these are the works that have been discovered so far, and that there is some evidence that this genre of writing, whether in astronomy or in other subjects, had already begun earlier.[18]

For astronomy in particular, the major work achieved during the previous two centuries was not unrelated to the development of planetary theories, although at first glance it appears to have been restricted to the adjustment of basic parameters that were found to be at variance with the Ptolemaic ones. The sources speak of the extensive astronomical activities conducted during the reign of al-Ma'mūn (813–833) by such famous astronomers as al-Khwārizmī (fl. 830), al-Marwarūdhī (fl. 832), al-Jawharī (fl. 832), Sind Ibn ᶜAlī (d. after 864), Ibn Kathīr al-Farghānī (d. c. 850), and Yaḥya Ibn Abī Manṣūr (fl. 830). Just after that period, or, according to some, contemporaneously with it, Ḥabash al-ᶜḤāsib (d. c. 864–874) was supposed to have done his work. And so did the three brothers who were known as the Sons of Mūsā Ibn Shākir (all died during the second half of the ninth century). The next generation included Thābit ibn Qurra (d. 901), followed by the generation of Muḥammad Ibn Jābir al-Battānī (d. 929) and later by Abū al-Wafā' al-Būzjānī (d. 998). By way of correcting the Ptolemaic parameters, the activities of these early astronomers included the reinvestigation of the position of the solar apogee, the motion of precession, and the size of the solar equation, among other things, all concepts related in one way or another to the improvements in the observational methods that were introduced during Islamic timcs.

One need only refer to the famous *fuṣūl* method which was devised sometime during the nith century in order to understand the full significance of the new observational techniques that began to expose the shortcomings of Ptolemaic astronomy. Of course, the mere span of time separating Ptolemy from ninth-century Baghdad must have played an important role in exaggerating the mistakes that were too small to be noticed during the time of Ptolemy. Values such as those used for precession or for the position of the solar apogee were in all likelihood not too different from the values that were determined by Hipparchus a mere two centuries earlier. But after another seven hundred years, the variations in these parameters became too large to be tolerated. As a result, astronomers of Islamic times applied themselves to the reexamination of these parameters and corrected Ptolemy's basic values without too much fanfare. After that it was difficult to find any astronomer who would still use the Ptolemaic values.

This step was important in itself for the reconstruction of the new astronomical theories; ultimately it also had something to do with the kind of planetary theories that would be developed later. But more importantly, it stimulated a new kind of theoretical research independent of the application for which this research was designed. It raised the question of the adequacy of the methodology Ptolemy used to determine these parameters in the first place. In the case of the solar apogee, the old method of determining the length of the seasons by observing the times of equinoxes and the solstices came under severe attack, and rightly so because of the immense difficulty associated with the determination of the exact times of the solstices. The alternate *fuṣūl* method which required the observation of the declination of the sun during the middle of the seasons, when that declination could be much more precisely determined, became the new method of choice. Shortly after that, a variation on the new method was also introduced where the process was further refined to require only three observations, two of which were taken at opposition from one another. The improved values for precession and the inclination of the ecliptic were in all likelihood obtained through the use of more refined methods and instruments.

But the import of these activities, at this early period, went beyond the establishment of more accurate parameters and also questioned the theoretical foundation of astronomy. The liberating effect that such activities must have engendered must have been felt by all practicing astronomers, giving them the confidence to push their own research to the frontiers of the field.

It was in this environment that new genres of astronomical literature began to appear. Some undertook to write commentaries on the *Almagest,* others translated it yet another time, while still others tried to abridge it or to put it in the context of other astronomical writings. Works such as those of Ibn Kathīr al-Farghānī, Thābit Ibn Qurra, al-Battānī, and Abū al-Wafā' al-Buzjānī, al-Nayrīzī (d. 922) and later al-Ḥāzimī (fl. c. eleventh century) were all concerned with this new approach to astronomy, in one way or another, and each according to the level of his own interest in the subject.

By the eleventh century, this process of reexamination reached its maturity, both on the theoretical level of methodology and procedures and on the level of observations and practical applications. Once the obvious errors were noted, analyzed, and corrected, attention was directed to the deeper theoretical issues, namely the issues regarding the foundations of the science of astronomy and the need for the harmonization between its mathematical and physical aspects. In all probability, this type of questioning could not have begun if the new Arabic astronomical tradition had not emerged sometimes during the ninth and tenth centuries, when the two traditions of the *Almagest* and the *Planetary Hypotheses* of Ptolemy were merged into the nascent *hay'a* texts. The emergence of this *hay'a* tradition should be investigated more thoroughly in order to determine the conditions under which it came into being.

The historical biographical sources are not very clear on the difference between *hay'a* texts and the type of texts dealing with the structure of the celestial spheres. One reads, for example, that the same Yaᶜqūb b. Ṭāriq who was active during the reign of the Abbasid caliph al-Manṣūr (754–775) produced two types of astronomical texts: a *zīj*-type claimed to have been based on one of the Indian *sidhhantas,* obviously resulting from Yaᶜqūb Ibn Ṭāriq's cooperation with al-Fazzārī in the translation of such *sidhhantas* from Sanskrit into Arabic, and another type of texts referred to in the sources as *Tarkīb al-Aflāk.*[19] This second type of text is of great importance to our discussion at this point.

The current presumption is that Ibn Ṭāriq was working before the time of the great translation movement which produced Arabic versions of such Greek scientific masterpieces as the *Almagest* and the *Elements*. This movement is usually dated to the early Abbasid period and is rarely connected with the previous reign of the Umayyads. The assumption then is that no Arabic versions of the *Almagest* or of the *Planetary Hypothesis* were available to Ibn Ṭāriq on the basis of which he could begin to raise such theoretical questions as the ones which were assumedly raised in *Tarkīb al-Aflāk*. It is unfortunate that the text itself did not survive to be subjected to modern scrutiny.

Others whose work was recognized by biographers as belonging to the same *hay'a* tradition and who came slightly later, during the next century, included Ibn Kathīr al-Farghānī, whose text was known under several titles, among them *Jawāmiᶜ ᶜilm al-falak,* and which was alternatively also known as *Kitāb al-hay'a,* at least according to one manuscript.[20] If we disregard the reference by Ibn al-Nadīm to a *hay'a* text by Jābir b. Ḥayyān (eighth century?), for reasons that have to do with the time this author flourished and the authenticity of such a text, we can still refer to various other texts with the same or similar titles about which we are slightly more certain, such as the work of Sahl b. Bishr (c. 850), *Kitāb al-hay'a wa-ʿilm al-ḥisāb,* ʿUṭārid b. Muḥammad (ninth century), *Kitāb tarkīb al-aflāk,* Abu Maʿshar (d. 886), *Kitāb hay'at al-falak,* and Abū Bakr al-Rāzī (d. 925) during the next century, *Kitāb hay'at al-ʿālam.* In the western part of the Muslim world, we also know of a similar text, *Kitāb al-hay'a,* attributed to a traditionalist and Quranic exegete by the name of Qāsim b. Muṭraf, who must have lived in Andalusia during the tenth century.[21] Unfortunately, none of these texts is known to have survived, and we cannot be certain about their contents. The only surviving text from the ninth century which is referred to as a *hay'a* text is the one attributed to Qusṭā b. Lūqā (c. 860) according to one manuscript, and to the sons of Mūsā according to another. This text does indeed represent the beginnings of what came to be known later as a *hay'a* tradition.

If we were to speculate about the other texts, beginning with Ibn Ṭāriq's *Tarkīb al-Aflāk,* or even the earlier work of Jābir b. Ḥayyān, they were most likely written in the environment in which two other traditions were coming together at that time or slightly earlier. The first tradition was that of Greek astronomy. It included star names, elementary mathematical astronomy required for horoscope casting and the like, and elementary general astronomy. The latter was represented by astrological Byzantine texts such as the *Eisagogeka* of Paulus Alexandrinus, which was known and paraphrased in the Syriac tradition some two centuries earlier than the Arabic translations.[22] The second was the tradition of pre-Islamic Arabic astronomy relating to *anwā'* (a type of investigation relating to seasonal variations thought to be produced by the rising and setting of the fixed stars), which, by the time of Fazzārī and Ibn Ṭāriq, had already merged with the Islamic cosmology as depicted in the Quranic text. Added to this can be the active participation of early Arabic lexicographers and Quranic exegetes who were interested in exhaustive treatments of *anwā'* and *manāzil* (lunar mansions) concepts, specifically because such studies were already spurred by the cosmological doctrines of the Qur'ān. This cosmological tradition of the Quranic text would later produce a separate type of astronomical literature usually referred to as *al-hay'a al-sunnīya.*[23] The use of the term *hay'a* to describe this tradition as well is of special significance, for it indicates the direction from which this tradition had developed. It is not a coincidence that the mathematical astronomical tradition which dealt with the theoretical foundations of astronomy also defined itself as a *hay'a* tradition, even though it rarely touched upon the Quranic references to the cosmological doctrines.

The other type of astronomical texts, about which we know a little more, is that known as the *azyāz* type. Although this type of literature was more in the Ptolemaic *Handy Tables* tradition, it nevertheless crossed paths with the other type at various points of its development. To take one instance that proved to be very influential in the development of a critical attitude toward Ptolemaic astronomy, we refer to the early astronomical observations which were conducted during the early part of the ninth century and whose purpose was specifically to update the *zījes,* which were inspired by the *Handy Tables*. As already noted, during this updating procedure it was easy to see that the Ptolemaic parameters were no longer true and could no longer be defended. No astronomer working in the early part of the ninth century could still accept the Ptolemaic values for precession, solar apogee, solar equation, or the inclination of the ecliptic. The variations were so obvious that they must have become intolerable and could no longer be explained without full recourse to a long process of questioning the very foundation of the validity of all the precepts of Greek astronomy.

This confrontation with the facts, as they were derived from direct observations, produced the questioning attitude that gave rise to the development of the new observational methodology, namely the so-called *fuṣūl* method. Although this method was developed to answer the specific question of the position of the solar apogee and the value of the solar equation as a by-product, it was also important for the process of evaluating the Greek astronomical tradition, which at the time came into conflict with the Indian tradition that had penetrated the Arabic sphere sometime during the middle of the eighth century, if not earlier. This questioning attitude must have raised the issues connected with the instrumentation, procedures, and practices of Ptolemy. At the same time, it led to a careful consideration of the practices and the instrumentation that were used from the early ninth century on. Echoes of this questioning are heard time and time again in connection with the increase in the size and precision of instruments, which became a major subject of research during Islamic times.[24] As a procedure, this questioning must have also highlighted the importance of continued observation and deepened the understanding of the theory of error evaluation, the conditions under which errors occur, and the most secure methods that would yield better values.

As a result, observational astronomy, in its attempt to secure more updated *zījes,* did not only produce new and more precise parameters, such as the new values for precession, solar apogee, solar equation, and the inclination of the ecliptic, but also managed to raise the level of theoretical discussion that fed into the other stream already developing in the *hay'a* texts. People like Thābit b. Qurra were presumed to have raised the question of precession variation on a theoretical level and attempted to develop a theory of trepidation that would answer this specific question. More recent research on the astronomical works of Thābit b. Qurra has also demonstrated the mathematical skills with which Thābit attempted to approach the Ptolemaic texts.[25] The same research also claims that Thābit was indeed conscious of the questions relating to the physical implications of the mathematical models described in Ptolemy's *Almagest*.

Therefore, by the time the *hay'a* tradition was beginning to emerge—that is, sometime during the first half of the tenth century—with an emphasis on the theoretical but sometimes more qualitative side, it came into direct contact with the more rigorous mathematical and observational reevaluation of Greek astronomy. The consolidation of this new genre of literature, which included the latest findings in the observational field, began to be expressed in the texts of *tarkīb al-aflāk* and *hay'a*. So it is not surprising that one finds such texts being written contemporaneously with the more updated *azyāj* texts which were themselves sometimes called *mumtaḥan*-type *zījes* to signal their overall new nature as resulting from fresh observational procedures. Sometimes the same people wrote both types of texts, as we have seen with the earlier case of Yaᶜqūb Ibn Ṭāriq. But most importantly, the new literature must have also benefited from the theoretical reconsideration to which the received Greek tradition was being subjected.

Development of Shukūk-Istidrāk *Literature*

The new attitude toward Greek astronomy was translated on the theoretical level into another novel tradition, namely that of writing texts that dealt explicitly with the contradictions in the Greek astronomical tradition. As already noted, the focal point of these texts was their attempt to uncover the inherent contradictions in the Ptolemaic tradition when one attempted to match its physical assumptions with the mathematical models used to describe that physics. We have already stated that the eleventh-century text of Ibn al-Haytham, *al-Shukūk ᶜAlā Baṭlamyūs,* represented the climax of that critical tradition.

That should not, however, mean that the history of that tradition is any less significant, and that Ibn al-Haytham's text was the novelty of the eleventh century. The few references in the scattered and poorly investigated sources demonstrate that the beginnings of this tradition may have very well extended as far back as the ninth century. We have already signaled the importance of Régis Morelon's new research in the works of Thābit b. Qurra, and the light it now sheds on Thābit's analytical attitude toward the Ptolemaic tradition. We have noted that it was Thābit who sometime during the ninth century began to ask questions regarding the mathematical implications of the Ptolemaic physical assumptions.

A century later, we begin to note the appearance of various texts, mostly known through their titles only, where the criticism of Ptolemaic astronomy seems to have been the main subject matter. The famous al-Qabīṣī (Latin Alchabetius), the personal astrologer of Sayf al-Dawla, the Ḥamdānid ruler of Aleppo, has left us a text concerning the testing of astrologers, in which he mentions, among other things, that he had written a critique of the *Almagest* that he had called *al-Shukūk fī al-majisṭī* (Doubts Regarding the *Almagest*).[26] The contents of this text seem to have been lost forever, but they must have been written from the perspective of the criticism that began to be developed a century earlier.

Another work by an eleventh-century Spanish astronomer, which apparently has not survived, mentions explictly the problematic nature of the Ptolemaic text. This Spanish astronomer, whose name is still unknown, speaks of his famous contemporary al-Zarqāel (fl. 1075) as a personal friend. Of his own works we seem to have a unique copy of a book called simply *Kitāb al-hay'a,* which is kept at the Osmania Library in Hyderabad, India. In this *Kitāb al-hay'a,* which is mainly an elementary rendering of Ptolemaic astronomy, we also find a fairly thorough analysis of the essentials of the Ptolemaic texts. Whenever the author encountered a contradiction or a difficulty, he drew attention to it and promised that he would treat that special point in a separate book called *al-Istidrāk* [*ʿalā Baṭlamyūs*] (Recapitulation in Regard to Ptolemy).[27] From a review of these references we can conclude that the text was indeed critical of Ptolemaic astronomy.

In a recent article, included in this collection, I have noted the existence of a yet to be located book by the famous eleventh-century polymath Abū al-Raiḥān al-Bīrūnī (d. c. 1050), which was apparently also critical of Ptolemaic astronomy.[28] What Bīrūnī seems to have doubted was the Ptolemaic astronomy's veracity regarding the planetary latitudes and the techniques Ptolemy employed to describe them.

Taken together, these texts seem to have laid the foundation for the kind of detailed analysis leveled by Ibn al-Haytham in his *al-Shukūk ʿalā Baṭlamyūs*. But they could not have developed during the two centuries preceding Ibn al-Haytham if it had not been for the combination of the various activities, including the new observational techniques, the updating of parameters and *zījes,* the combination of the two Ptolemaic traditions represented by the *Almagest* and the *Planetary Hypotheses,* and finally the attempt to harmonize the physical and the mathematical aspects of Ptolemaic astronomy.

I have stated above that the *Shukūk* writers did not propose new models to replace those to which they were objecting, and that is why I did not include their works in this book. Their criticism remained also within the theoretical realm, and they did not attempt to fully investigate the implications of this criticism. At a later stage, the model builders, such as Mu'ayyad al-Dīn al-ʿUrḍī (d. 1266), took this same attitude toward the *Shukūk* writers, and blamed them for not proposing alternative solutions. To be fair to the *Shukūk* writers, their project seems to have been slightly different from that of the model builders, and to blame them for their lack of interest in proposing their own alternative models, is to miss the subtlety of this difference. For to the critic, it was the foundations of the science that were being discussed, and not the reform of Ptolemaic astronomy. They were interested in highlighting the significance of the commitment that Ptolemy should have made to the physical principles when he tried to describe his astronomy in mathematical models. They wished him to say that the world that he was describing was in itself made of real physical bodies capable of real motions, and thus should be described by the kind of mathematics that allows such motions. That by itself is different from taking the next step, which required that one agree with the Ptolemaic presuppositions and then attempt to develop mathematical models that could render the implications of those presuppositions more consistent and true to the observations.

At any rate, the full motivation of the critics, the *Shukūk* writers, will not be fully understood until we locate these texts, produce critical editions for them, and then study them in relation to one another and to the Ptolemaic text itself. But since most are still unidentified, the prospect of understanding their motivation is still far in the future. The motivation of the reformers, however—that is, those who have attempted to build their own alternative models—is slightly easier to determine, for we have a fairly good representative sample of such texts, and a good number of them are highlighted in this collection of articles.

Motivation of the Model Builders

I would like to return now to the question of motivation, upon which I touched very briefly before. Now that we have analyzed the historical development of the literature that was critical of Ptolemaic astronomy, and after noting that the critics involved in this process were divided into two main groups—those who criticized Ptolemaic astronomy without attempting to replace it, and those who took it upon themselves to produce an alternative to it—let us try to sharpen the theoretical positions assumed by those critics. From that perspective, it is also useful to divide those critics into two other categories: those whose criticism was indeed motivated by philosophical considerations only, who were mostly incapable of producing the mathematical models that would satisfy their own philosophical presuppositions; and those who were more mathematically competent, who objected to Ptolemaic astronomy for purely scientific reasons of consistency and considered their activity as a reconstruction of Ptolemaic astronomy on firmer mathematical scientific grounds.

Before we proceed to analyze the general attitudes of each of these groups, it will be useful to discuss this distinction briefly. Those to whom we shall refer as the philosophically oriented group were active mainly in the western part of the Islamic world, in al-Andalus in particular, and included figures such as Ibn Bājah (1139), Ibn Ṭufayl (1185), Ibn Rushd (1198), and al-Biṭrūjī (c. 1200).[29] Their main concern was to recapture the Aristotelian purity of the astronomical system, and they did not accept any configuration that was not consistent with the Aristotelian propositions. To this group the main objection to Ptolemaic astronomy stemmed from its inclusion of such concepts as eccentrics and epicycles.

The reasoning behind their objection was rather simple. Since Aristotle had argued in his book *De Caelo* that the shape of the universe was necessarily spherical, it followed that the center of this universe, like the center of any moving sphere, was at rest and must coincide with the earth, the element of heaviness. If there had not been an actual earth, such as the one we live on, the Aristotelian analysis required that such an earth be postulated, since it was the concentration of heaviness and thus must be placed motionless at the center of the universe, with respect to which all directions of up and down can then be defined as being away from such an earth and toward such an earth. Under these conditions, eccentrics would violate this principle, for they would require a fixed point, a center of a revolving sphere, which did not coincide with the earth, thus creating a new center of heaviness and requiring that the element of heaviness that we call earth be, by assumption, not unique, which is impossible. Epicycles, on the other hand, required that a sphere, different from the one that surrounds the earth, revolve around a center of heaviness, which is now placed in the realm of the celestial spheres, which could not be possibly tolerated. According to the Aristotelian arguments, that realm was supposed to be made of a fifth element, the ether, of which such terms of heaviness and lightness could not be used.

To this philosophically oriented group, the whole enterprise of developing mathematical models to describe the celestial phenomena remained flawed as long as it included eccentrics and epicycles as part of its configurations. One must therefore devise a new astronomy that did not imply the use of eccentrics and epicycles in order to remain true to the Aristotelian principles that were indeed accepted by Ptolemy.

The second group, represented mainly by the astronomers of the east, now summarily referred to as the Maragha astronomers, raised the objections to Ptolemaic astronomy in a slightly different manner. Their objections were concerned more with scientific consistency than with consistency with Aristotelian presuppositions.

One could say that they would accept a center of heaviness other than the earth, or a center in the celestial realm around which an epicycle could move, but they could not accept the physical impossibility that a sphere move uniformly around an axis that did not pass through its center. To them, if such a requirement were introduced, as was indeed done by the Ptolemaic concept of the equant, then the term ''sphere'' would lose its meaning, for then it would no longer be the physical object we commonly refer to as a sphere. A sphere moving uniformly would, in their language, require that it describes equal arcs in equal times around its own center. Otherwise that sphere would not be moving uniformly. Put differently, this group of astronomers was ready to accept the Ptolemaic violation of the Aristotelian principles of the shape and form of the universe and the distribution of the elements within that universe, but they were not prepared to sacrifice the scientific principles of consistency as well—that is, when a sphere is used in a system, that sphere, as a physical body, has some physical and mathematical properties that could not be changed at will without violating the system.

Of the eastern astronomers, only Ibn al-Shāṭir would push this argument further and, in an attempt to respond to the philosophical concerns of the first group, try to devise a mathematical system in which there were no eccentrics.

As far as we can now tell, none of the others objected to the presence of the eccentrics and the epicycles, provided those eccentrics and epicycles behaved like spheres as they were supposed to: by revolving at uniform speeds around their own centers and not around some other center which is called an equant.

Dividing the astronomers responding to Ptolemaic astronomy into such subgroups and characterizing them as westerners and easterners should in no way imply that all the astronomers of al-Andalus were of such persuasion or that all the eastern astronomers did not pay attention to the philosophical concerns. We have just mentioned the work of Ibn al-Shāṭir in connection with this philosophical direction. For Ibn al-Shāṭir, eccentrics were to be avoided if one could do so in order to preserve the harmony of the total system. But when it came to epicycles, which are observational necessities that could not be avoided like eccentrics, he would allow them, accusing Aristotle of inconsistency in claiming that the stars and the planets as well as the spheres that carry them in their daily motion are all made of the same simple element, ether. If that were so, according to Ibn al-Shāṭir, how could one explain the presence of a shining star at a particular position of a sphere that is obviously different from all the other parts of the sphere? If that were not so, all parts of the sphere would give the same light as the star. To Ibn al-Shāṭir, the mere presence of such stars in all the spheres below the ninth sphere meant that the celestial spheres with which astronomy is concerned have some sort of composition and are not made of the simple element, ether. If this composition were allowed—and it must be allowed in order to avoid the inner contradiction of Aristotle—Ibn al-Shāṭir would say that the required epicycles are of the same composite nature as the stars in the celestial spheres.

Of the Andalusian astronomers, on the other hand, there were those, like al-Zarqāel and Jābir Ibn Aflaḥ (c. 1120) who were concerned with the lack of mathematical consistency of Ptolemaic astronomy, irrespective of its position vis-à-vis the Aristotelian presuppositions. To al-Zarqāel, for example, the mere difference between the value reported by Ptolemy for the solar equation and the one found by observation necessitates a new configuration that would explain the phenomena better.[30] To Jābir Ibn Aflaḥ, it was intolerable that one would expound such mathematical rigor in establishing his astronomy and then assume, without proof, that for all the superior planets the center of the sphere that carries the epicycle is simply placed halfway between the center of the world and the equant.[31] In other words, if

Jabir had been given the mathematical proof for the position of the equant, he may have accepted its existence.

Only al-Biṭrūjī stayed very close to the Andalusian philosophers in his attempt to reform Ptolemaic astronomy. He ended up with a configuration that did not have eccentrics or epicycles in the classical sense, but it also did not describe the phenomena as well as the Ptolemaic astronomy it was supposed to replace.

From the eastern domain, one of the articles in this book raises another question not dealt with in detail yet, namely the issue of the relationship between the observations and the model-building activity. It was also Ibn al-Shāṭir who seems to have raised a new objection to Ptolemy's solar model, not because it contained an eccentric (which he would not have accepted) or an epicycle (which he would accept), but because it did not account well for the observations. Even when he was ready to accept the epicyclic model of Ptolemy, he still claimed that the Ptolemaic model did not save the phenomenon of the solar motion in a manner that was based on observations. Therefore he found himself proposing a new model for the solar motion, which of course did not contain any eccentrics.

This quick overview should clarify why we cannot describe all reformers of Ptolemaic astronomy with the same adjectives and why we cannot restrict the trends to specific geographic areas. The motives behind these different attempts at reforming Ptolemaic astronomy were almost as varied as the astronomers who were proposing them. The bias of this book is toward the works of the eastern astronomers, and I explore only the different approaches employed by the various astronomers that have so far been discovered. Future research promises to produce more works, more motivations, and more variations on the themes that we have plotted so far. The relationship between the eastern and western astronomers will also undergo many more permutations as more and more works come to light. In that regard, it goes without saying that all we have stated thus far has to remain strictly tentative.

A final word about the place of Ptolemy's observations within the scope of Arabic astronomy. As mentioned earlier, in the various cases such as precession, solar apogee, and ecliptic inclination where the observational mistakes had led Ptolemy to adopt faulty parameters, the early observations of the ninth century produced much better values as well as a critique of the observational methodology used by Ptolemy. But for later astronomers, who had already assimilated the early observational results into their works, the problem was no longer that of disagreeing with Ptolemy on observational results, except in very few cases where new values could still be found, as in the case of Ibn al-Shāṭir's new observational results for the apparent size of the lunar and solar disks. The majority of the astronomers concerned with the theoretical foundation of Ptolemy's astronomy, that is, its inner consistency were prepared to take Ptolemy's observations at face value.

This was explicitly done by Mu'ayyad al-Dīn al-ʿUrḍī, who repeatedly stressed, in several places of his major work, that he had no difficulty with the observational results of Ptolemy, and that he himself had not produced any observations of his own.[32] He was also not prepared to be dishonest like the *zīj* writers by changing the parameter values ever so slightly in order to give the false impression that they had conducted fresh observations of their own.[33]

In fact, ʿUrḍī stressed his agreement with Ptolemy about the observational results in order to establish that his disagreement with Ptolemy is of a higher conceptual order. Observational errors could easily be fixed, but conceptual fallacies are much harder to account for. ʿUrḍī goes on to say that his own regard for observation is so high that they are his basis for any theoretical formulation.[34] He claims that Ptolemy had the same attitude and that he was in perfect agreement with him in that regard. But it is the conceptualization produced by Ptolemy to account for those observations that he found deficient. It is this project that ʿUrḍī undertook to complete.

Model Building and Copernicus

The relationship between the reform of Ptolemaic astronomy discussed in this collection of articles and Copernican astronomy needs to be clarified even further at this point. To start with, there was no question of doubting the originality or the genius of Copernicus by implying that he was less brilliant because he used two fundamental theorems that had already been discovered and used in Arabic astronomy some two to three centuries earlier. Nor was there any doubt that anyone else could lay claim to the theory of heliocentricity with which Copernicus had become so firmly associated. In fact, if the Copernican revolution is understood to mean the abandonment of geocentricity and the adoption of heliocentricity, which was the centerpiece of Copernicus's work, then it is clear that he remains the unchallenged master of that revolution, and there is no precedent within Arabic astronomy which is in any way similar to heliocentricity.

On the other hand, when we read the introduction of Copernicus's *Commentariolus,* the first of his astronomical works, we find that he was much more concerned with the violations of uniform motions expressed in Ptolemaic astronomy by the equant spheres and the like than he was with heliocentricity, which he discussed as a second point.[35] From that perspective, his adoption of heliocentricity was confirmed only after he had already cleansed Ptolemaic astronomy from the same defects that the earlier Arabic astronomers were pointing to, and by using the same techniques they had used.

Therefore, when we speak of the connection between Arabic astronomy and Copernicus, we only mean the connection of similarity of purpose and the use of similar mathematical techniques. The article titled "Arabic Astronomy and Copernicus" explores the second point in some detail, and focuses on a theorem that was first invented by Mu'ayyad al-Dīn al-ʿUrḍī (d. 1266) and was used to reform the Ptolemaic model for the upper planets; it was later used by Copernicus for exactly the same purpose. No special article is devoted to Copernicus's use of a second theorem, which was first invented by Naṣīr al-Dīn al-Ṭūsī (d. 1274), now called the Ṭūsī Couple, but I refer to it several times in the general articles.[36]

The identical purposes of Copernicus and his Arabic predecessors however, are much more important than the use of one or two mathematical theorems, in that those purposes touched on the theoretical issue regarding the foundation of science. They stressed the fact that any science must be inherently consistent, and its premises must always have the same meaning throughout its development. In this particular case, if a sphere is a physical body with certain properties, as was accepted by Ptolemy and all medieval astronomers after him, then that sphere cannot, through the mechanism of an equant or the like, be made to move in a mathematical system in a manner that is not consistent with its properties as a sphere. The original accepted notion of a sphere is that the sphere is capable of uniform motion in place around an axis that passed through its center. That notion would no longer make sense if the axis was later assumed to pass through a point other than the center.

The similarities between Copernican and Arabic astronomy at this level are overwhelming. At every juncture, one hears the same objections being raised against Ptolemy, and the same hesitation about announcing one's new findings. In one instance, when ʿUrḍī confesses that he was afraid of publishing the astronomical theory proposed in his book because it was so different from what was commonly accepted,[37] and that he held on to that theory for several years before he finally published it, one cannot help but think of the similar fate of Copernicus's *De Revolutionibus.*[38] It seems to me that both men knew that they were stepping into new territory. Both required a more consistent astronomy than the one inherited from Ptolemy. In the case of Copernicus, the problematic requirement of heliocentricity was a further addition to their list of complaints. Incidentally, I call this new Copernican requirement problematic because it is not obvious to me why Copernicus would abandon the Aristotelian cosmology with its consistent definition of the nature and function of the earth at the center of the world, when he did not have a gravitational theory to explain his shift to the heliocentric theory. For him, it was probably this second point that caused the most hesitation in publishing his new theory.

For such reasons, and independently of the fate of the criticism of Ptolemaic astronomy in medieval Islamic times, the relationship between Arabic astronomy and Copernican astronomy has proved in the last few decades to be very important for Copernican studies themselves. Even if the heliocentric theory originated with Copernicus alone, one cannot assume that his motivation for replacing Ptolemaic astronomy, his research program, and his mathematical techniques were historical breakthroughs introduced by Copernicus into the field of astronomy, especially when there are no such precedents in the Latin tradition to which he could have referred. After the masterful publication of the *Mathematical Astronomy in Copernicus's De Revolutionibus* by Swerdlow and Neugebauer (Springer, New York, 1984), it has become clear how the historical process unfolded: I do not think that anyone can now deny the relationship between Copernicus and the earlier and very similar Arabic astronomy. In fact, it was Swerdlow and Neugebauer who first referred to Copernicus as the last of the Maragha astronomers, as I have noted in more than one of the articles collected here.[39] By placing Copernicus as the heir of Arabic astronomy, we can at least account for a natural process for scientific development.

Like all historical phenomena where the solution of one problem requires the solution of several intermediary ones, this relationship between Arabic astronomy and Copernicus generated new studies regarding the modes, routes, and methods of transmission of astronomical ideas from Arabic to Copernicus, with a special emphasis on intermediary areas that could have been the conduits of such results. In that regard, I have already hinted to the second field that benefited from the study of this relationship between Copernican and Arabic astronomy, namely, the field of late medieval Byzantine astronomy. I have already stated that it was Neugebauer who first pointed to the direction of possible transmission of ideas from east to west and who first produced the concrete proof for the existence of revolutionary mathematical and astronomical ideas, first in Arabic sources and then in late Byzantine Greek sources, which were explicitly dependent on the Arabic and Persian traditions. I have said that he had in fact located a Greek manuscript (Vatican Gr. 211) in which there was, among other things, a diagram representing the famous Ṭūsī Couple. He also established that the manuscript was completed in Constantinople before it fell to the Ottomans, and that after the fall it was brought to the Vatican. I also said that a page of that manuscript was first published in his monumental work, *A History of Ancient Mathematical Astronomy*.[40] Two other pages followed later in Swerdlow and Neugebauer's work on Copernicus's *De Revolutionibus*.

The section of the Greek manuscript, which has the mathematical theorems that could have reached Copernicus, has not yet been published (though David Pingree of Brown University has been working on it). Once that text is published and studied, Neugebauer will probably be more than vindicated, and he will have rendered an unparalleled service to the Byzantinists who would then be able to reconstruct the history of Byzantine theoretical astronomy for that period. Such a study will also demonstrate how close that tradition was to the Arabic tradition which had already reached its maturity by the end of the thirteenth century and was beginning to forge new grounds thereafter.

Important and exciting as these new areas of research are, the connection between Arabic and Copernican astronomy should not become the focal point for the history of Arabic astronomy.

First, we should not assume that there was a linear progression in the development of astronomical thought from one astronomer to the other, all with the purpose of discovering Copernican astronomy and later modern astronomy. No medieval astronomer should be judged in terms of how close he was to Copernicus or to the accepted tenets of modern astronomy. The job of the historian is to understand the works of each astronomer in their own context, irrespective of their implications for later generations. Of course, if such an implication does exist, one should not disregard it. But it should not be sought as the central plan of the research.

Second, by stressing the connection between Arabic and Copernican astronomy, one tends to neglect the conditions under which Arabic astronomy itself was first conceived and developed. One would no longer ask the questions that every historian of science should ask, namely, what research environment led to the development of which research programs, and which solutions were conceived at what time to answer which questions, and whether those kinds of solutions were adequate to the purpose, and so on. Only when these circumstances are understood can one begin to understand the more general picture. If in this collection of articles I have managed to highlight concerns that were prevalent throughout the five centuries of Arabic astronomy covered here, to give a sample of the kinds of solutions that were being discussed, and to establish some kind of reference points as to who was doing what and when, then I would think that I have made a small contribution to the study of the history of Arabic astronomy on its own, irrespective of its relationship to that of Copernicus.

Third, the connection with Copernican astronomy has already been overemphasized at the expense of understanding the exact research programs in Arabic astronomy. More articles have been published with that purpose in mind, while the rest of the astronomical works from which the study of this special connection is extracted are left mostly untouched by modern scholarship. From the perspective of the historian of Arabic astronomy, this situation is deplorable, because in this fashion the general scope of Arabic astronomy will remain unexplored. For the general historian of Arabic science who is constantly counting on the historian of astronomy to corroborate results reached in other fields or to help dispel them, the situation is much more than deplorable, for no other field in the history of the Arabic sciences profits in any way from the continued exploration of this special connection between Arabic and Copernican astronomy. For such historians this isolated instance, important as it is for the historian of astronomy, does not complement the ongoing research in the other fields of Arabic science, and more exploration of its dimensions and circumstances does not increase our knowledge of the exact manner in which Arabic science operated within the larger social context.

I do not mean to say that we should henceforth drop this program of research and redirect our efforts to other areas of Arabic science, as much as this can be done from within the confines of Arabic astronomy. But with the limited resources and manpower at the disposal of the few people working in the field, to continue to explore this special relationship between Copernicus and Arabic astronomy is a bad allocation of resources and a misleading scale of priorities. The question that should become the focus of future research is how well did this phenomenon of reformulating Ptolemaic astronomy, the antecedent of Copernican astronomy, sit within the larger body of Arabic astronomy. In what contexts was it formulated, what purposes did it serve, how well did it answer other issues raised in the texts where it occurs, who were the people pioneering this revolutionary and exciting research, and how well did they relate to other scientists and their own society at large? Simply put, the study of Arabic astronomy for the sake of understanding its history within the framework of the general Arabic intellectual history should by itself be the program of research. Part of that program would be to continue to document the sources in which there are ideas that were later transmitted to other cultures.

In a very real sense, I imagine this research can also produce some very interesting results, if it can be shown that it did continue beyond the seventeenth century (that is, beyond the period covered in this collection of articles), and at a time when Copernican astronomy began to return to the east as the new import of the modern mode of astronomical theory. It would be interesting to find out how well the Copernican astronomy was accepted within the continuing Arabic tradition, which had generated the most powerful mathematical tools for Copernican astronomy or if there *was* such a continuing tradition. Such results could also be very useful to historians of Arabic science who are interested in the phenomenon of the decline of that science, which seems to have occurred around the same time.

The main beneficiary of such a program, however, will always be the student of Arabic social and intellectual history. The problems connected with periodization, already discussed, which were imposed on the study of Arabic intellectual history for reasons that were extraneous to the field, would also be seen under a new light. As I have argued in various places, and in several of the articles collected here, such a reorientation in our understanding of the role of the schematic periodization of intellectual history is very important for the total understanding of Arabic intellectual history, Arabic science, and Arabic astronomy as a whole. In fact, I have already noted that the subtitle of this book is in itself an attempt to jolt the student of Arabic intellectual history out of the accepted norm, and to steer him into the direction of reevaluating that history from within its own premises. I intended the subtitle to call attention to the criteria by which golden and silver ages of Islamic history were assigned in the first place, and by whom.

The Context of Arabic Astronomy

I have argued in "The Development of Astronomy in Medieval Islamic Society"[41] that the astronomers who were producing the original astronomical results—that is, the model builders—and the relationship they had with their own society constitute a very interesting phenomenon. Most important, we find, for example, that the majority of them produced theoretical astronomy only and had very little, if anything, to do with astrology, the twin sister of astronomy since the times of antiquity.

We also find that these astronomers were sometimes employed by the mosques as *muwaqqits* (time keepers), as in the case of Ibn al-Shāṭir, and they were therefore perceived by society as religious functionaries of the mosque. When we remember that the mosque was the focal point of the intellectual and social life of the community throughout medieval Islamic times, and that it was sometimes at odds with the political power, it becomes significant that the astronomers were accepted into the bosom of the Muslim community in such a fashion. I have also stressed in that article that their acceptability into the central life of the community hinged on their ability to draw a distinction between theoretical astronomy and astrology and to present their work as belonging to the first.

In the same article, I have also noted that this revolutionary change—which must have occurred toward the beginning of the eleventh century made theoretical astronomy, now defined as different from astrology,[42] religiously acceptable. This conceptual shift was contemporaneous with the change that took place among the functionaries of the mosque and resulted in the creation of the office of the *muwaqqit* himself. The type of theoretical astronomy the model builders were engaged in became part of the functions of the *muwaqqit* whenever he was competent enough to do so. My contention was then, and still is, that as far as I knew the office of the *muwaqqit* did not exist in the earlier period, and it seems that it was created specifically as a result of the change in the conception of the role of the astronomer in the society.

From that perspective, the practice of astronomical research within medieval Islam must have generated a different conceptualization of the role and function of astronomy. The astronomer, who was a century earlier employed by the government as an astrologer or who practiced astrology to make a living, was no longer obliged to do so. Under the new reorientation he was welcome to practice his craft within the mosque in perfect harmony with the community that supported his research, provided that he abandoned the practice of astrology. This may indeed explain the creation and remarkable increase, after the twelfth century, in the literature produced by these new *muwaqqits* who were now engaged as mosque functionaries. Their new works were commonly referred to as *mīqāt* literature.

This does not mean that all medieval astronomers who were engaged in theoretical astronomy were practicing *muwaqqits* in their respective mosques. But the fact that some of them were does indeed imply that their kind of practice was considered acceptable to the larger community. Some of them may have continued to be engaged in astrology and may have worked for the political authority, as was the case with Naṣīr al-Dīn al-Ṭūsī a century before Ibn al-Shāṭir. But that can only mean that the community could distinguish between the functions practiced in the mosque and the community at large, and those that were practiced within the confines of the political office. Someone like Ṭūsī was probably perceived first as a politician employing his astrological skills in the service of his patron,[43] and the acceptable part of his theoretical astronomical work was secondary to his functions, but it would have been accepted within the confines of the mosque had he wished to pursue it there.

In this new reorganization of the field, the astrologer was not completely out of a job, however, since we know that he continued to practice in the street, in the shop, and obviously in the various political courts of medieval Islam.[44] The community must have tolerated his activities, but it did not condone them. The intellectual posture of the community was definitely antipathetic to the functions of the astrologer, and there are enough elaborate treatises written from the ninth century onward that were critical of such functions. The last of these treatises that I know of, *Miftāḥ Dār al-Saʿāda,* written by Ibn Qayyim al-Jawzīya (d. 1350), the Ḥanbalite theologian of Damascus, devotes more than 250 pages to the attack on astrology, all in the context of defining what is acceptable to the Muslim community, and which beliefs would lead to salvation.[45]

It was in this environment that the astronomer *muwaqqit* and the theoretical astronomer working on his own as a teacher or an engineer felt safe to ply their trade in total agreement with the practices of their community. In return, the discerning community could distinguish between the various branches of astronomy, encourage those that were religiously acceptable, and limit the applications of others. As an example of that, we find that despite the political and astrological functions of Ṭūsī, his theoretical astronomical work, the *Tadhkira fī ᶜilm al-hay'a* (Memento on the Science of Astronomy), was in all likelihood acceptable to the community and may have become part of the school curriculum (when that curriculum itself was mainly devoted to legal and religious studies), while the practice of the astrologer was being regulated by the chief of police, the *muḥtasib*, like any other trade in the marketplace.[46]

As a type of astronomical literature, the *Tadhkira*, like the others in this genre, included a theoretical exposition of astronomy without encumbering it with geometric proofs or mathematical analysis of the relationships between the observations and the final models, as was done in the *Almagest*. In the words of Ibn al-Akfānī, the fourteenth-century ophthalmologist and encyclopedist who lived in Egypt,[47] this genre of literature was perceived as being intentionally devoted to the theoretical exposition of astronomical models without reference to geometric proofs. About this type Ibn al-Akfānī says: "As for these texts which are devoid of geometric proofs and which are devoted to the description of these matters without proofs *(taṣawwur hādhihi al-umūr dūn al-taṣdīq)* the introductory one among them *(mukhtaṣara)* is the *Tadhkira* of Khwāja Naṣīr al-Dīn al-Ṭūsī, the intermediate is the *Hay'a* of [Mu'ayyad al-Dīn] al-ᶜUrḍī, and the elaborate *(mabsūṭa)* is the *Nihāyat al-Idrāk* of al-Quṭb al-Shīrāzī."[48]

In a very interesting additional comment, Ibn al-Akfānī goes on to say: "The ancients continued to restrict themselves to pure circles in regard to the representations of the configurations of the celestial spheres until Abū ᶜAlī Ibn al-Haytham explicitly stated the corporeality of the latter and mentioned the conditions and implications resulting therefrom. The later [astronomers] followed him in that."[49]

In that regard, the contents and composition of the *Tadhkira* made it an excellent introduction to that type of theoretical astronomy, which was clearly distinguished from astrology, and thus may have become suitable for school instruction. The number of commentaries written on it from within those schools,[50] and the direct evidence from later astronomers who studied the commentaries on the *Tadhkira* as part of their school curriculum, attest very well to its popularity.[51]

This type of astronomical literature allowed people to discuss highly sophisticated astronomical matters, but this time in terms of real physical bodies, as was required by Ibn al-Haytham. It is this intersection of the mathematical and the physical disciplines that formed the core of this type of texts. From that perspective, the inclusion of the *Tadhkira*, along with other *hay'a* texts, in the school curriculum must have meant that the subject matter of *hay'a* was no longer restricted to the few astronomers who were interested in reforming Ptolemaic astronomy. It must have then become the subject of various discussions by jurists and theologians who would have been among the regular students and teachers of such schools. In that regard, the faults of Ptolemaic astronomy and the need to reform it must have also been well understood by the larger community.

In fact, we find that such widespread knowledge about the disagreements among the astronomers in regard to their discipline led to its exploitation by at least one theologian who cast doubt on the validity of that mathematical discipline, whose practitioners could not agree among themselves about its theoretical formulation. This disparaging remark about astronomy came from the pen of Ibn Taymīya al-Ḥarrānī (d. 1328), another Ḥanbalite theologian who was also the teacher of Ibn Qayyim al-Jawzīya.[52] If the subject matter of the reform of Ptolemaic astronomy, together with the various possible alternatives suggested by the various proposed models, had not been within the reach of the students, the knowledge of its faults and the disagreements among the practitioners would not have been so well known to the outside world.

A contrasting remark that reveals the respect with which the astronomers, that is those who studied the *Almagest,* were held was made by a fourteenth-century man of letters, Khalīl Ibn Aybak al-Ṣafadī (d. 1365). In a book that is rarely looked at by historians of science, namely his book on the biographies of the blind, Ṣafadī discusses the causes of blindness. In that context, and while discussing the faults of the astrologers who claim that blindness is caused by astrological reasons, Ṣafadī singles out the astronomers for praise by saying that the celestial sphere "has been proven to be of simple nature by the people of the *Almagest (aṣḥāb al-majisṭī)*... And the people of the *Almagest* are the people of the fundamentals of astronomy *(aṣḥāb al-uṣūl fī ʿilm al-falak.)*"[53]

Seen in a different light, the criticisms of Ibn Taymīya and al-Ṣafadī were not necessarily inimical to the subject of astronomy. They can be understood to raise fundamental questions regarding the nature of mathematical disciplines such as astronomy, and the nature of their validity. This in itself is indeed a healthy sign, especially when we remember the context in which these remarks were raised. In the case of Ibn Taymīya, the remark was made in the context of a book in which he was attempting to deny the incompatibility between religion and reason. For Ṣafadī, it was in the context of a general literary work, which could have been addressed to the belles lettristes of his time.

Both remarks also corroborate my contention that the model builders dealt with the fundamental consistency of scientific disciplines. From these two remarks just quoted it is obvious that such questions regarding the nature of scientific disciplines were not only asked by the scientists themselves, but were also raised by others who had a general religious and literary education. Participants in such discussions would likely have been rubbing shoulders with colleagues who would address the same questions from the vantage points of their own varied disciplines. All this activity apparently took place during a time often characterized as a period of decline in Islamic science. In light of the present discussion, I hope that such general characterizations will from now on be radically reconsidered.

Arabic reforms of Ptolemaic astronomy were therefore part of a much wider phenomenon that included an intellectual debate across disciplines and looked into the foundations of science in a way that was not completely investigated before. The participation of the astronomers in this debate, from their own position as students of a mathematical demonstrative science (as astronomy was conceived since classical times) and as accepted members of the intellectual center of the community, was one of the basic motivations that must have been responsible for the continued production of novel astronomical texts. Elsewhere I shall argue that by the sixteenth century this investigation of the foundations of scientific activity, and the role of mathematics in such investigations, reached such sophisticated levels that it became possible for someone like Shams al-Dīn al-Khafrī (c. 1522),[54] a contemporary of Copernicus, to apply a whole variety of mathematical solutions to the same physical phenomena, thereby demonstrating the exact linguistic nature of mathematics in the context of the physical sciences.

With such considerations in mind, the relationship between Arabic and Copernican astronomy becomes quite secondary and at best accidental to the general enterprise of Arabic astronomy. By refocusing on the general context of the Arabic astronomical treatises, on the other hand, we find that its dimensions were multiple and developed quite naturally within the intellectual environment of the time. Students were engaged in the debates of astronomical questions as were men of letters. As for the astronomers, they must have felt that their discipline was under continuous scrutiny by outside observers, which must have contributed to their pursuit of improving the understanding of their own work. In a way, this could explain the continuous production of astronomical texts during this period, each trying to outdo the earlier ones. But most important, I maintain that, as a result, there must have emerged a better understanding of the nature of astronomy as a scientific discipline in particular, and the nature of science in general. Most significantly, I also think that the role of mathematics as a language of science was much better understood during those debates.

Concluding Remarks

The introduction of some theoretical astronomy into the school curriculum must have passed through various stages during the long life of medieval schools. In the beginning, elementary texts such as Kharaqī's (1138) *Tabṣira fī al-Hay'a* (Insight into Astronomy) were in all likelihood used for the purpose of elementary astronomical education. In the next century they were probably followed by similar texts, such as the simpler text of Jaghmīnī (c. 1221) called *al-Mulakhkhaṣ fī al-Hay'a* (A Compendium of Astronomy). In some schools this tradition must have continued and simpler and simpler texts such as the commentary of Qāḍīzādeh al-Rūmī (fl. 1440) on Jaghmīnī's *Mulakhkhaṣ* must have continued to be used until our own century.[55]

The schools in which Ṭūsī's *Tadhkira* was introduced toward the end of the thirteenth century (about fifty years after it was written) must have been more demanding, or the teachers who taught such texts were more competent. As we were told by Mullā Shirwānī, the instruction in the relatively difficult text of Ṭūsī's *Tadhkira* was done through a famous commentary, such as that of Nīsābūrī (1300), which would make the text slightly easier to comprehend. Nīsābūrī's commentary could very well have been intended from the very beginning for school use, since it served such a purpose in the fifteenth century. Other commentaries, which also contained original material of their own, such as *Nihāyat al-Idrāk fī Dirāyat al-Aflāk* by Quṭb al-Dīn al-Shīrāzī (d. 1311), one of Ṭūsī's students, were probably used in the same capacity.[56] Nevertheless, teachers who ventured to go through the *Tadhkira* or through one of its commentaries, with their students must have been quite competent astronomers.

In a different context, I have argued that this school tradition was itself responsible for the continued production of such texts in Arabic, even when they were written by Persian-speaking authors.[57] The evidence for that, as far as it can be verified, attests to the fact that as time went on more and more texts were produced in the Persian-speaking parts of the islamic world, and yet these theoretical astronomical texts were almost always written in Arabic. Students going to the traditional Islamic schools of Persia studied these texts in Arabic, and must have discussed them in that language as well. This should not be surprising, for most of the curricula of these schools were centered around religious studies, and therefore they must have also been conducted in Arabic. This is the case till our very own day.[58] From a different perspective, the abundance of such Arabic astronomical texts within a Persian-speaking milieu can only be explained by the inclusion of such texts in the school curriculum where Arabic was studied in earnest, and where the texts could have been understood.

The interesting phenomenon, however, is that there were other texts from outside the school environment that were written in Persian. These were mainly *zījes* (astronomical tables), whose main purpose was to locate the actual positions of the planets for a specific time.[59] These texts were used primarily by astrologers, and the assumption is that such astrologers practiced outside the school environment, most probably in the political court, as can be attested by the existence of the office of *munajjim bāshī* (chief astrologer), a well-known government office from the Safavid period onward, if not before.[60] The main occupation of Ṭūsī himself, during the Ilkhanid period, is not too different from that of a *munajjim bāshī,* although I do not know if such a formal title existed at the time, or that it was ever bestowed on him.

Independently of that, I noted before that several of the *zījes* written in the geographical area designated by modern-day Persia were also written in Persian, while the theoretical astronomical texts were usually written in Arabic. This is certainly true of the work of Ṭūsī himself, who wrote his *Tadhkira* in Arabic and his *Zīj-i Ilkhānī* in Persian. Although Ṭūsī's earlier treatises, the *Muᶜīnīyah* and its supplement *Dhayl al-Muᶜīnīyah,* were both written in Persian and dealt with theoretical astronomy, Ṭūsī still felt that he needed to write the *Tadkhira,* the more comprehensive theoretical astronomical text that followed them, in Arabic. Similarly, two other important *zījes* were also written in Persian rather than Arabic, namely the *Zīj-i Khāqānī* of Kāshī (d. 1429), who worked at Ulugh Beg's (d. 1449) observatory in Samarqand, and the *Zīj-i Sulṭānaī* of Ulugh Beg himself. There are other Persian *zījes*[61] as well, but very few Persian texts in the *hay'a* tradition.

In order to explain this phenomenon, I have stressed the role of the school in the propagation of astronomical texts, and the clear distinctions which were drawn between astrology and astronomy. I have also explained it by trying to look at the clientele who would have used such texts, and found the court astrologers and their colleagues practicing outside the court requiring such *zījes,* while the school masters condemning astrology and writing commentaries on the theoretical astronomical texts of the *hay'a* tradition. As for the linguistic differences, I stipulate that the court astrologers, who were probably not so well educated in the religious sciences, did not have a very good command of Arabic and thus needed texts that were written in Persian, the language they used in their daily practice. The school students and the school masters, on the other hand, who were by the nature of the school itself more religiously inclined, were masters of both Persian and Arabic, but mainly Arabic, since they had to study all the primary religious texts in that language. It was therefore natural that they would write, read, and comment on theoretical astronomical texts in Arabic.

This brings me back to the title of this book, where the term "Arabic" rather than "Islamic" astronomy is used. In light of the last point made in this introduction,. I thought it was appropriate that the linguistic adjective applied to the type of astronomy studied in this collection of articles should be "Arabic" because the texts under discussion were written in that language. Designating these texts as "Arabic" does not mean that, because they were "Arabic," they were any less Islamic, if one were to use the term "Islamic" to designate the intellectual work of all the lands, Arab and non-Arab, that constituted classical Islamic civilization. As I have just argued, my contention is that more of such texts were produced in the religious circles of the Islamic civilization, and because the religious circles communicated intellectually in Arabic the texts were written in Arabic as well. Only at a much later period, which falls well outside the limits of this book, when Arabic was no longer mastered by the school population, one finds some theoretical astronomical texts written in languages other than Arabic, be they Persian, Turkish, or Urdu.

As for the age of decline, I can only ask the reader to go through the results reported in these articles, compare them to the results that were supposed to have been achieved before the eleventh century, during the "golden age" of Islam, and then judge for himself or herself the validity of such periodization. I hope that the reader can be persuaded at least to reconsider that periodization scheme.

NOTES

1. These texts were in all likelihood modeled after the Ptolemaic *Handy Tables.* See, for example, E. S. Kennedy, *Survey of Islamic Astronomical Tables, Transactions of the American Philosophical Society,* new series, vol. 46, part 2, 1956, pp. 123–177.
2. See, for example, David King, "Universal Solutions in Islamic Astronomy," in *From Ancient Omens to Statistical Mechanics: Essays on the Exact Sciences Presented to Asger Aaboe,* ed. J. L. Berggren and B. R. Goldstein, Acta Historica Scientiarum Naturalium et Medicinalium, edidit Bibliotheca Universitatis Hauniensis, vol. 39, University Library, Copenhagen, 1987, pp. 121–132; ID., "Universal Solutions to Problems of Spherical Astronomy from Mamluk Egypt and Syria," in *A Way Prepared: Essays on Islamic Culture in Honor of Richard Bayly Winder* (New York University Press, New York, 1988), pp. 153–184.
3. Sayılı, Aydın, *The Observatory in Islam and Its Place in the General History of the Observatory,* Publications of the Turkish Historical Society, series 7, no. 38 (Türk Tarih Kurumu Basimevi, Ankara, 1960).
4. Reference is made here to the famous attack against Greek philosophy by Abū Ḥāmid al-Ghazzālī (d. 1111) in his *Tahāfut al-Falāsifah* (Incoherence of the Philosophers).
5. The works referred to here were later republished in *Studies in the Islamic Exact Sciences* by E. S. Kennedy, colleagues and former students, ed. D. King and M. H. Kennedy (American University of Beirut, Beirut, 1983), pp. 50–107.
6. See, for example, E. S. Kennedy, "Late Medieval Planetary Theory," *Isis* 57 (1966):365–378, esp. p. 366, and my article, "Astrology/Astronomy, Islamic," *Dictionary of the Middle Ages,* ed. Joseph R. Strayer (Scribner's Sons, New York, 1982), vol. 1, pp. 616–624, esp. p. 621 (reprinted here).
7. G. Saliba, "Theory and Observation in Islamic Astronomy: The Work of Ibn al-Shāṭir of Damascus (d. 1375)," *Journal for the History of Astronomy* 18 (1987):36–43 (reprinted here).
8. As far I can tell, the designation of *hay'a* as a separate science is not found in the literature before the tenth century. Fārābi (d. 950), for example, considers, in his *Iḥṣā' al-ᶜulūm* (Census of the Sciences), ed. Osman Amine (Anglo-Egyptian Press, 1968), p. 103, this branch of astronomy under the title *ᶜilm al-nujūm al-taᶜlīmī* (mathematical science of the stars). While al-Nadīm (d. 990), author of thc *Fihrist,* who wrote toward the last quarter of that century, refers to some authors as being famous for their work in *ᶜilm al-hay'a,* which we can translate as Science of Astronomy. Cf., e.g. *Fihrist,* ed. R. Tajaddud (Teheran, 1971), pp. 333, 337, *et passim.*
9. These texts were apparently first conceived during the ninth and tenth centuries, but did not reach, as far as we can tell from the existing evidence, the sophisticated level addressed here. We note, for example, in the work of the famous astrologer of the Hamdānid ruler Sayf al-Dawla (d. 976), al-Qabīṣī (fl. c. 960), *fī imtiḥān al-munajjimīn,* the mention of another work dealing with the criticism

of Ptolemaic astronomy. In one instance while classifying the various types of astrologers, he says, "in our *Doubts on the Almagest,* there are several questions with which the members of this class of perfect astrologers can be tested. I will enumerate these questions in the large book." Ẓāhirīya Ms. 4871, fol. 67r. There is some evidence that earlier critiques of Ptolemy were also composed. See F. Sezgin, *Geschichte des Arabischen Schrifttums* (Leiden, Brill), vol. 6, pp. 204, 293, *et passim.*

10. I have already edited two of these texts, namely, *Kitāb al-Hay'a* of Mu'ayyad al-Dīn al-ʿUrḍī (d. 1266), published as *The Astronomical Works of Mu'ayyad al-Dīn al-ʿUrḍī,* Markaz Dirāsāt al-Waḥda al-ʿArabīya (Beirut, 1990), and *Nihāyat al-Sūl fī Taṣḥīḥ al-Uṣūl (The Final Quest Regarding the Rectification of Astronomical Principles* [forthcoming]), but none of them is yet translated and commented upon. F. J. Ragep has also produced an edition, translation, and commentary on a section of the text of Naṣīr al-Dīn al-Ṭūsī (d. 1274) as a Ph.D. dissertation at Harvard University, 1982, and the full text is promised.
11. As far as I can tell, it was Victor Roberts who first coined the term "Maragha School" in his article, "The Planetary Theory of Ibn al-Shāṭir: Latitudes of the Planets," *Isis* 57 (1966):365–378, esp. p. 365. As our research is beginning to show, that name was not quite felicitous since the type of activities conducted at the Maragha Obervatory, namely the criticism of Greek astronomical models and the development of new models to replace them, was not restricted to Maragha nor to that time period. The name "Maragha School" can therefore be sometimes misleading, especially when it is used in the sense of direct relationships among astronomers who lived centuries apart, or when it designates Maragha as a point of origin for such activities when we know that these activities began before the building of the Maragha Observatory.
12. See, for example, A. I. Sabra, "The Scientific Enterprise," in *Islam and the Arab World,* ed. B. Lewis (Thames and Hudson, London, 1976), pp. 181–200, esp. pp. 186–188, where he asserts over and over again that "observations play no essential part in this story, either as causes or as consequences," where "story" refers to the activities of the Maragha astronomers. See also Owen Gingerich, "Islamic Astronomy," *Scientific American* 254 (1986):74–83, where he speaks of "Refining Ptolemy," "Doubting Ptolemy," and that the attacks against Ptolemy "were invariably launched on philosophical rather than on observational grounds." A similar attitude toward Arabic astronomy was already expressed during the nineteenth century by Baron Carra de Vaux in "Les sphères célestes selon Nasîr-Eddîn Attûsî," in Paul Tannery, *Recherches sur l'histoire de l'astronomie ancienne* (Gauthier, Paris, 1893), app. 6, pp. 337–361, where he uses such terms as "faiblesse" and "mesquinerie" to describe the same Maragha activities; and François Nau, *Livre de l'ascension de l'esprit* (E. Bouillon, Paris, 1899), p. xiv, where he describes such activities as "*adjuncta* dus aux Arabes."
13. The latest discussion of the use of the Ṭūsī Couple by Copernicus is in N. Swerdlow and O. Neugebauer, *Mathematical Astronomy in Copernicus's De Revolutionibus* (Springer, New York, 1984), p. 46f.

14. W. Hartner, "Copernicus, the Man, the Work, and Its History," *Proceedings of the American Philosophical Society* 117 (1973):413–422, esp. p. 421.
15. See A. Grafton, "Michael Maestlin's Account of Copernican Planetary Theory," *Proceedings of the American Philosophical Society* 117 (1973):523–5520.
16. This subject was first raised by O. Neugebauer in *A History of Ancient Mathematical Astronomy* (Springer, New York, 1975), p. 1035.
17. A. Sabra and N. Shehaby, *Ibn al-Haytham al-Shukūk ʿAlā Baṭlamyūs (Dubitationes in Ptolemaeum)* (Cairo, National Library Press, 1971).
18. See the work of al-Qabīṣī, *supra,* and the work of the famous tenth-century physician, Abū Bakr al-Rāzī (d. 925), *al-Shukūk ʿAlā Jālīnus,* which is extant but not yet critically edited and published. See Sabra and Shehaby, *op. cit.,* p. "*nūn*" of the Arabic introduction, and S. Pines, *Dictionary of Scientific Biography,* s.v. "Rāzī."
19. See, for example, Sezgin, *GAS,* vol. 6, p. 125.
20. See, for example, the copy of this work at the Bibliotheque Nationale, Paris, Arabe 2504,3, Sezgin, *GAS,* vol. 6, p. 150.
21. See Sezgin, *GAS,* vol. 6, p. 196.
22. The Syriac text of Sergius Rasʿaina (d. 536) which was published by Sachau in *Inedita Syriaca,* 1870 (reprinted by Georg Olms, Hildesheim, 1968), pp. 125–126, was shown by the present author to have been a liberal translation of the twenty-eighth chapter of the *Eisagogeka* of Paulus Alexandrinus (forthcoming).
23. See the excellent study of this tradition by Anton Heinen, *Islamic Cosmology: A Study of As-Suyūṭī's al-Hay'a as-sanīya fī l-hay'a as-sunnīya,* Beiruter Texte und Studien, vol. 27 (Beirut, 1982, in Kommission bei Franz Steiner Verlag, Wiesbaden).
24. See, for example, the description of a large instrument (quadrant of 80 cubits diameter) by Abū Maḥmūd al-Khujandī (d. 992) in Cheikho's *"Risālat al-Khujandī fī al-mayl wa-ʿarḍ al-balad," Mashriq* 11 (1908):60–69; and E. Wiedemann with Th. W. Juynbol, "Avicennas Schrift über ein von ihm ersonnenes Beobachtunginstrument," *Acta Orientalia* xi,5 (1926):81–167. See also Ghiyāth al-Dīn al-Kāshī (d. 1429) in Aydın Sayılı, *Ghiyâth al-Dîn al-Kâshî's Letter on Ulugh Bey and the Scientific Activity in Samarqand* (Türk Tarih Kurumu Basimevi, Ankara, 1985).
25. See, for example, the work of Régis Morelon in *Thābit Ibn Qurra, Œuvres d'astronomie,* edition, translation, and commentary (Les Belles Lettres, Paris, 1987), and his more recent article in *Arabic Sciences and Philosophy,* where he demonstrates how Thābit Ibn Qurra began the process of mathematization of astronomical phenomena, i.e., applying rigorous mathematical methods in order to explain observational phenomena, and the first inkling of the questions related to the harmonization between the physical and the mathematical sides of Ptolemaic astronomy, which were to become later on the major concern of the *hay'a* texts.
26. See note 9 above, Ẓāhirīya, ms. 4871, fol. 67r, line 23. Incidentally, this same text gives a clear indication that such famous astronomers and astrologers as al-Qabīṣī did indeed instruct students who read such subjects with them.

27. For a detailed description of what is known about this text, see G. Saliba, "Early Criticism of Ptolemaic Astronomy: The Andalusian School" (forthcoming).
28. Cf. below G. Saliba, "The Astronomical Tradition of Maragha: A Historical Survey and Prospects for Future Research," *Arabic Sciences and Philosophy* 1(1991):67–99, esp. p. 88.
29. Although I seem to be agreeing with Gauthier and Sabra in this general characterization of the two responses to Ptolemaic astronomy, namely the Andalusian and the eastern, I have argued elsewhere that such a generalization is not very useful for conceptual reasons. Later on I refine this distinction further to include people like Jābir Ibn Aflaḥ and al-Zarqāel, as well as Ibn al-Shāṭir from the east. See L. Gauthier "Une Reforme du Système Astronomique de Ptolemée tentée par les Philosophes Arabes du XIIe Siècle," *Journal Asiatique,* 10e ser., 14 (1909):483–510; A. I. Sabra, "The Andalusian Revolt against Ptolemaic Astronomy," chap. 7 in *Transformation and Tradition in the Sciences,* edited by Everett Mendelsohn (Cambridge University Press, New York, 1984), pp. 133–153; and G. Saliba, "Early Criticism of Ptolemaic Astronomy: The Andalusian School" (forthcoming).
30. G. J. Toomer, "The Solar Theory of Az-Zarqāl: An Epilogue," in *From Deferent to Equant: A Volume of Studies in the History of Science in the Ancient and Medieval Near East in Honor of E. S. Kennedy,* ed. D. King and G. Saliba (New York Academy of Sciences, Annals 500, 1987), pp. 513–519.
31. Noel Swerdlow, "Jābir Ibn Aflaḥ's Interesting Method for Finding the Eccentricities and Direction of the Apsidal Line of a Superior Planet," *From Deferent to Equant,* pp. 501–512.
32. Cf., for example, ʿUrḍī, *Kitab al-Hay'a,* p. 250.
33. *Ibid.,* p. 219.
34. *Ibid.,* p. 228.
35. In Swerdlow's translation, the very first paragraph of the introduction to the *Commentariolus* by Copernicus says: "I understand that our predecessors assumed a large number of celestial spheres principally in order to account for the apparent motion of the planets through uniform motion, for it seemed highly unreasonable that a heavenly body should not always move uniformly in a perfectly circular figure." Copernicus goes on to describe how the previous astronomers accounted for these motions, and in the third paragraph he says: "Nevertheless, the theories concerning these matters that have been put forth far and wide by Ptolemy and most others, although they correspond numerically [with the apparent motions], also seemed quite doubtful, for these theories were inadequate unless they also envisioned certain *equant* circles, on account of which it appeared that the planet never moves with uniform velocity either in its *deferent* sphere or with respect to its proper center. Therefore a theory of this kind seemed neither perfect enough nor sufficiently in accordance with reason." Noel Swerdlow, "The Derivation and First Draft of Copernicus's Planetary Theory: A Translation of the Commentariolus with Commentary," *Proceedings of the American Philosophical Society* 117 (1973):423–512. Even the concepts

of "doubtful," "equant," "uniform motion," and so on are reminiscent of the wordings of Arabic astronomers.

36. See particularly "The Astronomical Tradition of Maragha: A Historical Survey and Prospects for Future Research," pp. 78f *et passim*.
37. See ʿUrḍī, *Kitāb al-Hay'a,* p. 340.
38. I am thinking of the famous statement in the dedication of the *De Revolutionibus,* where he says that he had resisted "letting come to light a work which I had kept hidden among my things for not merely nine years, but for almost four times nine years," and the earlier statement in the same dedication where he says: "For a long time I was in great difficulty as to whether I should bring to light my commentaries." In the same dedication he also complains about Ptolemaic astronomers: "But even those who have thought up eccentric circles seem to have been able for the most part to compute the apparent movements numerically by those means, they have in the meanwhile admitted a great deal which seems to contradict the first principles of regularity of movement." I use here the translation of Charles Glenn Wallis, Great Books, *Encyclopaedia Britannica* (University of Chicago, 1952).
39. See, for example, G. Saliba, "The Role of Maragha in the Development of Islamic Astronomy: A Scientific Revolution before the Renaissance," *Revue de synthèse* 4 (1987):371, note 22; *idem,* "The Astronomical Tradition of Maragha: A Historical Survey and Prospects for Future Research," p. 77, and Swerdlow and Neugebauer, *Mathematical Astronomy,* pp. 47, 295.
40. O. Neugebauer, *A History of Ancient Mathematical Astronomy* (Springer, New York, 1975).
41. *Arabic Studies Quarterly* 4(1982):211–225.
42. Regarding the distinction drawn by Bīrūnī between astrology and astronomy, see Shlomo Pines, "The Semantic Distinction between the Terms *Astronomy* and *Astrology* according to Al-Bīrūnī," *Isis* 55 (1964):343–349.
43. In the words of the Ḥanbalite theologian Abū ʿAbbās Taqī al-Dīn Aḥmad b. ʿAbd al-Ḥalīm Ibn Taymīya, *"wa-hal kān* [p. 68] *al-Ṭūsī, wa-amthāluhu yanfuqūna ʿinda al-mushrikīn min al-tatar illā bi-akādhīb al-munajjimīn, wa-makāyid al-muḥtālīn, al-munāfiya li-l-ʿaql wa-l-dīn?"* (would Ṭūsī and his likes have found success with the unbelievers the Tatars except through the lies of astrologers, and the tricks of the deceivers which are contrary to reason and to religion?), in *Dar' Taʿāruḍ al-ʿAql wa-l-Naql,* ed. Muhammad Rashad Salim, printed at the Islamic University of the Imam Muhammad b. Saʿūd, part of the library of Ibn Taymīya, first part, al-Mu'allafāt 3, first printing 1979, vol. 5, 1981, pp. 67–68.
44. For a more detailed description of the role of the astrologer in medieval Islam, see G. Saliba, "The Role of the Astrologer in Medieval Islamic Society," *Bulletin d' Études Orientales* 44 (1992):45–68.
45. For earlier attacks on astrology, see, for example, the work of the Ashʿarite theologian al-Bāqillānī (d. 1013), *Kitāb al-Tamhīd,* ed. J. McCarthy (Librarie Orientale, Beirut, 1957), where he devotes the fifth chapter to an attack on the astrologers.
46. See, for example, the proscriptions regarding the practice of the astrologers and

other craftsmen given by the *ḥisba* manual of Ibn al-Ukhuwwa, Muḥammad b. Muḥammad b. Aḥmad al-Qurashī (d. 1329), *Maʿālim al-Qurba fī' Aḥkām al-Ḥisba,* ed. Reuben Levy, Gibb Memorial Series, n.s. 12 (Luzac, London, 1938). Although this regulation is somehow late, it is in all likelihood safe to speculate that similar practices were probably introduced one or two centuries earlier, if not before.

47. See Ibn al-Akfānī, Shams al-Dīn Muḥammad b. Ibrāhīm b. Ṣāʿid al-Sinjārī al-Miṣrī (d. 1348), *Irshād al-Qāṣid ilā Asnā al-Maqāṣid,* ed. A. Sprenger, fasc. 1, vol. 6, no. 21 (Bibliotheca Indica, 1849).
48. *Irshād al-Qāṣid,* p. 85. In fact, ʿUrḍī's text is almost twice as long as Ṭūsī's *Tadhkira,* and the *Nihāya* of Shīrāzī is about four times as long. The theoretical context in which this characterization was made can best be understood in light of the remark made by Ibn al-Akfānī in the introduction of his book, where he says: ''*Wa-l-ʿilm maḥṣūr fī al-taṣawwur wa-l-taṣdīq. Wa-l-taṣawwur yuṭlab bi-l-aqāwīl al-shāriḥa min al-ḥudūd wa-l-rusūm wa-naḥwiha. Wa-qad tuʿqal ḥaqīqat al-shay' wa-qad yutakhayyal timthāluhu. Wa-l-taṣdīq yakūn ʿan ashyā' hiya muqaddamāt fī ashyā' hiya ṣuwar al-qiyāsāt li-ashyā' hiya natā'ij. Wa-qad yaḥṣal bihā al-yaqīn wa-qad lā yaḥṣal illā iqnāʿ,*'' which can be translated very freely as: Science *(ʿilm)* is restricted to being either speculative *(taṣawwur)* or demonstrative *(taṣdīq).* The speculative is sought after with statements that are descriptive of definitions, figures, and the like. (Through it) one could come to comprehend the reality of the thing or imagine its likeness. The demonstrative results from postulates regarding things that are themselves forms of analogies for other things that come out as results. Certainty may result from it, or only conviction may ensue therefrom.
49. *Ibid.*
50. One of the fifteenth-century commentators on the *Tadhkira* is none other than the famous Ḥanafite theologian al-Sharīf al-Jurjānī, ʿAlī b. Muḥammad b. ʿAlī al-Sayyid al-Zain Abū al-Ḥasan al-Ḥusainī (d. 1413), whose biography by al-Sakhkhāwī, Shams al-Dīn Muḥammad b. ʿAbd al-Raḥmān, in *Al-Ḍaw' al-Lāmiʿ li-Ahl al-Qarn al-Tāsiʿ* (Maktabat al-Qudsī, Cairo, 1935), vol. 5, p. 328, includes the following statement: ''He undertook to teach, compose and issue legal opinions. Many an excellent *imām* (a distinguished scholar, usually religious) graduated with him. His followers and students increased, while his fame and reputation became widespread in distant lands.'' He was obviously well established within the school system.
51. In a relatively unstudied text, a commentary on Ṭūsī's *Tadhkira,* written during the reign of Ulugh Beg by Mullā Fatḥ Allāh al-Shirwānī (c. 1440), the author attests to the fact that he was a student of Qāḍīzādeh at the Ulugh Beg school in Samarqand. The author goes on to describe the actual conduct of the class, where the students were studying Nīsābūrī's commentary on Ṭūsī's *Tadhkira,* under the professorship of Qāḍīzādeh and in the presence of Ulugh Beg himself. In the same text a reference is made to Ulugh Beg's visits to the said school twice or three times a week, where he would listen to the students reading Nīsābūrī's text and interrupted them at critical points to ask for spontaneous responses to the

subtle difficulties raised in the text; then he would add comments of his own to their responses. Such pedagogical procedures are also confirmed in Kāshī's letter to his father; see E. S. Kennedy, "A Letter of Jamshīd al-Kāshī to His Father: Scientific Research at a Fifteenth Century Court," *Orientalia* 29(1960):191–213, esp. p. 205. Additional evidence for the use of such *hay'a* texts in schools can be gathered from the possession statements usually marked on the flyleaves of such manuscripts. See, for example, Ibn al-Shāṭir's text of *Nihāyat al-sūl,* ms. Bodleian, Marsh 139, where it is marked as having been owned by a teacher *(mudarris),* and Shīrāzī's *Faᶜaltu fa-lā talum,* Majlis Shūrāy, ms. 3944, where it is marked as "belonging to the Manṣūrīya school." Two other autobiographical remarks from the turn of the century or the twentieth century also attest to the use of such *hay'a* texts in schools. See, for example, the reports of Aḥmad Kasravī (d. 1945), *Zandegānī man,* Tehran, 1323 (=1945), p. 59, and Hasan Taqīzādeh (1878–1970), *Yādnāmeh,* Tehran, 1349 (=1971), p. 290, which reveal that such *hay'a* texts as Jaghmīnī's and *Tashrīḥ al-Aflāk* of al-ᶜĀmilī were included in the regular *madrasa* curriculum as late as the early part of the twentieth century. I am grateful to my colleague, Professor Hamid Dabashi, Columbia University, for the reference to Taqīzādeh's biography.

52. Ibn Taymīya, *Dar' Taᶜāruḍ al-ᶜAql wa-l-Naql* vol. 1, pp. 157–158, where he says: "Nothing brings them (i.e. the philosophers) together, and they are at greater variance than all the sects of the Muslims, Christians and Jews. The philosophy followed by al-Fārābī and Ibn Sīnā is the peripatetic philosophy, the followers of Aristotle, the author of the mathematical sciences *(ṣāḥib al-ta' ālīm?).* The difference between him and his predecessors takes a long time to describe. And the difference among his own followers is also long to describe. As for the remaining sects, if one were to tell only about their differences in regard to astronomy *(ᶜilm al-hay'a)* it would be more than all the differences of all the sects of Islam *(ṭawā' if ahl al-qibla).* That is so, despite the fact that astronomy is a mathematical computational discipline *(ᶜilm riyāḍīy ḥisābīy)* and is the most valid of their sciences *(min aṣaḥ ᶜulūmihim).* And if their differences regarding it are so great, what could one say in regard to their differences in the physical [sciences] or logic? or even metaphysics?

"Consider this in connection with what was reported about them by al-Ashᶜarī in his book *Statements of the non-Muslims,* and by the Judge Abu Bakr in his book *al-Daqā'iq* in regard to the mathematical and the physical sciences. Their differences in that regard are many many times more than those which were mentioned by Shahrastānī and his like who report their statements. Their differences in regard to the mathematical sciences—which is the most valid of their sciences—could almost be uncountable. Even the same book regarding which their majority agreed—which is the book of the *Almagest* of Ptolemy—contains many problems which cannot be proven correctly *(fi-hi qaḍāya kathīra la yaqūm ᶜalayhā dalīl ṣaḥīḥ),* and has many problems disputed with him [i.e., Ptolemy] by others, and it contains issues based on reported observations which could be erroneous and faulty."

53. Khalīl Ibn Aybak al-Ṣafadī, *Nakt al-Humyān fī Nukat al-ᶜUmyān,* al-Maṭbaᶜa al-

Jamālīya (Cairo, 1900; reprint Maktabat al-muthanna, Baghdad, 1963), pp. 63–65.

54. The work of Khafrī intended here is his commentary on Ṭūsī's *Tadhkira,* in which he surveys earlier mathematical models that were proposed for the reform of Ptolemaic astronomical problems, and concludes by parading more than four mathematical solutions for the problem of the motion of Mercury, for example. One cannot help but feel that he advances these mathematical solutions with such abundance only to illustrate how easy it is to arrive at equally valid solutions of physical problems by mathematical means.
55. In a seventeenth-century autobiographical note, Ḥājjī Khalīfa (Kātib Chelebī) (1608–1657), the famous author of *Kashf al-Ẓunūn,* ed. Sharaf al-Dīn Yaletqaya (Istanbul, 1941), p. 16, tells us that he himself had lectured on a similar *hay'a* text written by ʿAlā' al-Dīn al-Qushjī (d. 1474).
56. We have already seen that Mulla Fatḥallāh Shirwānī was primarily a religious scholar before he was an astronomer. His works on religious issues such as *ʿIbādāt* are still extant. See, for example, H. O. Fleischer, *Catalogus Codicum Manuscriptorum Orientalium: Bibliothecæ Regiæ Dresdensis* (Leipzig, 1831), no. 144,4. Al-Sharīf al-Jurjānī, who was also mentioned above as a religious scholar, was also employed as a *madrasa* professor. See, for example, C. Brockelmann, *Geschiche der Arabischen Literature,* suppl. 2, p. 305.
57. G. Saliba, "Persian Scientists in the Islamic World: Astronomy from Maragha to Samarqand" (forthcoming).
58. The autobiographical reports of Aḥmad Kasravī, and Hasan Taqīzādeh both reveal the emphasis laid on the study of the Arabic language. In the case of Kasravī, that part of the curriculum proved to be painful at first for it was restricted to the study of grammar and syntax, and did not include a good grasp of the language as such.
59. See the discussion that follows about the production of such *zījes.*
60. See, for example, the reference to such an office in *Tadhkirat al-Mulūk: A Manual of Ṣafavid Administration,* trans. V. Minorsky, Gibb Memorial Trust (London, 1943), pp. 57, 66, *et passim.*
61. See, for example, the list of such *zījes* like the *Zīj-i Mufrad* and others assembled by E. S. Kennedy in his *Survey of Islamic Astronomical Tables, American Philosophical Society Transactions* 46 (1956).

I. General Background of Arabic Astronomy

The Development of Astronomy in Medieval Islamic Society

George Saliba

General surveys of Islamic astronomy tend to agree on the following basic outline: Before the seventh century of the Christian era, the Arabs possessed a rudimentary knowledge of the stars, enough to guide them in their desert travels. By the end of the eighth century and during the ninth century, most of the Greek corpus in the exact sciences as well as the medical sciences found its way into Arabic either directly from Greek, or through intermediaries such as Syriac, Pahlevi, etc. Then the contention is that the Arabs—and here we mean those who wrote in Arabic—seem to have held that Greek heritage in awe and at best introduced some slight modifications into it until the time of Ghazzali in the twelfth century. Ghazzali's famous attack on the philosophers seems to have closed the gate on the "foreign sciences"—as this Greek heritage came to be called—and led the Muslim world into an antiphilosophical slumber from which it was never to recover. Around the same century, i.e., the twelfth, the Latin West was experiencing a Renaissance that could profit from the sciences that were preserved in Arabic, and thus the Greek sciences luckily found their way back to Europe together with the "trivial" Arabic modifications.

This picture, although too simplistic and quite nonhistorical, is nonetheless the one described by most of the secondary literature about Islamic science.[1] There is no space here to thoroughly review this proposition(s). I will limit the discussion to the discipline of astronomy and attempt to isolate the factors within Muslim society that led to the emergence of a "Muslim astronomy"—irrespective of whether or not that astronomy was textually transmitted to the Latin West—thereby hoping to cast some doubt on the basic assumptions of the above outline.

George Saliba is Assistant Professor of Arabic, Department of Middle East Languages and Cultures, Columbia University, New York. He is the author of some twenty-five articles on Islamic science and is currently editing the two astronomical texts of Mu'ayyad al-Din al-'Urdi (d. 1266 A.D.) and of Ibn al-Shatir (d. 1375 A.D.), both of Damascus.

1. Cf., for example, L.P. Williams and H.J. Steffens, *The History of Science in Western Civilization* (University Press of America, 1977), vol. 1, chap. 2, pp. 170–215, esp. 170–78.

THE TRANSLATION MOVEMENT

It is quite unfortunate that we have no sources dealing directly with the status of astronomy during the first century of Hijra. Whatever fragments we have point to a genuine interest on the part of Muslims in the sciences that were foreign to Islam—be they from India, Persia, or Byzantium.[2] By the end of the second century of Hijra and the beginning of the third, a veritable explosion of interest in the "foreign sciences" seems to have taken place, particularly in Baghdad. This still inexplicable phenomenon produced an unprecedented number of translations of the Greek scientific sources, all within a relatively short period. Moreover, these translations included the best of the Greek scientific corpus. I propose that this phenomenon could not have happened in a society that was only interested in the stars that led travelers across the vast deserts of the Muslim Empire. The best Greek sources were by then all but neglected in the Greek world, and had been so for about four to five hundred years.

Why was there such a concentrated interest in the Greek sciences during the eighth century, and in Baghdad in particular during the early part of the ninth? This question will remain unanswered until a thorough study is completed of the social, economic, and political conditions during the latter part of the Umayyad times and the early Abbasid ones. I suspect that the answer may profitably be sought by concentrating on the technocratic and bureaucratic makeup of late Umayyad and early Abbasid times. Several hints pointing in that direction are preserved in the literary sources: The *Fihrist* of al-Nadim, for example, connects the translation movement with the "Arabization" of the administration under al-Hajjaj b. Yusuf (governor of Iraq, 694–714) from Persian, and Hisham b. 'Abd al-Malik (724–743) from Greek. Ạdd to that the anecdote preserved in Jahiz's *Bukhala'* about the Arab physician Asad b. Jani (before 850) who complained about his lack of success as a physician because he was of Arab stock and spoke Arabic eloquently without a foreigner's twist. These two anecdotes, taken together within their historical context, reveal a tension between educated Arabs and the foreign civil servants who were still monopolizing the civil administration. From that perspective, they may also explain why some private individuals, aspiring to greater administrative and social prestige for themselves or for their protégés, would patronize translation activities.

The participants in this dramatic activity, from translators to patrons, were not all Muslims by faith, but it was in the Muslim milieu that the drama

2. For a comprehensive survey of this fragmentary evidence, cf. C.A. Nallino, *'ilm al-Falak* (Rome, 1911) (reprinted by Maktabat al-Muthanna, Baghdad), esp. pp. 1–148, which is still very useful.

unfolded. If we take the statement of al-Nadim's *Fihrist* seriously, and there is no reason not to, one should note that even the bishop of Mousil, al-Habib Ibn Bahrij, a church official, obviously did not translate for his church but rather for the Caliph al-Ma'mun of Baghdad.

This whole translation movement, with all its social, political, and historical implications, was never repeated in history, although to some the translation movement of the Greco-Arabic sciences to the Latin West constitutes a parallel case. My contention is that the two movements are quite distinct, motivated by completely different reasons, patronized by different patrons, and produced distinctly different results. A comparative study of the two movements, however, promises to produce unprecedented results in the analysis of cultural transmissions.

Neither the drama of the translation movement in Islam, nor its comparison with that of Spain can be discussed at length here; both subjects will have to remain as points of departure for future research. What concerns us here, however, is the conscious effort made by the eighth- and ninth-century Muslims to incorporate the Greek legacy.

THE FOREIGN SCIENCES IN ISLAM

The Greek legacy did not become the dominant legacy in Islam without a significant struggle with the native sciences, as hinted above. In addition, another foreign tradition—that of India—was quite significant during the latter part of the eighth century and the early part of the ninth. In terms of astronomical texts, the Indian tradition came to be the main tradition relied upon by men such as Ya'qub b. Tariq, Fazzari, and Khwarizmi, to name only a few.[3] It took a generation or two before the Greek tradition, more sophisticated than the Indian one and backed by a body of philosophical literature that made it more systematic and coherent, began to replace this inadequate tradition and to engage Muslim thinkers in a dialogue that continued to be articulated throughout Muslim history. One should emphasize here that within this new Greek tradition the philosophical assumptions of any branch of science were an explicitly integral part of that science, and one could not, for example, be a good physician without being a good philosopher, as Galen would have put it. It was mainly this Greek tradition that was referred to as the "foreign sciences" from the ninth century onward.

3. D. Pingree, "The Fragments of the Works of Ya'qub Ibn Tariq," *Journal For Near Eastern Studies* (JNES) 27 (1968): 97–125; idem, "The Fragments of the Works of Fazari," *JNES* 29 (1970): 103–23.

In 1916 Goldziher extensively reviewed the whole question of these foreign sciences in Islam and the Muslim reaction to them.[4] The gist of his article is that although the foreign sciences were negatively received by the pious Muslims, they nevertheless were attacked on the theoretical level only and managed to survive within the ordinary life of the Muslims. At no stage did Goldziher ask, however, why Islam rejected these sciences in the first place, nor what it did after it had rejected them. I propose to address these questions with respect to astronomy, and to show that an Islamization process did take place some time between the tenth and the twelfth centuries. Moreover, I will show that theoretical astronomy—planetary theory, at least—was condoned and pursued even by religious men.

It is true that by the beginning of the third century of Hijra, there developed a tension between Islam as a religion and the foreign sciences, inasmuch as those sciences had any bearing on religious metaphysical questions. This tension was complementary and not a substitute for the tension among the civil servants and the Arabs educated in the native sciences. The most obvious grounds for a conflict between religion and the foreign sciences were in the field of astrology, a discipline that infringed directly on religious dogma on matters concerning, for example, the eternity of the world,[5] the problem of free will, and predestination; astrology was also singled out, for the same reasons, by the Christian theologians of pre-Islamic times as a controversial discipline in direct competition with religion.[6] Mas'udi tells us in his *Muruj al-Dhahab* (chap. 69) that even the astronomers (*al-falakiyyin*) proclaimed the doctrine of the eternity of the world, together with the Indians and the Greeks, the implication being that if the world has no beginning, it has no end, and therefore, man need not worry about punishment and reward.

Moreover, in Islam, the issue of the unity of the Creator led to a total aversion to any discipline that questioned that unity in any way. Astrologers, and adherents of the foreign sciences in general, seem to have taken the issue

4. I. Goldziher, "Stellung der Alten Islamischen Orthodoxie zu den Antiken Wissenschaften," *Abhandlungen der Akademie der Wissenschaften*, Bd. 8 (1916).

5. Cf. Mas'udi, *Muruj al-Dhahab*, ed. and trans. C. Barbier de Meynard and Pavet de Courteille (Paris: Imprimerie Imperiale, 1861) (reprinted in Teheran, *Matbu'at-i Isma'iliyyan*, 1970), vol. 4, p. 100f.

6. For pre-Islamic attacks on astrology, cf., Gregory of Nyssa (c. 335–395 A.D.), *Kitab Tabi'at al-'Insan* (Zahiriyyah Ms [Damascus]), 4871, fol. 57r–60r. For Ghazzali's attack and Ibn Rushd's response, cf, S. Van den Bergh, *Averroes' Tahafut al-Tahafut* (London: Luzac, 1969), p. 311f. Ghazzali, in his attack on the philosophers, does not even confront astrology directly and takes issue with the philosophers on matters dealing with the natural sciences only on four points; three of these points concern the problem of the soul and one the problem of the logical formulation of the relationship between cause and effect inasmuch as that reflects on the problem of the existence of miracles.

too lightly, hence leaving themselves wide open for attack. The politico-religious implications of this issue are only too obvious. In one of his treatises on the planets, the philosopher Kindi, considered the spokesman for the foreign sciences and an astrologer by conviction, gives us a flavor of the doctrines that must have been accepted by the astrologers of his time: "... the planets are rational (*natiqat*) spiritual beings capable of intelligence and speech, and [themselves] cause (*fa'ilat*) and administer (*mudabbirat*) everything in this world by the order of the prime Creator who controls all."[7]

In spite of the fact that the ultimate control of human destiny remains in the hands of God, it is not hard to see why such a doctrine smacks of polytheism, if not outright atheism. There is no doubt that it was perceived as such by Kindi's contemporaries and by the following generations of believers who saw in it a threat to Islam as a belief and as a culture. In one case, for example, we are told that Abu Ma'shar, the famous Albumassar of the Latin West, studied astrology until he became an atheist (*hatta 'alhada*).[8] It was the same Kindi who seduced Abu Ma'shar into astrology through geometry and arithmetic; Abu Ma'shar was at first one of the scholars of *Hadith*.[9] The importance of this anecdotal history is that it singles out astrology as the main culprit and makes geometry and arithmetic religiously commendable. Hence, one should not be led to believe with Goldziher that the foreign sciences were censured by Islam, for it is obvious that the commendable sciences such as the mathematical ones, were promoted and encouraged as long as they did not transgress outside their domain and dabble with theological questions.

As far as pure religious reaction to astrology is concerned, we do not have any early religious texts that deal with the attack on astrology, except for the few vague references in the *Hadith* collections; in this early period the legal schools were not yet formalized, and the attacks were not yet well articulated. What we know, however, is that the stigma of atheism was so widespread that it endangered the mathematicians and the astronomers because of their mere association with philosophy and astrology,[10] with astrology remaining the main culprit of the two.

Reaction of the Philosophers to Astrology

The philosophers' reactions were quite clear. Several treatises from the tenth

7. L.V. Vaglieri and G. Celentano, "Trois Epitres d'Al-Kindi," *Annali, Instituto Orientale di Napoli* 34 (N.S. 24) [1974]: 523–562, esp. p. 537.
8. Tannukhi, *Nushwar al-Muhadarat* (Beirut ed., 1973), vol. 4, p. 66; also Yaqut al-Hamwi, *Mu'jam al-Udaba'*, vol. 5, p. 467.
9. *Ibid.*
10. Cf., the convincing evidence collected by Goldziher, "Stellung der Alten."

and eleventh centuries by Farabi,[11] 'Isa b. 'Ali,[12] and Ibn Sina[13] are still preserved, each, in turn, attacking astrology. These attacks, important as they are in elaborating the pitfalls of astrology, do not concern us here in any major way. Suffice it to say that, with the sole exception of Fakhr al-Din al-Razi[14] of the thirteenth century, no philosopher of any repute would defend astrology. Razi's case should be studied, on account of its late date, under quite a different light from that of mere adherence to astrology or its rejection, for he belongs to a period when the occult sciences, including astrology, had themselves been reformulated to allow the writing of a book such as *Shams al-Ma'arif* by Al-Buni.[15]

As soon as the religious texts began to be standardized and codified, from the tenth century onward, there were systematic religious attacks on astrology, beginning with the attack of the Andalusian Ibn Hazm in his *maratib al-'ulum*[16] and *al-fasl fi al-milal*,[17] and culminating in the most organized attack, that of the fourteenth-century Hanbalite theologian Ibn Qayyim al-Jawziyyah in his *Miftah Dar al-Sa'adah*.[18] A systematic study of the religious attacks on astrology that isolates the purely Muslim parts of these attacks from the earlier Greek and Syriac ones that were translated into Arabic would be very instructive about the Muslim point of view.[19]

But, here again, we will come to see that the attack on astrology did not entail an attack on astronomy except inasmuch as the astronomers wanted to be astrologers. Moreover, the attack on astrology did not entail a rejection of the foreign sciences altogether, thereby heralding a decadence in scientific spirit as we are often led to believe.[20]

11. *Nukat Abi Nasr al-Farabi fima Yasuhhu wa-ma la Yasuhhu min 'ahkam al-nujum*, Hrsg. by Fr. Dietrici in *al-Farabi's Philosophische Abhandlungen* (Leiden, 1890), pp. 104 13. Cf. T. A. Druart, "Astronomie et Astrologie selon Al-Farabi," *Bulletin de. Philosophie Medievale*, Louvain 20 (1978): 43–47.

12. Quoted by Ibn Qayyim al-Jawziyyah, *Miftah Dar al-Sa'adah* (Beirut: Dar al-Kutub al-'Ilmiyyah), (reprint of the Cairo edition of 1939 with new pagination), vol. 2, pp. 148f.

13. M.A.F. Mehren, "Vue d'Avicenne sur l'Astrologie et sur le rapport de la responsabilitie humaine avec le destin," *Museon* 3 (1884): 383–403.

14. Fakhr al-Din al-Razi considers the legal status of astrological practices under one of five categories: (1) obligatory (*wajib*), (2) forbidden (*haram*), (3) recommended (*mandub*), (4) reprehensive (*makruh*), (5) permitted (*mubah*), as quoted in Escoral Ms 909, fol. 66v.

15. (Beirut: al-Maktabat al-Thaqafiyyah, n.d.).

16. ed. Ihsan Abbas (Cairo: Khanji, n.d.).

17. (Cairo: Khanji, 1903), vol. 5, p. 36f.

18. (Beirut: Dar al-Kutub al-'Ilmiyyah).

19. For the Arabic translation of Gregory of Nyssa's attack, see *Kitab Tabi'at al-'Insan*.

20. Actually the problem of the decadence of Islamic science has been most

Reaction of the Mathematicians to Astrology

In the Arabic sources dealing with the classification of science, the *Fihrist* of al-Nadim,[21] the *'ihsa' al-'ulum* of Farabi,[22] the *mafatih al-'ulum* of al-Khwarizmi[23] and others, confusion between astronomy and astrology is often the norm. Both disciplines are usually discussed under *'ilm al-nujum* and only formally separated into *'ilm al-hay'ah* (astronomy proper) and *'ilm al-'ahkam* (judicial astrology). The practitioners of either discipline are generally referred to as *munajjimun* by al-Nadim.

The reason for this confusion is far from clear, but is definitely connected with the original place of these two disciplines within the Greek legacy, and the fact that most early astronomers in Islam found employment as astrologers, for they were serving political patrons first and foremost.

In light of the above discussion, it is easy to imagine the dangers to the livelihood of astronomers and mathematicians who may have been subject to atheistic stigmatization because of their association with astrology, even if the association were only by name. Here again, we lack the texts that illustrate their reaction to the social environment. But from a few surviving fragments, and from the general trend in astronomical writings from the eleventh century onward, we can discern the unfolding of the events that gave birth to the new "Muslim Astronomy," the subject of our discussion. For the sake of organization and coherence, this new astronomy will be discussed under two different perspectives: the theoretical perspective and the philosophical one.

THE THEORETICAL PERSPECTIVE

To rescue themselves from the attacks on astrology, astronomers and mathematicians had to speak out against astrology in an attempt to carve out a separate identity for themselves. A few fragments have survived to illustrate this trend.

1. The biography of Abu Ma'shar and his implied approval of geometry and arithmetic as religiously condoned disciplines was mentioned earlier. A corollary of that is the implication that arithmeticians and geometers had, by the ninth century, already identified themselves as dealing with religiously *useful* subjects.

absurdly explained as a result of the currency of astrological and occult dogmas by A. Abel in "La Place des sciences occultes dans la decadence," *Classicisme et declin culturel dans l'historie de l'Islam* (Paris, 1957).

21. Ed. R. Tajaddud (Teheran, 1971).
22. Ed. Othman Amin (Cairo, 1968).
23. Ed. G. Van Vloten (Leiden, 1895).

2. This trend is further confirmed by an arithmetical text from the tenth century, written by 'Uqlidisi of Damascus in 952 A.D. In it 'Uqlidisi describes all the elementary arithmetical operations as they were to be performed on the *takht* (dustboard). But in Book IV he says:

> In this book we state all that is done by Hindi (schemes), not with *takht* (dustboard) or erasure, but with inkpot and paper. This is because many a man hates to expose the *takht* between his hands when he finds the need to use this art of calculation, for fear of the misinterpretation of the attendants or whoever may see it. It belittles him, for it is seen between the hands of the misbehaved who earn their living by astrology in the streets.[24]

This text not only confirms the condemnation of astrologers by the mathematicians, but also celebrates the introduction of the new technology of paper and pen into the conservative world of arithmetic. 'Uqlidisi is overjoyed to be finally rid of the dust, the dirt, and the crippling inability to review any arithmetical operations on the dustboard (for it would have been erased). He also says that he had seen no one in Baghdad perform these operations with paper and ink. But most significantly, he sets himself apart from the astrologers who used the same instruments, and kept on using them well into the seventeenth century.[25]

3. A text by Thabit b. Qurrah, the mathematician and astronomer of the ninth–tenth centuries, also attacks astrologers. The text has not yet been found, but it was quoted in the fourteenth century by Ibn Qayyim al-Jawziyyah as one of the instances of mathematicians attacking astrologers.[26] He mentions the title of Thabit's work as *tartib al-'ulum* which is the same as the one mentioned by Qifti as *tartib qira'at al-'ulum*, in all probability a classification of the sciences in the style of Farabi, but predating it. It is unfortunate that Ibn Qayyim al-Jawziyyah does not mention the other works of the mathematicians, nor the mathematicians by name. But the implication is very clear that mathematicians were consciously setting themselves apart from astrologers.

4. In the next century we witness a new attack on astrology authored by one of those who were often suspected of it, namely, an astronomer. Biruni, the author of a comprehensive manual on astrology that he wrote at the

24. A.S. Saidan, *The Arithmetic of Uqlidisi* (Boston and Dordrecht: Reidel, 1978), p. 247.

25. In a famous miniature painting from seventeenth-century India, the astrologers are depicted as using an astrolabe, an ephemeris (*taqwim*), and a dustboard (*takht*); cf. C. Welch, *Imperial Moghul Paintings* (New York: Braziller, 1978), pl. 16.

26. *Miftah Dar al-Sa'adah*.

instigation of his patroness, found himself in a very awkward position.[27] An astronomer at heart, he wrote the astrological manual in a very didactic style, almost always reporting what the astrologers said and not what he himself believed. But when astrological doctrines became too absurd, he hinted, within the same book, to the fact that he was definitely against it. Even in that book, which one would take to be a statement of belief in astrology, he spends half of the text discussing mathematics and astronomy proper, and when he reaches the section on astrology, he says:

> By the majority of people the decrees of the stars are regarded as belonging to the exact sciences, while my confidence in their results and in the profession resembles that of the least of them.[28]

Later, he discusses the details of astrological predictions:

> That is the point where astrology transgresses its proper limits and assumes the responsibility of what it cannot do, for it then departs from general principles and comes to deal with minute details. As such, it resembles the principles discussed before (i.e., of exact sciences) on the one hand, and becomes more like divination on the other.[29]

In his other works, Biruni is much more obvious in his attack on astrology. In *al-Athar al-Baqiyah* he condemns Abu Ma'shar and those of his ilk:

> . . . they abuse all religions, (and) make the cycles of Sindhind, and others, the means by which to revile those who warn them that the hour of judgement is coming, and who tell them, that on the day of resurrection there will be reward and punishment in yonder world. It is the same set of people who *excite suspicion against—and bring discredit upon—astronomers and mathematicians, by counting themselves among their ranks, and by presenting themselves as professors of their art*, although they cannot even impose upon anybody who has only the slightest degree of scientific training.[30]

This is indeed the same accusation leveled against the astronomers (*falakiyyun*) by Mas'udi above.

27. Abu al-Raihan al-Biruni, *Kitab al-Tafhim li-'Awa'il Sina'at at-Tanjim*, trans. R. Wright, *Elements of Astrology* (London: Luzac, 1934).
28. *Ibid.*, p. 210.
29. *Ibid.*, p. 319. My translation.
30. *The Chronology of Ancient Nations*, trans. E. Sachau (London: Allen & Co., 1879), p. 31. The italics are mine.

A similar attitude is expressed by Biruni in his *al-Qanun-al-Mas'udi*, where he again discusses astrology, only to warn the intelligent man away from it.[31] And, as if that were not sufficient, he also wrote a book attacking the astrologers, called *kitab al-tanbih 'ala sina'at al-tamwih;* it, unfortunately, is lost.[32]

5. Another astronomer, contemporary with Biruni, left us a book that we know only by title, in which he attacks the astrologers. The work is *al-Radd 'ala al-munajjimin* by Ibn al-Haitham, otherwise famous for his work on optics. His *Radd* is mentioned by both Ibn Tawus, *Faraj al-mahmum*; and al-Najashi, *Rijal*.[33]

6. The algebraist al-Samau'al al-Maghribi of the latter part of the twelfth century, continued this tradition in a treatise attacking the methods of the astrologers, not only to show that they were ignorant of their mathematics, but also to state that he in no way wished to be confused with them.[34]

This by no means exhaustive list indicates the extent of the evidence showing that astronomers and mathematicians were trying to present themselves in a garb quite different from that imposed on them by the Greek astronomical tradition.

In a positive vein, Biruni, an astronomer at heart, attempted in two of his works, namely, *The Coordinates of Cities*[35] and *The Exhaustive Treatise on Shadows*,[36] to define astronomy as a religiously useful science; again the key word is *useful*.

He argues that astronomy is not only to be distinguished from astrology, but also to be thought of as a handmaiden of religion, for it helps determine the *qibla*, the times of prayers, and the similar religious duties that are incumbent upon every Muslim. If one were to determine any of these with any precision and earnestness (*ijtihad*), one would require an extensive amount of spherical astronomy and mathematics.

31. (Hyderabad: Da'irat al-Ma'arif al-Osmania, 1954–1956), 3 vols. in continuous pagination, p. 1469, line 18f.

32. *Chronologie Orientalischer Volker von Alberuni* (Leipzig: Hrsg. E. Sachau, 1923), pp. xxxv, 79.

33. F. Sezgin, *Geschichte des Arabischen Schrifttums*, Bd. VI (Leiden: Brill, 1978), p. 261.

34. *Kashf 'uwar al-munajjimin wa-ghalatihim fi'akthar al-'a'mal wa-l-'ahkam* [The exposure of the errors of the astrologers] Leiden University Ms, Or. 98.

35. Trans. Jamil Ali (A.U.B., 1967), pp. 1–33, where Biruni's concern for the status of the exact sciences is most apparent.

36. Trans. E.S. Kennedy (Aleppo: Institute for the History of Arabic Science, Aleppo University, Syria, 1976), p. 8: "*The learned in religion who are deeply versed in science know that Muslim law does not forbid anything of what the partisans of the craft of astronomy* [*concern themselves with*] *except the lunar crescent.*" My italics.

Biruni must have been conscious of the fact that he was joining hands with those who had earlier vindicated arithmetic and geometry, and he must have had enough followers among the astronomers themselves, for the argument finally convinced a man of the stature of Ghazzali. In *al-Munqidh min al-Dalal*, Ghazzali not only distinguishes astrology from astronomy, but warns the believer not to contradict, in his zeal for religion, the truths of astronomy such as eclipses and the like, for then the believer would endanger religion by posing it against such obvious truths.[37] In *'Ihya''Ulum al-Din*, he classifies the truths of astrology as being of the same uncertain nature as those of medicine but yet to be condemned in accordance with a tradition going back to the Prophet himself.[38]

This attitude was adopted outside the religious circles as well, a fact that indicates a widespread acceptance of the astronomers and a rejection of the astrologers, at least in theory. Similar arguments were repeated by people such as Khalil b. 'Aybak al-Safadi (d. 1362) in *Nakt al-Humyan fi Nukat al-'Umyan*,[39] Ibn Qayyim al-Jawziyyah (d.1350) in *Miftah Dar al-Sa'adah*,[40] and Damiri (d. 1341) in *Hayat al-Hayawan al-Kubra*.[41] In short, the religious opposition was clearly directed against astrological dogmas and not against astronomy. Astronomy received a much wider acceptance than hitherto believed. With that type of religious sanction, astronomy could now enter into the service of religion and be allowed to survive within the religious institutions. That such a step was indeed taken is attested to by the establishment of the office of the *Muwaqqit* (time-keeper), which came into being only after the eleventh century, and the resulting dramatic increase in *Miqat* literature.

In this new environment Islamic astronomy was finally freed from political patronage and was able to be more responsive to the religious needs of the society. It was now issuing from the mosque—where the office of the *Muwaqqit* was mainly found—and was thus accepted by layman and learned alike. The current research is to determine the theoretical contributions of this new astronomy and its implictions for sundial theory, astrolabes, *miqat* tables, *qibla* computations, etc., all of which require a high standard of mathematical sophistication.

37. Ghazzali, *al-Munqidh min al-Dalal* (Cairo: Anglo-Egyptian Press, 1964), esp. pp. 68–69.

38. *Idem.*, *'Ihya''Ulum al-Din* (Cairo: al-Maktabat al-Tijariyyat, n.d.), vol. 1, p. 29.

39. (Cairo: al-Matba'at al-Jamaliyyah, 1900), (repr. Baghdad: Maktabat al-Muthanna, c. 1963), pp. 63–65.

40. (Beirut: Dar al-Kutub al-'Ilmiyyah).

41. (Cairo: Matba'at al-'istihqaq, 1963), vol. 1, pp. 11–14.

THE PHILOSOPHICAL OUTLOOK OF THE NEW ASTRONOMY

The critical approach to the foreign sciences, and specifically to astrology, led to a further reaction among the astronomers. This reaction was of a slightly different nature than the dissociation from astrologers and the redefinition of astronomy that we discussed above. The astronomers, freed of the earlier respect for the Greek sciences,[42] their discipline now accepted by society under the rubric of *miqat*, found themselves free to formulate their astronomy on new philosophical principles. In that, they were probably under the influence of the Islamic philosophical tradition in which truth was supposed to be within a system that is consistent, harmonious, and well articulated, with religion having an essential position in that system.

The old Greek dictum of "saving the phenomena" was now considered to be insufficient, for at times the phenomena were saved at a high cost, namely, a contradiction between the physical world and its mathematical representation. A few problems were first identified in the major text of Greek astronomy, the *Almagest* of Ptolemy, where the Greek astronomer did indeed save the phenomena with a mathematical system that sacrificed the physical reality. One such problem was that of the equant, which can make sense only as a mathematical point and not as a physical one. In essence it is a mathematical device used by Ptolemy in his planetary models which implicitly assumes a sphere to be moving uniformly at an axis different from the one that passes through its center, an assumption which is physically impossible to find. Other problems included the "prosneusis" and the lunar distance from the earth, to name only a few.

In the eastern part of the Muslim world, Ibn Sina and his student Abu 'Ubayd al-Juzjani began the attempt to reformulate the Ptolemaic problem of the equant so that both the mathematical and the physical realities could be satisfied. A short treatise by Juzjani dealt with that problem; in it he mentions that Ibn Sina too had a solution but would not tell him about it. His own solution, which has survived in a summary fashion, is not quite successful.[43]

42. A similar attitude was also developed by the physicians as is clearly evident from the works of Razi, Abu Bakr, *al-Shukuk 'ala Jalinus* (unpublished but studied in a modern Persian study by M. Muhaqqiq, *Filusif-i-Rayy* [Teheran, 1974], pp. 291–345), and 'Abd al-Latif al-Baghdadi, *al-'Ifadah wa-l-I'tibar* (pp. 61–62) when he clearly states that his own observations are to be trusted much more than the authority of Galen, quoted in S. Kataye, *Les manuscrits medicaux et pharmaceutiques dans les bibliotheques publiques d'Alep* (Aleppo: Institute for the History of Arabic Science, Aleppo University, Syria, 1976), p. 23.

43. This text is now edited by the present author with an English translation and a commentary in "Ibn Sina and Abu 'Ubayd al-Juzjani: The Problem of the Ptolemaic Equant," *Journal for the History of Arabic Science* 4 (1980): 376–403.

In the same century, and apparently quite independently, Ibn al-Haitham devoted a full treatise to these problems in the Ptolemaic works under the title *al-Shukuk 'ala Batlamyus* (Dubitationes contra Ptolemeum).[44] In this work Ibn al-Haitham clearly formulates, for the first time perhaps, the objections to Ptolemy as well as the requirements for the new alternative astronomy if there were to be one. His work has been justifiably referred to as the new program of research in Islamic astronomy.

The response to the call for such a program of research came first from Andalus. Ibn Baja of Saragossa (d. 1139), Ibn Tufayl of Granada (d. 1185/6), Ibn Rushd of Cordova (1126–1198), al-Bitruji, probably of Seville (1200) and a student of Ibn Tufayl, and Jabir Ibn Aflah of Seville (1200), all from Andalus and all known to the Latin scholastics, attempted to reformulate Ptolemaic astronomy. It is not at all clear whether any of these astronomers were responding directly to Ibn al-Haitham's challenge, although it is quite clear that their research seems to have been motivated by the same considerations. Of all the works of these astronomers, the most extensive treatise that has come down to us dealing directly with the subject of the reformulation of Ptolemaic astronomy is that of Bitruji under the innocent title *Kitab al-Hay'ah* (The book of astronomy).[45] Although the new astronomy that he proposes is not as successful as one would have liked it to be, Bitruji, nevertheless, made the reform of Ptolemaic astronomy a necessity. After Bitruji, no astronomer could tolerate the *Almagest*'s problems without any criticism, least of all an astronomer of the stature of, say, Copernicus, who knew of the works of these Andalusian critics.[46] The exact indebtedness of Copernicus to these Andalusian astronomers will not be fully understood, however, until all their works are edited, both in Arabic and Latin, and made available for research.

We are now beginning to understand the works of a group of astronomers in the eastern part of the Muslim world who had similarly attempted to formulate a new, non-Ptolemaic astronomy. We have already mentioned the humble attempt of Abu 'Ubayd al-Juzjani.[47] But of a much greater significance are the attempts of Mu'ayyad al-Din al-'Urdi (d. 1266), Nasir al-Din al-Tusi (d.1274), Qutb al-Din al-Shirazi (d. 1311), and Ibn al-Shatir al-Dimashqi (d. 1375). All of these astronomers have left us complete texts, in some cases even more than one, in which they describe their new non-Ptolemaic astronomy. It is worth noting at this point that Ibn al-Shatir, who worked as a *muwaqqit* at the Umayyad mosque of Damascus, thought very

44. Ed. A. I. Sabra and Nabil Shehaby (Cairo: Dar al-Kutub, 1971).
45. Trans. B. Goldstein (New Haven: Yale University Press, 1971).
46. J.L.E. Dreyer, *A History of Astronomy from Thales to Kepler* (New York: Dover, 1953), p. 262.
47. "Ibn Sina and Abu 'Ubayd al-Juzjani."

little of astrologers;[48] his work was read, copied, and owned by Shafiʿites and Hanafites—in one case an imam, as is noted on the flyleafs of the surviving manuscripts. In a way this confirms our earlier analysis of the new status of Islamic astronomy and its social acceptability.

None of the works of these astronomers have been published, but enough articles are now in print, starting in the late 1950s, to give us some idea of the kind of research these astronomers were doing. Their importance seems to have been in their emphasis on the mathematical rigor of their astronomy, for all of them were essentially tackling the mathematical models of Ptolemy's planetary theories. However, we will remain totally ignorant of their real achievements until their texts are properly edited and surveyed. Only during the last few years have some of these works begun to receive some attention in the direction of establishing their actual texts.[49]

During the 60s, several articles were published by E.S. Kennedy and his students; the articles mainly dealt with the text of Ibn al-Shatir. Because of their efforts, we now know the basic outline of Ibn al-Shatir's astronomy. That outline showed many points of agreement between the astronomy of Ibn al-Shatir and that of Copernicus who lived about 150 years later. In the words of Noel Swerdlow, who edited the earliest work of Copernicus, *De Commentariolus*, when describing the Copernican model for the superior planets:

> One may seriously wonder whether he (i.e., Copernicus) understood the fundamental properties of his model for the first anomaly, and this, of course, bears strongly on the important question of whether the model was his own invention or something he learned from a still undiscovered transmission to the West of a description of Ibn al-Shatir's planetary theory. My own inclination is to suspect the latter, not because I think Copernicus incapable of carrying out such an analysis of the first anomaly in Ptolemy's model . . . but rather because the identity with the earlier planetary theory of Copernicus' models for the moon *and* the first anomaly of the planets *and* the variation of the radius of Mercury's orbit *and* the generation of rectilinear motion by two circular motions seems too remarkable a series of coincidences to admit the possibility of independent discovery[50]

48. Bodl. Ms. Marsh 139, fol. 48r; 5.

49. G. Saliba, "The Original Source of Qutb al-Din al-Shirazi's Planetary Model," *Journal for the History of Arabic Science* 3 (1979): 3–18, where ʿUrdi's text for the model of the upper planets is edited, translated, and commented upon. The important text of Tusi's *Tadhkirah* is now edited by Jamil Rajab of Harvard University as a Ph.D. dissertation; it includes an English translation, a commentary, and an extensive historical introduction.

50. "The Derivation and First Draft of Copernicus's Planetary Theory: A Translation of the Commentariolus With Commentary," *Proceedings of the American Philosophical Society* 117(6) [1973]: 423–512, quote from p. 469.

CONCLUSION

In the light of this quick survey, limited to the fragmentary evidence that we now have on astronomy, the new picture that emerges seems to define in broad lines a slow movement away from the foreign sciences, because of their conflict with religion and the social tensions that they created when held by the foreign few, but most importantly because of their inner inconsistencies, to a reformulation of a new astronomy that was distinctly Islamic—patronized by the mosque and not the palace—in which the pursuit of pure theoretical research could go on unhampered by the pitfalls of an occult science such as astrology. The main feature of this new astronomy was its responsiveness to the social environment, which produced the office of the *muwaqqit* as one aspect of its dimensions.

As for the problem of the decline of Islamic science—including Islamic astronomy—hinted at in the introduction of this paper, this brief survey should have made it clear that we can no longer blame it on Ghazzali, nor on the Muslim zealots of the twelfth century, for although it incontestably took place, it did so at a much later date than Ghazzali, and most probably for completely different reasons, that are yet to be identified.

Moreover, recent research in Islamic theoretical astronomy has begun to show that the most original results began to emerge almost a full century after the death of Ghazzali and culminated in the fourteenth century in the works of the Damascene *muwaqqit* Ibn al-Shatir. With this in mind, and if one were to adopt genuine scientific originality as a criteria, rather than mere abundance of scientific activity, I suspect that a comprehensive study of the works of Jazari (c. 1205) in mechanics, Athir al-Din al-Abhari (c. 1240) in astronomy, Mu'ayyad al-Din al-'Urdi (d. 1266) in astronomy, Nasir al-Din al-Tusi (d. 1274) in astronomy and mathematics, Qutb al-Din al-Shirazi (d. 1311) in astronomy, Ibn al-Shatir (d. 1375) in astronomy, Kamal al-Din al-Farisi (d. 1320) in optics, Ibn al-Baytar (d. 1248) in pharmacology, and Ibn al-Nafis (d. 1288) in medicine, may revolutionize our conception of Islamic intellectual history and shift the "golden age" of Islam from the 9th–10th century—when the Greek scientific legacy was being assimilated—to the 13th–14th century—when a genuine Islamic science came into full bloom.

Astrology/Astronomy, Islamic

George Saliba

The expression *ʿilm al-nujūm* (science of the stars), as used by most Muslim authors, referred to both astrology and astronomy. More precisely, astrology—defined by the ninth-century astrologer, Abū Maʿshar, as "the knowledge of the effects of the powers of the stars, at a given time, as well as the future time"—was referred to as *ʿilm 'aḥkām al-nujūm* (science of the decrees of the stars), *ʿilm al-'aḥkām,* or simply *'aḥkām* or *tanjīm* (divining by the stars). Astronomy, on the other hand, was commonly referred to as *ʿilm al-falak* (science of the spheres), or more commonly *ʿilm al-hay'a* (science of the [heavenly] configurations).

Early encyclopedists treated both disciplines under the same rubric, with the implication that astrology was the natural sequel to, yet distinguishable from, astronomy, as was expressed by Ptolemy himself. Al-Nadīm around 990 characterized the works of al-Nayrīzī, the commentator on the *Almagest* and the *Elements* of Euclid, as more *hay'a* (astronomy) than *nujūm* (astrology).

In the usual classifications of the sciences, the two disciplines were commonly considered as branches of the same science. It is only at a later date, around the thirteenth century, that astronomy was made fully distinct from astrology. Astronomy was thereafter counted as a mathematical science; and astrology was shifted to the applied physical sciences, together with agriculture, medicine, and alchemy.

Astrology

The early history of astrology in Islam is closely connected with divination. Tradition attests to the presence of astrologers even before the time of Muḥammad. An astrologer named Qays Ibn Nushbah was supposed to have predicted the coming of the Prophet, who later called him *ḥabr qawmih* (chief of his people), a title usually reserved for the learned men of the Jews, the Christians, or the Sabaeans. But the Muslim religious rejection of the ancient Arabian institution of the *kāhin* (diviner priest) had a negative effect on astrology, inasmuch as the latter was identified with that divinatory practice. The Prophet supposedly said that whoever studies anything of the stars *(nujūm)* would have studied some magic, and astrology leads to divination. Other than the divinatory aspect of astrology, the native Arabs probably had a limited knowledge of the lunar mansions and the heliacal rising of certain stars. But by the ninth century several texts had been translated into Arabic from Greek, Pahlavi, Syriac, and Sanskrit. These texts included the masterpieces of Hellenistic astrology, namely the *Tetrabiblos* of Ptolemy and the five books of Dorotheus of Sidon. The latter text had already been translated into Pahlavi sometime during the sixth century, from which source the work became known to the Arabs. The text of Vettius Valens's *Anthologies* seems to have followed the same route but has not survived in Arabic except in scattered fragments quoted by later authors.

Ptolemy's *Tetrabiblos,* on the other hand, was taken much more seriously than any other text and was by far the most influential source of medieval Islamic astrology. It was translated more than once and was paraphrased several times by early writers such as Ibn al-Farrukhān, Ibn al-Ṣalt, al-Nayrīzī, and al-Battānī.

An extensive commentary that became famous during the Middle Ages was made in the eleventh century by Ibn Riḍwān and was later translated into Latin. All of these surviving texts, whether translations, paraphrases, or commentaries, are older than the earliest surviving Greek manuscript (thirteenth century) that was used to prepare the modern Loeb edition of the *Tetrabiblos*. In addition to the Arabic tradition there is also a Syriac fragment (Paris, Bibliothèque Nationale, MS Syriaque 346) containing a paraphrase of book II, 9 to the end. No study has yet been done of these sources and their relationship either to the edited Greek text or to the Greek paraphrases, such as that of Proclus. The negative Muslim attitude toward astrology had taken on a new form by the ninth century, by which time the translations were almost completed. Astrology was now seen as part of a coherent but foreign body of Greek philosophy, primarily that part which dealt with problems such as the eternity of the world and free will.

The religious leaders, feeling that such subjects were within their own domain and already backed by a prophetic tradition against astrology, took a definite position against the new Greek formulation. Their rejection centered on the astrologers' main claim, namely, the ability to foretell the future in a world predetermined by the stars. At times their attacks included the serious charge of atheism. Abū Maʿshar (Albumasar) was supposed to "have studied astrology until he became an atheist," the implication being that atheism was a natural end of such studies. The suspicion against astrology was not restricted to such passing remarks or the religious men alone. By their association with the "foreign sciences" the astrologers also endangered their colleagues the astronomers, the philosophers, and the physicians. These men in turn had to defend themselves by dissociating themselves from the astrologers.

The earliest known attack on the astrologers came from the famous eighth-century Arabian prosodist al-Khalīl ibn Aḥmad in a few lines of poetry. A ninth-century poet, Abū Tammām al-Ḥabīb ibn Aws, supposedly celebrated the error of the astrologers, who predicted that al-Muʿtaṣim would not be able to conquer Amorium in 838, with the famous poem: "The sword is much more telling than the [astrologer's] books. . . ."

Of much greater significance, however, is the attack leveled by the two most prominent men of the tenth century, the famous philosopher al-Fārābī, and ʿAlī ibn ʿĪsā al-Asṭurlābī, the astronomer and astrolabist, as his name implies. Al-Fārābī's text comprised a brief introduction and thirty short sections devoted to polemics against astrology.

Al-Asṭurlābī, a convert from astrology to orthodox Islam, is quoted at length, with supplementary remarks, by the Ḥanbalī theologian Ibn Qayyim al-Jawzīya. His main argument involves the issue of the eternity of the world, a problem already faced by the *mutakallimūn* (speculative theologians?). The astrologers, who are called the atheists *('ahl al-'ilḥād* or *zanādiqa),* seem to have held the world to be uncreated, a view diametrically opposed to orthodox Islam.

Abū Ḥayyān al-Tawḥīdī, a tenth-century philosopher and man of letters, devoted two seances of his literary work *al-Muqābasāt* to refuting astrology as a discipline and a profession. In one of the seances an important association was drawn between the astrologer and the physician, a remark already made by Ptolemy in defense of astrology as an "empirical science." The virtue of medicine, al-Tawḥīdī says, is not to be put in any doubt, but it is somehow unfortunate that its method belongs to the same class as that of astrology.

Another philosopher, of comparable stature to al-Fārābī, was Ibn Sīnā (Avicenna), who also devoted a treatise to the refutation of astrology. In his argument against the astrologer's ability to foretell the future, he uses only verses from the Koran and a reported tradition from the Prophet. This may indicate the strength of the religious opposition to astrology: even the philosophers felt they had to dissociate themselves from astrology by appealing to religious dogma.

Al-Bīrūnī, a contemporary of Ibn Sīnā, an astronomer, and a compiler of what remains the best encyclopedic work on medieval Islamic astrology, found himself in a very awkward position. Asked by his patroness to write a text on astrology, but feeling the pressure of religious objections and his own skepticism toward the subject, he could leave only a few remarks throughout the work disavowing astrological doctrines. On another occasion, he even went so far as to attack astrology directly. And in still another work he says that he discussed astrology only to warn the intelligent man away from it. He tolerated it only as a means of livelihood for the astronomer, whose research might otherwise not be supported. From the other end of the Muslim world, medieval Spain, the Ẓāhirī theologian Ibn Ḥazm had a different reason to attack astrology. His chief contention was that any science, especially astrology, that does not serve to understand theology is worthless.

Although Abū Ḥāmid al-Ghazzālī, the most influential theologian and jurist of Islam, devoted a full treatise to attacking the philosophers, in two separate works he seems to accept the validity of astrology inasmuch as he accepts medicine, even though both sciences are conjectural. But in view of the prophetic tradition against astrology, he maintains that one can dispense with this conjectural discipline.

Ibn Rushd (Averroës), on the other hand, clearly rejects astrology: it "does not belong to physical science; it is only a prognostication of future events, and is of the same type as augury and vaticination."

Fakhr al-Dīn al-Rāzī was the only philosopher thereafter to have had some sympathy toward astrology. But he could not have any serious impact, for by the early thirteenth century arguments against astrology had become well articulated and formalized, leading in the next two centuries to the most elaborate and comprehensive attack on astrology by Ibn Qayyim al-Jawzīya, and by the historian Ibn Khaldūn. It is in these treatises that the "official" orthodox position against astrology is found.

The astrologer's defense was elaborately formulated as early as the ninth century by Abū Maʿshar. In his work, *Kitāb al-madkhal ilā ʿilm 'aḥkām al-nujūm* ("Introduction to Astrology"), he fills some twenty folios in defense of astrology against its enemies, whom he classifies into the following types: those who denied the influence of the planets on the sublunar world of generation and corruption; those who believed that the planets influence only general events but not particular ones; traditionalists and speculative philosophers; those who studied the general things *(ʿilm al-kull)* of the science of the stars (astronomers and philosophers?); those who studied the generals; mathematicians *(ʿaṣḥāb al-ḥisāb);* those envious of the astrologers; physicians; the general masses *(al-ʿāmma)* who do not know the virtue of any science; and the general masses who are misled by the mistakes of those claiming to be astrologers.

With the exception of the feeble defense of Ibn Ṭāwūs and the sympathies of Fakhr al-Dīn al-Rāzī, there is no other Islamic defense of astrology of the same thoroughness.

Thus astrology seems to have been distinguished from astronomy at an early stage in Islam, although the same expression was used to designate both disciplines. The religious reaction to astrology in particular, and to "foreign sciences" in general, forced physicians, philosophers, and mathematicians to dissociate themselves from the astrologers. The religious position most often quoted in the sources is that astronomy is to be considered as permissible and astrology as forbidden. The argument most often presented against astrology is that "God has reserved for himself the knowledge of the future to the exception of his angels and prophets."

The attacks on astrology apparently did not stop astrologers from practicing in almost every domain of public life—in the streets, in shops, in the company of armies, on ships, at deathbeds, and in official positions at court. Administrative manuals specify the duties of such astrologers, especially the court astrologers. Sometimes they were carefully tested, and their salaries fixed. The areas of their competence were supposed to include every facet of human existence. The extant sources attest to the following categories of astrological work.

Horoscopic (genethliac) astrology, the most common type, dealt with the problems of the individual, mainly through a reading of the heavenly configurations at his time of birth, starting from the point of the "horoscope," that is, the point of the ecliptic that is ascending at the eastern horizon at that time. In the *Tetrabiblos,* Ptolemy made only an ambiguous reference to that point, as well as to the divisions of the ecliptic known as "houses." With Muslim astronomers, on the other hand, both concepts (as well as others) were mathematically defined with great precision. In this category one also finds *mawālīd* (nativities). In typical prognostication from one of these texts, if the native is born "with the moon within the limits of Mercury, and Mercury is beholding it from humid places, the native will have the inclination for painting, engraving, embroidering, and the like."

Katarchai, including both the *ikhtiyārāt* (elections) and the *interrogationes,* was another common type of prognostication in which the moon plays a very important role. The elections are devoted mainly to determining the opportune time to begin any kind of action: "If you wish to start an alchemical work, or anything requiring fire, or any kind of work you may have to repeat, start that when the moon is in a bicorporeal sign." A typical example of *interrogationes* is: "If you are asked about an army whether it is small or large, count the signs between the moon and Mercury, and if they come out to be even the army is large, otherwise, it is small."

World and year's cycles have their origins in the repetitive nature of astronomical phenomena. One such cycle is that of the repeated conjunction of Saturn and Jupiter, which takes place approximately every twenty years on a point on the ecliptic that moves so as to cover the entire ecliptic in 960 years. Political events were assumed to have been determined by such conjunctions. Another cyclical event is the return of the sun to the vernal equinox. The planet having the greatest number of "honors" at that moment was called the *aphetis* ("significator") or *hylāj.* The prognostication connected with this phenomenon was called the year's revolution *(taḥwīl al-sana).* Similarly, the yearly return of the sun to the native's "horoscope" produced prognostications for an astrological birthday. The consideration of such cycles in connection with the native's birth chart, and permutations of these and similar cycles, could increase the astrologer's treasury to meet practically any situation.

Fortune, rays, and lots. The point on the ecliptic that is in the same position to the "horoscope" as the moon is to the sun was called the lot of fortune *(sahm al-saʿāda).* Once determined, it was used in the same capacity as a planet to foretell a number of events, including the length of one's life. Other lots were similarly defined and allowed to increase beyond reasonable limits. Planets were supposedly able to project rays in order to attack, support, capture, or obstruct another planet. Such concepts apparently stem from the works of Vettius Valens and Ptolemy; Muslim astrologers only gave them a mathematical definition. Other concepts, such as *tasyīr* (astrological computations based on planetary trajectories), "equalization of houses," and transit, were also given similar mathematical formulation.

In all of these problems, and in the type of question the astrologer asked of the astronomer, definite progress was made toward making astrology itself more of an exact science. Al-Bīrūnī's text on astrology, for example, includes a long introduction to mathematics and to mathematical astronomy, a clear indication of the interdependence of these disciplines.

Astronomy

Although a distinction between astrology and astronomy was drawn in early Islamic times, the two disciplines did overlap in more than one area. Astronomers, physicians, philosophers, and mathematicians who were endangered by the religious attacks on astrology were quick to dissociate themselves from the astrologers, thus allowing astronomy to develop as an independent discipline. Its sources are essentially the same as those of astrology and the other "foreign sciences," namely, Indo-Persian and Hellenistic.

Tradition has it that an embassy from the province of Sind visited the caliph al-Manṣūr in Baghdad sometime during the 760s and that this embassy included an Indian astronomer who brought along a Sanskrit astronomical text known as the *Sindhind (siddhānta).* The caliph supposedly assigned two men to translate an abridged version of this text into Arabic, with the assistance of the Indian astronomer himself. If this tradition is true, it would explain why soon afterward several texts were written in Arabic based on the text of the *Sindhind.* Unfortunately, only one of these texts has survived in extensive form, that of Muḥammad ibn Mūsā al-Khwārizmī, who was also distinguished as the originator of the discipline of algebra. That his text has survived only in a Latin version, and that the others have been all but totally obliterated, clearly indicates the quick neglect of the Indo-Persian tradition.

The Hellenistic tradition, on the other hand, is represented mainly by the transmission of the *Almagest.* Ptolemy's *mathematical collection,* arabized as the *Almagest* through a yet unknown route, was first translated under the patronage of Yaḥya ibn Khālid the Barmacid sometime during the late eighth/early ninth century. The sources agree as to the unsatisfactory nature of this early translation; and within the next sixty-odd years two authoritative translations were made available, first by al-Ḥajjāj ibn Maṭar and then by Isḥāq ibn Ḥunayn; the latter was later edited by Thābit ibn Qurra sometime during the second half of the ninth century.

Once available in Arabic, the *Almagest* generated a tradition of its own, giving rise to epitomes, commentaries, and paraphrases. The relatively new tradition also managed quickly to replace both the Sanskrit tradition of the *Sindhind* and the Pahlavi one represented by the nonextant *Shahrayar zīj*. In the following centuries the astronomical texts that were produced looked at first like mere amalgamations of these traditions, but they very quickly became more and more homogeneously Islamic. Among the most important types are the *anwa'* texts, the *hay'a* books, and the *'azyāj,* and works devoted to observational astronomy, instruments, timekeeping for religious purposes, and uranography.

There is no unanimous agreement as to the exact meaning of the word *anwa'* (singular, *naw'*) usually included in the titles of works in this category. But the closest approximation that covers most of the sources is the concept of the setting of one lunar mansion and the rising of another. The material discussed in these texts emphasizes weather prognostications associated with each *naw'*. The pre-Islamic Arab, Indian, Pahlavi, and Greek traditions are also juxtaposed without much coherence or synthesis.

Falak (or *hay'a*) books (epitomes of astronomy) constitute a second category of astronomical writings. The text of the *Almagest* was thought of even by Ptolemy himself as comprising three major parts: statements of the general principles and configurations of the heavenly bodies; mathematical proofs (demonstrations) of these principles and configurations; and tables for each planet that allow the prediction of its position. It was Ptolemy who later treated two of these parts in separate books, the *Planetary Hypotheses* and the *Handy Tables*.

In the style of the *Planetary Hypotheses,* several books were written that varied greatly in their contents. A text attributed to Muḥammad ibn Mūsā ibn Shākir (Bānū Mūsā), for example, extant in a Damascus manuscript, gives a general description of the major circles on the heavenly sphere and of the star constellations but unfortunately breaks off just before it begins to treat the planets. Muḥammad ibn Kathīr al-Farghānī, on the other hand, wrote a much more extensive text that also dealt with elementary astronomy but included almost all topics treated in the *Almagest*. With time, this genre of literature became more sophisticated and formalistic in structure, and was used as a vehicle to launch criticism of the *Almagest,* as well as to propose new models for planetary theories.

Another type of astronomical writing attempted mainly to summarize the *Almagest* itself and, more often than not, to bring "its terminology more in line with the terminology of the time." Ptolemy's Menelaus theorem, for example, was often replaced by the equivalent sine theorem. That genre too was also formalized with time and reached a standard form with Naṣīr al-Dīn al-Ṭūsī's *Taḥrīr al-Majisṭī,* which itself was the subject of several commentaries.

Those activities that centered on the *Almagest* were also often critical of its contents. Certain phenomena, admittedly of a minor nature, were observed to be at variance with Ptolemy's description. One such phenomenon is the movement of the solar apogee, which according to Ptolemy was fixed at Gemini 5;30°. The reaction of the Muslim astronomers varied from simple corrections of Ptolemy's statement, without further comment, to special attention to the problem and explict discard of the Ptolemaic value in favor of that found by observation. Bīrūnī went a step farther, becoming the first Muslim astronomer to state explicitly that the solar apogee not only partakes of the precession motion, as Ptolemy prescribed for the other planets, but also that it has a motion of its own, totally unknown to Ptolemy. Observations also forced Muslim astronomers to correct the precession value adopted in the *Almagest* and to give it a value much closer to the modern one.

More serious criticism of Ptolemy's astronomy was directed at its inherent philosophical contradictions. Ptolemy argued, for example, in the *Planetary Hypotheses* that the planetary spheres were actual physical bodies and not merely a mathematical hypothesis, as he seemed to imply in the *Almagest;* he speaks, for instance, of solid spheres versus empty ones. If the two hypotheses are supposed to be describing the same universe, as they seemed to be doing, then the mathematical hypothesis adopted in the *Almagest* leads to several problems, with the problem of the "equant" being the most outstanding. Put briefly, the planetary models proposed by Ptolemy presuppose the existence of a mathematical point, later called the equant, around which the planetary epicycles were supposed to move at a uniform speed. This concept becomes totally absurd when this point is thought of in terms of physical spheres, for then one would have to accept the mechanical impossibility of allowing a physical sphere to move at a uniform speed around an axis that does not pass through its center. The realization of this problem in the Ptolemaic theory gave rise not only to several treatises that discussed this point specially but also to books in which this and other problems were treated at great length.

It was Ibn al-Haytham (Alhazen) who devoted a comprehensive treatise to the criticsm of Ptolemy, although we are not sure whether he himself produced an alternative system. In a later work he is blamed for "raising doubts; but (failing to) produce anything more than doubts."

In Muslim Spain, the problem of the equant also received some attention, but in the context of several other problems. Jābir ibn Aflaḥ, for example, criticized Ptolemy for not being rigorous enough and for "taking the center of the deferent [in the model of the upper planets] to be halfway between the 'equant' and the center of the universe without proof." Ibn Rushd, on the other hand, blamed Ptolemy for not being Aristotelian enough, taking him to task mainly in the context of his own commentary on Aristotle's *Metaphysics*. The only Andalusian who attempted to produce an alternative astronomy was al-Biṭrūjī, although it did not meet with much success.

In the eastern part of the Muslim world, sometime during the first half of the thirteenth century, a Damascene named Mu'ayyad al-Dīn al-ᶜUrḍī wrote a full treatise devoted to a reform of Ptolemy's astronomy. At about the same time, al-Ṭūsī wrote two texts, one in Persian and the other in Arabic, in which he not only argues against Ptolemy's astronomy but also proposes new alternatives to some planetary models that avoid most of its pitfalls. In his discussion of the lunar model, he introduced a new mathematical theorem, now known as the Ṭūsī-couple, which was subsequently incorporated into the works of every original astronomer up to and including Copernicus.

We are not very clear on the works of other astronomers of this period who worked mainly from the Ilkhanid capital city, Marāgha, in northwest Iran. Among them was Quṭb al-Dīn al-Shīrāzī, who proposed one of the most sophisticated models for the motion of Mercury. He also mentions several other texts, which have not yet been studied or even identified, that contain original material.

In the fourteenth century this model-building activity was brought to a very successful conclusion by Ibn al-Shāṭir of Damascus. He not only incorporated al-Ṭūsī's mathematical theorem but also managed to avoid the mistakes of the earlier Ptolemaic reformers. He also drew attention to the need for combining the philosophical treatment, which had characterized most earlier astronomical attempts, with observation and hence produced the first realistic model of the motions of the moon.

These attempts at reforming Ptolemy's astronomy are not totally unrelated to the Copernican revolution. Not only was Copernicus motivated by the same considerations, but recent research has shown that the Copernican model for the upper planets (as discussed in *De revolutionibus*) uses the same techniques proposed three centuries earlier by al-ʿUrḍī, and his model for the moon is identical to that of Ibn al-Shāṭir. Moreover, the similarities between Copernicus and Ibn al-Shāṭir in the Mercury model add one more link in the chain of apparent coincidence to bring the whole issue of independent discovery into question.

The *ʿazyāj* (astronomical handbooks), probably the most extensive genre of Islamic astronomical literature, should be seen as a continuation of the tradition of the *Handy Tables* of Ptolemy. In these works, the authors do not deal with the configuration of the planetary spheres as such but rather assume some configuration as given and set out to compute the actual positions of a planet at any given time.

Since all reforms of Ptolemaic astronomy were in essence philosophical reforms, these tables cannot be expected to vary too much from the *Handy Tables,* except for the necessary fixing of calendars, longitudes, latitudes, and so forth. In format, however, these handbooks changed considerably between the ninth century, when they were first computed, and the late seventeenth century, when they started to become scarce. Most of this change was motivated by the concept of "simplicity of use." The ultimate result of simplicity was finally reached sometime in the fifteenth century, when one astronomer managed to change the method of computation and the format of his tables to such an extent that all he required of his reader was the mastery of the operation of addition. One cannot but feel these works were compiled especially for less educated astrologers who were mainly interested in quick determination of planetary positions and not in the kinematics of the celestial spheres as such.

Excluding the treatises on instruments, discussed below, we find a scarcity of texts dealing with observational astronomy. Yet we know that some of the observations produced new parameters, either correcting those of Ptolemy, as in the case of precession and solar apogee, or refining them by applying new methods of observation. An example of these methods is contained, for instance, in the work of Thābit ibn Qurra and al-Bīrūnī, who used the new method of observing the solar declination at midseason instead of at the solstices, as was done by Ptolemy.

Observatories were also established especially for these activities. But although we know some details connected with these observatories as institutions, we do not yet have enough records of the actual observations conducted there or of the methods by which individual parameters were tested and later incorporated into the tables. We are fortunate in this regard to have the text of al-Maghribī, which was wrongly described by Suter as a compendium *(cholasa)* of the *Almagest,* with some new observations conducted at Marāgha. The text, which is still extant at Leiden, is not a compendium of the *Almagest* but, rather, a *hay'a* (astronomy)-type text written in the style of the *Almagest* but based solely on observations conducted in Marāgha between 1263 and 1274. In it we are told in great detail how each parameter, such as eccentricity and epicyclic radius, of each planet was determined. Unfortunately, neither al-Maghribī's text, nor the *Īkhānī zīj,* nor most of the other texts written in Marāgha during this period has ever been studied in any detail by modern scholars.

Another text that might have been of the same nature, *Taᶜlīq al-'arṣād* ("Comments on Observations") of Ibn al-Shāṭir, is known only by name. It has not yet been located, nor have we come across anything similar to it from the famous fifteenth-century observatory of Ulugh Beg in Samarqand. All of this evidence—or lack of it—amounts to saying that although observational astronomy managed to attack and solve individual problems, it did not on the whole develop a conceptual framework that analyzed the relationship between theory and observation.

Islamic treatises on instruments were devoted either to large-scale construction of observatories or to individual instruments; of the latter the most popular remains the astrolabe.

Although the theory of stereographic projection was known at least from the time of Hipparchus, and a treatise expounding it was known as early as Ptolemy's time, the theory itself was not put to full use in the construction of the planispheric astrolabe until just before that instrument reached Islam. Once it did, the astrolabe was further perfected and new elements introduced, so that by the early tenth century its capabilities as an observational instrument as well as a slide rule-type computer were fully developed to include some three hundred problems in mathematical astronomy, geography, and spherical trigonometry. In the hands of Muslim astronomers, the astrolabe became sophisticated enough to be useful for any latitude.

The surviving specimens, dating from the late tenth century to our own, are in most cases superb examples of the blending of precision craftsmanship and fine Muslim metallic artwork. Literary and iconographic evidence scattered over many centuries confirms that the astrolabe became the most popular symbol of the professional astrologer. Quadrants, a further development of the astrolabe and produced by using only one quarter of it, are not known from non-Islamic sources and seem to have been developed by Muslims as a natural consequence of their work on the astrolabe. In this sophisticated form, the quadrant could be used to solve "all standard problems of spherical astronomy."

Spherical astrolabes and celestial globes are much scarcer but, like the planispheric astrolabe, seem to have been of little use in observations and were in all probability intended only to exhibit how the celestial spheres rotated. Connected with this high technology were sundials and equatoria, the former used mainly to determine the time of Muslim prayers, while the latter exhibited the planetary movements at any given time.

The times for observing the prescribed five daily prayers of Islam were all defined by the daily passage of the sun. Because of this dependence, the time varied from one day and place to another. Muslim astronomers devised several methods that specifically often tabulated their results to simplify the solution of what were essentially problems of spherical trigonometry. Finding the time from the altitude of the sun, for example, was one such problem solved by tables given in the *miqāt* (timekeeping) texts, as this literature was known. Special curves designating the times of prayers were also engraved on astrolabes.

Although there was a religious prohibition on beginning the lunar month of fasting according to the computed time, a *zīj* text often included tables of lunar visibility to answer that problem specifically. Moreover, the beginning of the daily fasting during that month was also astronomically defined by the onset of dawn, a problem that spurred much research of its own.

Following Ptolemy's description of the "fixed stars" in the *Almagest*, Muslim astronomers devoted special texts to describing the constellations. One such work that became very famous in the Islamic world and in Europe, especially because of its artistic value, was *Ṣuwar al-kawākib* of ʿAbd al-Raḥmān al-Ṣūfī. In these texts old Arabian star names and constellations were matched with those described by Ptolemy, thus allowing pre-Islamic traditions to survive. Through such texts most modern star names still bear the imprint of Arabic.

During the ninth and tenth centuries the religious attacks on astrology began to endanger the astronomers, whose profession had previously been conceived to be the same as that of the astrologer. For the sake of survival, the astronomers of the eleventh and twelfth centuries began a process of redefinition of their field that entailed a rejection of the astrologer's craft and a greater emphasis on religious matters.

In this confrontation, the religious authorities seem to have won and hence forced the astronomers to become increasingly dependent on religious patronage. The office of the *muwaqqit* (timekeeper) was introduced into the bureaucracy of the mosque, the main center of the Islamic community, during the thirteenth century.

Most of the astronomical texts thereafter were written by such *muwaqqits;* the net result was less emphasis on astrological subjects and more concern for religious issues. The importance accorded to these issues led to further redefinition of the religious prescriptions, this time in mathematical terms. As a consequence, all problems that had any religious bearing were incorporated into mathematical astronomy and treated in those texts irrespective of the religious injunctions.

Freed from political patronage, the *muwaqqits* could then, in principle, direct their attention to any astronomical problem and no longer had to produce astrological texts. It is still very difficult, however, to assess the significance of this new orientation; for there has never been a full study devoted to the impact of this new patronage on Islamic astronomy.

Bibliographical Essay

An example of the several Arabic texts on the classifications of the sciences is al-Fārābī, *'Iḥṣā' al-ʿulūm,* ed. Osman Amine (1968). The English translation of al-Nadīm's *Fihrist* by B. Dodge (1970) should be used with extreme care.

For the sources of Arabic astrology, see Dorotheus Sidonius, *Carmen Astrologicum,* ed. David Pingree (1976); and Ptolemy, *Tetrabiblos,* ed. and trans. F. E. Robbins (1971). For overview and manuscript material, see M. Ullmann, *Die Natur und Geheimwissenschaften im Islam* (1972); and Fuat Sezgin, *Geschichte des arabischen Schrifttums,* vol. 7 (1979).

For a flavor of the texts themselves, see al-Bīrūnī, *Elements of Astrology,* trans. Ramsay Wright (1934); and the less available work of Abū Maʿshar, *Kitāb al-madkhal ilā ʿilm 'aḥkām al-nujūm,* Carullah MS 1508.

For a treatment of astrology in Islam, see al-Khaṭīb al-Baghdādī, *Risālat fī ʿilm al-nujūm,* Asir MS 190. For the social status of the astrologer, see G. Saliba, "The Role of the Astrologer in Medieval Islamic Society," in *Bulletin d' Etudes Orientales* 44 (1992).

Attacks on astrology are numerous, the most extensive being Ibn Qayyim al-Jawzīya, *Miftāḥ dār al-saʿāda,* Dār al-Kutub al-ʿIlmīya, II, and Ibn Khaldūn, *The Muqaddimah,* trans. F. Rosenthal. Along different lines, see Ibn Ḥazm, *Marātib al-*

ʿulūm, ed. Iḥsān ʿAbbās (n.d.); and *Kitāb al-faṣl fī al-milal wa-l-'ahwā' wa-l-niḥal,* vol. 5 (1903). See also M.A.F. Mehren, "Vues d'Avicenne sur l'astrologie et sur le rapport de la responsabilité humaine avec destin," *Le Muséon* 3 (1884); and Averroës, *Tahāfut al-Tahāfut* ("The Incoherence of the Incoherence"), trans. S. van den Bergh (1969).

The most extensive defense of astrology is in Abū Maʿshar's work, *Madkhal,* to which add Ibn Ṭāwūs, Ali ibn Mūsā, *Faraj al-Mahmūm fī ta' rīkh ʿulamā' al-nujūm* (1949); the former was partially translated in Jean Claude Vadet, "Une defense de l'astrologie dans le Madhal d'Abu Maʿšar al-Balḫi," *Annales islamologiques* 5 (1963).

For the "world-year" type of astrology, see E. S. Kennedy, "Ramifications of the World Year Concept on Islamic Astrology," in *Proceedings of the 10th International Congress of the History of Science* (1964), pp. 23–45.

On the mathematization of astrology in Islam, see E. S. Kennedy and H. Krikorian-Preisler, "The Astrological Doctrine of Projecting the Rays," *Al-Abhath* 25 (1972); and O. Schimmer, *"Al-Tasyīr,"* in *Encyclopedia of Islam,* 1st ed., vol. 4.

Among the general references for Islamic astronomy are F. Sezgin, *Geschichte des arabischen Schrifttums,* vol. 6 (1978), and H. Suter, *Die Mathematiker und Astronomen der Araber und ihre Werke* (1900).

On the transmission of ancient science to Islam, consult C. A. Nallino, *ʿIlm al-falak* (1911), translated into Italian in *Raccolta di scriti editi et inediti* (1944), vol. 5; and D. Pingree, "The Greek Influence on Early Islamic Mathematical Astronomy," *Journal of the American Oriental Society* 93 (1973).

For the important transmission of the *Almagest* and its influence, consult Sezgin, *Geschichte,* vol. 6, pp. 88–94; and O. Pedersen, *A Survey of the Almagest* (1974).

For books written in the tradition of the *Planetary Hypotheses* and the *Almagest,* see Muhammad ibn Musa ibn Shaker, *Kitāb ḥarakat al-falak,* Falak 4489; Muhammad ibn Kathir al-Farghani, *Elementa astronomica* (1669); Baron Carra de Vaux, "L'Almagest d'Abu-lwefa albuzdjani," *Journal asiatique,* 8th ser., 19 (1892); and for a discussion of the later genre of this literature, J. Livingston, "Naṣīr al-Dīn al-Ṭūsī's al-Tadhkirah: A Category of Islamic Astronomical Literature," *Centaurus* 17 (1972–1973).

For the term *anwā'*, see C. Pellat, *Encyclopedia of Islam,* new ed., vol. 1; and for the most comprehensive survey of the *'azyāj* works, see E. S. Kennedy, *A Survey of Islamic Astronomical Tables, Transactions of the American Philosophical Society* 46 (1956); and, for later developments in these texts, G. Saliba, "The Planetary Tables of Cyriacus," *Journal for the History of Arabic Science* 2 (1978), which contains a bibliography of the most recent literature on the modifications of the *zīj.*

There are several studies dealing with the Islamic reaction to Ptolemaic astronomy mainly gathered in E. S. Kennedy and I. Ghanem, eds., *The Life and Work of Ibn al-Shāṭir* (1976); to which should be added O. Neugebauer, "Thabet ben Qurra 'On the Solar Year' and 'On the Motion of the Eighth Sphere,' " *Proceedings of the American Philosophical Society* 106 (1962); W. Hartner and M. Schramm, "Al-Bīrūnī and the Theory of the Solar Apogee: An Example of Originality in Arabic Science," in A. C. Crombie, ed., *Scientific Change* (1963); G. Saliba, "Ibn Sīnā and Abū ʿUbayd al-Jūzjānī: The Problem of the Ptolemaic Equant," *Journal for the History of Arabic*

Science 4 (1980); "The First Non-Ptolemaic Astronomy at the Marāghah School," *Isis,* 70 (1979); and "The Original Source of Quṭb al-Dīn al-Shīrāzī's Planetary Model," *Journal for the History of Arabic Science* 3 (1979); B. Goldstein, *al-Biṭrūjī on the Principles of Astronomy* (1971); L. Gauthier, "Une réforme du système astronomique de Ptolémée tentée par les philosophes arabes du XIIe siècle," *Journal Asiatique,* 10th ser., 14 (1909); and for the relationship of these modifications of the Ptolemaic system to the works of Copernicus, see N. Swerdlow, "The Derivation and First Draft of Copernicus's Planetary Theory: A Translation of the Commentariolus with Commentary," *Proceedings of the American Philosophical Society* 117 (1973).

For observatories and instruments, consult A. Sayılı, *The Observatory in Islam* (1960); W. Hartner, *"Asṭurlāb,"* in *Encyclopedia of Islam,* new ed., vol. 1; D. King, "An Analog Computer for Solving Problems of Spherical Astronomy," *Archives internationales d'histoire des sciences* 24 (1974); C. Schoy, *Gnomonik der Araber in die Geschichte der Zeitmessung und der Uhren* (1923); E. S. Kennedy, *The Planetary Equatorium of Jamshīd ibn Ghiyāth al-Dīn al-Kāshī* (1960).

For astronomical responses to religious questions, see E. S. Kennedy, "The Lunar Visibility Theory of Yaʿqūb ibn Ṭāriq," *Journal of Near Eastern Studies* 27 (1968); and "Al-Biruni on the Muslim Times of Prayers," in Peter Chelkowski, ed., *The Scholar and the Saint* (1975); and with M. L. Davidian, "Al-Qayini on the Duration of Dawn and Twilight," *Journal of Near Eastern Studies* 22 (1961).

For Arabic star names and their transmission to Europe, see P. Kunitzch, *Untersuchungen zur Sternnomenklatur der Araber* (1961); and *Arabische Sternnamen in Europa* (1959).

II. Development of Planetary Theories

Ibn Sīnā and Abū ᶜUbayd al-Jūzjānī: The Problem of the Ptolemaic Equant

George Saliba*

Introduction

The Ptolemaic model for the upper planets assumes that the epicycle centers of those planets move on a circle, called the *deferent*, whose center does not coincide with the earth, and that they describe equal angles around yet another center, called the *equant*. This arrangement violates the principle that any celestial motion must be a combination of uniform circular motions.

This, in a nutshell, is the essence of the equant problem which greatly exercised Muslim astronomers, and which was also one of the main motivations for the Copernican astronomy. It would be naive to suppose that Ptolemy was not aware of it, or that he was incapable of solving it. What it reveals, though, is that Ptolemy's main concern in the *Almagest* and in the *Planetary Hypothesis* was quite different from that of the later medieval astronomers. For Ptolemy it was sufficient to produce mathematical models that are capable of describing the planetary motion in longitude and in latitude, in spite of the fact that, at times, one were to "use something contrary to the general argument".[1] For later medieval astronomers, harmony between the physical and the mathematical worlds was essential, and they thought of the Ptolemaic equant as a contradiction between those two worlds.

We do not know when this alleged blemish in the Ptolemaic system was first singled out as a problem. But we do know that several Muslim astronomers, in the period extending between the eleventh and the fourteenth centuries, tried to construct new planetary models which would be free of this fault.[2] According to present knowledge, the earliest explicit criticism of the Ptolemaic system came from Ibn al-Haytham, in the first part of the 11th century.[3]

In this paper we give an edition of a very short Arabic text, with an English translation, written by Abū ᶜUbayd al-Jūzjānī, a younger contemporary of Ibn al-Haytham, and apparently independently of him, in which he also

*Department of Middle East Languages and Cultures, Columbia University, New York, New York, 10027, U.S.A.

1. *Almagest* IX, 2 and Ibn al-Haytham, *Al-Shukūk ᶜala Baṭlamyūs*, ed. A. I. Sabra and N. Shehaby (Cairo, 1971), p. 33.

2. Sezgin, F., *Geschichte des arabischen Schrifttums*, Bd. VI, (Leiden, 1978), p. 34f.

3. *Shukūk*, *op. cit.*

criticises the equant of Ptolemy. Abū ᶜUbayd, however, goes a step further than Ibn al-Haytham and attempts to construct his own models which were to avoid the pitfalls of the Ptolemaic ones.

Sources

Abū ᶜUbayd is supposed to have written on the subject of planetary configurations a book having the title *Kayfiyyat tarkīb al-aflāk*, which apparently has not been preserved.[4] What has reached us, however, is a compendium of the book by the author himself, which has been preserved in three copies. Two of these are at the Bodleian Library, Thurston 3 and Marsh 720, while the third is at Leiden, Or. 174/2.[5]

Bodleian Marsh 720 is a later copy of Thurston 3. Hence we must assume that we really have two independent copies of Abū ᶜUbayd's text, neither of them being an autograph. The scribe of the Leiden copy, however, explicitly states that he made it from an autograph that Abū ᶜUbayd used in his own teaching.

Abū ᶜUbayd's other work *Khilāṣ tarkīb al-aflāk*, Meshhed MS No 5593/9, may have some bearing on our text. But, under the circumstances, I have to accept Sezgin's statement that it is only a commentary on Farghānī's *Jawāmiᶜ*, and as such assume that it is not essential for the determination of the language of the present text.

What is given here, therefore, is an edition and translation of *Mulakhkhas kayfiyyat tarkīb al-aflāk* based on three copies which are on the whole quite legible and rather consistent, with very few variations. This does not mean that the text is totally free from problems, and, should the original full-length work ever be found, we may have a slightly different version of the text. The essential material for our purposes, i.e. the problem of the equant, will probably remain unchanged due to the fact that the full text was quoted by Quṭb al-Dīn al-Shīrāzī (c. 700 H) in essentially the same language as that of the compendium.[6]

4. Sezgin, *op. cit.* pp. 280–281.

5. *Ibid.*, Thurston 3, fol. 144b–146a, Marsh 720, fol. 288a–292b, Leiden Or. 174, fol. 63b–67b. The author wishes to thank the keepers of these libraries for their kind assistance in procuring the necessary films for this research.

6. *faᶜaltu fa-lā talum*, MS Majlis-i Shura (Tehran) No. 3944, fol. 63f. The author wishes to express his gratitude to Mr. Jamil Ragep of Harvard University for allowing him to examine this text. This author also differs with A. I. Sabra (*JHAS*, 3 (1979), 391) concerning the title of this work, for two main reasons: 1) Shīrāzī himself gives us a clue as to what he intended with the title, for on fol. 13 he refers to it as *nafthat maṣdūr* (the cough of someone sick in the chest, i. e. a release of anger) for which one can not be blamed, and 2) the scribe, probably copying the original vowels, vocalizes the verb as *faᶜaltu*. The vocalization *faᶜalta* on the flyleaf is in a later hand and less trustworthy than that of the scribe.

Plate 1: MS Thurston 3, f. 144v. (Courtesy of the Bodleian Library)

The First Page of al-Jūzjānī's Treatise الصفحة الاولى من كتاب أبي عبيد الجوزجاني

The Author

The manuscript refers to the author as Abū ᶜUbayd ᶜAbd al-Wāḥid b. Muḥammad al-Jūzjānī, with the possible variation Abū ᶜUbayd Allāh. There is little doubt that he is the same student of Ibn Sīnā known from the *Kitāb al-Shifā'*. The introduction to our compendium, quoted by Quṭb al-Dīn al-Shīrāzī, confirms this association with Ibn Sīnā.

Abū ᶜUbayd's Proposals

Abstracted from the verbiage of the manuscript, the basic idea is equivalent to the following:

> A point, called the *fixed epicycle center*, moves at constant speed along a circle called the *deferent*. Extending from the point is a line segment, of unspecified length, the endpoint of which is called the *movable*, or *real*, *epicycle center*. The segment desplaces itself parallel to the line of apsides. The circle which is the trace of the movable epicycle center is called the *equant*.

Presumably the earth is at the center of the "deferent", and presumably the planet itself rotates about the "movable epicycle center". But there is no indication that Abū ᶜUbayd realizes that (1) the orbit of the epicycle center must have an eccentricity determined by observational considerations, and (2) observation also imposes on the epicycle center a periodic acceleration and deceleration (as viewed from the earth) which is roughly twice the magnitude of that imparted to i+ by the eccentricity.

Thus, far from solving the equant problem, Abū ᶜUbayd, has failed to understand what it was. He does understand the equivalence of the eccentric and epicyclic hypotheses, demonstrated in *Almagest* III, 3, and well known ever since.

To the extent that his ideas make sense, they constitute an unconscious throwback to some non-equant pre-Ptolemaic planetary model which was indeed a conbination of uniform circular motions.

Conclusion

We have established that as early as the middle of the eleventh century the attempts to reform Ptolemaic astronomy had begun. We are told by Abū ᶜUbayd that Ibn Sīnā himself had a solution of the equant problem, which he refused to teach to anybody. Whether he was merely boasting, and all evidence points in that direction, or not, we can not yet determine with absolute certainty.

Our text, for what it is worth, illustrates the kind of discussions that were being conducted in the Avicennian circle in the eleventh century, and it imparts the flavor of the valid solutions which would eventually be propounded. It falls towards the beginning of a historical process that was to mature only two centuries later at the hands of ᶜUrḍī, Ṭūsī, and Shīrāzī, and finally to culminate in the brilliant work of Ibn al-Shāṭir in the fourteenth century. Within that historical development, it is understandable that Abū ᶜUbayd's work should be ignored by astronomers generally. Only Quṭb al-Dīn al-Shīrāzī refers to him, and then to state that Abū ᶜUbayd disgraced himself (*faḍaḥa nafsahu*). In a forthcoming article I shall give the full criticism of Abū ᶜUbayd's solution by Shīrāzī. Let it suffice here to say that Shīrāzī was vigorous in his rejection of Jūzjānī's astronomy, referring to it as false (*bāṭil*), obvious mistake (*khaṭa' ṣarīḥ*), and grave error (*ghalaṭ fāḥish*).

Translation

(fol. 63r)

A compendium concerning the meaning (*maᶜnā*) of the equant sphere, and the meaning of deviation (*mayl*), twisting (*iltiwā'*) and slant (*inḥirāf*) of the spheres of the epicycle.

I extracted it from the book *on the Nature of the Construction of the Spheres*, by the honorable Shaykh Abū ᶜUbayd ᶜAbd al-Wāḥid b. Muḥammad al-Jūzjānī, may God have mercy on his soul.

The original manuscript was in his own handwriting and was also collated and read with him.

(fol. 63v)

In the name of God the Merciful, the Compassionate. God grant assistance. Praise be to the Lord of all creation, and prayers be upon the best of His creation, Muḥammad, and all of his kin and companions.

The honorable Shaykh Abū ᶜUbayd Allāh ᶜAbd al-Wāḥid b. Muḥammad al-Jūzjānī, may God have mercy on his soul, said: I was always eager to acquire knowledge of the science of astronomy, and diligent in reading the books composed in it, until I reacned the content (*maᶜnā*) of the equant, the deviation, the twisting and the slant of the epicyclic spheres. I could not understand that, nor was I able to comprehend its import. I started to meditate about it and apply myself to it for a long time until God, may He be exalted, facilitated that for me and it was revealed to me. Then I could imagine it and understand its nature, and could not know whether they (i.e. the astronomers) niggardly held it back from others, or it escaped them altogether, as in the case of al-Shaykh al-Ra'īs Abū ᶜAlī, may God have mercy on his soul. When I asked him about this problem, he said: "I came to understand this problem after great effort and much toil, and I will not teach it to anybody. Apply yourself to it and it may be revealed to you as it was revealed to me". I suspect that I was the first to achieve these results.

I, then, say: Firstly, the uncertainty (*shubhat*) concerning the question of the equant is, as we know, that the celestial bodies could not have variable motions in themselves so that they move quickly at times and slowly at others, as is established in physical science (*al-ᶜilm al-ṭabīᶜī*).

As for the observable variations in the planetary motion on the zodiacal sphere, they result from the planets' nearness or remoteness from us.

Accordingly, the arcs described by the centers of the epicycles in equal times must (themselves) be equal. And the angles subtended at the centers of the deferent spheres carrying these epicycles in these equal motions must (also) be equal. The facts, however, are not so, for the equal angles described by the epicycles in equal times were found to be equal with respect to yet another point. I will mention the reason for that in accordance with what was revealed.

Thus I say: the explanation of this problem involves several things; of which, one ought to know that the epicyclic sphere is not a unique one, but

(fol. 64r)

is composed of several spheres, assembled in a fashion similar to that of the spheres surrounding the earth. To illustrate that we mention the epicyclic sphere of Mercury and then we explain the details of the remaining epicycles of the planets.

Thus I say: the first of its spheres (i.e. Mercury's) is a sphere of uniform thickness whose center is always fixed within the thickness of the eccentric sphere, just as the center of the earth is in relation to the spheres surrounding the earth. The motion of these spheres is from west to east in the order of the signs, around two fixed poles as we will explain below in detail.

Below this sphere (there is) another sphere of uniform thickness, and it is the one that moves the diameter passing through the apogee and perigee of the epicycle to the north and to the south, and thus, the epicycle's apogee and perigee are sometimes to the north and at other times to the south.

Below this (there is) another sphere of uniform thickness that moves the diameter passing through the two mean positions at times to the south and at other times to the north. The centers of these two spheres are the same as the fixed center of the first sphere.

Next is a sphere of unequal thickness similar to that of the apogee of the spheres that surround the earth. The conditions for this sphere are identical to those (of the apogee) such that the center of its outer surface is the fixed center, and the center of its inner surface is eccentric.

That is followed by a sphere of uniform thickness in which Mercury itself is embedded. And with the motion of this sphere, Mercury moves in what is called the motion in anomaly. Through it, also, direct and retrograde motions take place. The conditions attributed to the epicycle are with respect to this eccenter, and through the motion of this sphere the moon (*sic.*) moves fast or slows down.

Below that (there is) a solid (*muṣmatat*) sphere with two centers: one is for its outer surface and that is the eccenter and the other is the fixed center. This sphere is similar to the complement (*mutammim*) of the spheres that surround the earth as we show in the following figure (Fig. 1 in the Arabic text).

(fol. 64v)

As for the epicycle of Venus, it is similar to that of Mercury, each being composed of six spheres.

As for the moon its epicyclic sphere does not include a mover for the two diameters. Hence, it will have only four spheres.

The spheres of the epicycles of the superior planets do not include the mover of the diameter that passes through the two mean positions. Thus the spheres of their epicycles are composed of five (spheres) each.

The total sum of these spheres is thirty-one. And when it is added to the spheres surrounding the earth the number will then be seventy-three. These spheres, however, are known and determined through their motions.

The poles of these spheres are at variance, just like the poles of the spheres that surround the earth.

Since you know that the sphere of the epicycle is not only one sphere, but that it is rather composed of several spheres, some inside the others, and some are of uniform thickness, while others are not; and that the whole of the epicyclic sphere is embedded in the thickness of the deferent carrying the epicycle, then the motion of the center of the epicycle, which is called the motion in anomaly, is that of the center of the inner sphere of unequal thickness. And through the motion of this eccentric sphere, the direct and the retrograde motions are achieved, as well as the hastening and the slowness, as we have shown.

Now if the outermost sphere moves on itself the eccenter will then move around the fixed center,[7] thereby producing a small circle, and itself is sometimes speeded up, at other times slowed down, while it ascends or descends.

As a result of the motion of the center of the epicycle in this fashion, another circle is drawn such that it intersects the circumference of the deferent sphere that carries the epicycle, and that is the circle of the equant.

It is inconceivable that the motion of the center of the epicycle with respect to the center of the deferent will produce equal angles, because that center (of the epicycle) sometimes draws away from the center of the deferent and at other times it draws close to it. On the contrary, the equal angles are with respect to the center of the imaginary circle which is called the equant.

7. The text has *al-khārijat* "the eccentric", which could not be the innermost sphere, for the motion described can only be achieved if the whole epicycle moves around the fixed center and not only the eccentric sphere as in the text.

From such things one ought to know that the distance between the center of the deferent and the center of the equant must be the same as the distance between

(fol. 65r)

the fixed and the moving center of the epicycle.

Moreover, one ought to know that the motion of the outermost sphere of the epicycle is equal to that of the deferent.

It is then necessary that the motion of the eccenter of the epicycle on the small circle be equal in time to the motion of the deferent itself, so that if the sphere of the deferent moves, for example, by one quarter of its motion, the center of the epicycle would then move by one quarter of the small circle. And if (the deferent) moves by one half of its circle, the center will move by one half of its (own) circle. The remaining parts of the two circles are then related in the same fashion.

If that which we mentioned is clear, let us assume now that the sphere of the epicycle is at the apogee of the deferent, and the moving center of the epicycle is on the line that passes through the centers, above the fixed center, in the direction of the apogee of the epicycle. (At that position) it will be at its farthest distance from the center of the deferent. And when the fixed center of the epicycle is moved west to east in the direction of the signs, on account of the motion of the deferent, and the outermost sphere of the epicyclic spheres moves on itself towards the east (*sic*),[8] then the moving center will also move towards the east (*sic*)[8] with a descent downwards. Now, if the fixed center is carried around one quarter of the deferent, th, movable center would move by an equivalent quarter circle. (The movable) center would be delayed behind the (fixed) center and would reach the tip of the diameter at quadrature and would almost intersect the first circle.

But if the fixed center is carried towards the perigee of the deferent and the movable center also moved, with some descent, it would then touch the circle of the deferent and would intersect it, until the fixed center reaches the perigee of the deferent and the movable center reaches the line that passes through the centers, each of the two centers would then have moved by one half of its own circle. Then the movable center will be at its closest distance to the center of the deferent and would be above the fixed center, with the distance between them being the same as before.

Then the fixed center is moved towards the third quarter of the deferent,

(fol. 65v)

and when it reaches the end of the quarter the movable center would have gone ahead of it and completed its own quarter circle, and would have inter-

8. This cannot happen if the outermost circle does not move towards the west, *not* the east. The mistake is also noted by Quṭb al-Dīn al-Shīrāzī.

sected the circle of the deferent. And because the movable center was above the fixed one, it is inevitable that it will go ahead of it as it used to trail it in the first quarter. Then the fixed center continues to be raised until it reaches the apogee of the deferent and the movable center returns to its place after completing its own circle.

If this is evident, then the movable center, in all of these positions, draws sometimes near to the center of the deferent and at other times draws away from it. As a result of that, it is impossible to have equal angles described at (the center of the deferent) in equal times. Its distance, however, from the equant is always the same, and at that point equal angles are described in equal times.

If our statement is taken to be true, we then draw an example (illustrating the way in which) the circle of the equant is achieved. I will represent the spheres with circles.

I say: let the circle *ABGD* be the deferent, with center *E*, and diameter *AEG* passing through the apogee and perigee.[9] Let the second diameter, at quadrature, be *BED*, The circle is then divided into four parts by points *A*, *B*, *G*, *D*. We then draw at these points the circles of the epicycles. (Let) the one at point *A* be circle *WZHT*, at *B* be *YKLM*, at *G* be *SOFN*, and the one at point *D* be the circle *QRXC*. Let the deferent apogee be point *A*. And point *A* is itself the fixed center of the epicycle. And let its movable eccenter be point *P*, *P* being above *A*.

If point *A* is moved, circle *ABGD* moves towards the east and circle *WZHT* moves on itself. Then point *P*, which is the movable center, moves with the epicycle towards the east and begins to descend slowly until point *A* reaches point *B* (*sic*)[10] and completes a quarter of a circle. But (point *P*)| does not reach (*B*) in the same way *A* does, because point *P* was above point *A*, and hence remains behind at point *J*, after having completed its own quarter circle that is equal to one quarter of the circle of the deferent, i.e. arc *PJ*.

(fol. 66r)

The arc between the two points *P* (and) *J* is equal to the arc between *A* and *B*. Then point *B* is moved towards point *G* until it reaches it and coincides with the deferent perigee. Point *J* is then on diameter *AG*, on point *x* (of it), which is the movable center, (and) at its nearest distance from *E*, the deferent center.

Then point *G* moves towards *D*, and *x* moves in such a way that when *G* reaches *D*, then point *x* would have bypassed point *D* by the distance that is between the two centers. Since point *x* was above point *G*, then it must

9. The reference is to Figure 2 in the Arabic text.

10. If *A* moves eastwards it should coincide with *D* in the diagram of the three MSS. We have redrawn the figure to correspond to the text. Cf. Plate 2, p. 387, a facsimile from one of the MSS.

bypass it and reach point *d*. At that time the fixed center would have been moved by three quarters of the circle of the deferent, and the movable center would have covered an equivalent three quarters of a circle.

Point *D* then moves towards point *A* and point *d* begins to rise. When point *D* reaches point *A*, point *d* would coincide with point *P*, and would have then completed another circle *PJxd*. The center of this circle is (itself) the center of the equant circle which is point *t*.

Then the movement of point *P* describes equal angles in equal times around point *t*, and point *P* is the real[11] center of the epicycle. (In contrast) equal angles are not described in equal times around point *E*, which is the center of the deferent, because (*P*) draws near to it at times and away from it at other times.

This condition does not take place when *P* revolves around *t*, and thus the equal angles around *t* are described in equal times.

And that is the reason by which the circle of the equant is achieved.[12]

Farghani said in his *Topics* (*Fuṣūl*) that if the center of the epicycle moves

(fol. 66v)

from the apogee of the deferent, the diameter of the epicycle deviates (*yamīl*) towards another point. These words are connected with the preceeding as I will show.

I say: If the epicycle is at the apogee of the deferent, then the diameter of its sphere would then be continuous with that of the deferent. When the center of the epicyele moves towards the east and the sphere of the epicycle moves around itself, then the movable center of the epicycle moves, as we have said, producing with its motion the circle of the equant with some descent. For had it not been for the motion of the epicycle on itself, the circle drawn by the motion of the movable center would be concentric (*muwāziyah*) with the circle of the deferent sphere. But if they both move, then the movable center describes the circle that we have mentioned, and thus there will be two diameters. One of (these diameters) is the diameter of the deferent and the second the diameter of the equant, but both equal and coinciding.

Then (the two diameters) depart from one another and a rhomboid is produced, with its longer sides being equal to the radii and its shorter sides equal to the distances between each (pair) of the (four) centers (see, e.g., Fig.3).

11. Abū ᶜUbayd misunderstands the Ptolemaic requirement, that, although equal angles are measured around the equant in equal times, the center of the epicycle, however, never departs from the circumference of the deferent as the resultant path. All later attempts at the solution of the equant, by ᶜUrḍī, Ṭūsī, and Ibn al-Shāṭir, approximated this path.

12. Abū ᶜUbayd misses the point completely and ends up with a model that can produce an equant circle rather than with a model that produces the deferent, retains the property of the equant, and satisfies the conditions of uniform motion. Such results seem to have been successfully achieved for the first time only in the thirteenth century.

The more the two centers descend towards quadrature, the more the figure increases in width until they reach the first quarter, when the figure becomes a right-angled quadrilateral.

The two centers then move towards the perigee, and when they reach it, the two lines coincide and become like one line. As soon as they bypass the perigee, the movable center begins to ascend and the rhomboid is produced (again) and continues to increase in width until they reach the second quadrature, when the figure becomes a rectangle.

Then the two diameters move towards the apogee until they coincide, as they did before. In all of these conditions, the diameter passing through the movable center of the epicycle is always connected with the diameter of the circle, which is the equant.

I will draw an illustration for that. I repeat, then, the first example and say: if the epicycle were at the apogee of the deferent, then the diameters of the epicycle and the deferent would be as one line, which is line *EtP* (in Fig. 3).

If the two centers move, the movable center begins to descend, and the fixed center will be ahead and the two diameters separate. The movable center will remain behind, for it is descending from above until they reach, for example, one eighth of their circles, and point *P* coincides with point *H*[13] and point *A*

(fol. 67r)

coincides with *B*, thereby producing the rhomboid *EBHt*.

Then they descend to quadrature and the square (*sic*)[14] *tJBE* is produced, for the figure was increasing in width.

Then they descend to the second (*sic*) eighth, at which time the square begins to get narrower and produces the rhomboid at the two points *G* and *Z*, for example, and figure *EtZG* is produced.

They further descend to the perigee and the two diameters coincide to form one line *tExG*. If, however, they begin to move and start to ascend, point *x* will then move ahead of point *G* and produce, at the third eighth, for example, the rhomboid *tEGd*.

When they ascend to reach the second quadrature, the square *tEDd* is produced, because the figure begins to widen.

They (keep on) ascending to reach the fourth eighth when the rhomboid *tEAP* is produced.

They (finally) ascend to return to the original position, and that (Fig. 3) is the illustration for the five planets.

13. Abū ᶜUbayd seems to be confused about the direction of motion. The diagram accompanying the three MSS shows a westward motion which is contrary to assumption. We have left the illustration as is because the direction of motion here is not essential to the argument.

14. Read *rectangle*.

The moon, however, is different from these for its epicycle moves in a direction contrary to that of the other epicycles. For if the moon's epicycle is at the perigee of the deferent, it then moves on itself in the direction of the west. Due to that, the movable center of its epicycle would then be below the fixed center when it is at the apogee of the deferent. If the epicycle moves on itself westwards and the apogee of the deferent also moves westwards, then the perigee of the deferent moves to the east, and the movable center follows

(fol. 67v)

in its motion the motion of the perigee. Whatever takes place in connection with the other planets, it does so on account of the motion of the fixed center eastwards, as we have seen. The example for all that is in the following diagram (Fig. 4) and God knows best.[15]

The compendium is thus completed and praise be upon His friend and prayers be upon His prophet.

Collated with the original. And much praise be to the Lord, and His prayers be upon our lord Muḥammad and his kin and his chaste companions.

15. The confusion of directions is obvious. Moreover, the author does not seem to have worked out the model for the moon, which is understandable, for the lunar motion is more complicated than that of the superior planets.

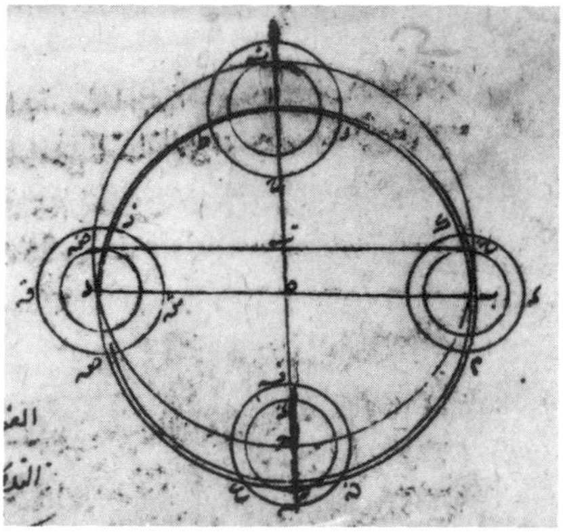

Plate 2: Facsimile drawing from MS Thurston 3, f. 145v.
(Courtesy of the Bodleian Library, Oxford).

ابن سينا وأبو عبيد الجوزجاني :
قضية معدل المسير عند بطلميوس

جورج صليبا *

ان الهيئة التي وضعها بطلميوس لافلاك الكواكب العليا فرضت فيما فرضت ان مراكز التداوير لهذه الكواكب يجب ان تدور بانتظام حول نقطة سمّاها بطلميوس مركز الفلك المعدل للمسير . والواقع ان هذا الفلك وبالتالي مركزه لم يكن مجسماً طبيعياً ، فلذلك لم ينطبق مركزه على مركز الأرض ولا انطبق على مركز الفلك الحامل لفلك التدوير كما كان متوقعاً . فالمشكلة التي وقع فيها بطلميوس اذن تلخص في كونه فرض كرة تدور بانتظام حول محور لا يمر بمركزها .

ولما وصلت الهيئة البطلمية الى الفلكيين العرب والمسلمين أخذ بعضهم الفلك المعدل هذا على انه تناقض بين الجزء الطبيعي في الهيئة البطلمية وبين جزئها الرياضي . والجدير بالذكر ان هذه المشكلة هي مشكلة فلسفية بالدرجة الأولى .

وما نعرفه الى الآن عن تاريخ هذه المشكلة هو فقط ما كشفت عنه الابحاث القليلة التي تمّت خلال السنوات القليلة الماضية . فهذه الابحاث تشير الى ان الفلكيين العرب والمسلمين تسابقوا خصوصاً بعد القرن الثالث عشر الميلادي الى وضع عدة حلول تتحاشى الشبهات التي المّت بهيئة بطلميوس .

ولكي لا يتبادر الى الذهن ان بطلميوس لم يكن على بيّنة من امر هيئته ، أو انه كان عاجزاً عن تحاشي شبهاتها ، يجب ان نشير هنا الى الاولويات التي عمل عليها بطلميوس ،

* جامعة كولومبيا – الولايات المتحدة الاميركية

الا وهي وضع هيئة تمثل حركة الكواكب طولاً وعرضاً بصرف النظر فيما اذا شملت تلك الهيئة بعض المسلّمات التي تتنافى مع طبيعة الحركات السماوية . أما الاولويات التي عمل عليها الفلكيون العرب فقد فرضت انسجام الحركات السماوية على انها حركات لمجسمات مع أوضاع تلك الحركات الرياضية .

ولا بدّ ان تكون قد اثيرت شبهات عديدة ، وخاصة في حلقات الفلاسفة ، حول هذه المشكلة في هيئة بطلميوس . غير ان ابن الهيثم كان اول من اثار هذه الشكوك بشكل صريح منظم في كتابه الذي سمّاه « الشكوك على بطلميوس » . ولم نكن نعرف الى الآن ان احداً آخر اثار شكوكاً اخرى او اتى بهذه الشكوك عينها في هذه الفترة المبكرة .

ففي هذا البحث نورد نصاً قصيراً جداً وضعه ابو عبيد الجوزجاني ، تلميذ ابن سينا ، ومعاصر ابن الهيثم ، يعالج فيه قضية فلك المعدل للمسير . فأبو عبيد لم يثر شكوكاً على بطلميوس فحسب بل تعدى ذلك الى محاولة وضع هيئة تتحاشى المشاكل الواردة في هيئة بطلميوس .

لذلك رأينا ان نورد هنا النص كاملاً نظراً لأهميته ، كذلك رأينا ان نرفقه ، بعد تحقيقه على النسخ الثلاث الباقية ، بترجمة انكليزية للنص بكامله ليتسنى للقارئ الذي لا يجيد العربية الاطلاع على هذه الهيئة الجديدة التي حاول ابو عبيد وضعها كبديل لهيئة بطلميوس .

ان اهمية هذا النص لا تكمن في كونه يشير الى نوعية المشاكل الفلكية التي كانت تطرح في الحلقات الفلسفية كحلقة ابن سينا فحسب ، بل في انّه يعطينا نموذجاً في الحلول المطروحة آنذاك لهذه المشاكل والتي ان اتسمت بشيء فتتّسم بالبديهية الرياضية وبقصر النظر الرياضي .

اما من الناحية التاريخية فقد يتساءل القارئ عن سبب اهمال الفلكيين التابعين لابي عبيد لهيئته تلك . ونحن لا نعرف ان احداً ذكر هذه الهيئة من قريب أو بعيد سوى قطب الدين الشيرازي في أوائل القرن الرابع عشر الميلادي ، ولكن ليشير الى ان ابا عبيد قد « فضح نفسه » في تلك الهيئة الباطلة . والسبب في رأيي يكمن في ان ابا عبيد كفيلسوف وكواضع لهيئة اوّلية لم يوفق تماماً الى الوصول الى حل سليم لمشكلة معدل المسير بسبب خلطه بين جهات حركات الفلك الحامل وحركات افلاك التداوير . كذلك لقد توهم خطأ ان باستطاعته ان

يجعل مركز التدوير يدور على دائرة المعدل نفسها عوضاً عن كونه يدور على دائرة الحامل .

ولكن بالرغم من ذلك ، فان هذا النص يثبت فيما يثبت ان تطور علم الفلك لم يأتِ فجأة ولا كان مقصوراً على فلكيي القرن الثالث عشر الميلادي بل انّه مرّ طبيعياً كغيره من العلوم في محاولات فاشلة قبل ان يرتقي الى النضج الذي وصل اليه على ايدي مؤيد الدين العرضي ونصير الدين الطوسي وقطب الدين الشيرازي وابن الشاطر الدمشقي .

الرموز المستخدمة في التحقيق

ه — نسخة مكتبة ليدن OR 174 هولنده ، وهي الاصل المعتمد .

ب — نسخة بودليان ثورستون ٣

م — نسخة بودليان مارش ٧٢٠

لقد حاولنا قدر الامكان ان نشير الى الحروف التي سقط اعجامها ولكن صححناها احياناً ليستقيم النص دون الاكثار من الهوامش .

مختصر في معنى فلك[1] ٦٣ و

معدل المسير ومعنى الميل والالتواء والانحراف لافلاك التداوير .

استخرجته من كتاب كيفية تركيب الافلاك .

مصنـــف

الشيخ الجليل ابي عبيد عبد الواحد بن محمد الجوزجاني

رحمه الله تعالى .

وكان الأصل بخطه مقابلاً معه مقروءاً عليه .

٦٣ ظ بسم الله الرحمن الرحيم[2] . عونك يا لطيف . الحمد لله رب العالمين وصلواته على خير خلقه محمد وآله وصحبه أجمعين .

١ — ورقة العنوان ساقطة من ب و م .

٢ — الرحيم : سقطت من ب .

قال الشيخ الجليل ابو عبيد الله[٣] عبد الواحد ابن محمد الجوزجاني رحمه الله . اني لم ازل كنت شديد الميل الى معرفة علم الهيئة ومتوفراً على قراءة[٤] الكتب المصنّفة فيه الى ان بلغت الى معنى[٥] فلك معدل المسير ومعنى الميل والالتواء[٦] والانحراف لافلاك التداوير فلم اكن أعرف ذلك[٧] ولم يكن يتبيّن لي وجهها . فأخذت اتفكر في ذلك واجتهد زماناً طويلاً الى ان يسّر[٨] الله تعالى[٨] ذلك لي[٨] وانفتح عليّ وتصورتها وتبيّنت كيفيتها وانا لا أدري ابخلوا بذلك على غيرهم ام لم يفطنوا له مثل الشيخ الرئيس ابي علي رحمه الله ، فاني سألته عن هذه المسألة فقال : اني تبينت[٩] هذه المسألة بعد جهد وتعب كثير ولا أُعلّمُ احداً[١٠] . فأجتهد انت فيها فربما انكشفت لك كما[١١] انكشفت لي . واظن اني ما سبقت[١٢] الى معرفة هذه المسايـــل .

فأقول : أولاً الشبهة في مسئلة معدل المسير انّا نعلم ان الاجرام السماوية لا يجوز ان تختلف حركاتها بالسرعة والبطء[١٣] في ذاتها حتى تكون مرة اسرع ومرة ابطأ وهـــذا مبرهن[١٤] في العلم الطبيعي .

وأما ما نرى من سرعة الكواكب وبطئها[١٥] في فلك البروج فانما هي بالاضافة الينا لقربها وبعدها منا .

فعلى هذا يجب ان تكون القسي التي تقطعها مراكز افلاك التداوير في ازمان متساوية متساوية . والزوايا التي تحصل عند مراكز الافلاك[١٦] الحاملة لافلاك التداوير بهذه الحركات المتساوية متساوية . وليس الامر كذلك بل وُجد تساوي الزوايا في أزمان متساوية بسبب مراكز التداوير[١٧] عند نقطة اخرى . وانا اذكر سبب ذلك على حسب[١٨] ما تبين .

٤– قراءة : قرآة في ه ، قراة في ب و م ؛ ٥بلغت الى معنى : بلغت فيه الى معنى ذلك في م ٦ – والالتواء : الاليواز في م . ٣ – عبيد الله : عبيد في ه . ٧ – ذلك : سقطت في م .

٨ – يسر : بين في م ؛ تعالى : سقطت في م ؛ ذلك لي : لي ذلك في م .

٩ – تبينت : تثبت في م . ١٠ – احداً : واحداً في ب و م .

١١ – كما : لما في م . ١٢– سبقت : تتبعت في م .

١٣– البطء : البطؤ في ه . ١٤– مبرهن : مسيرهن في م .

١٥– وبطئها : وبطؤها في جميع النسخ . ١٦– الافلاك : لافلاك في م .

١٧– التداوير : التدوير في م . ١٨– حسب : على مامش م .

فأقول : ان بيان هذه[١٩] المسئلة ينثني على اشياء ، منها ان تعلم ان فلك التدوي[ر][٢٠] ليس كرة واحدة بل هو كرات كثيرة مجتمعة كما[٢١] هو في كرات الافلاك المحيطة بالارض. ٦٤ و
ونحن نذكر لمثال ذلك فلك تدوير عطارد ثم نُفصّل ونبيّن تداوير ساير الكواكب السيارة .

فأقول[٢٢] : اول كرة من كراته كرة متساوية الثخن ومركزها لازم لموضع من ثخن[٢٣] الفلك الخارج المركز مثل مركز الارض للاكر المحيطة بالارض. وحركة هذه الكرات[٢٤] من المغرب الى المشرق على توالي البروج على قطبين ثابتين كما نذكره بعد هذا ونشرحه[٢٥] .

وتحت هذه الكرة كرة متساوية الثخن وهي التي تحرّك القطر المارّ بالاوج والحضيض من فلك التدوير الى الشمال والجنوب فيصير اوجه تارة الى الشمال وتارة الى الجنوب وكذلك حضيضه .

وتحتها كرة متساوية الثخن وهي التي تحرك القطر المار بالاوسطين منه تارة الى الجنوب وتارة الى الشمال . ومركزا[٢٦] هاتين الكرتين مركز الكرة الاولى الثابت .

وتحتها كرة مختلفة الثخن مثل ما هو[٢٧] (كذا) كرة الاوج من الكرات المحيطة بالارض. وحكم هذه مثل حكم تلك من حيث ان مركز سطحها الخارج يكون المركز الثابت ومركز سطحها الداخل خارج عن المركز الثابت .

وتحتها كرة متساوية الثخن وعطارد نفسه[٢٨] مركوز فيها. وبحركة هذه[٢٨] الكرة يتحرك عطارد الحركة[٢٩] التي يقال لها حركة الاختلاف . وبها يكون الرجوع والاستقامة . والاحكام التي تُنسب الى مراكز التداوير + هو هذا المركز الخارج +[٣٠] وبحركة هذه الكرة[٣١] تكون سرعة القمر (كذا) وبطؤه .

١٩– ان بيان : البرهان في م .
٢٠– التدوير : سقطت الراء من هـ .
٢١– كما : لما في م .
٢٢– فاقول : سقطت وعوض عنها بـ " ان " في ب و م .
٢٣– ثخن : سقطت في ب و م .
٢٤– الكرات : الكواكب في م .
٢٥– ونشرحه : ونسده في م .
٢٦– ومركزا هاتين : مركزها بين في م .
٢٧– هو : كذا في جميع النسخ .
٢٨– نفسه : منه في م ؛ هذه : بهذه في م .
٢٩– الحركة : والحركة في م .
٣٠– +...+ وردت على هامش هـ . اقرأ : « هي الى هذا ... »
٣١– الكرة : الحركة في ب و م .

وتحتها كرة مصمتة[٣٢] ويكون لها مركزان . احدهما لسطحها[٣٣] الخارج وهو المركز الخارج . والثاني المركز الثابت[٣٤] . وهذه الكرة مثل المتمم للاكر المحيطة بالارض كما[٣٥] بينّا في هذه الصورة .

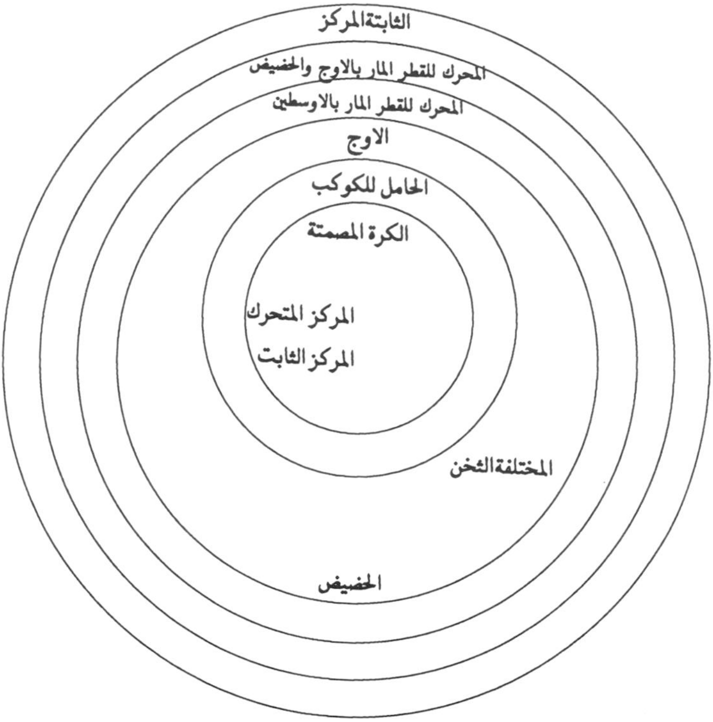

[الشكل الاول Fig. 1]

اما فلك تدوير الزهرة مثل تدوير عطارد وكل واحد منهما مركب من ست اكر . ٦٤ ظ

واما القمر فليس لكرة تدويره[٣٦] محرك القطرين فيبقى له اربع اكر .

٣٢– مصمتة : مضمته في م . ٣٣– لسطحها الخارج : لسطحها الثابت الخارج في ب و م .
٣٤– الثابت : سقطت في ب و م . ٣٥– كما : لما في م .
٣٦– تدويره : تدوير في م .

واما اكر تداوير[٣٧] الثلثة العلوية فليس لها محرك القطر المار بالاوسطين . فتكون اكر تداويرها[٣٨] خمسة خمسة .

فجملة هذه الاكر احدى وثلثون كرة . واذا[٣٩] جُمع الى الاكر المحيطة بالارض تكون ثلثة وسبعين[٤٠] كرة . وانما وقفوا على هذه الاكر وعرفوها[٤١] بسبب حركاتها .

واقطاب هذه الاكر متخالفة مثل اقطاب الافلاك المحيطة بالارض .

فاذا عرفت ان فلك[٤٢] التدوير ليس كرة[٤٣] واحدة بل هو مركب من اكر بعضها في جوف بعض . وبعضها متساوي الثخن وبعضها مختلف الثخن . وفلك[٤٤] التدوير بجملته جزء من ثخن الكرة[٤٤] الحاملة لفلك التدوير . فيلزم من ذلك ان تكون حركة مركز فلك التدوير التي[٤٥] يقال لها حركة الاختلاف هو (كذا) حركة مركز الكرة الداخلة المختلفة الثخن . وبحركة هذه الكرة الخارجة المركز يكون الرجوع والاستقامة والسرعة والبطء[٤٦] على ما بينّا .

فاذا تحركت الكرة الخارجة منها على نفسها تحرك[٤٧] المركز الخارج حول[٤٧] المركز الثابت. ويحصل من حركته دائرة صغيرة فيتأخر ذلك المركز مرة ويتقدم اخرى ويعلو ويسفل .

ويرتسم من حركة مركز التدوير على هذا الوجه دائرة اخرى تقاطع منطقة الفلك الحامل للتدوير وهي دايرة معدّل المسير .

ولا يمكن ان يحصل من حركة مركز التدوير بالقياس الى مركز كرة[٤٨] الحامل للتدوير زوايا متساوية لان ذلك[٤٩] المركز تارة يبعد من مركز الحامل وتارة يقرب منه . بل الزوايا المتساوية تكون بحسب مركز تلك الدائرة الموهومة التي يقال لها[٥٠] المعدل المسير .

٣٧– تداوير : تدوير في م .
٣٨– تداويرها : تداويره في م .
٣٩– واذا : واخرا في م .
٤٠– سبعين : سبعون في ب و م .
٤١– عرفوها : عرفواها في م .
٤٢– فلك : ذلك في م .
٤٣ – كرة : حركة في ب و م .
٤٤– وفلك : وذلك في م ؛ الكرة : سقطت في ب و م .
٤٥– التي يقال لها : الذي يقال بها في م .
٤٦– البطء : البطؤ في جميع النسخ .
٤٧– تحرك : بحركت في ب ، وبحركة في م ؛ حول : حوالي في ب و م .
٤٨– كرة : الكرة في ه ، سقطت من ب و م .
٤٩– ذلك : فلك في م .
٥٠– لها : فيها في م .

ومن تلك الاشياء يجب ان تعلم انه يلزم ممّا ذكرنا[٥١] ان يكون البعد بين مركز الحامل وبين مركز[٥٢] المعدّل للمسير مثل البعد بين مركز فلك التدوير الثابت وبين مركزه[٥٣] المتحرك . ٦٥ و

ومنها انه يجب ان تكون حركة الكرة الخارجة من اكر التداوير مساوية لحركة الكرة الحاملة لفلك[٥٤] التدوير بالزمان .

فيلزم من هذا ان تكون حركة مركز الخارج من اكر التداوير في الدايرة الصغيرة مساوية في الزمان لحركة حامل التدوير على نفسها . حتّى اذا تحرك كرة الحامل مثلا رُبع حركة[٥٥] كرتها يكون قد تحرك مركز التدوير ربع دائرتها الصغيرة . واذا تحركت هي نصف دائرتها يكون المركز تحرك نصف دائرته . وعلى هذا جميع اجزاء الدائرتين .

فاذا بان ما ذكرنا فلنفرض الآن ان كرة التدوير على أوج الحامل ومركز التدوير المتحرك على الخط المار بالمراكز فوق المركز الثابت نحو اوج التدوير . فيكون اذن[٥٦] في ابعد ما يكون من مركز الحامل لفلك التدوير . فاذا تحرك مركز التدوير الثابت من المغرب[٥٧] الى المشرق على توالي البروج بحركة كرة الحامل للتدوير ، والكرة الخارجة من اكر التداوير تتحرك[٥٨] على نفسها ايضاً نحو المشرق ، فيتحرك المركز المتحرك منه ايضاً نحو المشرق مع نزول من العلو الى السفل . فاذا قطع المركز الثابت ربع دائرة الحامل يحصل من حركة المركز المتحرك ربع دائرة مساوٍ لمثل الربع الاول . الاّ ان هذا المركز يتأخر عن ذلك المركز ويبلغ راس القطر المربع له[٥٩] ويقرب من ان يقطع تلك الدائرة الاول .

ثم[٦٠] اذا تحرك المركز الثابت نحو الحضيض من الحامل وتحرك ايضاً المركز المتحرك مع نزول يماس[٦١] دائرة الحامل ويقطعها الى ان يبلغ المركز الثابت حضيض دائرة الحامل ويبلغ

٥١– ذكرنا : ذكرها في م . ٥٢– مركز : سقطت في م .
٥٣– مركزه المتحرك : مركز المعدل للمسير المتحرك في ب و م .
٥٤– لفلك : لذلك في ب و م . ٥٥– حركة : سقطت من ه ، حركت في م .
٥٦– اذن : اخرى في م . ٥٧– المغرب الى المشرق : المشرق الى المغرب في م .
٥٨– تتحرك : محرك في م . ٥٩– له : سقطت في م .
٦٠– ثم : سقطت في م . ٦١– يماس : مما بين في م .

المركز[٦٢] المتحرك الخط المارّ بالمراكز ، وقد قطع كل واحد من المركزين[٦٣] نصف دائرته[٦٣]. ويحصل المركز المتحرك في اقرب بعده من مركز دائرة الحامل للتدوير فوق المركز الثابت . والبعد بينهما ذلك البعد الاول .

٦٥ ظ ثم يأخذ المركز الثابت نحو الربع الثالث من دائرة الحامل . فاذا بلغ هو آخر الربع فيكون المركز المتحرك قد سبقه وتمّم رُبع دائرته ، وقد قطع دائرة الحامل . لان المركز[٦٤] المتحرك كان فوق المركز الثابت فلا محالة يسبقه كما كان في آخر الرُبع الاول[٦٥] يتأخّر عنه. ثم يأخذ المركز الثابت يعلو[٦٥] حتى يبلغ اوجَ الحامل، والمركز المتحرك عاد[٦٦] الى حيث كان وتمّم دائرته .

فاذا بان هذا فان المركز المتحرك في هذه الاحوال كلها تارة يقرب من مركز[٦٧] الحامل وتارة يبعد . فلا يمكن ان يحصل من ذلك زوايا متساوية+ عنده في أزمنة متساوية . وبُعده من مركز المعدل للمسير يكون متساوياً. فيحصل هناك زوايا متساوية في ازمنة متساوية+.[٦٨]

فاذا ثبت ما قلنا فانا نمثّل لحصول[٦٩] دائرة معدل المسير مثالا . واقتصر من الكرة على الدائرة .

فأقول : لتكن[٧٠] دائرة ا ب ج د دائرة حامل التدوير على مركز ه وقطرها[٧١] ا ه ج ، وهو المار بالاوج والحضيض . وقطرها[٧٢] الثاني المربع لها ب ه د . فصارت الدائرة بأربعة اقسام على نقط ا ب ج د .

ثم ندير على هذه النقط دوائر[٧٣] التداوير . أما التي عـلى نقطة[٧٤] آ فدائرة و ز ح ط.

٦٢– المركز : الخط في ب و م .
٦٣– المركزين : المركز في ب و م ؛ دائرته : دائرة في ب و م .
٦٤– المركز المتحرك : المر الحامل في ب ، المركز الحامل في م .
٦٥– الاول : سقطت في ب و م ؛ يعلو : يعلوا في ه .
٦٦– عاد : عالي في م . ٦٧– مركز : المركز في جميع النسخ .
٦٨– +...+ الجملة ساقطة في ب و م . ٦٩– لحصول : بحصول في ب و م .
٧٠– لتكن : ليكن في ه . ٧١– وقطرها : وقطرين في م .
٧٢– وقطرها الثاني : وقطرين الباقي في م . ٧٣– دوائر التداوير : داير التدوير في م .
٧٤– نقطة : فقط في ه ؛ و ز ح ط : د ز ح ط في ب و م .

والتي على نقطة ب دائرة ي ك ل م . والتي على نقطة ج دائرة س ع ف ن[٧٥] . والتي على نقطة[٧٦] د دائرة ق ر ش ص. واوج الحامل نقطة آ . ونقطة آ هي المركز الثابت لكرة التدوير . ومركزها الخارج المتحرك نقطة ث و ث فوق آ .

فاذا تحركت[٧٨] نقطة آ تحركت[٧٨] دائرة ا ب ج د نحو المشرق وتحركت[٧٨] دائرة و ز ح ط[٧٧] على نفسها . وتحركت[٧٨] نقطة ث الذي هو المركز المتحرك بحركة كرة التدوير نحو المشرق وأخذ ينزل قليلاً قليلاً الى ان تبلغ نقطة آ الى نقطة ب ويقطع ربع دائرته . ونقطة ث ايضاً[٧٩] تتحرك نحو نقطة ب . ولكن لا تبلغ اليها بلوغ نقطة آ اليها لان نقطة ث كانت فوق نقطة آ بل تتأخر عنها عند نقطة خ وقد حصل من حركتها ربع دائرة مساوية لربع دائرة الحامل وهو قوس ث خ .

ويكون البعد بين نقطتي ث خ كالبعد بين نقطتي ا ب . ثم تتحرك نقطة ب نحو ج ٦٦ و
فتبلغ اليها وقد حصل على حضيض الحامل وحصل نقطة خ على قطر ا ج على نقطة ذ ، وهو المركز المتحرك . وهو اقرب بعده من نقطة ه الذي هو مركز الحامل .

ثم تأخذ نقطة ج نحو د وتتحرك ذ[٨٠] فاذا بلغت[٨١] نقطة ج الى نقطة د فتكون نقطة ذ قد سبقت نقطة د بقدر ما بين المركزين . لان نقطة ذ كانت[٨٢] فوق نقطة ج . فاذن تسبقه وتبلغ نقطة ض . ويكون قد تحرك المركز الثابت وقطع ثلثة ارباع دائرة الحامل وحصل من حركة[٨٣] المركز المتحرك ثلثة ارباع دائرة مساوية للاولى[٨٤] .

ثم تتحرك[٨٥] نقطة د نحو نقطة آ ونقطة ض تأخذ تعلو . فاذا حصلت[٨٦] نقطة د عند نقطة آ تحصل نقطة ض عند[٨٧] نقطة ث . وتم دائرة اخرى وهي دائرة ث خ ذ ض .

فمركز هذه الدائرة هو مركز دائرة معدل المسير التي هي نقطة ت .

٧٥– س ع ف ن : س ع ف ج في م . ٧٦– نقطة : نقط في ه .
٧٧– و ز ح ط : ه ز ح ط في ب و م. ٧٨– تحركت : تحرك في جميع النسخ .
٧٩– ونقطة ث أيضاً : نقطة ث تتحرك أيضاً في ب و م .
٨٠– ذ : سقطت في م . ٨١– بلغت : بلغ في ه .
٨٢– كانت : كان في ب و م . ٨٣– حركة : سقطت في ب و م .
٨٤– للاولى : للاول في م . ٨٥– تتحرك : تحرك في م .
٨٦– حصلت نقطة : حصل من نقطة في م . ٨٧– نقطة ض عند : سقطت في م .

فاذن من مسير نقطة ث في الازمان المتساوية يحصل عند نقطة ت زوايا متساوية ونقطة ث هي مركز التدوير الحقيقي . ولا يحصل من حركة نقطة ث عند نقطة ه التي هي[88] مركز الحامل في الازمان المتساوية زوايا متساوية لانها تقرب[89] منها تارة وتبعد اخرى .

ولا يكون هذا المعنى لنقطة ث عند نقطة ت فتحصل الزوايا عند نقطة ت في الازمان المتساوية متساوية .

فهذا هو السبب في حصول دائرة معدل المسير .

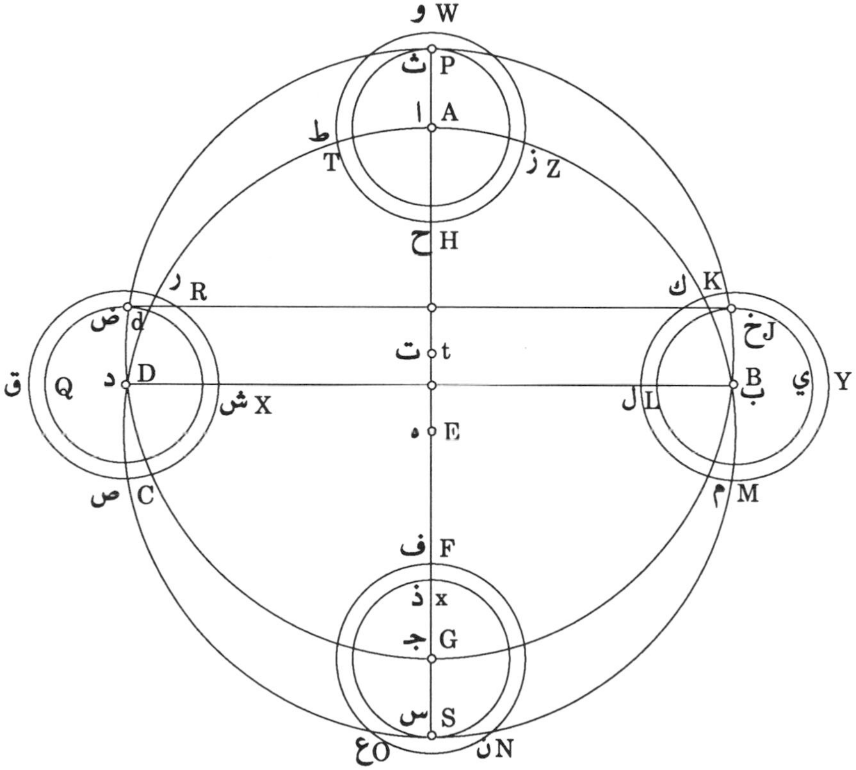

[Fig. 2 الشكل الثاني كما ورد في جميع النسخ]

٨٨– هي : سقطت في ب و م .　　٨٩– تقرب : سقطت من ه .

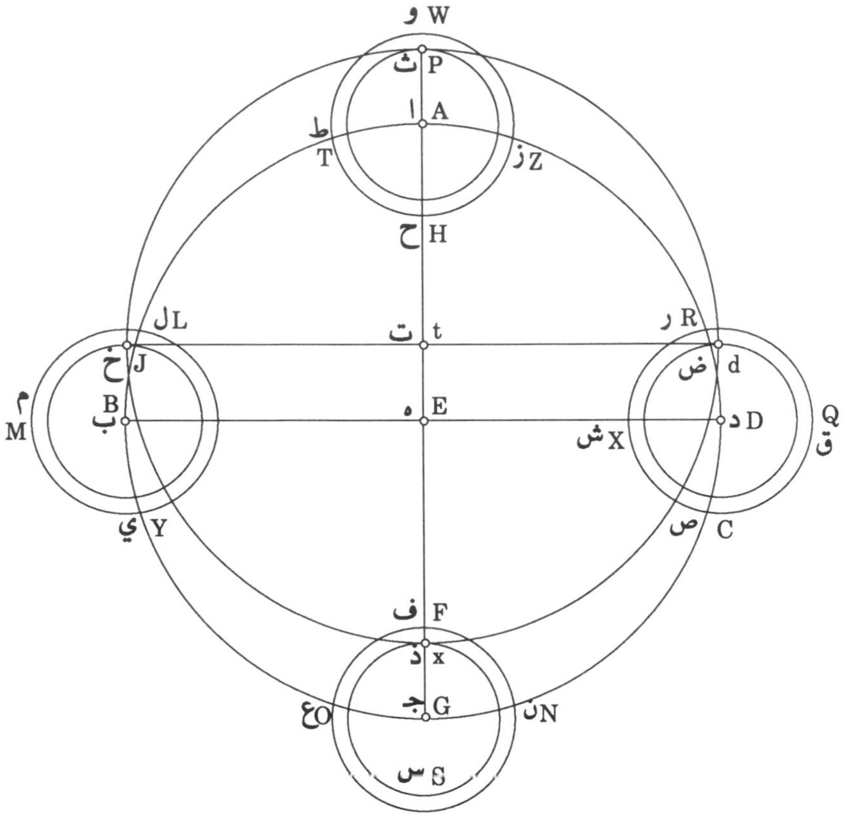

[الشكل الثاني المصحّح Fig. 2, corrected]

٦٦ ظ قال الفرغاني في فصوله انه اذا تحرك **فلك** التدوير عن اوج الحامل فان قطر **فلك**[٩٠] التدوير يميل الى نقطة اخرى . فان هذا الكلام متصل بالذي قبله وانا ابيّن كيفية **ذلك** .

فأقول : انه اذا كان **فلك** التدوير على اوج الحامل فان قطر فلكه يكون متصلاً بقطر **فلك** الحامل . فاذا تحرك مركز التدوير نحو المشرق وتحرك **فلك** التدوير على نفسه فان مركز **فلك** التدوير المتحرك يتحرك[٩١] كما قلنا . ويحدث من حركته دائرة معدل المسير مع نزول[٩٢]

٩٠– فلك : ذلك في م ؛ فان : وان في م .
٩١– يتحرك : سقطت في م .   ٩٢– نزول : نزل في م .

لانه لو لم يتحرك فلك التدوير على نفسه فان الدائرة التي ترتسم من حركة المركز المتحرك كانت موازية لدائرة منطقة كرة[٩٣] الحامل لمركز التدوير . فاذا تحركا وحصل من المركز المتحرك الدائرة التي ذكرنا فيحصل هناك قطران . احدهما قطر كرة الحامل للتدوير والثاني قطر دائرة معدل المسير . ويكونان متساويين ومنطبقين .

ثم تفترقان فيحصل شكل شبيه بالمعين وضلعاه الاطولان نصفا القطرين وضلعاه الاقصران الخطان اللذان بين كل واحد من المركزين .

وكلما نزل المركزان نحو التربيع فالشكل يزداد اتساعاً الى ان يبلغا الربع الاول فيصير الشكل مربعاً مستطيلاً .

ثم يأخذ المركزان نحو الحضيض . فاذا بلغا[٩٤] الحضيض فينطبق الخطان ويصيران كخط واحد. ثم اذا جازا[٩٥] الحضيض اخذ المركز المتحرك يعلو[٩٥] فيحدث الشكل الشبيه بالمعين ويزداد سعة[٩٦] كل وقت الى ان يصير المركزان عند التربيع الثاني فيصير الشكل مربعاً مستطيلاً .

ثم يأخذ القطران نحو الاوج والى ان ينطبقا كما كانا أولاً . وفي هذه الاحوال كلها يكون القطر المارّ بمركز التدوير المتحرك متصلاً بقطر الدائرة التي هي معدل المسير .

وامثل لذلك مثالاً . فأعيد[٩٧] المثال الاول وأقول : اذا كان فلك التدوير على اوج الحامل فان قطر التدوير وقطر الحامل يكونان كخط واحد+ وهو خط+[٩٨] ه ت ث .

فاذا تحركا ، اعني المركزين فان المركز المتحرك يأخذ في النزول والمركز الثابت يسبق ذلك المركز ويتفارق القطران ويتأخر المركز المتحرك لانه ينزل[٩٩] من علو الى ان[٩٩] يبلغا
موضعي الثمن مثلاً[١٠٠] من دائرتيهما وتحصل نقطة ث على نقطة ح ونقطة آ على نقطة ب ٦٧ و
فيحصل الشكل الشبيه بالمعين ه ب ح ت[١٠١].

٩٣– كرة : الكرة في جميع النسخ .
٩٤– فاذا بلغا : سقطت في م .
٩٥– جازا : حار في ب و م ؛ يعلو : يعلوا في ه .
٩٦– سعة : معه في م .
٩٧– فاعيد المثال الاول : سقطت في ب و م .
٩٨– +...+ على هامش ه .
٩٩– ينزل : ينز في م ؛ ان : على هامش ه .
١٠٠– مثلا : سقطت من ب و م .
١٠١– ه ب ح ت = ه ب ح ب في ب و م .

ثم ينزلان الى التربيعين فيحصل مربع[١٠٢] ت خ ب ه لانه يزداد سعة الشكل .

ثم ينزلان الى موضع الثمن الثاني فيأخذ المربع ينقص سعته ويحصل الشكل الشبيه بالمعين على نقطتي ج ز مثلاً[١٠٣] ويحصل شكل ه ت ز ج .

ثم ينزلان الى الحضيض فينطبق[١٠٤] القطران ويصيران كخط ت ه ذ ج . فاذا تحركا ويأخذان[١٠٥] الى العلو وتسبق نقطة ذ وتتأخر نقطة ج الى ان يبلغا موضع الثمن الثالث فيصير الشكل الشبيه بالمعين ت ه ج ض مثلاً .

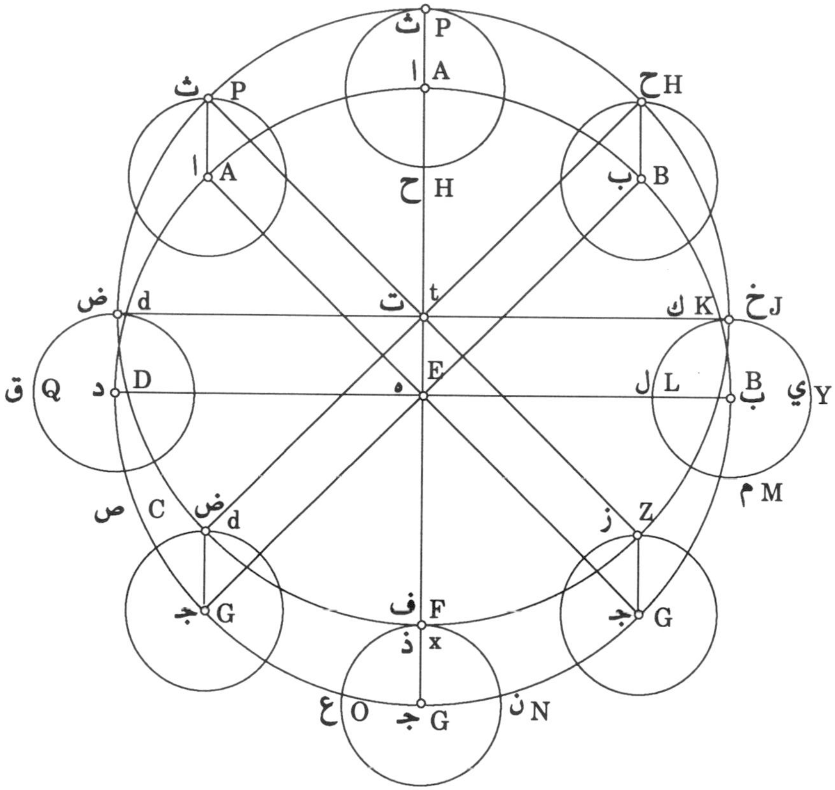

[الشكل الثالث Fig. 3]

١٠٢– مربع : اقرأ المربع المستطيل .
١٠٣– مثلا : ميلا في م .
١٠٤– فينطبق : وينطبق في ب و م .
١٠٥– يأخذان : ياخذا في ه ، ياخذ في ب و م .

ثم يصعدان[١٠٦] الى ان يبلغا التربيع الثاني فيحصل مربع ت ه د ض ، لان الشكل يأخذ يتسـع .

ثم يأخذ في الصعود الى ان يبلغا الثمن الرابع فيحصل الشكل الشبيه بالمعين ت ه ا ث .

ثم يصعدان[١٠٧] حتى[١٠٧] يصيرا كما كانا وهذا مثاله[١٠٧]. فهذا هو الكلام في الخمسة المتحيرة .

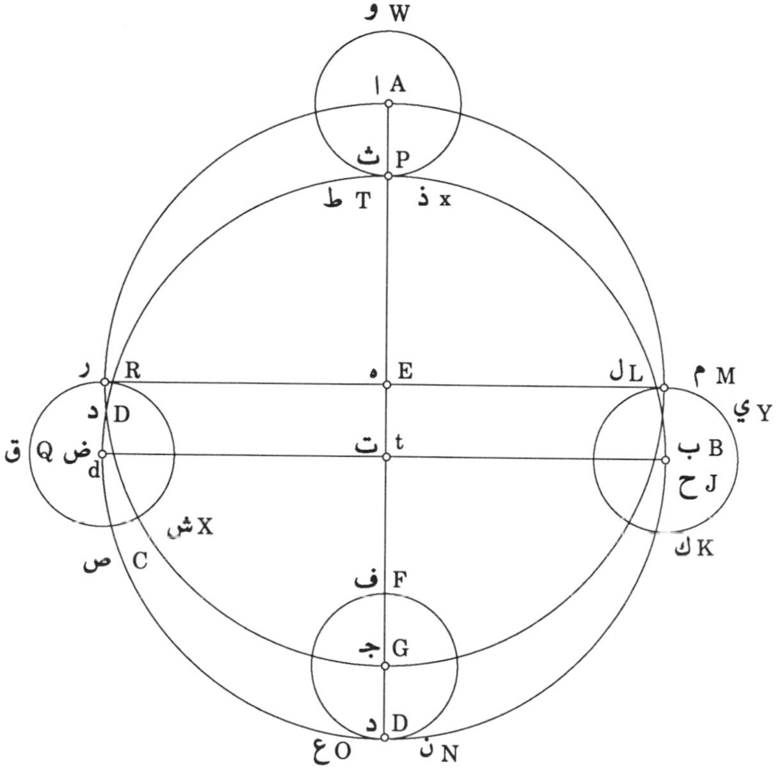

[Fig. 4 الشكل الرابع كما ورد في جميع النسخ]

١٠٦– يصعدان : يصعد في جميع النسخ .

١٠٧– يصعدان : يصعدا في ه و ب ، نصعدا في م ؛ حتى : وحتى في ب و م ؛ وهذا مثاله : وهذا مثاله فهذا هو المثال في م .

وأما القمر فانه يخالف هذه لان فلك تدويره يخالف في حركته حركة افلاك تداويرها . لان القمر اذا كان فلك تدويره على اوج الحامل فانه يتحرك في نفسه نحو المغرب . فيلزم من هذا ان يكون مركز تدويره المتحرك حالة كونه على اوج الحامل تحت مركزه[١٠٨] الثابت . فاذا تحرك فلك التدوير في نفسه نحو المغرب واوج الحامل يتحرك نحو المغرب ، فان
حضيض[١٠٩] الحامل يتحرك نحو المشرق ويتبع المركز المتحرك في حركته حركة[١١٠] حضيضه ٦٧ ظ
ويحصل ما يحصل في تلك الكواكب لان مركزه الثابت يتحرك نحو المشرق كما بينا مثاله في هذه الصورة . والله اعلم[١١١] .

تم المختصر والحمد لوليه والصلوة على نبيه . قوبل بالاصل ولله الحمد كثيراً وصلواته على سيدنا محمد وآله وصحبه الطاهرين[١١٢] .

١٠٨– مركزه : مركز في ب و م .

١٠٩– حضيض : حضيضه في ه .

١١٠– حركة : سقطت في م .

١١١– اعلم : اعلم بالصواب في ب و م .

١١٢– في ب و م : " تم المختصر في معنى فلك معدل المسير ومعنى الميل والالتواء والانحراف لافلاك التداوير وهو مستخرج من كتاب كيفية تركيب الافلاك مصنف الشيخ ابي عبيد عبد الواحد بن محمد الجوزجاني رحمه الله تعالى".

THE FIRST NON-PTOLEMAIC ASTRONOMY AT THE MARAGHAH SCHOOL

*By George Saliba**

In 1893 Bernard Carra de Vaux published a translation of a chapter of an astronomical text written by Naṣīr al-Dīn al-Ṭūsī (d. A.D. 1274), in which Ṭūsī proposed a non-Ptolemaic model for the moon.[1] Carra de Vaux's translation and commentary asserted that Islamic scientists did not hold Ptolemy in such high regard. The text itself remains unpublished, and during the past sixty years or so, historians of science have failed to take note of it. Between 1957 and 1966, however, Victor Roberts, Edward Kennedy, and Fuad Abbud published several studies of Arabic texts in *Isis,* each dealing with defects in the Ptolemaic models.[2] As a result of these publications, Kennedy created a new terminology with a view toward describing the activities in Islamic astronomy between the second half of the thirteenth century and the middle of the fourteenth. Increasingly, historians of Islamic astronomy refer to the "Maraghah School" and to the "Tusi Couple" (the two circles that transform circular motion into a linear one and vice versa). Otto Neugebauer, moreover, has connected the work of Ibn al-Shāṭir with that of Copernicus, as reflected in Roberts' article of 1957. Finally, Noel Swerdlow argues that the similarities between the works of Copernicus in the *Commentariolus* and that of Ibn al-Shāṭir are "too remarkable a series of coincidences to admit the possibility of independent discovery."[3]

Such, briefly, are the results reached so far. This contemporary research, moreover, has uncovered some of the works of members of the Maraghah School, including Ṭūsī, Quṭb al-Dīn al-Shīrāzī (d. A.D. 1311), and the later Ibn al-Shāṭir (d. A.D. 1375).[4] Because a manuscript located at Konya, Turkey (Yusef Agha Library No. 6829)[5] was thought to be unique and inaccessible, the work of Mu'ayyad al-Dīn al-ʿUrḍī (d. A.D. 1266), another member of the Maraghah School, has not been made available. But, as this paper will show, the Konya manuscript is not unique, and the anonymous manuscript Marsh 621 at the Bodleian Library, Oxford, is the work of ʿUrḍī known as *Kitāb al-Hay'ah* (A Book on Astronomy), which will now be made available.[6] I will also show that ʿUrḍī's work definitely predates that of Ṭūsī and

*Hagop Kevorkian Center for Near Eastern Studies, New York University, New York, N.Y. 10003.

[1]Appendix VI in Paul Tannery, *Recherches sur l'histoire de l'astronomie ancienne* (Paris: Gauthier, 1893), pp. 337–361.

[2]Victor Roberts, "The Solar and Lunar Theory of Ibn ash-Shāṭir," *Isis,* 1957, *48*:428–432; Edward S. Kennedy and Victor Roberts, "The Planetary Theory of Ibn al-Shāṭir," *Isis,* 1959, *50*:227–235; Fuad Abbud, "The Planetary Theory of Ibn al-Shāṭir: Reduction of the Geometric Models to Numerical Tables," *Isis,* 1962, *53*:492–499; Victor Roberts, "The Planetary Theory of Ibn al-Shāṭir: Latitudes of the Planets," *Isis,* 1966, *57*:208–219; E. S. Kennedy, "Late Medieval Planetary Theory," *Isis,* 1966, *57*:365–378. Now all these articles are gathered in one volume in *The Life and Works of Ibn al-Shāṭir,* ed. E. S. Kennedy and I. Ghanem (Aleppo: Aleppo University, 1976). See also Willy Hartner, "Naṣīr al-Dīn al-Ṭūsī's Lunar Theory," *Physis,* 1969, *11*:287–304.

[3]Noel Swerdlow, "The Derivation and First Draft of Copernicus's Planetary Theory: A Translation of the *Commentariolus* with Commentary," *Proceedings of the American Philosophical Society,* 1973, *117*:423–512, esp. p. 469.

[4]For a summary of the results of the research see Kennedy, "Late Medieval Planetary Theory."

[5]Aydin Sayili, *The Observatory in Islam* (Ankara: Türk Tarih Kurumu Basimevi, 1960), p. 435.

[6]I have already described the planetary model with an edition and a translation of the relevant text in a forthcoming article *(Journal for the History of Arabic Science).* The Mercury and the lunar models are now being prepared for publication as well as an edition of the complete text of ʿUrḍī. The author wishes

hence is to be considered as the very first Arabic work to come out of the Maraghah School which offered alternative models to those of Ptolemy. In terms of comprehensiveness and success it is probably the first Arabic work ever to achieve this result.

Finally, it should be stated that the genesis of the ideas discussed by the Maraghah School is not at all clear and should be reconsidered to establish the chronological sequence of the Maraghah activities. I have proved, in a forthcoming article, that the planetary model so far attributed to Shīrāzī[7] is actually due to ᶜUrḍī and goes back to the years before 1259.

THE AUTHORSHIP OF THE BODLEIAN MANUSCRIPT MARSH 621

Uri's catalogue of the manuscripts at the Bodleian Library ascribes Marsh 621 to Ibn Sīnā (Avicenna).[8] Goldstein and Swerdlow have already stated, on the basis of internal evidence, that the text could not have been written by Ibn Sīnā.[9] A closer reading of the text revealed that their hypothesis is well confirmed. The author, who is called al-Shaykh al-Imām (fol. 126r), quotes the works of Jābir Ibn Aflaḥ and al-Kharaqī. Both of these astronomers lived a century later than Ibn Sīnā.[10] But this closer reading also revealed that al-Shaykh al-Imām had written another text, called *Risālat fī al-kura al-kāmila* (fol. 175r), or *R. fī al-ᶜamal bi-l-kura al-kāmila* (fol. 199r) or simply *R. al-kura al-kāmila* (fol. 176v) (A Book—or Treatise—on the Complete Sphere). This title is not known in the literature collected by Suter and Brockelmann,[11] and hence is assumed to be nonextant.

On the other hand, ᶜUrḍī described the observation instruments constructed for the Maraghah observatory in a treatise that was translated first by Jourdain and then by Seeman.[12] In it ᶜUrḍī claims authorship of *Risālat fī ᶜamal al-kura al-kāmila*,[13] proving, among other things, that the meridian line could be determined by the Indian Circle (a method for the determination of the meridian by two observations of the gnomon shadows). Similarly, in the three instances in Marsh 621 in which this treatise is mentioned the discussion is about some mathematical problem in geography, a subject one imagines could very well be discussed in such a treatise. This identification makes ᶜUrḍi the most likely candidate for the authorship of Marsh 621.

Ultimately, Sayili, in *The Observatory in Islam,* solved the problem unequivocally

---

to thank the keeper of Oriental Books at the Bodleian Library for his assistance in procuring the necessary material to edit the manuscript Marsh 621, as well as B. Goldstein and N. Swerdlow.

[7] See Kennedy, "Late Medieval Planetary Theory," p. 367.

[8] *Bibliotheca Bodleinae Codicum Manuscriptorum Orientalium,* pars prima (Oxford: Oxford University Press, 1787), No. 1012, p. 219.

[9] Bernard R. Goldstein and Noel M. Swerdlow, "Planetary Distances and Sizes in an Anonymous Arabic Treatise Preserved in Bodleian MS Marsh 621," *Centaurus,* 1970, *15*: 135–170, esp. pp. 145–146.

[10] This result was first reported in a commentary I read before the Boston Colloquium for the Philosophy of Science, Dec. 12, 1978. The full text of that commentary is forthcoming with the proceedings. For Jābir Ibn Aflaḥ see R. P. Lorch's biography in *Dictionary of Scientific Biography,* Vol. VII (New York: Scribner's, 1973), pp. 37–39, and for Kharaqī see Heinrich Suter, *Die Mathematiker und Astronomen der Araber und Ihre Werke* (Leipzig: Abhandlungen zur Geschichte der mathematischen Wissenschaften mit Einschluss ihrer Anwendungen, X. Heft, 1900), p. 116.

[11] Suter, *Die Mathematiker,* and Carl Brockelmann, *Geschichte der arabischen Literatur* (2nd. ed., Leiden: Brill, 1943–1949).

[12] Amable Jourdain, "Mémoire sur les instruments employés à l'observatoire de Maragha," *Magasin encyclopédique au journal des sciences, des lettres et des arts,* 1809, *6*:43 ff.; Hugo J. Seeman, "Die Instrumente der Sternwarte zu *Maragha* nach den Mitteilungen von *al-ᶜUrḍī,*" *Sitzungberichte der physikalisch-medizinischen Sozietät zu Erlangen,* 1928, *60*: 15–126.

[13] Seeman, "Die Instrumente," p. 25.

by translating in a rather literal style a passage from the Konya manuscript of ʿUrḍī's work:

> Intellects are in agreement and minds are in accord as to the excellence of science and the worthiness of scientists. Through science happiness is obtained and ranks are elevated; it sharpens the intellect and strengthens it; it increases sagacity and augments perspicuity. It is by it that the indolent is embellished and the obscure is rendered illustrious, and it is with its help that the true is distinguished from the false. All this is especially true for those sciences whose object of investigation is demonstrative and whose principles are indisputable and self-evident. Indeed, this kind of science is common to people of different religions and does not show variation with the passage of time or change of location.[14]

This paragraph, I claim, is an honest translation of the section enclosed by brackets in Figure 1, which comes from Marsh 621 (fol. 95v).

***Figure 1.** From the first page of Marsh 621, folio 95v. Text between brackets, lines 6–11; text underlined, lines 11–17. (Courtesy Bodleian Library, Oxford.)*

[14] Sayili, *The Observatory in Islam*, p. 11.

In the other two instances where ʿUrḍī's work is quoted by Sayili, the Konya manuscript is then paraphrased and not quoted directly; the citation, however, is of sufficient length to allow a positive identification. The first paragraph reads thus:

> . . . the excellence of each science comes either from the excellence of its subject or from the solidity of its proofs, or that it may come from both, and he [i.e., ʿUrḍī] says that this latter case is true of astronomy; for its subject-matter deals with God's most admirable achievements, the most magnificient things he has created, and the most sagacious of his acts and its proofs are geometrical and arithmetical and therefore clear and final. He then adds that the usefulness of astronomy is enormous to those who contemplate on stellar marvels and the motions of the heavenly bodies and that to the reflecting mind there are in these matters remarkable circumstances and solid proofs concerning God's existence. He concludes by asserting that astronomy leads to the science of theology and gives evidence of God's magnificence. . . .[15]

This statement of ʿUrḍī is undoubtedly made on folio 95v of Marsh 621, as underlined in Figure 1. The second paraphrase given by Sayili reads thus:

> Shortly before the construction of the Maraghah observatory Mu'ayyad al-ʿUrḍī complained that no real patron sufficiently interested in astronomy was available and that therefore systematic observations on which any serious work in astronomy had to be based, could not be undertaken.[16]

This same complaint is voiced by the author of Marsh 621 on folio 158r and is here enclosed between brackets in Figure 2.

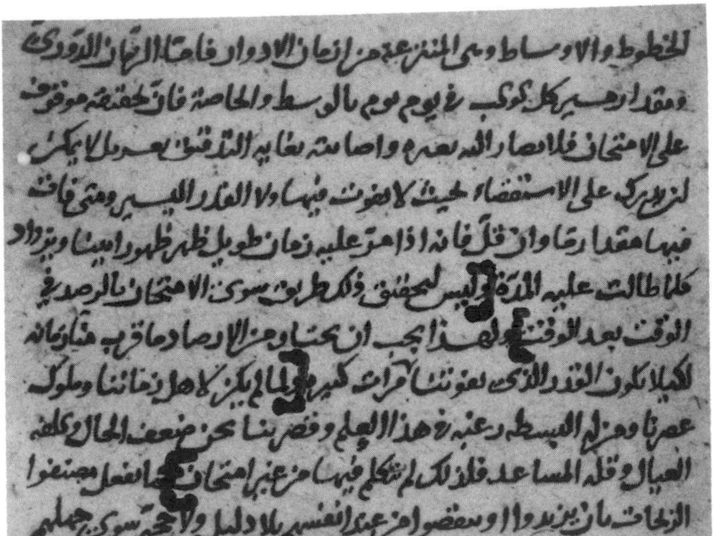

***Figure 2.** From Marsh 621, folio 158r. Text between brackets, lines 6–7 and 8–10. (Courtesy Bodleian Library, Oxford.)*

[15] *Ibid.*, p. 17.
[16] *Ibid.*, p. 224.

PRIORITY OF ᶜURḌĪ

Ironically, on an earlier occasion I used this last quotation to doubt the authorship of Marsh 621 by ᶜUrḍī, being at the time still under the influence of the generally accepted opinion that Ṭūsī was the first to initiate these non-Ptolemaic models.[17] ᶜUrḍī, or so ran my reasoning, wrote his text after he came to Maraghah, and by then he had all the observations and the patrons that he needed. I am now inclined to think that ᶜUrḍī wrote his text before the building of the Maraghah observatory in 1259, just as Sayili claims. ᶜUrḍī, it is now clear, invented his non-Ptolemaic models before 657 H. (= A.D. 1259), and in fact even before Ṭūsī wrote his *tadhkira* in which he first proposed his own non-Ptolemaic models.

In ᶜUrḍī's description of the Maraghah instruments he states that he is going to describe the instruments built before and up to the year 660 H. (= A.D. 1261/1262). From the description itself one can safely say that the instruments must have been under construction for at least a couple of years, if not more. This corroborates the information we have in the introduction of the *Zīj-i Īlkhanī* and in *Jamīᶜ al-tavārīkh,*[18] which attest to the fact that ᶜUrḍī was brought to Maraghah for the express purpose of building the observatory, which seems to be safely dated in the year 657 H.[19]

We must conclude then that ᶜUrḍī's work was written some time before the year 657 H. Moreover, even though he may have completed his text "shortly before the construction of the Maraghah observatory," as Sayili thinks, he certainly must have invented his non-Ptolemaic models well before that time; for he says, speaking of his new models: "When I saw this result, I hesitated *for a long time* to include it in this book of mine, for it varies greatly from what is known to people. But then I thought of including it for I became certain of the validity of the method by which I achieved it."[20]

The suggestion that ᶜUrḍī may have written his text early and added the non-Ptolemaic models after he came to Maraghah is untenable, for the whole text is written with the express purpose of reforming Ptolemaic astronomy, and the objections to Ptolemy and the suggested alternatives are interlaced throughout. Moreover, if ᶜUrḍī had ever re-edited his text after he came to Maraghah, would he not then edit the statement about observations and especially about his patrons, of whom he speaks with such gratitude in the treatise on the instruments in 660 H.?

His priority is further confirmed by his own sense of originality, for he says:

> No one came after him [i.e., Ptolemy] to complete this Art in a correct fashion. And no one of the moderns [*muta'akhkhirīn*] added anything to his work or deleted anything from it, but rather they all followed him. There were some though, such as Abū ᶜAlī b. al-Haytham and Ibn Aflaḥ al-Maghribī, who raised doubts; but they produced nothing more than doubts.[21]

[17] See n. 10 above.

[18] J. Boyle, "The Longer Introduction to the 'Zij-i-Ilkhani' of Naṣīr-ad-Dīn Ṭūsī," *Journal of Semitic Studies,* 1963, *8*:244–254, esp. p. 247; Rashīd al-Dın, *Jamiᶜ al-tavārīkh,* ed. Bahman Karīmī (Teheran: Eqbāl, 1960), Vol. II, p. 718.

[19] April–May 1259; see Sayili, *The Observatory in Islam,* p. 190.

[20] Marsh 621, fol. 196v; emphasis is mine.

[21] *Ibid.,* fol. 156v, lines 6–9. See also Ibn al-Haytham, *al-Shukūk ᶜalā Baṭlamyūs,* ed. A. Sabra and N. Shehaby (Cairo: Dar al-Kutub, 1970), *Dictionary of Scientific Biography,* Vol. VI (1972), pp. 189–210.

All this evidence leads to only one conclusion: the *Book on Astronomy* of ᶜUrḍī in the form extant in Marsh 621 was written before the building of the Maraghah observatory in 657 H.

Ṭūsī, on the other hand, did not compose his *tadhkira* until 659 H. (= A.D. 1260/1261), at least two to three years after the work of ᶜUrḍī, if not more. This date is designated in the colophon of a copy of the *tadhkira* kept at Meshhed.[22] Ibn al-Fuwaṭī, the librarian appointed by Ṭūsī himself at Maraghah, in effect adds corroborating evidence. Ṭūsī, according to the librarian, composed his *tadhkirah* for ᶜIzz al-Dīn al-Zinjānī. But the latter did not reach Tabriz until after a journey of several years from Central Asia, a trip which could not have started before 654 H., when he was still in Baghdad.[23]

CONCLUSION

Mu'ayyad al-Dīn al-ᶜUrḍī, who was born in a small village near Aleppo[24] early in the thirteenth century and lived his later life in Damascus and Maraghah, was the first Arab astronomer associated with the Maraghah School to initiate a process of constructing planetary models. Ṭūsī and the other Maraghah astronomers continued his work, which led in the fourteenth century to the final formulation of the planetary theory of Ibn al-Shāṭir. As research unravels the chronological problems, so, too, researchers should begin to explore the patterns in the relationships among members of the Maraghah School. But much more work needs to be done before a proper assessment of their relationships and activities can be made.

[22] Muhammad Mudarris Rizavi, *Aḥval wā-āṯār . . . Naṣīr al-Dīn* (Teheran: Farhang Iran, 1976), pp. 399–400.

[23] *Ibid.*, pp. 284 f. A note in the catalogue of the Meshhed Library mentions another copy of the *tadhkira* as being composed in 569 H., an obvious mistake for 659 H. Ukta'i, *Fihrist . . . Quds Rizavī* (Meshhed, 1926), Vol. III, p. 337.

[24] Mudarris, *Aḥvāl*, pp. 228–229; *Jāmiᶜ al-tavārīkh*, Vol. II, P. 665. For the village ᶜUrd, see Yāqūt al-Rūmī, *Muᶜjam al-Buldān* (Beirut: Ṣāder, 1957), Vol. IV, p. 103.

The Original Source of Quṭb al-Dīn al-Shīrāzī's Planetary Model

George Saliba*

Introduction

A STUDY[1] published some twelve years ago reviewed the information then available concerning late medieval planetary theory. In this article, more space was devoted to the work of Quṭb al-Dīn al-Shīrāzī (fl. 1280 A.D.) than to any other individual. The model he uses for all the planets except Mercury differs from those of his contemporaries, Naṣīr al-Dīn al-Ṭūsī and Ibn al-Shāṭir. It was then remarked that perhaps the unique feature of Quṭb al-Dīn's arrangement had not been invented by him, but had been inherited from a predecessor.

This paper introduces a text,[2] anterior to that of Quṭb al-Dīn, in which the distinctive device is fully described and motivated. As such, it constitutes the earliest successful effort thus far discovered to eliminate a supposed fault in the Ptolemaic system. It was a belief widely held in antiquity that the motion of any celestial body must be circular and uniform, or a combination of uniform circular motions. Ptolemy's equant device (see Fig. 1 below), although imposed by the facts of observation, violated this principle. The mechanism here explained conforms fully to the requirement of uniform circularity, retains the effect of the equant and yields predictions differing only slightly from those obtainable with the Ptolemaic model.

In a separate article, the involved problem of authorship and priority as well as the relationships among the members of the "Marāgha School" has been treated in some detail, and further research is still going on to unravel the intricate relationships and historical questions involved. Nevertheless, there seems to be no way in which future research can change the thesis of

*Department of Near Eastern Languages and Literature, Faculty of Arts and Sciences, N. Y. U., Washington Square, New York City 10003.

1. E. S. Kennedy, "Late Medieval Planetary Theory", *Isis*, 57 (1966), 365-378.

2. Bernard R. Goldstein and Noel Swerdlow, "Planetary Distances and Sizes in an Anonymous Arabic Treatise Preserved in Bodleian Ms. Marsh 621", *Centaurus*, 15 (1970), 135-170. The author wishes to thank Prof. N. Swerdlow of the University of Chicago for bringing this Ms to his attention. The author is also indebted to the courtesy of Prof. B. Goldstein of the University of Pittsburgh for allowing him to investigate this manuscript.

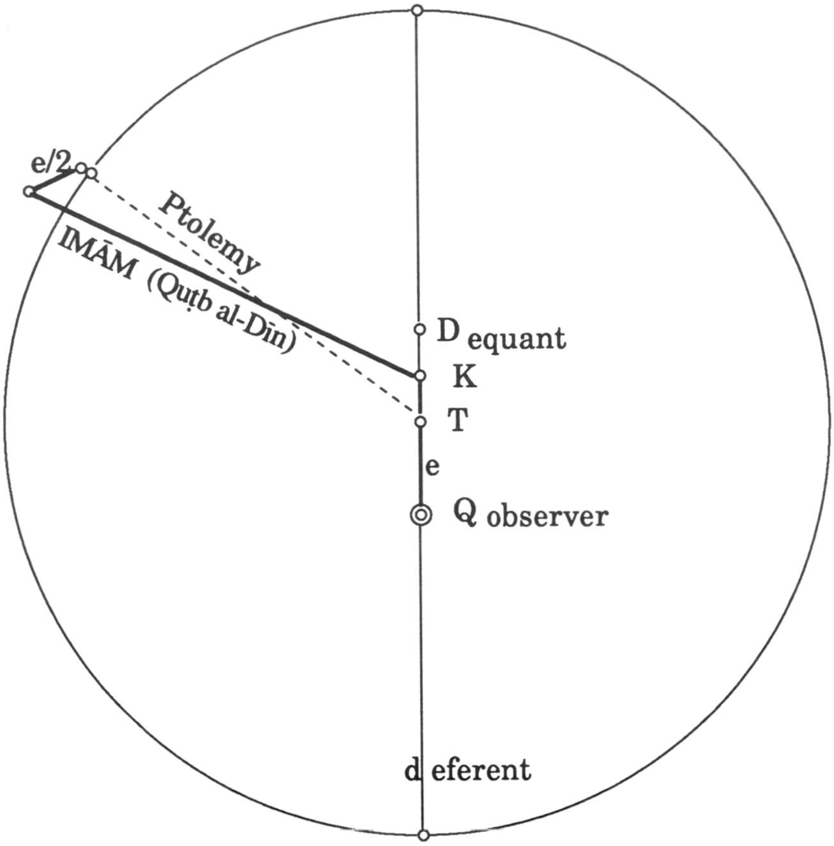

Figure 1. Sketch (not to scale) illustrating the two models.

this paper. We summarize here the tentative results reached so far and reported in the article mentioned above.[3]

The author of Marsh 621, at this stage, can be called al-Shaykh al-Imām as the scribe refers to him on fol. 126r. He must have lived between 1138 A.D. and 1272 A.D.

Shaykh Imām did not participate in the activities of the Marāgha observatory, for he says that he has no access to new observations. Hence he was probably writing before 1259. This author suspects that Shaykh Imām was not Mu'ayyad al-Dīn al-ᶜUrḍī, a likely candidate.*

Shaykh Imām was not known to Ibn al-Shāṭir except through the works of Quṭb al-Dīn al-Shīrāzī.

And finally, it is highly probable that the "Ṭūsī couple" grew out of Imām's model as a logical consequence.

Due to the historical significance of this source, this author has undertaken a full transcription of it, but will give here only the relevant section on the planetary model with an English translation for the benefit of the reader who is not familiar with Arabic.

Quṭb al-Dīn and Shaykh Imām

The first reading of Marsh 621 revealed the identity of Shīrāzī's planetary model and that of Shaykh Imām. A first working hypothesis, however, was to assume that Marsh 621 was some earlier work of Shīrāzī reproduced in the *Nihāyat al-'idrāk* of Quṭb al-Dīn in a different format. That hypothesis ran into immediate problems, for the author of Marsh 621 is referred to as deceased by 1272 A.D., as was already noticed by Goldstein and Swerdlow,[4] whereas Quṭb al-Dīn was still writing in 1281 A.D. and lived till 1311 A.D.

The task remained, however, to prove beyond doubt that the phrase *qaddasa 'Allāhu rūḥahu* (May God bless his soul) is to be taken literally, and hence to establish Shaykh Imām as different from and earlier than Quṭb al-Dīn.

Hence it was necesary to examine the work of Quṭb al-Dīn with this question in mind. The present writer did so, braving Quṭb al-Dīn's "exasperating traits" of prolixity and repetition, coming upon the following passage of the *Nihāyat al-'idrāk*:

« قال بعض افاضل المتاخرين من اهل الصناعة ههنا ان الشيء الذي يجعل علامة لمبدأ حركة يجب ان يكون ساكناً بالنسبة الى المتحرك ليكون تباعد المتحرك عنه وتقاربه اليه بحركة المتحرك وحده » .

3. These results were first reported on December 12, 1978, in a commentary read at the Boston Colloquium for the Philosophy of Science. The full text of the commentary will be published in the proceedings of the Colloquium.

4. *Op. cit.*, p. 146.

* *Note added in proof*: In an article appearing in *Isis* the present author has now established that al-Shaykh al-Imām was indeed alᶜUrḍī (d. 1266) and that the text preserved in Marsh 621 was written before the building of the Marāgha observatory in 1259.

"Some of the esteemed modern workers in this science (*ṣināᶜa*) say in this place: If something is to be taken as a reference point for any motion, it must be stationary with respect to the moving thing so that motion will be due only to the moving body as it draws away from it or comes close to it."[5]

This same statement is made by Shaykh Imām in Marsh 621 in the relevant discussion of the moving center of the lunar deferent and which he uses as his own axiom to begin his new model. Furthermore, Quṭb al-Dīn, as usual, takes issue with this statement, hence proving that the author of Marsh 621 is a different person. In addition, this demonstrates that the work of Shaykh Imām was available to the Marāgha scholars and was actually incorporated into their works.

In what follows we give a translation of the text appended to this paper, from Marsh 621, fol. 157v-160r, attempting to be as literal as possible, only inserting a few explanatory words in brackets here and there to facilitate comprehension on the part of the reader.

Translation

f. 157v

As for the correct astronomy which agrees with what is obtained by observation and is apparent to the eye and (also) agrees with the accepted principles without any variation, we will explain it in the simplest way we can. We will also show the position of the spheres, which produce the continuous simple motion that is uniform with respect to their centers. The uniform motion is the one through which the moving (body) describes equal angles at the center of its mover in equal times. The non-uniform one is the one that is not so.

You must know that achieving such a momentous result in a correct fashion is of the highest human intellectual degrees and it is actual perfection of the theoretical part of the mathematical (sciences).

The researcher ought to accept in this science the ancient observations that he thinks are true, such as those of Hipparchus and Ptolemy, for they were trustworthy in knowledge and in practice. Let us accept what they have recorded by way of observations through which he (i.e. Ptolemy) himself used to work and upon which he based his computations, that he derived through

f. 158r

geometry (*khuṭūṭ*), and mean motions that are taken from periods of revolution.

As for the period of revolution and the daily motion of the planet in mean longitude (*wasaṭ*) and in anomaly, its verification depends upon testing (*imti-*

5. We transcribe here the text from Marsh 621, fol. 124v:1-3, to facilitate the comparison.
« إن أنشيء الذي يفرض علامة لمبدأ حركة متحرك يجب ان يكون ساكناً بالنسبة الى المتحرك ليكون تباعد المتحرك عنه وتقربه اليه انما هو بحركة المتحرك وحده » .
Quṭb al-Dīn's text comes from the *Idrāk*, British Mus. Add 7482, fol. 52v:10-12.

ḥān) and is not obtainable otherwise. Its accurate determination is very difficult and rather cannot be achieved with high refinement (*istiqṣā'*) in a way that no slight inaccuracy is incorporated into it. And when any amount (of error) is incorporated into it, even if it be small, it will become quite apparent after the passage of time and will increase as the time increases.

The verification of that can only be achieved through testing by observations time after time. For that reason we must select the observations that are close to us in time so that the amount that we miss (i.e. the error) does not get multiplied several times.

And since our contemporaries and the kings of our times and those who have the authority have no bent toward this science, and we ourselves are lacking on account of our weakness and the expenses of our dependents and the lack of a helper, we did not say anything about it (i.e. observation) without testing as would the authors of *zījes* do when they add and subtract on their own without any evidence nor do they have any proof except their ignorance of the method by which these things are derived. They are (encouraged ?) to do so by what they see of the variations in the books of the people of this science and hence each of them selects mean motions for himself and sets them down.

For that reason the contradictions in these *zījes* are obvious. But let us return now to our discussion of the planets and say:

The center of the epicycle appears to be carried by an eccentric sphere, and its motion appears to be uniform with respect to the center of a sphere other than the one by which it is carried on account of the motion of the epicycle center which Ptolemy thinks is simple, but it is not so. (On the contrary) it is composed of two equal and uniform motions around two centers other than the ones described above, i.e. the centers of the carrier (deferent) and of the equant that he had mentioned.

But when the center of the epicycle moves with the two motions that we will describe the resulting uniform and composite motion will look as if it is simple with respect to the center of the equant.

Let us then introduce that with a useful reminder (*tadhkira*) by saying: Every straight line upon which we erect two equal straight lines on the same side so that they make two equal angles with the (first) line, be they alternate or interior, if their edges are connected, the resulting line will be parallel to the line upon which they were erected.

Erect on line AB the two lines AG and BD so that they surround with it the two equal angles described (above). Let line GD be connected.

Then I say: Line GD is parallel to line AB. Its proof is to produce AB to E. Then if the exterior angle DBE is equal to the interior angle GAB as in the first two cases, it is obvious that the two equal lines AG and BD are parallel.

But if

158v

the two equal angles were the interior ones that are on the same side, i.e. angle $GAB = DBA$ as in the remaining two cases, then we produce from D a line parallel to AG and let it meet line AB at point Z.

Since AG is parallel to DZ then angle $GAB = DZE$. Therefore $DZB = DBZ$ and line $DZ = DB$, i.e. AG and is parallel to it.

Then the two lines AB and GD are parallel, and that is what we wanted to show.

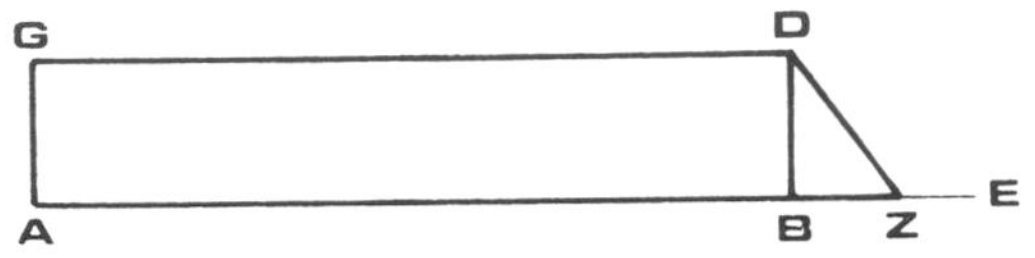

In the same way, if two equal circles intersect on a plane surface and their centers are joined with a straight line that is produced in both directions to their circumference, and if we mark the midpoint of the line joining their centers and make it a center of a circle whose radius is equal to the radius of either of the two circles, then the circumference of this circle cuts the two segments of the straight line that is between the two circumferences of the two circles at their midpoints.

This circle intersects each of the two circles at two points other than the points of their original intersection.

If we make the point at which this circle cuts the two segments that are between the two circumferences a center and with it draw a small circle tangent to the two original circles, then the diameter of this circle is equal to the distance between the centers of the two original circles.

When the center of the small circle moves along the circumference of the third circle, which is the middle one of the three circles, until it reaches the diametrically opposite position on this line, then the small circle will also be tangent to the two circles to which it was tangent in the previous position, internally and externally, so that it will be externally tangent to the one to which it was internally so, and conversely with the other circle.

If one were to imagine the center of the epicycle of a planet to be carried on the circumference of this small circle, and (the circle) itself were assumed to be moving around its center in the direction of the zodiacal signs on the upper arc, i.e. the direction of the movement of the center, and in the reverse on the lower arc, and if the two motions were equal and the two original circles assumed to be fixed, and the eye (*baṣar*) were assumed to be on the line that passes through the centers and distant from the center of one of the two circles by as much as the distance between the two centers, and if the center of the epicycle of the planet were imagined to be at the point where the small circle is externally tangent to the one of the two original circles whose center is closer to it, then if the small circle moves and with it the point of tangency, i.e. the center of the epicycle, in the direction opposite to that of the motion of the center. And if the center moves with the motion of its deferent, then the center of the epicycle moves with its motion, i.e. with the motion

f. 159r

of the small circle and its own motion on itself, in a motion composed of these two motions in such a way that it is thought to be simple and uniform at the center of the circle that is more eccentric from the eye, which is called the equant.

As for the center of the epicycle, i.e. the point of tangency mentioned above, it looks as though it were carried along the circle whose center is closer to the point of sight, on account of the fact that the center of the epicycle will be on this circle at its two distances, i.e. its farthest distance from the eye and its closest distance to it. And since it is very close to its circumference at the remaining portions of its distances (*dhurwa*), that has led Ptolemy to believe that the center of the epicycle is coincident with its circumference, and it describes it with its motion (Fig. 2).

Let us give an example to illustrate (that) very clearly. Let there be two equal circles intersecting in the same plane. The first of them, which is called the equant by Ptolemy, has points *ABG* on it and its center is point *D*. The second, which he calls the sphere carrying the center of the epicycle (i.e. deferent), is circle *EZH* with center *T*. Let the two (circles) intersect at points *W* and *Y*. We join the line *DT* that passes through the centers and produce it to the circumference on either side. Let it intersect circle *ABG* at the points *E* (and) *H*. We then bisect line *DT* at point *K* and with it as a center we draw a circle with a distance *DA*, i.e. the radius of the first circle, and (mark) in it points *L*, *N*, (and) *M*. It will bisect each of the two lines *AE* and *GH* at points *L* and *M*.

With point *L* as a center and with distance *AL* we draw circle *ASE*. It will be tangent to circle *ABG* internally at point *A* and tangent to circle *EZH* externally at point *E*. Let

f. 159v

point *S* be on the right-hand side of the small circle.

It is obvious then that the radius of this circle, i.e. *EL*, is equal to line *DK*, i.e. half the line connecting the centers of the first two circles *ABG* and *EZH*.

If we then assume that the first two circles *ABG* and *EZH* are fixed, and that the sphere surrounding the epicycle of the planet is tangent to the epicycle,

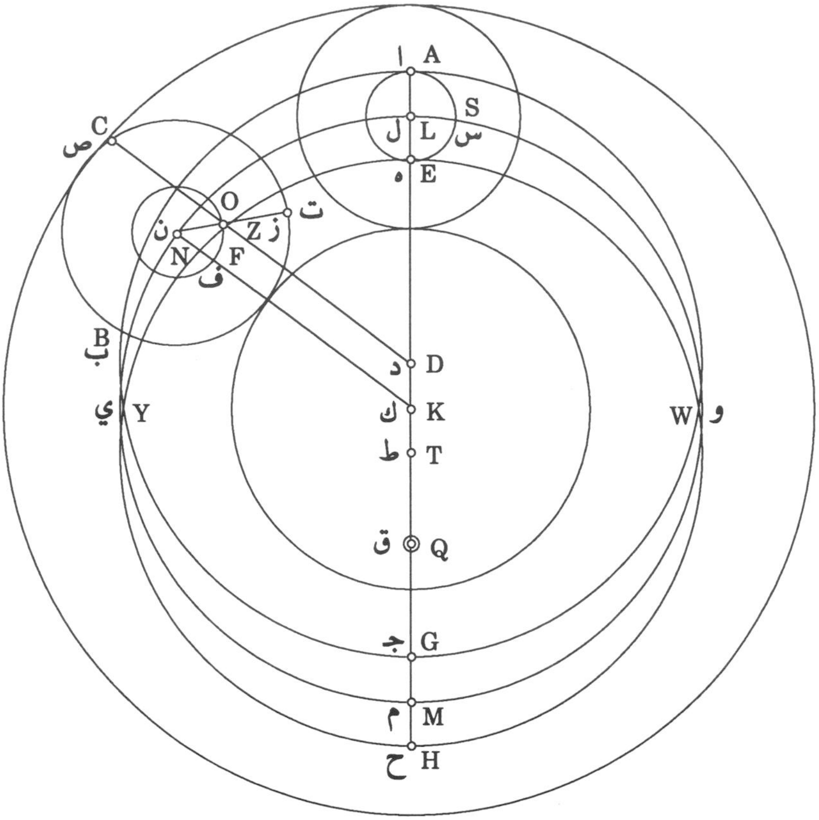

Figure 2. The planetary model of Shaykh Imām as reconstructed from Marsh 621.

then its center will be point *L* and the sphere will be called the director *(al-mudīr)* sphere of the epicycle.

Let this sphere be sunk into the thickness of (another) sphere whose curved parallel surfaces are around center *K*, so that it is tangent to its parallel surfaces in such a way that the surface of the director is tangent to its outer and inner surfaces. That sphere is called the carrier sphere (i.e. deferent).

When this sphere makes a full revolution the center of the director will then describe a circle whose center is point *K*, and that is the (above-)mentioned middle circle.

And as the director moves around center *L*, the epicycle of the planet, i.e. point *E*, will describe the small circle which is inside the sphere of the director, i.e. the (above-)mentioned circle *ASE*.

Now if the deferent moves uniformly, point *L* will move along the circumference of the third (circle) *LNM* whose center is point *K*. It will then move through its motion the sphere of the director. With the motion of the director sphere the center of the epicycle will also uniformly move along the small circle *ASE* and around its center, i.e. point *L*, at the same speed as point *L*.

So if point *L* moves along the circle *LNM* to point *N* and (then to) *M* on the left-hand side of circle *LNM*, then point *E* will move on circle *ASE* on the right-hand side to point *O*, then to point *H*.

Now if you imagine the situation as we described it, let the center of the director and the epicycle be at any assumed position. Then we join lines *KFN*, *DZOC*, and *NOR* to the circumference of the epicycle.

Then I say that the two lines *KFN* (and) *DZOC* are parallel.

Its proof is that arc *LN* of circle *LNM* in all positions of point *L*, i.e. *N* of circle *LNM*, is similar to arc *FO* of the small circle. Then the two angles *EKN* and *FNO* are equal. And lines *KN* and *DO* are parallel. Then *ADO* = angle *LKN*. And the motion of point *E*, i.e. *O*, around center *D* is similar to the motion of point *L*, i.e. *N*, around center *K* at any assumed time and place.

But the motion of point *N* around center *K* is uniform, hence the motion of point *O* around center *D*, i.e. the center of the equant, is uniform. This resulting motion of point *O* around center *D* is composed of the two uniform motions of points *L* and *E*, i.e. *N* and *O*.

That demonstrates what we said, that if point *E* moves with the sum of the two motions mentioned (above), it will have a uniform motion with respect to point *D* and equal in speed to the motion of circle *LNM*.

If the eye is assumed to be at point *Q* of line *TG*, and its distance from *T* were to be equal to the distance of point *T* from point *D*, then these distances, when their values are of the same quantities assumed (over a millenium before) f.160r

by Ptolemy for the distances between the deferent center and the equant from point *Q*, i.e. the center of the universe, for any planet, then what appears of these motions will be in agreement with what appeared to him (i.e. Ptolemy) by observation.

Appendix

[١٥٧ ظ] فاما الهيئة الصحيحة التي يتهيأ بها اصابة ما يخرج بالارصاد ويشاهد بالعيان ويجري على الاصول الموضوعة من غير مخالفة لشيء منها فنحن مثبتوها بابسط ما نقدر عليه . ونبين وضع الأكر التي تكون عنها الحركة البسيطة المتصلة على أن حركاتها مستوية عند مراكزها . والحركة المستوية هي التي يقطع المتحرك بها في الازمان المتساوية زوايا متساوية عند مركز المحرك له . والمختلفة هي التي ليست كذلك .

وينبغي ان تعلم أنّ إصابة مثل هذا الامر الجليل على الوجه الصواب في اعلى مراتب القوى الفكرية البشرية وهو تمام بالحقيقة للجزء النظري من التعاليم .

والذي ينبغي ان يسلّمه الباحث في هذا العلم هي الارصاد القديمة التي يظن بها الصحة مثل ارصاد ابرخس وبطلميوس اذ كانا ممن يوثق بعلمهما وعملهما . فلنسلم ما اورداه من هذه الارصاد وهي التي عليها كان يعمل هو ايضا وعليها عمل حسابه الذي اخرجه بطريق [١٥٨ و] الخطوط والاوساط وهي المنتزعة من ازمان الادوار .

فاما الزمان الدوريّ ومقدار مسير كل كوكب في يوم يوم بالوسط والخاصة فإن تحقيقه موقوف على الامتحان فلا يصار اليه بغيره . واصابته بغاية التدقيق يعسر بل لا يمكن ان يدرك على الاستقصاء بحيث لا يفوت فيها ولا القدر اليسير . ومتى فات فيها مقدار مّا وان قلّ فانه اذا مرّ عليه زمان طويل ظهر ظهوراً بيّناً ويزداد كلما طالت عليه المدة .

وليس لتحقيق ذلك طريق سوى الامتحان بالرصد في الوقت بعد الوقت . ولهذا يجب ان نختار من الارصاد ما يقرب منّا زمانه لكيلا يكون القـــدر الذي يفوتنا مضاعفا[١] مرات كثيرة .

ولما لم يكن لاهل زماننا وملوك عصرنا ومن له البسيطة[٢] رغبة في هذا العلم وقصر بنـــا نحن ضعف الحال وكلفة العيال وقلة المساعد فلذلك لم نتكلم فيها من غير امتحان كما يفعل مصنفو[٣] الزيجات بان يزيدوا او ينقصوا من عند انفسهم بلا دليل ولا حجة سوى جهلهم بالطريق التي استخرجت بها هذه الامور . وانما حملهم[٤] على ذلك كونهم يرون الخــلاف الواقع في كتب اهل هذه الصّناعة فاختار كل واحد منهم اوساطاً من نفسه فوضعها .

فلذلك صارت زيجاتهم على ما يرى من التناقض . ونعود الى كلامنا في افلاك الكواكب فنقول :

إنّ السبب الذي من اجله صار مركز التدوير يرى انه محمول على فلك خارج المركز ويرى مسيره المستوي عند مركز فلك آخر غير الذي هو محمول عليه ان نقلة مركز التدوير التي يظن بطلميوس انها بسيطة ليست كذلك . وانما هي حركة مركبة من حركتين بسيطتين مستويتين على مركزين غير المركزين الموصوفين اعني مركز الحامل ومركز معدّل المسير اللذين ذكرهما .

لكن فلك التدوير اذا تحرك بالحركتين اللتين سنوضحهما فانه سيحصل من تركيبهما حركة مستوية تخال انها بسيطة عند مركز معدّل المسير . ونقدم لذلك تذكرةً نافعة فنقول :

إنّ كل خط مستقيم نقيم عليه خطين[٥] مستقيمين متساويين[٥] في جهة واحدة فيصيران زاويتين من الزاويا التي تحدث مع الخط امّا الداخلة مع الخارجة واما الداخلتان اللتان في جهة واحدة متساويتين[٦] ثم يوصل بين طرفيهما[٦] بخط مستقيم فانه يكون موازيا الخط الذي قاما عليه .

١ – صححت على الهامش

٢ – البسطه في المخطوط .

٣ – مصنفوا

٤ – كذا .

٥ – خطان مستقيمان متساويان .

٦ – عبارة مكررة

فلنقم على خط اب خطي[٧] اج ، بد ويحيطان معه بالزاويتين الموصوفتين المتساويتين. ويوصل خط جد .

فاقول إنّ جد موازٍ لخط اب . برهانه أنّا نخرج خط اب على استقامة الى نقطة ه فإن كانت زاوية دبه الخارجة مساوية لزاوية جاب الداخلة على ما في الصورتين الاولتين فمن البيّن أنّ خطّي اج ، بد المتساويين يكونان متوازيين . فخطا اب ، جد كذلك .

واما إن كانت

[١٥٨ ظ]

الزاويتان المتساويتان هما الداخلتين اللتين في جهة واحدة اعني زاوية جاب مساوية لزاوية دبا كما في الصورتين الباقيتين فنخرج من نقطة د خطاً موازياً لخط اج وليلقى خط اب على نقطة ز .

فمن اجل ان اج موازٍ لدز تكون زاوية جاب مثل زاوية دزه . فلذلك تكون دزب مثل زاوية دبز . فخط دز مساو لخط دب اعني اج وموازٍ له. فخطا اب ، جد متوازيان . وذلك ما اردنا بيانه .

ومن ذلك ايضا ان كل دائرتين متساويتين يتقاطعان في بسيط مستوٍ يوصل بين مركزيهما بخط مستقيم وينفذ في الجهتين الى محيطها ثم نعلم على نقطة على منتصف الخط الذي بين مركزيهما ونجعل هذه النقطة مركزاً ويدار عليه دائرة يكون نصف قطرها مساويا لنصف قطر احدى[٨] الدائرتين الاولتين ، فان محيط هذه الدائرة يقطع كل واحدة من القطعتين اللتين تقعان من الخط المستقيم المار بالمراكز فيما بين محيطي الدائرتين بنقطتين نصفين .

٧ – خطا .

٨ – احد .

وتقطع هذه الدائرة كل واحدة[٩] من الدائرتين الاولتين على نقطتين غير نقطتي تقاطع الدائرتين الاولتين .

فاذا جعلنا موضع قطع هذه الدائرة لاحد قسمي الخط الذي فيما بين الدائرتين مركزاً وادرنا عليه دائرة صغيرة تماسّ الدائرتين الاولتين ، فإن قطر هذه الدائرة يكون مساويا لبعد ما بين مركزي الدائرتين الاولتين .

فمتى تحرك مركز هذه الدائرة الصغيرة على محيط الدائرة الثالثة وهي الوسطى من الدوائر الثلثة المتساوية الى ان يصير وضعها على هذا الخط من الجهة الاخرى مقاطراً لهذا الوضع فإن الدائرة الصغيرة تصير ايضاً مماسّة للدائرتين اللتين كانت مماسّة لهما في الوضع الاول من داخل ومن خارج فتماس التي كانت تماسها من داخل من خارج وبالعكس في الاخرى .

واذا توهم مركز فلك تدوير الكوكب محمولاً على محيط هذه الدائرة الصغيرة وفرضت متحركة على مركزها امّا في القوس العليا منها فالى التوالي اعني الجهة التي يتحرك مركزها اليها ، واما في القوس السفلى بالعكس وفرضت الحركتان[١٠] متساويتين[١٠] وفرضت الدائرتان[١١] الاولتان[١١] ثابتتين وفرض البصر على الخط المار بالمراكز وبعده من مركز احدى الدائرتين الاولتين مثل بعد ما بين مركزيهما . فاذا توهم مركز تدوير الكوكب على النقطة التي تماس الدائرة الصغيرة احدى الدائرتين الاولتين من خارج اعني التي مركزها اقرب من النقطة التي توضع عليها ثم تحركت الدائرة الصغيرة فحركت بحركتها النقطة المماسة اعني مركز التدوير الى خلاف الجهة التي يتحرك مركزها اليها . ويتحرك مركزها بحركة الحامل له . حصل لمركز التدوير بتحركها اعني بانتقال

[١٥٩ و]

جملة الدائرة الصغيرة وبحركتها ايضا على مركز نفسها حركة مركبة من هاتين الحركتين يظنّ انها بسيطة مستوية عند مركز الدائرة التي هي اكثر خروجاً عن موضع البصر وهي المسمّاة بمعدل المسير .

واما مركز التدوير اعني نقطة المماسّة المذكورة فقد يخال انه محمول على الدائرة التي

٩ – واحد .
١٠ – الحركتين متساويتين
١١ – الدائرتين الاولتين .

مركزها اقرب من النقطة التي عليها البصر من أجل أنَّ مركز التدوير يكون على هذه
الدائرة في بعديه المختلفين اعني اعظم ابعاده من البصر واقربها منه .

وكونها قريبا من محيطها في باقي ذروته جداً فلذلك ظنّ بطلميوس أنَّ مركز التدوير
لازماً لمحيطها وانه يرسمها بحر كته .

١٢ولنضرب لذلك مثالاً ليظهر ظهورا بينا . فليكن دائرتان متساويتان في بسيط واحد
متقاطعتان . الاولى منهما وهي يجعلها بطلميوس دائرة معدّل المسير عليها ابج مركزها١٣
نقطة د . والثانية منهما وهي التي يجعلها الفلك الحامل لمركز التدوير دائرة هزح ومزكزها
نقطة ط . وليتقاطعا على نقطتي وي . ونصل خط دط المار بالمركزين وننفذه في الجهتين الى
محيطها . وليقطع دائرة ابج على نقطتي اج ودائرة هزح على دح . ونقسم خط دط بنصفين
على نقطة ك ونجعلها مركزاً وندير عليها دائرة وبعد دا اعني نصف قطر الدائرة الاولى
عليها لنم . فتقطع كل واحد من خطي اه ، جح بنصفين على نقطة لم .

فنجعل نقطة ل مركزاً وندير ببعد ال دائرة صغيرة عليها اسه . فتماس١٤ دائرة ابج
من داخل على نقطة ا وتماس دائرة هزح من خارج على نقطة ه . ولتكن١٥

[١٥٩ ظ]

نقطة س في النصف الايمن من الدائرة الصغيرة .

فمن البيّن أنَّ نصف قطر هذه الدائرة اعني هل يكون مساويا لخط دك اعني نصف
الخط الذي بين مركزي دائرتي ابج ، هزح الاولتين .

فاذا توهمنا أنَّ دائرتي ابج ، هزح الاولتين ثابتتين وان الكرة المحيطة بتدوير الكوكب
يماس١٦ سطحها سطح التدوير يكون مركزها نقطة ل وتسمى هذه الكرة الفلك المدير
للتدوير .

___

١٢ – النص ، من هنا وصاعداً ، هو عينه النص الذي ورد في نهاية الادراك لقطب الدين الشيرازي مع
تغييرات طفيفة جداً لم تؤثر على الهيئة التي توهمها .

١٣ – مكررة .   ١٤ – فيماس .

١٥ – وليكن . يلي هذه الكلمة شكل يخال انه يمثل هذه الدوائر غير انه مرموز اليه على هامش الصفحة بالعبارة
التالية : " هذا الشكل خطأ " . لذلك اعدنا رسمه حسب مقتضيات النص . انظر الشكل ٢ المرفق بهذا المقال .

١٦ – تماس .

ولتكن هذه الكرة مغرقة في ثخن كرة محدبها سطحان متوازيان مركزهما نقطة ك ، فتماس[١٧] سطحيها المتوازيين بحيث يماس سطح المدير سطحيها الظاهر والباطن . وتسمى هذه الكرة الفلك الحامل .

فاذا تحركت هذه الكرة دورة تامة رسم مركز المدير دائرة مركزها نقطة ك وهي الدائرة الوسطى المذكورة .

واذا تحرك المدير على مركز ل رسم تدوير الكوكب اعني نقطة ه الدائرة الصغيرة التي في داخل كرة المدير اعني دائرة اسه المذكورة .

فاذا تحرك الحامل تحركت نقطة ل محيط دائرة لنم الثالثه التي مركزها نقطة ك حركة مستوية فانها تدير[١٨] بدورانها كرة المدير . فيدور بدوران كرة المدير مركز التدوير على دائرة اسد الصغيرة على مركزها اعني نقطة ل حركة مستوية ايضا ومساوية في السرعة لحركة نقطة ل .

فاذا انتقلت نقطة ل على دائرة لنم الى ن ثم الى م في النصف الايسر من دائرة لنم انتقلت نقطة ه على دائرة اسه في النصف الايمن من دائرة هسا الى نقطة ع ثم الى نقطة ح .

واذا تصورت هذا الامر على ما شرحناه فإنّ مركز المدير ومركز التدوير عل اي وضع فرضناه . ووصلنا خطوط لكفن ، دزعص ، نعت الى محيط التدوير .

فاقول إنّ خطّي ك فن ، درعص متوازيان .

برهانه انّ قوس لن من دائرة لنم تكون في جميع اوضاع نقطة ل اعني ن من دائرة لنم شبيهة بقوس فع من الدائرة الصغيرة . فزاويتا هكن ، فنع متساويتان . فخطا كن دع متوازيان . فزاوية ادع مثل زاوية لكن . فحركة نقطة ه اعني ع على مركز د شبيهة بحركة نقطة ل اعني ن على مركز ك في اي وضع وزمان فرض .

لكن حركة نقطة ن على مركز ك حركة مستوية فحركة نقطة ع على مركز د اعني مركز معدل المسير حركة مستوية . وهذه الحركة التي حصلت لنقطة ع على مركز د حركة مركبة من حركتي نقطتي له اعني نع المستويتين .

١٧ – يماس .

١٨ – يدير .

٦

فقد تبيّن ما قلنا انه متى تحركت نقطة ه بمجموع الحركتين المذكورتين حصل لها حركة مستوية بالنسبة الى نقطة د ومساوية في السرعة لحركة دائرة لنم .

فاذا فرض البصر على نقطة ق من خط طج وفرض بعده من ط مساويا[١٩] لبعد نقطة ط من نقطة د فإنّ هذه الابعاد متى كانت مقاديرها على وفق الاقدار التي وضعها

[١٦٠ و]

بطلميوس لبعدي مركزي الحامل والمعدّل من نقطة ق اعني مركز العالم في واحد من الكواكب كان ما يظهر من هذه الحركات موافقا لما يظهر له بالارصاد .

١٩ – مساو

A MEDIEVAL ARABIC REFORM OF THE PTOLEMAIC LUNAR MODEL

GEORGE SALIBA, Columbia University

Introduction

In a previous article, published in 1979, I have described in some detail the planetary model of Mu'ayyad al-Dīn al-'Urḍī of Damascus (d. A.D.1266).[1] In that article I published a working edition of the relatively short Arabic text describing the model, and appended to it an English translation and a commentary. The purpose of that article was to show that the planetary model, hitherto ascribed to Quṭb al-Dīn al-Shīrāzī (d. A.D. 1311), was in fact due to the Damascene astronomer Mu'ayyad al-Dīn al-'Urḍī.

In contrast, the remaining models of Mu'ayyad al-Dīn al-'Urḍī, namely his models for the Moon and Mercury, have received no attention beyond a brief mention here and there in public lectures. The most recent brief description of these models has now been incorporated in a chapter on Islamic planetary theories in a forthcoming trilingual book (English, Arabic and French) on Arabic science.[2]

The main purpose of this paper is to describe at some length the lunar model of Mu'ayyad al-Dīn al-'Urḍī, in order to demonstrate one of the several attempts, produced by medieval Arabic astronomers, all expressly aiming to reform the Ptolemaic lunar model, and to make the contributions of Mu'ayyad al-Dīn al-'Urḍī more accessible to students of the history of Arabic science.

After some hesitation the scheme followed in the previous article on the planetary model, namely to present an edition of the Arabic source, an English translation and a commentary, had to be abandoned here for the simple practical reason that the lunar model in 'Urḍī's work occupies a considerably much larger space, and thus makes the reproduction of an edited Arabic text in the form of an article indeed prohibitive. For purposes of comparison, the planetary model in 'Urḍī's text takes up some two-and-a-half folios, while that of the Moon is spread over a space of some thirteen folios.[3]

The Source

The source for the present paper is the critical edition mentioned in ref. 3, which was based on all three surviving manuscripts that have come to light so far. The most accessible of these manuscripts is the Oxford manuscript, Bodleian Marsh 621, in which the discussion of the lunar spheres occupies the folios between 118r and 130v. It should be noted, however, that, unlike the planetary model, in this case there is no diagram to illustrate the workings of the lunar model in any of the extant manuscripts, and the text itself does not seem to have depended on

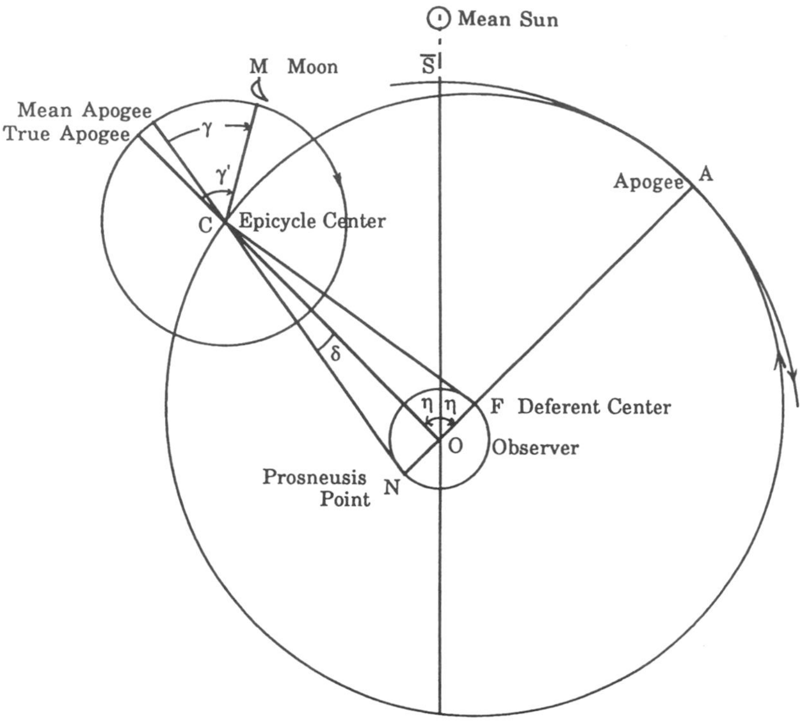

FIG. 1. Ptolemy's lunar model.

one. What 'Urḍī seems to have required of his reader is a thorough familiarity with the Ptolemaic lunar model, for he kept referring to it and described all the emendations that he wished to make with reference to the standard Ptolemaic lunar model.

Ptolemy's Lunar Model[4]

For those who are not familiar with the standard Ptolemaic lunar model, nor with the criticisms that were raised against it in medieval times, the main features are as follows:

In Figure 1, the observer is supposed to be at point *O*, the centre of the ecliptic. The outermost lunar sphere, also called the sphere of the nodes, the *Jawzahr* of medieval Arabic, moves in the direction marked on the diagram which is opposite to the direction of the order of the zodiacal signs, or from east to west. The motion of this outermost sphere moves the apogee of the second sphere, the deferent, in the same direction, at a speed equal to the daily elongation of the Moon from the mean position of the Sun, here marked by angle η at point *O*.

The second sphere, called the deferent, moves in the opposite direction around centre *F*, with a speed equal to double the daily elongation, carrying the epicycle of the Moon to point *C*. At this point, we should note the first objection raised by medieval Arab astronomers against this model. They did not fail to point out that although Ptolemy required the sphere of the deferent to move around centre *F*, its uniform motion, however, is measured around the observer at point *O*. This, in effect, violates the primary principle of uniform motion that was stated by Ptolemy himself earlier in the same book, the *Almagest*,[5] for here we have a sphere, the deferent, moving around its own centre *F*, while it describes equal arcs in equal times around another point *O*. Ptolemy himself had already demonstrated that if a sphere moved uniformly around one point, it will necessarily move at a variable speed around any other point. Therefore, the deferent uniform motion just described could not take place around the centre of the same deferent sphere once it is supposed to move uniformly around an eccentre *O*.

This contradiction in the Ptolemaic model was already noted by the famous eleventh-century astronomer al-Ḥasan Ibn al-Haytham, Latin Alhazen (d. 1048), although the name of Ibn al-Haytham is nowhere mentioned by 'Urḍī in this connection. Instead, 'Urḍī goes on to develop his own objections to this feature of the Ptolemaic model and asserts that such a position as the one taken by Ptolemy is indeed contradictory to his earlier position regarding uniform motion.

The significance of this problem in the Ptolemaic lunar model becomes obvious when we realize that it is essentially the same problem as that which bedevilled the model for the upper planets, where Ptolemy had to introduce a special sphere called the sphere of mean motion, to produce a similar motion, thus generating the famous medieval *equant* problem.

To continue with the main features of the Ptolemaic lunar model, the Moon is assumed to move in the direction opposite to that of the order of the signs, along an epicycle, whose centre is the point *C*, just mentioned. After carefully chosen observations, Ptolemy determined that the mean anomalistic motion of the Moon on its own epicycle takes place with respect to a starting point called the mean apogee, and not with respect to the true apogee. In his description of this phenomenon, Ptolemy asserts that if a line is drawn from the mean apogee through the centre of the epicycle, it would pass, when extended, through a prosneusis point, here called *N*, which is itself located diametrically opposite to point *F*, at the same distance *s* from point *O*.

This second feature of the Ptolemaic lunar model was indeed supported, and derived from two observations taken earlier by Hipparchus. Ptolemy argues, in *Almagest*, V, 5, that according to the two observations taken by Hipparchus (first, when the Moon was close to the perigee of its epicycle, and second, when it was close to the epicyclic apogee), the observed position of the Moon required that its mean anomalistic motion be measured from a point on the epicycle determined by the extension of *NC*, described above. Put differently, Ptolemy asserts that if the point of mean apogee on the epicycle were connected by a straight line to the centre of the epicycle, then when that line is extended it will not pass through the centre of the ecliptic *O*, nor through the centre of the epicyclic carrier *F*, rather it will pass through point *N*, just described.

Since this last line is in fact an imaginary line joining two imaginary points, and since the starting point, from which the mean anomaly was to be measured, is described in Ptolemy's model as a moving point, which depends on the position of the prosneusis point *N*, 'Urḍī correctly notes that such an arrangement does not befit the astronomical sciences,[6] and that an alternative astronomy has to be developed so that it would not suffer from such inconsistencies *muḥālāt* (literally, 'impossibilities').

'Urḍī's Lunar Model

In order to construct his own lunar model, 'Urḍī admits from the very beginning, that he has no alternative observations to contribute to the new model, and that as far as observations are concerned he would like to assume the veracity of the Ptolemaic observations. His main purpose is to take the same data from the Ptolemaic observational records, and to construct a model that would account for the observed phenomena, without suffering from the same inconsistencies. From that perspective, one can understand why 'Urḍī constantly refers to the Ptolemaic model in his discussion, and why he only wished to develop a mathematical alternative to the Ptolemaic model.

For his own model, 'Urḍī states explicitly that he was going to contradict Ptolemy only in matters not related to the actual observations. The direction for the various motions of the lunar spheres, for example, are, according to 'Urḍī, simply invented by Ptolemy, and nothing in the observations determines them one way or the other. He asserts that if, in Figure 2, the outermost sphere were to move at three times the mean daily elongation of the Moon from the Sun, in the same direction as that of the order of the signs, while the deferent were to move in the opposite direction at twice the mean daily elongation, then for an observer at point *O* the mean position of the lunar epicyclic centre would come to the same point *C* predicted by the Ptolemaic observations. At this point, 'Urḍī anticipates his critics by observing that he is talking of *mean* motions only, and for that purpose the direction *PD* is the same as *OC* for the observer at *O*, for mean motions should be measured in exactly the same manner as they were measured in the case of the solar model. There, in the solar model, we allowed the Sun to move around the centre of an eccentric at a uniform mean motion, while the actual mean motion was measured from the observer's position at the centre of the ecliptic in the same parallel direction. In the case of the Moon, 'Urḍī claims that we could do the same.

In fact, if the quantities assigned to the movements of the spheres in 'Urḍī's lunar model are taken in conjunction with the Ptolemaic lunar model, then one can show that, in Figure 2, line *PD* will always be parallel to line *OC*, and that the angle $\bar{S}OC$ is indeed the same η required by the Ptolemaic model. Moreover, 'Urḍī's lunar model would duplicate the positions predicted by the Ptolemaic model exactly at the four critical points, which were used for the construction of the Ptolemaic model, namely the syzygies and the quadratures. The rest of the

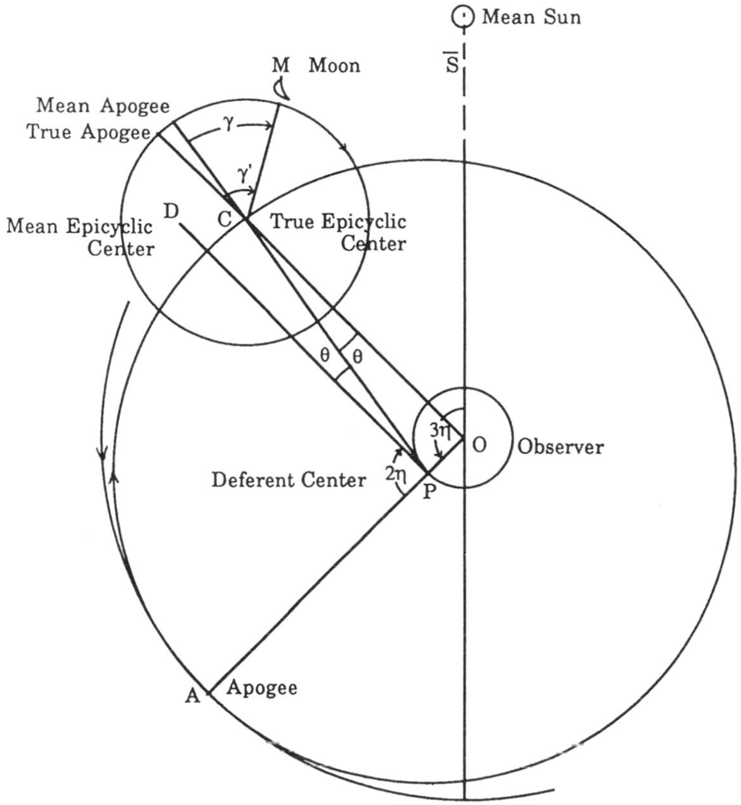

FIG. 2. ʻUrḍī's lunar model.

present discussion will be devoted to the analysis of the situation at the intermediate points.

Testing ʻUrḍī's Lunar Model

We have just noted that the two models predict identical positions for the Moon at the critical points, where eclipses take place, i.e. at the syzygies, and where the maximum apparent diameters of the lunar epicycle and of the Moon itself are observed, i.e. at quadratures. ʻUrḍī claims that much for his model. We should also add that the two models also predict identical positions at the octants, when the mean elongation is 45°. ʻUrḍī does not make this last statement.

But ʻUrḍī is aware of the fact that Ptolemy's model was also tested at two other points, namely at the two Hipparchian observations recorded in *Almagest*, V, 5, where the Moon was once near the perigee of its epicycle, and the other time near the apogee. In fact these were the critical observations that were

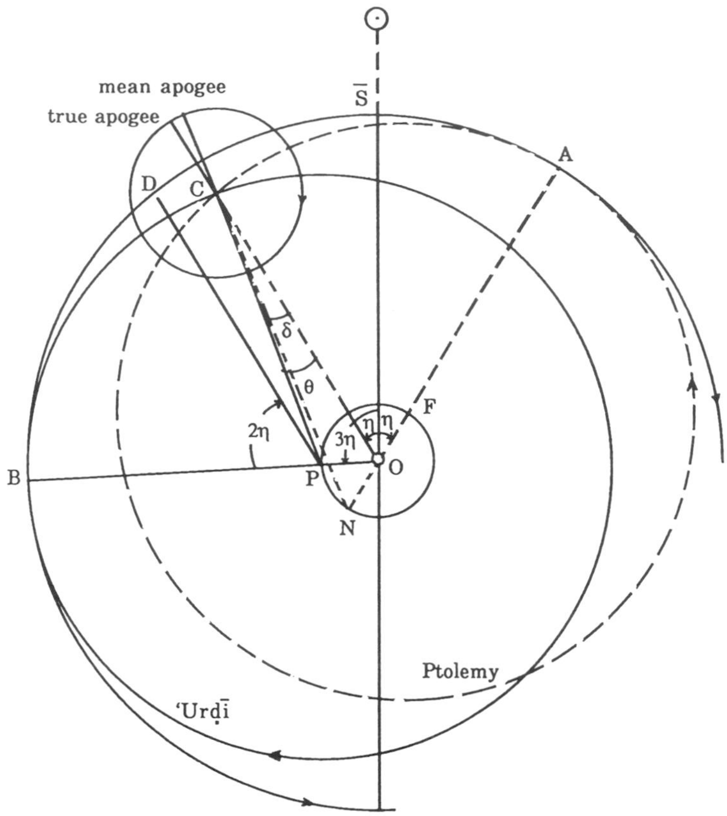

FIG. 3.

used by Ptolemy to determine the position of the prosneusis point *N*, and the equation between the mean and the true apogee. To be satisfied with his model, 'Urḍī felt that he should test his own model at exactly the same points, and by taking the same observational data.

At this point, 'Urḍī takes the Hipparchian observational values for the mean daily elongations, and applies them to his model, the sole object being the determination of the variation between his model and that of Ptolemy in regard to the equation determined at those points. Figure 3 demonstrates the two models superimposed, and represents the conditions at a general point described by both models. Since it is not drawn to scale it intentionally exaggerates the difference between the two models at such a point. 'Urḍī's aim was to calculate the difference between the equation angle θ, in his own model, and δ, the equation angle in the Ptolemaic model. After carrying out very elaborate calculations, in essence duplicating those which were applied by Ptolemy to his own model plus a calculation of the differences, 'Urḍī finds correctly that at these two testing points, and for the observer at point *O*, his model exhibits a variation from that of Ptolemy, amounting to less than half a minute in the first case, and about two minutes in the second. 'Urḍī then rightly concludes that such a variation could not be possibly detected by any known instrument, and "could very easily escape the most skilful observer".

'Urḍī was apparently satisfied with these results, and concluded correctly that his model, despite the changes it embodies, was essentially just as viable as the Ptolemaic model. In addition, his model had none of the contradictions noted in the Ptolemaic model; it solved the problem of uniform motion, where in 'Urḍī's model every sphere rotates uniformly around its own centre, and the problem of the prosneusis point, where in 'Urḍī's model the centre of the sphere itself is taken as the determinant of the mean apogee rather than a fictitious prosneusis point as was required by the Ptolemaic model.

But at no point did 'Urḍī raise the issue of the general agreement between his model and that of Ptolemy at all degrees of elongation. In fact, when such a comparison was indeed carried out, the variation in the first equation, between 'Urḍī's model and that of Ptolemy, reached as much as 3;32°, at two points symmetrically located about 20° away from each side of the quadrature points. But for an observer at point *O*, where the whole arc of 180 degrees of the epicycle appears to reach 7;40°, exactly at quadrature, a difference of 3;32° at points removed from quadrature could not possibly reach more than ten minutes. And even that variation is within the order of magnitude which would have been acceptable to Ptolemy himself.

As was stated above, such a discussion is nowhere carried out by 'Urḍī. One does not even know if 'Urḍī was at all conscious of the problem. All the indications, however, are that he was not. In fact such a comparison is somehow fictitious, for we should be interested in it only if we think that the trajectory of point *C*, in the Ptolemaic model, is supported by observation at all degrees of elongation. No such claim is made by Ptolemy for his own model, and there is no reason why any other astronomer should make that assumption. Since the few critical points, at which Ptolemy's model was tested, are the ones that really count in eclipse computations, one should accept 'Urḍī's model as yielding identical results to that of Ptolemy, and as a perfectly acceptable model for exactly these same purposes.

Acknowledgements

Research for this article was supported by the National Endowment for the Humanities and the Institute for Advanced Study, Princeton. This support is gratefully acknowledged.

REFERENCES

1. G. Saliba, "The original source of Quṭb al-Dīn al-Shīrāzī's planetary model", *Journal for the history of Arabic science* [Aleppo], iii (1979), 3 18.
2. The book is being edited by Prof. Roshdi Rashed, CNRS, Paris. A very brief description of

'Urḍī's lunar model was published in Arabic as part of "Falakīy min Dimashq yarudd 'alā hay'at Baṭlamyūs", *Journal for the history of Arabic science*, iv (1980), 3–17.

3. Those interested in the Arabic text will have to wait for the forthcoming full critical edition, which had been scheduled to appear in a publishing house in Beirut, Lebanon, and which has been understandably delayed due to the ongoing civil war in that country. The full English translation and the commentary are now scheduled to appear with the Islamic Texts Society, Cambridge, England, and may indeed appear before the Arabic text, although every effort is being made to reverse the process.
4. For a full description of this model see *Almagest*, IV–V, and Otto Neugebauer, *A history of ancient mathematical astronomy* (New York, 1975), 68–99.
5. See *Almagest*, III, 2, 3 for an explicit statement of the principle of uniform motion which is ascribed to the celestial spheres.
6. In the words of Ibn al-Haytham, imaginary lines have no motions of their own.

THE ROLE OF THE *ALMAGEST* COMMENTARIES IN MEDIEVAL ARABIC ASTRONOMY: A PRELIMINARY SURVEY OF ṬŪSĪ'S REDACTION OF PTOLEMY'S *ALMAGEST*

George Saliba

Introduction

The importance of Ptolemy's *Almagest* was apparently realized by Arabic-writing astronomers as soon as the text was translated into Arabic. The first translation was probably completed sometime during the latter part of the eighth century or the early part of the ninth. Once that was done, reportedly at the behest of Hārūn al-Rashīd's vizier [1], we are told that another translation immediately followed [2], and a 'correction' (*iṣlāḥ*) [3] came soon thereafter. Within

[1] According to al-Nadīm, *Kitāb al-Fihrist* (ed. by R. Tajaddud [Teheran, 1971], 327), the *Almagest* was first translated for Yaḥyā ibn Khālid al-Barmakī, the vizier of al-Rashīd, by the otherwise unknown Abū Ḥassān and Salm the director (?) (*ṣāḥib*) of Bait al-Ḥikma. This translation, we are told, was superior to yet an earlier one which was accomplished by a group of unknown people. Al-Nadīm continues to say that the text was also translated at this early period by al-Ḥajjāj ibn Maṭar, was commented upon by al-Nairīzī, and was corrected by Thābit ibn Qurra. For a detailed discussion of the *Almagest* translations and their transmission through later sources and into Latin, see Paul Kunitzsch, *Der* Almagest*: Die Syntaxis Mathematica des Claudius Ptolemäus in arabisch-lateinischer Überlieferung*, Wiesbaden, Harrassowitz, 1974.

[2] The second translation seems to have been done by the otherwise unknown al-Ḥassan ibn Quraysh, during the reign of al-Ma'mūn (813-833), and was also translated another time by al-Ḥajjāj ibn Maṭar in 827/828. See G.J. Toomer, *Ptolemy's* Almagest (New York: Springer Verlag, 1984), 2, and Paul Kunitzsch, "Zur Kritik der Koordinatenüberlieferung im Sternkatalog des *Almagest*", *Abhandlungen der Akademie der Wissenschaften Göttingen, Phil.-hist. Klasse*, 3F, Nr. 94 (1975).

[3] Al-Nadīm's evaluation of Thābit's second correction, that it was not as good as the first, implies that Thābit had completed an earlier correction before he accomplished the second one. It was the second version, however, which became the most popular and the one frequently used by Arabic-writing astronomers. Is it possible that the surviving version of Isḥāq–Thābit was confused with the first version by al-Nadīm?

a period of about one century the *Almagest* had several translations – maybe as many as five, had inspired a few corrections, and had at least one or two commentaries.

The *Fihrist* of al-Nadīm informs us that the first, and apparently the best [4], of the *Almagest* commentaries, was penned by al-Nairīzī, who must have completed his work sometime during the first half of the ninth century. It is unfortunate that this early commentary does not seem to have survived and that only two of the *Almagest* translations – one by Ḥajjāj and one by Isḥāq – are still extant.

We have sufficient reports, and enough surviving texts, however, to confirm that the text of the *Almagest* had generated a prolific literature, and attracted the attention of several authors, at various times, during the period stretching from the time of Nairīzī (in the middle of the ninth century) till, at least, the middle of the sixteenth century [5]. One would have expected that all this activity, and this abundant literature, would have engendered more interest on the part of modern historians of science for them to study the impact of the *Almagest* on Arabic astronomy.

With the exception of a single article by Bernard Carra de Vaux, which was devoted to Abū al-Wafā's commentary on the *Almagest* [6], I do not know of another study devoted to any of the other surviving commentaries. This, despite the fact that recent research has already revealed that, of all the Arabic astronomical writings, the theoretical analysis of two of Ptolemy's works, namely, the *Almagest* and the *Planetary Hypothesis*, as reflected in the various treatises on *hay'a*, was probably the most original research in medieval Arabic astronomy. One would have expected that the same type of analysis, to which the *hay'a* texts were subjected, would be carried over to the *Almagest* commentaries for they too probably contain remarks relevant to the on-going research on these *hay'a* texts. Yet, as far as I am aware, none of this was done.

This paper is therefore a limited attempt to fill that gap by drawing attention to one of these commentaries, which I think illustrates the importance of this genre of astronomical writings very well. I will begin by surveying the contents

[4] *Al-Fihrist*, *op. cit.*, where al-Nairīzī is mentioned as being among the first to comment on the *Almagest*, and Niẓāmī 'Arūḍī Samarqandī, *Chehār Maqāla* (tr. by Edward G. Browne, reprinted in 'Gibb Memorial Series' [London, 1978], 89), where Nairīzī's commentary is mentioned as the best.

[5] For a general list of the various commentaries on the *Almagest*, see Fuat Sezgin, *Geschichte des Arabischen Schrifttums* (E.J. Brill, 1978), Bd. VI, 88-94.

[6] See *Journal Asiatique*, 8[e] ser., *19* (1892), 408-471. The mathematical contents of the text had already been studied by M. Delambre, *Histoire de l'astronomie du Moyen Âge* (Paris, 1819), 156-170. Other historians have consulted the earlier commentaries, but none, as far as I know, has devoted a special study to them.

of *taḥrīr al-majisṭī* (Redaction of the *Almagest*), written by the famous astronomer Naṣīr al-Dīn al-Ṭūsī (d. 1274), who, at one point, was the director of the Maragha Observatory that gave its name to a group of very original astronomers, now known by the collective name of 'Maragha School' [7]. After identifying the main features of the *taḥrīr* that are relevant to its role in Arabic astronomy, I will isolate the problems in the *taḥrīr*, which shed light on the general theoretical issues discussed by Ṭūsī in his other works. I will then conclude by asserting that one can not understand the natural historical development of Ṭūsī's research in regard to highly technical issues without taking into consideration his work in the *taḥrīr*.

The text

The text of the *taḥrīr* is confidently dated to the period in Ṭūsī's life when he was under the patronage of the Ismā'īlī rulers [8]; as it is indicated in various manuscripts the text was completed "on the fifth of Shawwāl 644 A.H." = 13 February 1247, while Ṭūsī was still at the citadel of Alamūt [9]. In the introduction, Ṭūsī dedicated the book to a certain Ḥusām al-Dīn al-Ḥasan ibn Muḥammad al-Sīwāsī (?), to whom he referred as "the dear brother" (*al-'akh al-'azīz*), and "the supreme excellency" (*al-janāb al-rafī'*), who, in all likelihood, was a high ranking Ismā'īlī official as well as a competent astronomer [10].

Ṭūsī 's rationale for writing the book, aside from the fact that he seems to have been asked to do so by his patron, was that he had surveyed all the early epitomes (*ikhtiṣārāt*) of the *Almagest*, which were plentiful, and found them to be wanting in so far as they did not meet the set of criteria that he had set for himself. These criteria, which were used in his redaction (*taḥrīr*), included, among other things, the condition that his work should not omit the theoretical considerations of that book (*i.e.* the *Almagest*), nor its practical methods. It should even follow the order of the chapters, and include the computational sections, the tabular configurations, and follow the same arrangement of the

[7] Edward S. Kennedy, "Late Medieval Planetary Theory", *Isis*, *57* (1966), 365-378, esp. 365; reprinted in E. S. Kennedy Colleagues, and Former Students, *Studies in the Islamic Exact Sciences* (Beirut: American University of Beirut, 1983), 84-97.

[8] See Muḥammad Mudarris Riḍawī, *Aḥwāl wa-Āthār Qudwat-i Muḥaqqiqīn ... Naṣīr al-Dīn*, intishārāt Farhang Iran, 1976, 345 f.

[9] *Ibid.*

[10] This Ḥusām al-Dīn seems to have been the author of a commentary on the *taḥrīr*, which is still extant in two manuscripts. See Sezgin, *Geschichte des Arabischen Schrifttums*, cit., 93.

diagrams [11]. It should not be blemished by anything that was alien to it, except that which one needs to put forth in order to simplify a difficult (passage) or to offer a solution to a doubt (*ḥall ishkāl*). It should furthermore include what the moderns have invented (*istanbaṭahu al-muḥdathūn*), or what the later ones have adopted (*dhahaba ilaihi al-muta'akhkhirūn*), which made the theorems more elegant and splendid and reduced the pain and toil in the practical aspects. All of this on the condition that there should be preference given to brevity and conciseness, and one ought not to give in to repetition and prolixity [fol. 1ᵛ]. [12]

Ṭūsī then went on to say:

> I have noted quite explicitly that which was not of the main text of the book and which I myself have added in order to make it easily accessible. I have used various colors to draw the lines and the numbers of the diagrams, which I have added to the original text, in order that they could be distinguished at a glance without any excessive concern. I have gone to that extreme because this book is considered as a main reference for scholars who gather around it in their discussions and refer to specific points in its problems, its sections, and its diagrams. When I finished it I called it 'A Redaction of the *Almagest*' (*taḥrīr al-majisṭī*). [*Ibid.*]

It is therefore clear from this introduction that Ṭūsī intended to give a brief account of the contents of the *Almagest*, but also wished to add improvements to it that were invented by the moderns. He also intended to add propositions that would facilitate the solution of doubts (*ḥall ishkāl*). I translate this expression as literally as possible because I think it is crucial to the other works of Ṭūsī, and, as we will see below, it is vital when one considers the relationships of these works to one another.

In what follows, I will show that Ṭūsī did indeed live up to his promise and produced a text of pivotal historical importance, for it allows us, for the first time perhaps, to closely view the development of his thought during the time when he wrote his elementary text *al-risāla al-Mu'īniyya* (composed in the 1230s), this text of the *taḥrīr* (written in 644 = 1247 as we have seen above), the text of *ḥall-i mushkilāt-i mu'īniyya* (whose date we do not know), and the text of the *tadhkira*, whose date is firmly established in the year 659 A.H. = 1260/1261.

[11] It should be noted that, in this arrangement, Ṭūsī follows Isḥāq-Thābit version of the *Almagest*. See Kunitzsch, *Almagest*, cit., 47 f.

[12] The text used for this survey is that of the India Office Ms. No. Loth 741, a microfilm of which was kindly supplied by the keeper of the oriental manuscripts at that library. It is my pleasant duty to aknowledge his assistance.

Because of the recent interest in the chronological arrangement of Ṭūsī's works [13], one would hope that a close look at the *taḥrīr*, and a careful analysis of its contents might help to determine the relative date of Ṭūsī's *Ḥall*, the only one in this group of Ṭūsī's works that is not yet firmly dated. And since the claim has been made that Ṭūsī first proposed his non-Ptolemaic models for the moon and the upper planets in the *Ḥall*, its dating gains an added significance in relation to Ṭūsī's other work, namely the *tadhkira*, where these models were further developed.

The contents of the taḥrīr

In this preliminary survey, I will restrict my remarks to what I believe are the salient features of Ṭūsī's *taḥrīr*. I will divide these comments into two types: (1) those that shed light on other astronomical works in general, and (2) those that shed light on Ṭūsī's works in particular.

General remarks

I have referred above to Ṭūsī's claim in his own introduction that he would include in his book the inventions of the moderns and the opinions of the astronomers who came after Ptolemy. Viewed separately, these inventions were additions to the text of the *Almagest* that preserved the accretions of centuries of research in Arabic astronomy.

In the first treatise of the book, for example (fols 5 - 8), he discussed the table of chords *Almagest* I, 11, and concluded that section by saying:

> I say, since the method of the moderns, which uses the sines at this point instead of the chords, is easier to use, as I will explain below, I wished to refer to it as well. I then say: The sine of an arc is half the chord of the angle subtended by twice that arc. It could never be more than the radius itself, in the same way the chord could not be more than the diameter. Indeed, its relationship to the radius is the same as that of the chord to the diameter.

[13] See George Saliba, "The Original Source of Quṭb al-Dīn al-Shīrāzī's Planetary Model", *Journal for the History of Arabic Science, 3* (1979), 3-18; *id.*, "The First non-Ptolemaic Astronomy at the Marāgha School", *Isis, 70* (1979), 571-576; *id.*, "A Damascene Astronomer Proposes a non-Ptolemaic Astronomy" (Arabic with English summary), *Journal for the History of Arabic Science, 4* (1980), 97-98, 220-234; Jamil Ragep, *Cosmography in the* Tadhkira *of Naṣīr al-Dīn al-Ṭūsī* (Ph. D. Dissertation, Harvard University, 1982), 47-49; and Edward S. Kennedy, "Two Persian Treatises by Naṣīr al-Dīn al-Ṭūsī", *Centaurus, 27* (1984), 109-120.

> Moreover, every perpendicular, which is drawn from one end of a circular arc and makes a right angle with the diameter that passes through the other end (of the same arc), (that perpendicular) is the sine of (the arc). The (section) falling between the foot of the perpendicular and the center of the circle is itself the sine of the complement of that arc. [Fol. 5r]

This definition is then followed by two tables: one for the sines, and one for the tangents. And immediately after the exposition of the Menelaus Theorem, the alternate spherical sine theorem, called *al-shakl al-mughnī*, is given together with the tangent configuration, called *al-shakl al-ẓillī*. Neither one of those tables, nor these trigonometric theorems are found anywhere in the *Almagest*.

At the beginning of the third treatise, where the solar year is discussed, Ṭūsī uses the occasion to introduce the important calendars of his days, thus introducing the Jewish, the Persian (*i.e.* the Yezdigird), the Coptic, and the Hijra calendars, all new to the text of the *Almagest* [fol. 14v]. Moreover, at various points in the text, whenever the opportunity arose to quote an epoch for the longitude of a planet or some such parameter, always given in the Nabonassar Era in the *Almagest*, Ṭūsī would usually translate that to the Yezdigird epoch (June 16, 632 A.D. JD = 1952, 063), thus updating the *Almagest* to make it useful for his own time.

By way of criticizing the observational contents of the *Almagest*, Ṭūsī commented on the one hand on Ptolemy's use of the fixed solar apogee, which produced a variable tropical year, adding that

> according to the observations of the moderns, since the apogee was found to be moving together with the motion of the fixed stars – the latter having been determined by Hipparchus, the equal revolutions should then be taken with reference to the points on the [sun's] own sphere, *i.e.* the apogee or the perigee. The revolutions of the real sun that are taken with reference to particular points on the ecliptic are therefore variable. [Fol. 17v]

On the other hand, while discussing the difficult Ptolemaic passage on the relative sizes of the two luminaries as it affects eclipses, *Almagest* V, 14 [p. 252, and note 53], [14] Ṭūsī disproved Ptolemy's conclusion by reference to the observations of the moderns in regard to the annular eclipses. He then concluded

[14] References to the text of the *Almagest* are to G. Toomer's translation, *Ptolemy's* Almagest, New York, Springer Verlag, 1984.

that, contrary to Ptolemy's assertion, the solar disk must appear to vary in size and to be larger than that of the moon when the latter is at its farthest distance [fols 27ᵛ-28ʳ].

Moreover, in the first chapter of Book IX of the *Almagest,* Ptolemy reported his uncertainty concerning the order of the five planets, in particular whether Venus and Mercury were to be located above the sun or not. The reason for the hesitation was, according to Ptolemy, due to the fact that neither of these two planets had ever been observed to 'obscure' the sun. After explaining the reasons for his inability to determine the order of these two planets with certainty, Ptolemy finally accepted the arrangement of the 'older astronomers' and took the sun to be in the middle, *i.e.* above both Venus and Mercury, simply because this arrangement "is more in accordance with the nature [of the bodies]". Ṭūsī seems to have been aware of the crucial need for an observation that would settle the Ptolemaic argument, and thus could remove the uncertainty; namely an observation that would show that either Venus or Mercury could have ever 'obscured' the sun. At this point in his exposition of the contents of the *Almagest,* Ṭūsī discusses this possibility and then refers to the observations of the moderns as recorded by Avicenna in one of his works. He then reports:

> al-Shaykh al-Ra'īs, Abū 'Alī Ibn Sīnā, had mentioned in his books that he had seen Venus like a mole on the surface of the sun. Moreover, Ṣāliḥ b. Muḥammad al-Zaynabī al-Baghdādī [otherwise unknown] had also mentioned in his own book, which he called the *Almagest,* that al-Shaykh Abū 'Imrān, in Baghdad and Muḥammad b. Abī Bakr al-Ḥakīm, in Fersīn (?) of the district of Tulak (?), had both seen Venus across the face of the sun at two different times – separated by some twenty years. He said that Venus was in the first case at the apogee of the epicycle, while in the second time, it was at the perigee. This disproves the fact that they were in the same sphere as the sun, with the sun as their center. That is all I have found in this regard, and none of them have recorded the time of the observation. [Fol. 42ᵛ] [15]

By way of recasting the contents of the *Almagest,* Ṭūsī anticipated, at the beginning of the fourth treatise, the development of the lunar theory in *Almagest* IV, and V, and gave, in a very brief form, the reasons why the lunar

[15] With Venus being a solar satellite, the observation of its being in transit while at the apogee has to be discarded. For an evaluation of the other observations, and of Venus transits in general, see Bernard Goldstein, "Some Medieval Reports of Venus and Mercury Transits", *Centaurus, 14* (1969), 49-59.

variations could not be accounted for with either of the two models discussed before, namely the eccentric and the epicyclic models. He concludes by describing the final model of the moon, together with its three assigned motions, namely its own motion on the epicycle, its motion in longitude on its deferent, and its motion in latitude on the inclined plane [fol. 19ʳ]. Such an editorial style is definitely an improvement over the text of the *Almagest* where one does not find such pedagogical summations.

In an attempt to reevaluate the received recensions of the *Almagest*, and to decide which of them was a reliable version, Ṭūsī quotes, when discussing the mean lunar month, *Almagest* IV, 2, the Babylonian-Hypparchian value [16], and then comments that instead of 29 days, 31 minutes (of a day), 50 seconds, 8 thirds, and 20 fourths, "Ḥajjāj's copy (of the *Almagest* had the value) 9 fourths, 20 fifths and 12 sixths, which was the correct (value)" [fol. 19ᵛ].

On folio 39ᵛ, there is a marginal note in connection with the fixed stars, supposed to have been copied from a Syriac version (of the *Almagest*). If this note were intended to have been carried over from the original text, it would be the second reference we have from medieval times to the existence of a Syriac copy of the star tables of the *Almagest* [17], this time known to Ṭūsī. Moreover, since it is a marginal note, and could therefore have been added by a later writer, this could push the survival period of that Syriac version even further forward in time. Unfortunately, we can not make any further deductions at this point concerning this Syriac version.

Finally, in an attempt to critically evaluate the works of Ptolemy himself, Ṭūsī studied the various works of Ptolemy and tried to relate them to one another. He says, for example, in the section concerning the inhabited world, *Almagest* II, 6:

> Ptolemy had mentioned in another one of his books, known as the *Geography*, some inhabited areas south of the equator that have a significant latitude. Perhaps he wrote that book after he finished the *Almagest*. [Fol. 9ᵛ]

This remark was given as a comment on Ptolemy's statement that he had no reliable reports about localities south of the equator [*Almagest*, p. 83].

[16] A. Aaboe, "On the Babylonian Origin of Some Hipparchian Parameters", *Centaurus*, *4* (1955), 122-125.

[17] For a fuller discussion of the Syriac version of the *Almagest*, see Kunitzsch, *Almagest*, cit., 7 f., 59 f., *et passim*, and *id.*, "Über einige Spuren der Syrischen Almagestübersetzung", *Prismata: Festschrift für Willy Hartner* (Wiesbaden, 1977), 203-210.

The significance of the taḥrīr *to Ṭūsī's other works*

In terms of his other works, the most significant comments in Ṭūsī's *taḥrīr* are the ones that treat what was later known as the *ishkālāt* of the *Almagest.* After he finished explaining, for example, the lunar model as given in *Almagest* V, 2, Ṭūsī concluded:

> *wa-fī imkān ḥaraka basīṭa 'alā muḥīṭ dā'ira tastawī ḥaul nuqṭa ghair al-markaz naẓar yajib an yuḥaqqaq* (As for the possibility of a simple motion on a circumference of a circle, which is uniform around a point other than the center, it is a subtle point that should be verified). [Fol. 24ᵛ]

I take this comment to mean that Ṭūsī was definitely aware of the problem of the *equant* when he wrote this remark – which he also mentioned later on in connection with the model for the upper planets – but that he had not yet found a solution for it. Otherwise, this would be the place for him to comment on his solution of this *ishkāl* if he had had such a solution at the time. But since such a solution was indeed mentioned in Ṭūsī's *Ḥall,* I suspect then that, by 1247, the date of composition of the *taḥrīr,* the *Ḥall* was not yet written.

Moreover, in the same context of the lunar model, Ṭūsī mentions as well the problem of the prosneusis point (*nuqṭat al-muḥādhāt*) and supplies a rather lengthy comment in which he describes the irregular motion of the diameter of the epicycle, which has to be always pointing in the direction of the moving prosneusis point. He concludes by saying:

> *wa-hādhihi al-ḥaraka ka-ḥarakat aqṭār tadāwīr al-khamsa fī al-muyūl wal-inḥirāfāt 'alā mā yajī', illā annahā takūn fī al-'arḍ wa-hādhihi fī al-ṭūl. wa-l-naẓar fī kaifiyyat wujūd ḥarakāt mustadīra tāmma yaẓhar 'anhā amthāl hādhihi al-ḥarakāt fī al-ḥiss wājib. fa-l-yuḥaqqaq, wa-na'ūd ilā al-kitāb* (This motion is similar to the motion of the five [planets] in the inclination and the slanting, as will be shown later on, except that that is a motion in latitude while this one is in longitude. One must look into the possibility of the existence of complete circular motions that would produce such observable motions [*i.e.* similar to the oscillating prosneusis motion of the epicyclic diameter]. Let that be verified. We now return to the book). [Fol. 25ʳ]

Once again, the identity of the solution for the prosneusis point and that of the latitude, and the possibility of explaining such a motion, was proposed in the *Ḥall*, and Ṭūsī would have referred to it had the *Ḥall* been available. My earlier suspicion that the *Ḥall* had not yet been composed at the time when Ṭūsī wrote that remark, is here further strengthened.

Moreover, while discussing the problem of the equant in the model of the upper planets, *Almagest,* IX, 5, Ṭūsī explains the Ptolemaic arrangement, and then concludes by saying:

> Here too, I say, that there is a subtle point (*mawḍiʿ naẓar*) concerning motion on a circumference, and around a point other than the center of that circumference, which should be verified (*yajib an yuḥaqqaq*) as I have already pointed out in the case of the moon itself. [Fol. 46ᵛ]

As in the case of the moon, here too, Ṭūsī does not yet seem to have solved the problem of the equant, as he apparently does in the *Ḥall.* And here too, my suspicion is further confirmed that Ṭūsī's *taḥrīr* was written before his *Ḥall.*

The latitude theory

But the critical contribution of Ṭūsī's *taḥrīr* for the dating of Ṭūsī's *Ḥall* comes from the latitude theory of the lower planets, where the Ptolemaic text is desperately problematic, *Almagest,* XIII, 2. In order to give a general idea of the problem involved, I refer to the following set of figures. In figure 1, the observer is at point *0,* while the planet, say Venus, moves on the epicycle *SNRI,* in the direction *RIS.* Note that in this position, when the center of the epicycle is in the position of the apogee, the plane of the epicycle will be 'slanted' so that *R* will be to the North and *S* to the South, thus producing a component of the latitude equal to i_2. But, in that position, the plane of the deferent itself will also be 'inclined' by an angle i_0, which will vary in such a way that when the epicycle's center reaches 90 degrees away from the apsidal line (Fig. 2), that inclination will cease to exist, and the plane of the deferent and that of the ecliptic will coincide. In that position, the only latitude component left will be that of the epicyclic inclination measured as i_1. Once the epicycle moves towards the perigee, the plane of the deferent will incline again to reach a maximum value of i_0, when the epicycle reaches the actual perigee (Fig. 3).

In effect, therefore, the plane of the eccentric of the inferior planets seems to be performing a seesaw motion or a 'libration' with respect to the plane of the ecliptic.

To solve this problem, Ptolemy suggested that the diameters of the epicycles be carried by ill-defined circles that would allow this libration to take place. But in his description of these circles he stated that

> their revolution in uniform motion takes place, not about their own centers, but about some other point which will produce in the small circle

> an eccentricity corresponding to [the eccentricity] of the planet in longitude in the ecliptic,

once again iterating the problem of the equant [*Almagest*, p. 600].

This non-uniform non-circular motion seems to have bothered Ptolemy, for he says immediately after that, *Almagest*, XIII, 2:

> Let no one, considering the complicated nature of our devices, judge such hypotheses to be over-elaborated. For it is not appropriate to compare human [constructions] with divine, nor to form one's beliefs about such great things on the basis of very dissimilar analogies ... For provided that each of the phenomena is duly saved by the hypotheses, why should anyone think it strange that such complications can characterize the motions of the heavens when their nature is such as to afford no hindrance, but of a kind to yield and give way to the natural motions of each part, even if [the motions] are opposed to one another? ... In this way all [motions] will appear simple, and more so than what is thought 'simple' on earth, since one can conceive of no labor or difficulty attached to their revolution. [*Almagest*, p. 600]

To this, Ṭūsī responds by saying:

> This statement is, at this point, extraneous to the art [of astronomy] (*khārij 'an al-ṣinā 'a*), and unconvincing. For it is the duty of the worker in this art that he posits circles and parts that move uniformly in such a way that all the varied observed motions would result as a combination of these regular motions. Moreover, since the diameters of the epicycles had to be carried by small circles so that they could be moved northward and southward, which also entailed that they would be moved as well from the plane of the eccentric [*i.e.* the deferent] so that they would no longer point to the direction of the ecliptic center, nor would they be parallel to specific diameters in the plane of the ecliptic, but they would rather be swayed back and forth in longitude by an amount equal to their latitude, that, is contrary to reality. One could not even say that this variation is only felt in the case of the latitude, and not in the longitude, because they are equal in magnitude and equally distant from the center of the ecliptic.
>
> If one were to imagine the diameter of the small circle to be equal to the total latitude in either of the two directions, and imagine the center [of that first circle] to be moving on the circumference of another circle, which is *equal* to it, and whose own center is in the plane of the eccentric, and let the second circle move by an amount equal to one half the motion of the tip of the epicyclic diameter on the first circle, and opposite to it in direction, then there would be a northward and southward transposition

equal to the latitude without having any speeding up or slackening down in longitude.

To show that, let [in Fig. 2(a)] *AB* be a portion of the eccentric, and *GD* [a section] of the latitude circle that passes through the tip of the epicyclic diameter. Let them intersect at point *E*. And let *EZ*, *EM* be equal to the sum of the latitudes in both directions, while *EH* would be equal to half of [the latitude] in one direction. With *H* as center, and *EH* as radius, we draw circle *HZ*. With [center] *E*, and radius *EH*, we draw circle *HTKL*. Imagine the tip of the epicyclic diameter to be at point *Z*, and moving along circle *EZ* in the direction from *G* to *B*. Let the center *H* move along circle *HTKL* in the direction from *G* to *A*, by an amount equal to half [the previous] motion.

Then it is obvious that when *H* moves by one quarter [of a circle] and reaches *T*, *Z* would move by one half [of a circle] and would reach point *E*. Then if *H* moves by another quarter and reaches *K*, *Z* would move by another half and reach *M*. When *H* moves by yet another quarter to reach *L*, *Z* would then move by another half and would again reach *E*. [Finally], when *H* completes its revolution, *Z* would go back to its original place. [The tip of the diameter] would therefore always move back and forth between *Z* and *M* along line *GD* without ever slanting away from it in the direction of *AB*. And that is how this can be shown.

But we have one further reservation (*nalūm ʻalaih*) in this regard, and this is that the time the diameter takes in the northern direction is equal to the time it takes in the southern one. And the reality is contrary to that.

As for the statement of Ptolemy concerning the motion [of the diameter] along the circumference of a circle, but around a point that is not its center, that requires investigation (*yaḥtāj ila naẓar*) and we will verify it (*nuḥaqqiquhu*) as we have said above. We now return to the book. [Fol. 58^r^]

Now, the circles proposed by Ṭūsī to solve the problem of libration of the epicyclic diameters are essentially a rudimentary form of what later came to be called the 'Ṭūsī Couple'. The identity of both couples is obvious if we think of circle *HK* as the path of the center of the smaller sphere in the 'Ṭūsī Couple' as in Fig. 5(a), (b). The way these circles were proposed here, however, seems to require that they be taken as plane figures not yet related to the solid spheres that they were taken to be in the *Ḥall*. Moreover, there is no mention of solid bodies in the *taḥrīr*, nor is there any mention of the latitude theory of Ibn al-Haytham which were both referred to in the *Ḥall* and the *Tadhkira*. Therefore, the only conclusion that can be drawn at this point, is that Ṭūsī's *Ḥall*, with its incorporation of the solid bodies of Ibn al-Haytham's theory of latitude, and the reformulation of the 'Ṭūsī Couple' in spherical terms definitely represent an advanced stage in Ṭūsī's thought, and was not yet available by 1247 when the *taḥrīr* was composed.

Conclusion

With this short survey, it should have become clear that the so-called redactions of the *Almagest*, such as Ṭūsī's *taḥrīr*, are veritable short commentaries in which the contents of the *Almagest* were not only reformulated and paraphrased, but were also corrected, completed, criticized, and brought up to date both theoretically and practically. As such, these redactions constitute an integral part of the Arabic astronomical tradition, and no study of such a tradition can be complete without taking these redactions into full consideration.

On the theoretical level alone, the original contributions made in these redactions should not be ignored, for we have seen that they shed light on the other works of Arabic-writing astronomers and are probably the closest we can ever get to the kind of education these astronomers underwent when they studied the *Almagest*. I suspect that the *Almagest* was usually read through one such redaction or another.

In terms of Ṭūsī's own work, the *taḥrīr* is a milestone, for it seems to solve the problem of dating his other work, the *Ḥall-i Mushkilāt-i Mu'īniyya*. The evidence preserved in connection with the lunar theory, the equant problem of the upper planets, and the latitude theory, especially that of the inferior planets, seems to point to the fact that the problems 'solved' in the *Ḥall* were still being formulated in their rudimentary form in 1247, the date of the composition of the *taḥrīr*. The *Ḥall* therefore seems to have been written sometime after that date, and closer to the date of the *Tadhkira* (1260/1261), which it resembles much more closely.

Finally, since a rudimentary form of the 'Ṭūsī Couple' was only used once in the *taḥrīr*, in connection with the latitude theory of the inferior planets, the origin of the developed 'Ṭūsī Couple' seems to have been conceived first as a solution for the latitude theory, in a plane form, to restrict the variation in longitude of the epicyclic diameters of the inferior planets, and only later did this couple develop into a spherical form to become a universal solution for all linear motions that were composed of circular ones. *

* *Acknowledgment.* – The author wishes to thank Professor Dr Paul Kunitzsch for his valuable suggestions given on an earlier draft of this paper. Most of these suggestions were incorporated in the final version, without implying that he is in any way responsible for any of the remaining errors.

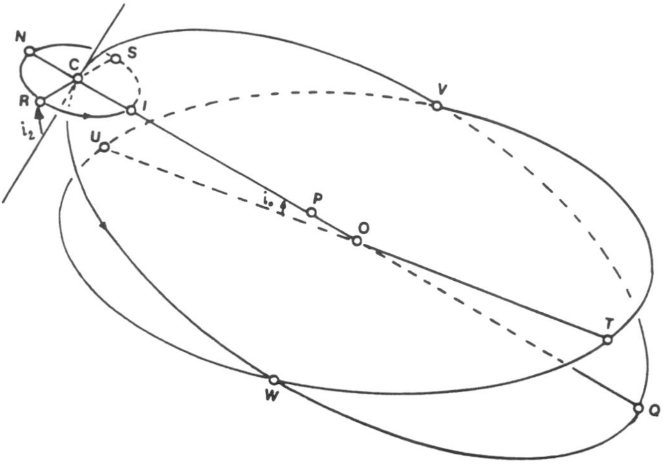

Fig. 1. – For an observer at point *0*, the epicycle for the inferior planet Venus is shown when its center is at the apogee. At that position, the deferent plane will reach its maximum inclination i_0, and the epicyclic diameter *NI* will lie in the plane of the deferent. The epicyclic diameter *RS*, perpendicular to the direction of *NI*, will be slanted by angle i_2.

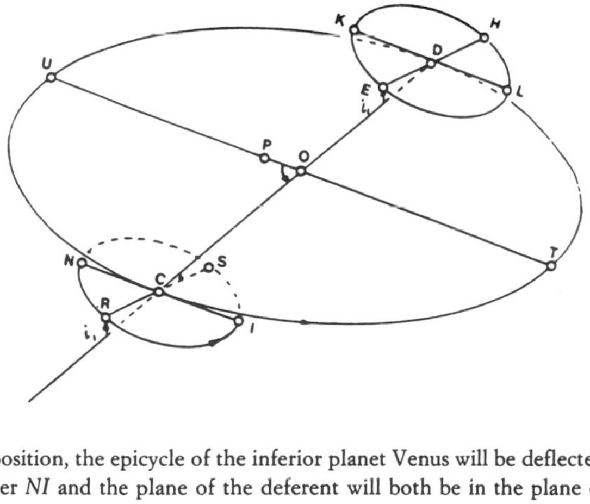

Fig. 2. – In this position, the epicycle of the inferior planet Venus will be deflected by an angle i_1, while the diameter *NI* and the plane of the deferent will both be in the plane of the ecliptic.

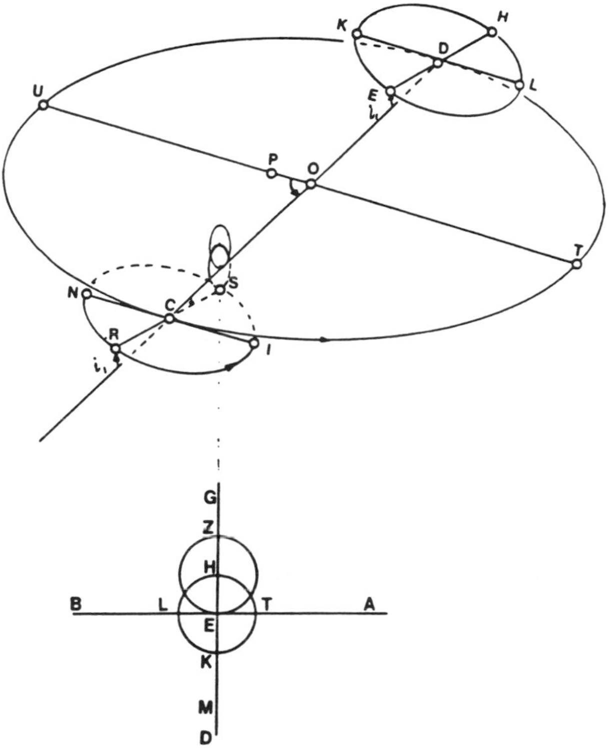

Fig. 2 (a). – To account for the deflection i_1, Ṭūsī allows the tip of the diameter *S* to move along circle *EZ*, whose center will in turn move along circle *KLHT* at half the speed and in the opposite direction. The combinedmotion of circles *EZ*, and *KLHT*, will produce a linear motion of point *S* along line *GD*. In principle this version of the 'Ṭūsī Couple' could be attached to any point that is required to oscillate in a linear harmonic motion, as in the case of point *C* in Fig. 5(a).

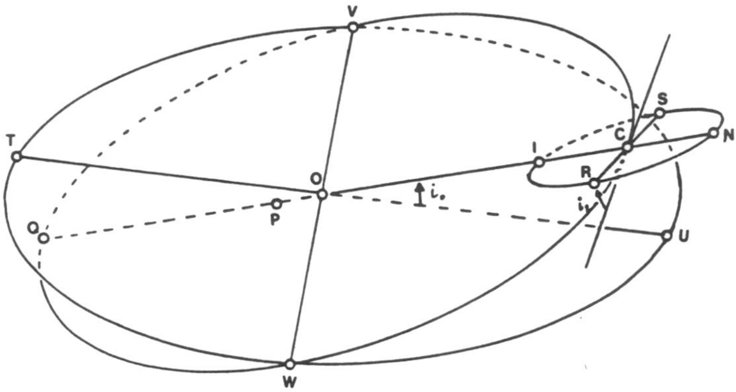

Fig. 3. – When the epicyclic center reaches the perigee, as in this diagram, the diameter *SR* will be slanted again by an angle i_2, and the deferent plane will have seesawed in the opposite direction to reach a maximum inclination of i_0 again.

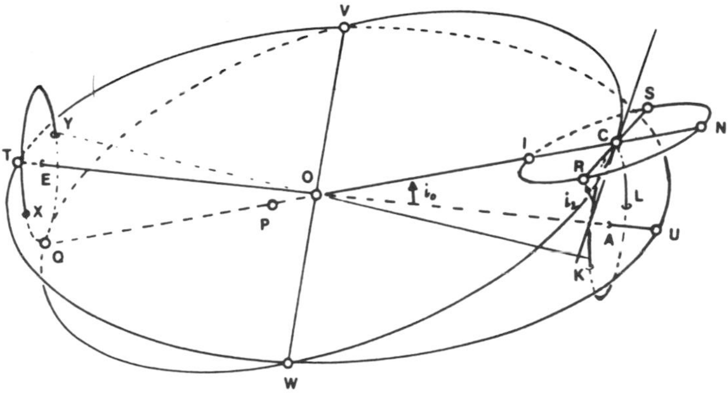

Fig. 4. – Ṭūsī seems to have understood the small circles of Ptolemy to be similar to circles *XQY*, and *KCL*, which will cause the diameter of the deferent to sway in a rocking motion. In Fig. 5(a), his own 'Couple' could restrain that motion to take place only along line *GD*, thus limiting the variation in longitude.

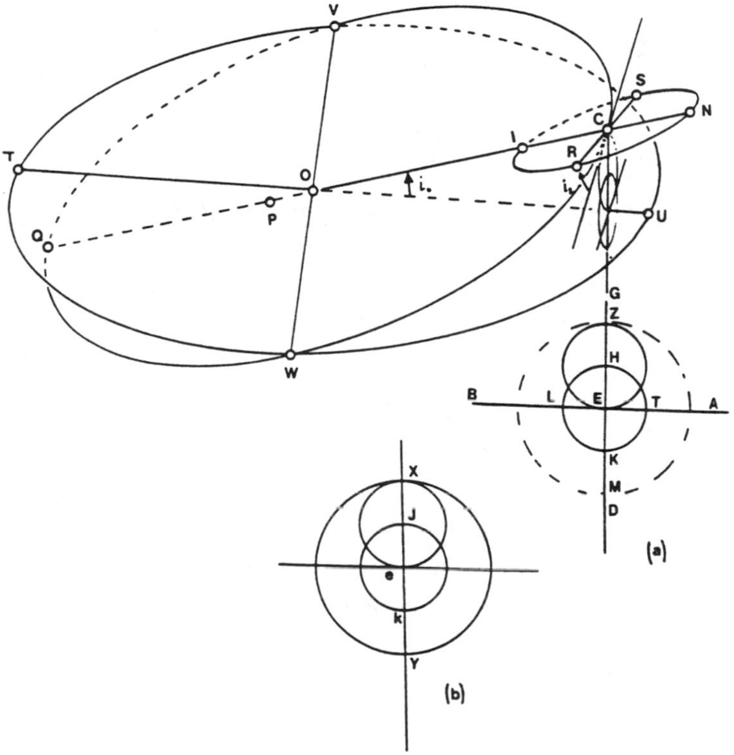

Fig. 5 (a). – An application of the 'Ṭūsī Couple' to the tip of the deferent diameter *C* would cause that point to move linearly along line *GD* only, thus preserving the longitude positions. Fig. 5 (b), represents a solid form of the 'Couple'.

Fig. 6. – Fol. 58[r] of Ṭūsī's *taḥrīr,* containing his comment on Ptolemy's latitude theory, *Almagest* XIII, 2, from India Office Manuscript, Loth 741. Courtesy of the India Office Library.

III. Observations and Observatories

An Observational Notebook of a Thirteenth-Century Astronomer

*By George Saliba**

THE ABILITY TO RETRIEVE the observational records and computational processes used by medieval Muslim astronomers is of no small significance, especially if these records have any bearing on the process by which astronomical parameters were determined. This is especially true in the case of the most common medieval Islamic astronomical writings, known as *zījes* (astronomical handbooks of the *Handy Tables* type). In his now classic survey of these *zījes*, E. S. Kennedy has drawn attention to the importance of the parameters used in the *zījes* in terms of their bearing on observational activities during medieval times; the hypothesis being that if a *zīj* contains a set of parameters unknown from earlier sources, it was in all likelihood based on observations conducted by the author himself.[1]

As far as I know, no Islamic source has been studied so far in which there is any detailed discussion of the actual observations used to determine a new set of parameters, irrespective of whether these parameters were later used to construct a *zīj* or not. Several *zījes*, such as *al-Qānūn al-Mas*ᶜ*ūdī* of Bīrūnī (d. ca. A.D. 1050), and the *Zīj al-Ṣābi*ᵓ of Battānī (d. A.D. 929), do mention observations that these astronomers performed, but the remarks are cursory and generally tend to omit the actual record and computational procedures by which the accepted parameters were finally determined from the observations. These *zījes* usually mention the last standardized values, but do not discuss the other values that must have been also obtained during the actual observations. What has long been wanted, therefore, is a clue to the methods of computation of these medieval astronomers, their actual observations, and their methods of se-

* Department of Middle East Languages and Cultures, Columbia University, New York, N.Y. 10027.

I wish to thank the librarians of the several libraries who allowed use of microfilms of manuscripts in their possessions, and the librarian of the Rijksuniversiteit for allowing publication of the photographs of Leiden MS Or. 110. This research was partially supported by a grant from the American Philosophical Society.

[1] E. S. Kennedy, "A Survey of Islamic Astronomical Tables," *Transactions of the American Philosophical Society*, 1956, *46*:168–169. The only drawback of such a hypothesis is its disregard of the possibility of fraud, which medieval astronomers themselves seem to have noted. One such astronomer flatly accused the *zīj* authors of intentionally fudging the parameters of their *zījes* specifically to give the impression that they were the result of new observations. See G. Saliba, "The Original Source of Quṭb al-Dīn al-Shīrāzī's Planetary Model," *Journal for the History of Arabic Science*, 1979, *3*:7.

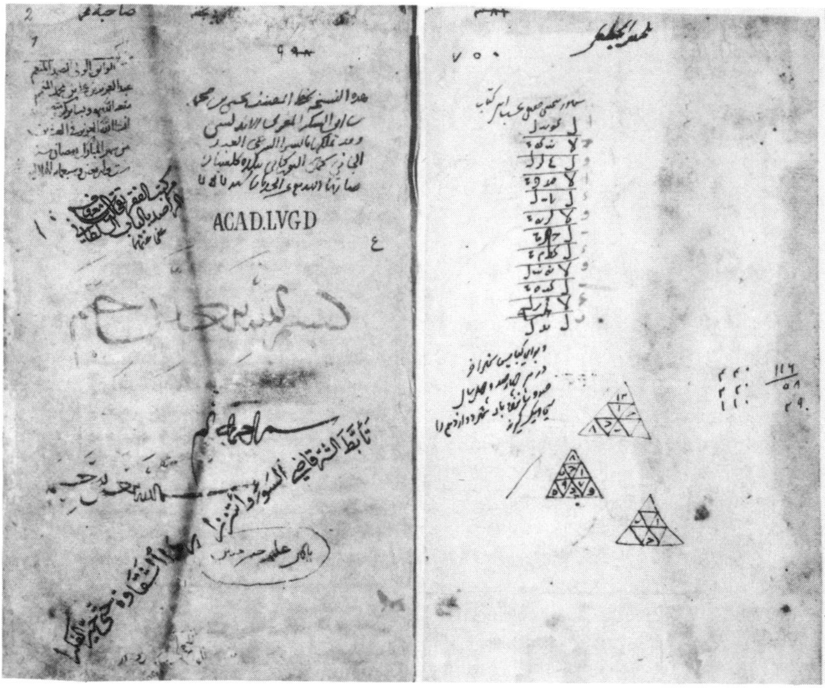

Figure 1. *Flyleaf (right) and folio 1r of Leiden Orientalis 110. Courtesy Leiden University Library.*

lecting parameters from observations. One document containing such information has recently come to light: the *Talkhīṣ al-majisṭī* of Maghribī, from the Arabic manuscript collection of the Rijksuniversiteit in Leiden. This article is the first to discuss this work.

LEIDEN ORIENTALIS 110

Although Heinrich Suter designated the manuscript as "Cholāṣa" (Compendium) in 1900, an owner's note on the flyleaf correctly identifies it as *Talkhīṣ al-majisṭī* (Compendium of the Almagest).[2] Suter redefined the work in the *Nachträge* as "einem Nachtrag oder Ergänzung . . . in welchem er mehr die neuern Beobachtungen, besonders die in Marāga gemachten." No other mention of this manuscript, which (as we shall see) is clearly different from Maghribī's *Khulāṣat,* has so far come to my attention. Of special significance is another owner's note on the flyleaf (see Fig. 1), which states explicitly that the manuscript is an autograph. The humble reference in the body of the text, "the slave who is in need of his Lord" (see Fig. 2, line 11), tends to confirm this claim, for scribes and copyists usually refer to authors with many more honorifics and flowery titles.

[2] Heinrich Suter, "Die Mathematiker und Astronomen der Araber und ihre Werke," *Abhandlungen zur Geschichte der mathematischen Wissenschaften,* 1900, *10,* on p. 156, and "Nachträge und Berichtigungen," *ibid.,* 1902, *14:*157–185, on p. 219, n. 78.

The manuscript is unfortunately incomplete, and ends abruptly on folio 137r with about one fifth of the text missing. So far no other copy of this manuscript has come to light, and we may never learn more of the last two treatises of the ten originally projected in this text, which seem, judging from the table of contents (translated below), to have treated planetary latitudes and the theory of stereographic projection. The observations quoted in the surviving parts are spread between 631 Yezdigird Era (= A.D. 1262) and 643 Y.E. (= A.D. 1274). We know from at least one other source that Maghribī, the author of this text, lived till A.D. 1283 and thus may have completed this text at a later date. But since Maghribī did incorporate his findings in a *zīj* composed in A.D. 1275 (see end of the next section), we have to assume that his observational activity came to an end around A.D. 1274. Why the last two treatises were not after all included in the manuscript is not entirely clear. Was this autograph copy then the first stage in finalizing a text that was already complete in a notebook form, which was also used as a basis for the A.D. 1275 *zīj,* and was this finalization process interrupted for some reason? Or are we really dealing with an incomplete later copy, rather than with an autograph copy, as the owner wants us to believe? The data at hand do not permit us to answer these questions with any certainty. But whatever the case, the manuscript does indeed contain detailed discussion of the methods of observations and extraction of parameters later used in the A.D. 1275 *zīj,* which makes even this remnant of considerable interest in its own right.

After this introductory essay (which concludes with a brief biography of Maghribī), the rest of this article is devoted to a translation of the opening section of the Leiden manuscript, containing Maghribī's introduction and table of contents, and a more detailed list of contents compiled from chapter headings within the individual treatises. The introduction establishes that this *Talkhīṣ* is different from a yet undiscovered text by the same author called *Khulāṣat al-majisṭī*. Contrary to Suter's contention, the author himself identifies these as separate works in the introduction, and the Leiden manuscript is the more recent. The scarcity of such texts from medieval times made translation of the surviving chapter headings and summary of their contents highly desirable. In the summary I have also called attention, whenever possible, to the parameters the author incorporated in his later *zīj*. Identifying these parameters also serves the more general purposes of allowing historians of science to detect whether the same parameters occur in later *zījes,* and hence to begin to appreciate the influence of the Maraghah observations on later astronomical works. These parameters also, conversely, when compared with those preserved in the *Zīj-i Īlkhānī* of Naṣīr al-Dīn al-Ṭūsī (d. A.D. 1274) become conclusive evidence that the *Zīj-i Īlkhānī* does not owe much to the observations of Maghribī, contrary to popular medieval affirmations about this indebtedness.[3] Moreover, a steady accumulation of these parameters and a determination of the time when and place where they were first made should also help answer the question whether *zīj* authors were really fudging the parameters in their *zījes* or simply updating their

[3] The whole question of Maghribī's relationship to the *Zīj-i Īlkhānī* (see Kennedy, "Islamic Astronomical Tables," No. 6) has been raised in the medieval sources themselves; see, e.g., A. Sayili, *The Observatory in Islam and its Place in the General History of the Observatory* (Ankara: Türk Tarih Kurumu Basimevi, 1960), pp. 204, 212, 214, 279, *et passim.*

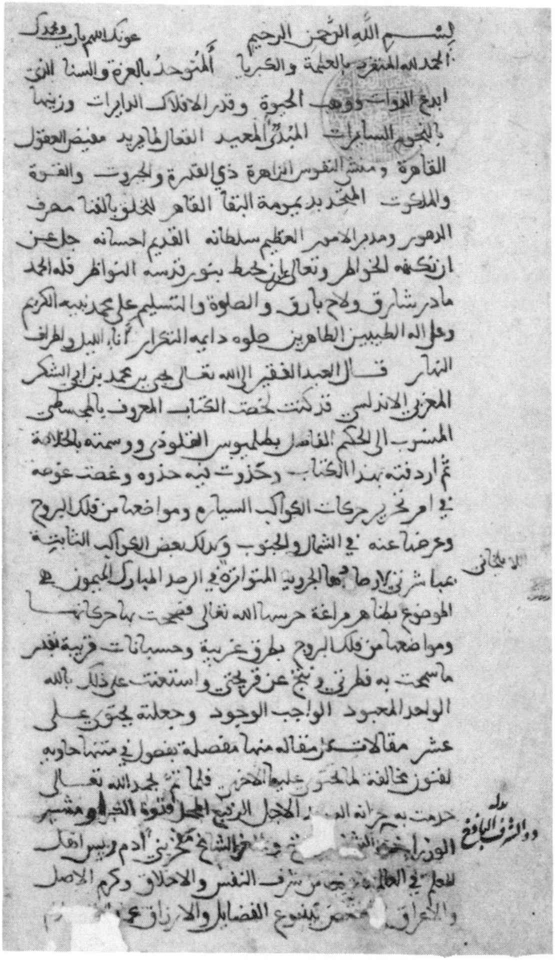

Figure 2. *Folio 1v of Leiden Orientalis 110. Courtesy Leiden University Library.*

zījes to conform to the latest observational results. There is some evidence that the latter was the case, for we have, for example, many more versions of the *zīj* of Ibn al-Shāṭir (d. A.D. 1375) and the *zīj* of Ulugh Beg (ca. A.D. 1440) than, say, the *zījes* of Battānī or Bīrūnī.

Finally, this preliminary survey of the contents of the Leiden manuscript Orientalis 110 should in no way be understood to be a substitute for an edition, translation, and analysis of the full text. My hope is only to whet the appetite for such an undertaking, which promises to shed much needed light on the actual workings of the Maraghah observatory.

THE AUTHOR OF LEIDEN ORIENTALIS 110

If this text is indeed an autograph, then we have the author's name in his own hand as Yaḥyā Ibn Muḥammad Ibn Abī al-Shukr al-Maghribī al-Andalusī (Fig.

2, lines 11–12). This is of some importance, since the same author was identified by a copyist of a manuscript preserved at the Escorial, Arabe 932, as Abū ᶜAbdallah Muḥammad Ibn Abī al-Shukr. This confusion in the name may have contributed to Kennedy's suspicion that we may be dealing with the works of father and son.[4] A careful review of the Escorial manuscript, however, reveals that the author is consistently called Yaḥyā Ibn Muḥammad, and not Muḥammad, in the body of the text, the more trustworthy part. We can assume, then, either that the author's name was Yaḥyā, his *kunya* Abu ᶜAbdallah, and his honorific name (which did not have to be always mentioned) Muḥammad; or that the copyist of the name on the flyleaf of the Escorial manuscript simply neglected to insert the word Ibn before Muḥammad, for the name of the author's father was indeed Muḥammad. The grandfather was Abū al-Shukr. The *nisbas* attached to Maghribī's name indicate that he was born in Andalusia. Ibn al-Fuwaṭī, the librarian of the Maraghah observatory, who must have met him in person, tells us that Maghribī had studied religious law according to the school of Mālik Ibn Anas (d. A.D. 795), one of the four major schools of Islamic law most widely spread in the western portion of the Muslim lands.[5] At some point in his life he was given the title (*laqab*) Muḥyī al-Dīn (The Reviver of Religion), probably by the Ayyubid ruler al-Malik al-Nāṣir of Damascus (A.D. 1250–1260), whom he served in Damascus perhaps in the capacity of an astrologer till at least 1257. It was in this year, while still in Damascus, that he composed his first major *zīj*, called *tāj al-azyāj* (Crown of *Zījes*). This *zīj* is, as far as I know, preserved in a unique copy at the Escorial library, Arabe 932.[6] Bar Hebraeus (d. in Maraghah A.D. 1286) recounts that Maghribī himself had told him how he escaped death at the hands of the Mongols who invaded Damascus around 1258, simply because he was an astrologer. Ibn al-Fuwaṭī also tells us that Maghribī joined the service of the Mongols under Naṣīr al-Dīn al-Ṭūsī (d. A.D. 1274) at the Maraghah observatory. After making at least one trip to Baghdad with Ṭūsī's son, which must have taken place between A.D. 1274 and 1283, he returned to Maraghah to teach and to enjoy a wide fame till the end of his days in Rabīᶜ I, A.H. 682 (= summer of A.D. 1283).[7]

As mentioned above, the observations that Maghribī quotes here were conducted at the Maraghah observatory between A.D. 1262 and 1274. In 1275 he incorporated the results of these observations in a new *zīj*, which he titled *Adwār al-anwār madā al-duhūr wa-l-akwār* (Everlasting Cycles of Light); it is preserved in several copies, the one used for this study being Meshhed Shrine Library manuscript 103.[8] There is also another *zīj* attributed to Maghribī, Mīqāt 188 in Dār al-Kutub, Cairo. Close investigation reveals that it is a hodgepodge of later *zījes* and not the work of Maghribī.

[4] Kennedy, "Islamic Astronomical Tables," p. 131.

[5] Ibn al-Fuwaṭī, *Talkhīs Muᶜjam al-Alqāb*, published in *Oriental College Magazine*, Lahore, 1939–1945, esp. 1942–1943, biography 889.

[6] Kennedy, "Islamic Astronomical Tables," p. 131.

[7] Bar Hebraeus, *Taᵓrikh Mukhtaṣar al-Duwal*, ed. Ṣālḥānī (Beirut: Catholic Press, 1890), pp. 489–490; Ibn al-Fuwaṭī, *Talkhīuṣ*, biog. 889.

[8] Other copies are at Chester Beaty, Dublin, MS Arab. 3665, and at Medina, Saudi Arabia, ᶜĀrif Ḥikmat Library, Mīqāt 1 (dated A.H. 691 = A.D. 1291). These additional copies were brought to my attention by Professor David King of New York University, who has kindly allowed me to study microfilms in his possession of Maghribī's works.

TRANSLATION

[folio lv] In the name of God, the merciful and the compassionate. God grant assistance, and may You be praised.

Praised be the Lord who is without peer in wisdom and magnificence, matchless in power and loftiness, who created the essences [*dhawāt*] and granted life. He predetermined the moving spheres and embellished them with the moving stars. [He is] the initiator and the destinator, the executor of his own wishes, emanator of the dominant intellects, and originator of the flourishing souls. [He is] the possessor of might and grandeur, power and royalty, identical with eternity, controls the annihilation of the created things, dispenser of generations and governor of all things. His authority is magnificent and his bounty is eternal. He is beyond access to onlookers. May praise be to him as long as the sun rises and the lightning flashes. Salutations and continuous prayers be upon His noble prophet Muḥammad and his goodly and pure family.

The slave who is in need of his Lord, may He be exalted, Yaḥyā Ibn Muḥammad Ibn Abī al-Shukr al-Maghribī al-Andalusī says: I had in the past summarized the book known as the *Almagest,* which is attributed to the honorable wise man Baṭlamyūs al-Qalūdhī [Ptolemaeus Claudius], and called it *al-Khulāṣat* [The Epitome]. Then I followed it with this present book, imitating it in method and depth, [and directing it] to the determination of the motions of the planets, and some of the fixed stars, their positions with respect to the ecliptic, and their latitudes from it to the north or to the south. That was done during the repeated detailed observations that I conducted at the blessed and auspicious Ilkhanid observatory, which was set at the outskirts of Maraghah, may God protect it. Thus I corrected the movements [of the stars and the planets] and their positions with respect to the ecliptic with admirable methods and simplified computations to the extent that my intellectual abilities could accomplish [this task] and my mind perform it; in that I sought the assistance of the One God, the worshipped, and the One who exists necessarily.

I composed it of ten treatises, each [treatise] containing several chapters, all different in nature from those [contained] in the other [treatises]. When I finished it, with the praise of the exalted, I submitted it [*khadamtu*] to the library of the highly esteemed master, the example of the noble ones, the counselor of ministers, of most high honors and lofty might, the pride of the sons of man, the chief of the scientists in this world, [endowed?] with nobility of soul and character and of descent and ancestry, [one illegible word] the source of virtues and bounty, [the supporter of Islam?] [folio 2r] and the Muslims, the bosom of truth and religion [i.e., Ṣadr al-Dīn] Abū al-Ḥasan ᶜAlī Ibn Muḥammad Ibn Muhammad Ibn al-Ḥasan Tūsī, may God strengthen his supporters, and multiply his fortunes and guard him against all calamities of this world.

Chapter: Concerning the table of contents of this book, and the details of each treatise, given first in a tabular form and later detailed with all their contents of chapters and computations.

GENERAL TABLE OF CONTENTS

Treatise	
I	On the derivation of chords occurring in circles and the sines of their arcs, as well as their tangents by calculation and through tables. Ten chapters [fol. 2v].
II	On the proof of the two figures *al-mughnī* [the sufficient] and *al-ẓillī* [the tangential], and the derivation of the unknown quantities from the known ones in them [23v].
III	On problems related to day and night with regard to celestial arcs that appear on the surface of the sphere [31r].

IV	Mention of the principles [*uṣūl*] governing the mean motion of the sun and the length of its year, and whatever is related to that [51r].
V	On the derivation of the movements of the moon by observation, of problems related to that, and the positions of its spheres [65v].
VI	On the derivation of the lunar parallax in longitude and latitude, the distances of the two luminaries from the center of the earth, and their eclipses [84v].
VII	On the derivation of the position of the fixed stars with respect to the ecliptic, their latitudes with respect to it, their movement, their conformation [*tashakkulāt*] with respect to the sun and the other [stars?], and the mention of some preliminary remarks related to the five planets [111r].
VIII	On the derivation of the positions of the five planets with respect to the ecliptic and their movements in longitude and their variations [*ikhtilāf*] [122r].
IX	On the derivation of the value of their [i.e., the planets'] retrograde and their latitude with respect to the ecliptic, and their heliacal rising and setting [text missing].
X	On the projection of circles found on the surface of the sphere onto the plane tangent to the sphere, and their tracing on the plates of the astrolabe [text missing].

DETAILED TABLE OF CONTENTS

Folio	*Treatise: Chapter*	*Contents*
2v	I:1	Definition of the arc and the sine.
2v	2	On the determination of the value of the chords of 1/4, 1/3, and 1/10 of a circle in the units that make the diameter 60 units.
3v	3	The derivation of the side of the inscribed pentagon by geometric means and by calculation.
4r	4	On the derivation of the sines of half the chords whose sines are known, and the sines of their double if the sines of their halves are known, both by geometric means [*bi-ṭarīq al-burhān*] and by calculation.
5r	5	On the determination of the sine of the sum of two known arcs and the sine of their difference by geometric means and by calculation.
6r	6	On the determination of the sine of one degree with the utmost precision [*bi-adaqq al-ḥisāb*]. [Here sin 1° = 0;1,2,49,43,13,24,50, or 0;1,2,49,42,17,35,12 as attributed to Ptolemy.]
8r	7	On the ratio of the circumference of a circle to its diameter [π = 3;8,29,53,34,39]. [Fol. 9r contains a sine table for every minute of arc 0° to 90° given to four sexagesimal fractions.]
18r	8	Preliminary remarks related to tangents.
19r	9	On the computation of the two tangents. [Fol. 19v contains a tangent table beginning with tangents of degrees and minutes to three sexagesimal fractions (0°–50°), then continuing in jumps of 15 minutes for four sexagesimal fractions (51°–89°).]
22v	10	On how to use the sine and tangents tables.

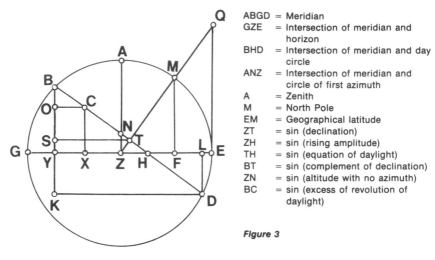

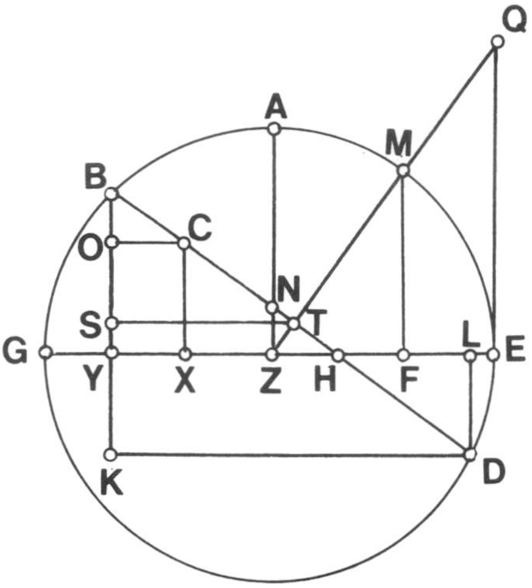

ABGD = Meridian
GZE = Intersection of meridian and horizon
BHD = Intersection of meridian and day circle
ANZ = Intersection of meridian and circle of first azimuth
A = Zenith
M = North Pole
EM = Geographical latitude
ZT = sin (declination)
ZH = sin (rising amplitude)
TH = sin (equation of daylight)
BT = sin (complement of declination)
ZN = sin (altitude with no azimuth)
BC = sin (excess of revolution of daylight)

Figure 3

23v	II:1	On the proof of the "equivalent configuration" [*al-shakl al-mughnī*] [i.e., the sine theorem for Menelaus theorem].
25r	2	The proof of the tangent configuration.
26r	3	The extraction of the unknown from the known quantities in the "equivalent configuration."
31r	III:1	Concerning our observation of the maximum declination of the ecliptic from the equator [ϵ] and the latitude of the locality of the observation [Φ]. [Observations conducted in 633 Yezdigird Era = A.D. 1264. The same values are found as the ones used in the Meshhed *zīj*, namely ϵ = 23;30°, and Φ_{Maraghah} = 37;20,30°.]
32v	2	Right and oblique ascensions. [Fols. 34v–35r contain tables of right ascension given in degrees, minutes, and seconds.]
34v	3	The distance of a planet from the equator and its transit at midheaven, and related matters. [Fols. 35v–36r contain a table of oblique ascension for Φ = 37;20,30° given in degrees, minutes, and seconds.]
37v	4	Discussion of the results [obtainable] from the simple and complete configuration. [Here Maghribī uses an analema construction to solve for the standard spherical astronomical quantities on the plane of the meridian.[9] These quantities are as listed (see also Fig. 3).] Equation of half daylight [*taʿdīl al-nahār*]. Rising amplitude [*siʿat al-mashriq*]. Excess of revolution of daylight [*faḍl al-daʾir*]. Altitude of no azimuth [*al-dāʾir wa-l-irtifāʿ al-ladhī lā samt lahu*]. Azimuth of altitude [*samt al-irtifāʿ*]. Altitude on the day circle [*al-irtifāʿ min al-dāʾir*].
39r	5	On the derivation of these results by calculation.

[9] In the translation of the technical terms I have followed the terminology used by E. S. Kennedy in al-Bīrūnī, *The Exhaustive Treatise on Shadows* (Aleppo: Univ. Aleppo, Institute for the History of Arabic Science, 1976).

40v	6	On the determination of the horoscope and the midheaven by tables and by calculation. [Fols. 41v–42r contain the method of computing horoscopes.]
42r	7	On the determination of the height of the zodiacal pole and the planet from the horoscope.
43v	8	Determination of the *qibla* [direction of Mecca on the local horizon], and the direction of cities, and the altitude at that direction. [The *qibla* of Maraghah = 16;59°, with Maraghah's longitude = 82°, latitude = 37;20,30°, Mecca's longitude = 77°, latitude = 21;40° (recomputed *qibla* value is 16;49°).]
45v	9	On the determination of the latitude of the incident horizon [*al-ufuq al-ḥādith*], and related matters.
47r	10	On the determination of the aforementioned questions by calculation [including the determination of astrological quantities such as *tasyīr*, projection of rays, etc., on 48v–49r.]
49r	11	On the determination of the longitude of a planet and its latitude.
51r	IV:1	On the mention of the eccentric model for the movement of the sun.
53r	2	On the mention of the eccentric and epicyclic models for its [i.e., the sun's] movement.
54v	3	On the proof of the configuration that combines these models.
57v	4	On the determination of the solar year according to verified observations. [On 57v the tropical year is given as 6,5;14,30 days.]
58v	5	On the determination of the eccentricity and the solar apogee by observation. [Observations conducted during 633–634 Y.E. = A.D. 1264–1265; Maghribī obtains the following values for eccentricity (e): (59v) e = 2;5,59 or 2;5,57 or (60r) 2;5,55; on 61r he selects the value e = 2;5,59. On 60r the solar apogee = Gemini 28;50,21.]
61v	6	On the determination of the solar mean longitude and apogee for the [epoch time] 630 Y.E. [= A.D. 1261]. [Precession is given, as in the Meshhed *zīj*, as 0;0,54,33°/year.]
62r	7	On the manner of determining the solar equation for the various points of the zodiac.
63r	8	On the determination of the position of the sun on the zodiac. [Fol. 64r contains a table of mean motions, epoch 600 Y.E. = A.D. 1231; 64v contains an equation table, e_{max} = 2;0,21 at 92°/242°.]
65r	9	On the configuration of the solar spheres.
65v	V:1	On the periods of the lunar revolutions, and a description of the lunar motion.
67v	2	That either of the two principles mentioned with respect to the sun [i.e., eccentric or epicyclic] will account for the variations of the lunar motion in the same way. [On 68v the epicyclic radius of the moon (r) is determined by observation to be r = 5;12^p.]
69r	3	On the method of the sage Ptolemy in determining the movements of the moon.
69r	4	On the determination of the epicyclic radius, and the maximum first equation. [Three eclipses are used for the computation, dated 28 Ardabhasht 631 Y.E. = JDN **2182070** = 8 March A.D. 1262 (Oppolzer

		#3821); 1 Tir 639 Y.E. = JDN **2185023** = 8 April A.D. 1270 (Oppolzer #3835); 18 Farwardin 643 Y.E. = JDN **2186410** = 24 January A.D. 1274 (Oppolzer #3841). On 70v it is determined that $r = 5;12^p$, and $C_4(\gamma)_{max} = 4;58°$[10].]
70v	5	On the determination of the mean longitude and mean anomaly of the moon.
71r	6	On the determination of the mean motions in longitude [$\dot{\lambda}$], anomaly [$\dot{\gamma}$], and nodes [☊ = ascending node]. [Here $\dot{\lambda}$ = 13;10,35,1,52,46,45°/day, $\dot{\gamma}$ = 13;3,53,42,51,59°/day, and ☊ = 0;3,10,37,37,12,20°/day as in the Meshhed *zīj*.]
72v	7	On the determination of the positions of the mean longitude, anomaly, and ascending node for the end of the year 600 Y.E. [= JDN **2171062** = 18 January A.D. 1232], and the number of months between the two eclipses, and the length of each month. [Here the lunar month = 29;31,50,8,18,50 days; fol. 73r contains a table of mean motions in longitude.]
73r	8	On the reasons for the double elongation. [Fol. 73v contains a table of mean motion of the anomaly; 74r a table of mean motion of the node.]
76r	9	On the determination of the eccentricity and the maximum second equation when the moon is at its mean velocity [i.e., on the line issuing from the center of the universe and passing tangentially by the epicycle], and when its center is at quadrature from the mean sun. [Observation made 12 Tir 633 Y.E. = JDN **2182844** = 20 April A.D. 1264. On 77r–v it is determined that $s = 9^p$, $C_4(\gamma)_{max} + C_5(\gamma)_{max}$ = 7;8°, β_{max} = 5;2°; the Meshhed *zīj* has β_{max} = 5;0,0°.]
77v	10	On the inclination of the epicyclic diameter, and the difference between the two apogees. [Observation made 23 Aban 633 Y.E. = JDN **2182975** = 29 August A.D. 1264.]
80r	11	On the determination of each one of the three particular variations with respect to the epicycle and to the zodiac by geometric means and by calculation. [Fol. 82r contains a table of the first lunar equation, in which $C_3(2\eta)_{max}$ = 10;51° at 110°–111°, and a table for the proportional parts $C_6(2\eta)$; 82v contains a table of the second equation of the moon, in which $C_4(\gamma)_{max}$ = 4;58° at 95°–100°; 83r contains a table of the third equation of the moon, in which $C_5(\gamma)_{max}$ = 2;10° at 97°–105°.]
83v	12	On the configuration of the lunar spheres.
84v	VI:1	On parallax with respect to the altitude circle.
84v	2	On the determination of lunar parallax by observation and the lunar distance from the earth assuming the latter's radius to be one unit. [Observation made 5 Khurdad 631 Y.E. = JDN **2182077** = 15 March A.D. 1262. Parallax = 1;25,37° and distance = 36;59,53 earth radii.]
86r	3	On the determination of the distance of the moon from the center of the earth in the same units as those that make the radius of the deferent sixty and the ratio between the two distances. [Distance = $37;37,42^p$ and ratio = 59/1.]

[10] Julian Day Numbers are given in boldface for ease of reference. For the symbols used in connection with Ptolemaic variables, I follow the terminology developed by O. Neugebauer, *Exact Sciences in Antiquity* (Providence: Brown University, 2nd. ed. 1957), Appendix I.

87v 4 On the determination of the lunar parallax in the altitude circle. [Fol. 90r contains a table of lunar parallax.]

91v 5 On the variation of the lunar parallax on the altitude circle, the longitude, and the latitude.

93v 6 On the [apparent] diameters of the two luminaries and their shadows.

95r 7 On the determination of the distance of the sun from the earth, assuming the earth's radius to be one unit, and the ratio of the diameter of the two luminaries to that of the earth.

[Diameter of the sun = 10955;1 diameter of the moon (text has 10955;10)
= $(22;12,34)^3$
= 268;4 diameter of the earth (text has 255;10)
= $(6;26,52)^3$
Diameter of the earth = 40;52 the diameter of the moon
= $(3;26,40)^3$]

96r 8 On the adjustment of the radius of the shadow circle.

97r 9 On the determination of the limits of eclipses of the two luminaries, and their distances from the nodes.

98v 10 On the positions of the luminaries and the shadow during eclipses; these are four positions.

99v 11 That the time of the true contact [*ittiṣāl*] is at variance from that of the mid-time of the eclipse by a negligible amount.

100r 12 On the duration of eclipses.

100v 13 On the demonstration of the eclipsed area of the lunar surface.

101v 14 On the derivation of the lunar eclipse by computation.

102v 15 On the various conditions for lunar eclipses.

103v 16 On the determination of what is eclipsed of the lunar surface or diameter on the assumption that each is twelve digits.

103v 17 On the statements [*rasāʾil*] relating to solar eclipses.

106r 18 On the duration between two eclipses.

111r VII:1 On the determination of the fixed stars with respect to the zodiacal belt, and related matters, and the mention of preliminaries connected with the five planets, which are:

First: On the mention of our observations of the fixed stars, and the first of them is *al-Simāk al-Rāmiḥ* [Arcturus]. I say: We measured its maximum altitude on the upper quadrant of the meridian circle and found it to be 75;48°. The clock [*minkām*] lasted [*khadama*] from the time of its transit till the sun was 8° high, three revolutions minus 2/5 of a degree [of a revolution]. That was on the morning of Friday the twentieth of Farwardin 636 Y.E. [= JDN 2183857 = 28 January A.D. 1267]. [The sun] was observed to be in Aquarius 15;41,34°, its oblique ascension 330;56,34°. The time [of calibration] of the clock is 15;24,44,26[11] and the time for each minute [1/60 of a revolution?] is 0;15,2,11. The revolution of the clock is 46;8,12. The revolution due

[11] The calibration is probably the ratio between the one revolution of the *minkām* and the number of degrees the equator goes through during that revolution. The minute of the revolution seems to be independent of the revolution as a whole. Were there two calibrations?

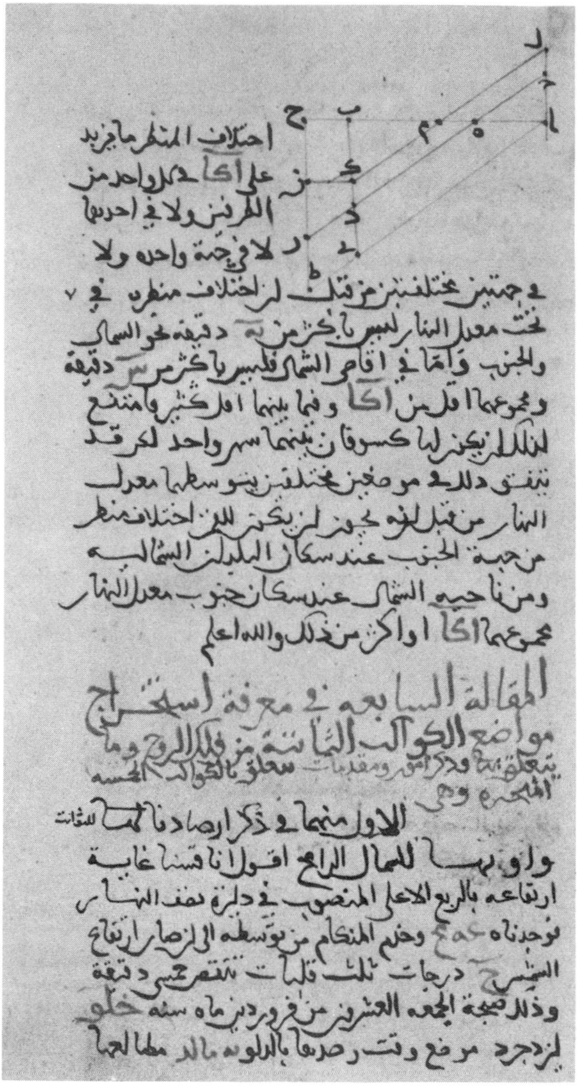

Figure 4. *Folio 111r of Leiden Orientalis 110. Courtesy Leiden University Library.*

to solar altitude is 11;1,29. The difference between them is 35;6,43. We subtract it from the oblique ascension of the ascendant, the remainder will be the ascension of the degree that reaches midheaven with the star, which is 295;50°. We search [*qawwasnā*] into the tables of right ascension of the zodiacal signs to get the degree that reaches midheaven with the star; that was found to be 27;50°. [Although this procedure is not entirely clear, Maghribī uses it to compute the ecliptic position of this star to be Libra 14;19°. He follows the same method in determining the longitude of the other fixed stars, as summarized in Table 1.]

114r 2 On the determination of the motion of these stars. [The precession is 1°/66 years; the precession since Menelaus (1170 years separation) is found to be 17;44°.]

Table 1. Ecliptic positions of the major fixed stars observed by Maghribī.

Symbol	Name	Coordinates	Meshhed *zīj* 640 Y.E. = A.D. 1271	Observation Date
α Boötis	Arcturus	Libra 14;19	Libra 14;22	20 Farwardin 636 Y.E. 28 January A.D. 1267 JDN **2183857**
α Leo	Regulus	Leo 19;49	Leo 19;52	23 Khurdad 636 Y.E. 11 April A.D. 1267 JDN **2183920**
α Scorpio	Antares	Scorpio 29;53	Sagittarius 0;2	23 Shahrayar 636 Y.E. 30 June A.D. 1267 JDN **2184010**
α Canis Major	Sirius	Cancer 4;59	Cancer 5;2	3 Dimah 636 Y.E. 8 October A.D. 1267 JDN **2184110**
α Canis Minor	Procyon	Cancer 16;28	Cancer 16;42	22 Dimah 636 Y.E. 27 October A.D. 1267 JDN **2184131**
α Virgo	Spica	Libra 14;2	Libra 14;2	14 Mirdad 637 Y.E. 21 May A.D. 1268 JDN **2184336**
α Aquila	Altair	Capricorn 21;10	Capricorn 21;12	6 Adhar 637 Y.E. 10 September A.D. 1268 JDN **2184448**
α Taurus	Debaran	Gemini 0;0	Gemini 0;2	13 Adhar 637 Y.E. 17 September A.D. 1268 JDN **2184455**

115v 3 On the aspects of these stars with respect to the planets.

116v 4 On the preliminary principles to be considered in the motion of the five planets. [This chapter discusses the practical observational difficulties and the principles of observation.]

118r 5 On the method of treating these principles and the variation resulting therefrom.

119v 6 On the determination of each of the variations that are attributed to the zodiac and to the epicycle.

120v 7 A reconsideration of preliminaries related to what was said at the beginning of this treatise [*maqālah*]. [This chapter proves, for example, that the maximum equation due to eccentricity occurs at quadrature, and discusses the methods by which one determines eccentricities from maximum equations and vice versa.]

122r VIII:1 Introduction

123r 2 The observations related to the planet Saturn. [Observations made Thursday, 19 Dimah 632 Y.E. = JDN **2182666** = 25 October A.D. 1263; Thursday 5 Isfandar 635 Y.E. = JDN **2183807** = 9 December A.D. 1266; and Monday, ? Ardabhasht 642 Y.E. = ? A.D. 1273.]

124r	3	On the determination of the eccentricity assuming the radius of the deferent to be 60 units. [On 126r it is determined that $2e = 6;30^p$, apogee = Sagittarius 18;37,37°.]
126v	4	On the determination of the epicycle radius. [On 127r it is determined that $r = 6;30^p$; but it is also determined to be $6;31^p$ from an observation taken in Shahrayar 640 Y.E. = A.D. 1271; Maghribī accepts $6;30^p$. On 127v it is determined that $C_6(\gamma)_{max} = 6;13°$.]
127v	5	On the determination of the mean motion of Saturn. [On 128r $\dot{\lambda}$ = 0;2,0,36,45,35,41°/day as in the Meshhed *zīj*. On 128r also the value is normalized to year 600 Y.E. as $\bar{\lambda}$ = 0,15;37,53°, and the apogee = Saggittarius 18;0,53° as in the Meshhed *zīj*.]
128r	6	On the observations connected with Jupiter. [Observations made Sunday, 14 Dimah 633 Y.E. = JDN **2183026** = 19 October A.D. 1264; Tuesday, 24 Isfandar 635 Y.E. = JDN **2183826** = 28 December A.D. 1267; and Saturday evening, 8 Aban 643 Y.E. = JDN **2186610** = 12 August A.D. 1274.]
129r	7	The determination of eccentricity. [On 131r it is determined that $2e = 5;30^p$; on 131v apogee = Virgo 27;56,32°.]
131v	8	Determination of the epicyclic radius. [Observations made Sunday, 2 Adhar 633 (text has 636 by mistake) Y.E. = JDN **2182984** = 7 September A.D. 1264; $r = 11;28^p$. But Maghribī accepts Ptolemy's $11;30^p$ on 132r. $C_6(\gamma)_{max}$ = 11;3°, as in the Meshhed *zīj*.]
132r	9	On the derivation of the mean motion. [On 132r $\dot{\lambda}$ = 0;4,59,16,40,55,8°/day, as in the Meshhed *zīj*, normalized to year 600 Y.E. as $\bar{\lambda}$ = 3,27;53,54°, and the apogee = 5,27;17,48°; the Meshhed *zīj* has the apogee at 5,27;17,50°.]
132v	10	On the observations related to the planet Mars. [Observations made Tuesday evening, 1 Bahman 633 Y.E. = JDN **2183043** = 5 November A.D. 1264; Sunday, 15 Isfandar 635 Y.E. = JDN **2183817** = 19 December A.D. 1266; and Wednesday evening, 20 Ardabhasht 640 Y.E. = JDN **2185347** = 26 February A.D. 1271.]
133v	11	Determination of eccentricity. [On 135r $2e$ = 11;53,46 or 11;58,24 or 11;58,48,6; but Maghribī accepts the value $2e = 12^p$.]
135r	12	Determination of the epicyclic radius. [Observation made Tuesday, 10 Dimah 639 Y.E. = JDN **2185212** = 14 October A.D. 1270; r = 39;37,30 (Ptolemy 39;30); $C_6(\gamma)_{max}$ = 41;20° (Ptolemy 46;59).]

[The text is interrupted just after Maghribī normalizes the mean values for the year 600 Y.E. as $\bar{\lambda}$ = 8,2;8,3° and apogee = 4,16;31,31°, the Meshhed *zīj* having apogee = 4,16;31,30°. The text ends on 137r with no colophon.]

SOLAR OBSERVATIONS AT THE MARAGHAH OBSERVATORY BEFORE 1275: A NEW SET OF PARAMETERS

GEORGE SALIBA, Columbia University

Introduction

Most of what we now know about the Maraghah observatory is derived from the thorough research of Aydin Sayili.[1] In his book, *The observatory in Islam*, Sayili has determined the founding date of this observatory, and collected all the information available from the primary sources about the activities in that observatory and the possible duration of its life.[2] It is now accepted, for example, that the observatory was founded during the reign of the Ilkhanid dynast Hulagu in 1259,[3] and survived in one form or another till at least 1316.[4]

The pretext for which the observatory was founded was, according to most primary sources, related to the need to update planetary parameters in order to obtain better astrological results. To do so, a group of professional astronomers were invited to Maraghah to build the necessary instruments, conduct the required observations, and hopefully produce an up-to-date astronomical handbook (*zij*) that could be used by a competent astrologer to answer whatever questions the patron wished to ask.

The fact that the observatory was actually built is confirmed by archaeological evidence.[5] The sources also speak of the lengthy process involved in the instruments' construction. It is doubtful, however, that the whole edifice was completed during the life time of the first patron Hulagu who died in 1265. But as we will see below, serious research, coupled with actual observations, did indeed start in 1262, and continued well after the death of the first patron.

As for the results of these observations, most sources agree that they are to be found in the astronomical handbook, known as *Zij-i Ilkhani*.[6] But even during medieval times, this conclusion was also put to doubt,[7] and various reports assert that an astronomer by the name of Muhyi al-Din al-Maghribi (d. 1283) was either the one who completed the observations used by Nasir al-Din al-Tusi (d. 1274) in his *Zij-i Ilkhani*, or the sole author of the true Maraghah observations.[8] This confusing state of affairs will not be cleared up until a detailed study of the *Zij-i Ilkhani* is undertaken, and then compared with the surviving works of Muhyi al-Din al-Maghribi to determine the exact nature of this alleged indebtedness to Maghribi.

As a contribution towards resolving this ambiguity I have recently drawn attention to a unique manuscript that contains a report of the actual observations conducted by this Muhyi al-Din al-Maghribi, whose full name is Yahya b. Muhammad b. Abi al-Shukr al-Maghribi al-Andalusi.[9] In this manuscript, we have detailed accounts of a set of observations conducted at the Maraghah observatory between the years 1262 and 1274. The document also contains elaborate mathematical analysis of these observations, and shows the method by which each parameter was determined. After a quick comparison between this report of Maghribi, and the parameters used in the *Ilkhani Zij*, I concluded that Maghribi had very little to do with the compilation of the *Zij-i Ilkhani*, and, instead, he compiled his own *zij* of which we have, as far as I know, a unique copy at the Meshhed Library in Iran.[10] To clear the issues further, it seems to me to be much more profitable to assume at this stage that Maghribi worked independently of Tusi, and whatever mistakes the medieval authors claim to exist in the *Zij-i Ilkhani* are to be attributed to Tusi himself. We can then proceed to study the observations conducted by Maghribi, the methods that he used to determine his new set of parameters from these observations, and the form in which he compiled his own planetary tables that he included in his own *zij*.

On another occasion, I have studied the observations used by Maghribi to determine the eccentricity of Jupiter.[11] I noted there that Maghribi applied the same iteration method that was used by Ptolemy in *Almagest* X,7, but that he had carried the iteration procedure four times instead of the two times performed by Ptolemy.

In this paper, I will discuss the observations and the method used by Maghribi to determine the solar apogee and eccentricity. But before I do so, I must note that the same problem was solved by Ptolemy in *Almagest* III,4, where the eccentricity was determined, by observing the equinoxes and the solstices, to be 1/24th part of the eccentre's radius, while the apogee was found to be fixed at Gemini 5;30°. Both of these values were successively criticized by Muslim astronomers beginning as early as the ninth century. In particular, the Hipparchian method, which was followed by Ptolemy – namely, to observe the time in days and hours separating solstices from equinoxes – was itself questioned on account of the difficulty of observing the solstices, and was deemed to be unreliable.[12] Once that was noticed, several alternative methods were proposed including the so-called method of seasons, where the Sun is observed in the middle of the seasons, i.e. at Taurus 15°, Leo 15°, Scorpio 15°, and Aquarius 15° (where the solar declination changes rather fast) and is therefore easier to determine with precision. But even that highly improved method was abandoned sometimes in favour of a much more general method (known to Ptolemy himself, *Almagest* IV,6, IV,11, X,7, XI,1, XI,5, best summarized by Neugebauer in the appendix to his *Exact sciences in Antiquity*[13]), that allows the determination of the required parameters by using three observations only, taken at random, or sometimes restricting this general method by requiring that two of the three observations be in opposition. This restriction will indeed simplify the computations dramatically (as can be easily noted by comparing the following computations with those of Ptolemy in, say, *Almagest* IV,6) without sacrificing the precision of the results. One of Maghribi's contemporaries, Mu'ayyad al-Din al-ᶜUrdi (1266), wrote a special treatise on the determination of the solar eccentricity using this restricted method.[14]

Maghribi's Observations

To determine the dimensions of the solar model, Maghribi conducted three observations:

(1) 8 September 1264 (JD = 2182985), where the Sun was on Virgo 22;53,59°,
(2) 26 October 1264 (JD = 2183033), where the Sun was on Scorpio 10;42,44°,
(3) 5 March 1265 (JD = 2183163), where the Sun was on Pisces 22;19,54°.

In each case, he says that he observed the maximum height of the Sun as it passed the meridian circle, by using the high quadrant (*al-rub*ᶜ *al-a*ᶜ*la*) that was erected at the Ilkhanid observatory. And in each case he takes the difference between the observed height and the complement of Maraghah's latitude, which he had previously determined as being $\varphi = 37;20,30°$ (fol.31r). The difference was then identified as being the declination of the Sun on that day, and thus the longitude of the Sun would be easily determinable from:

$$\sin \lambda = \frac{\sin \delta}{\sin \varepsilon}, \text{ where } \varepsilon \text{ was also determined to be } \varepsilon = 23;30°.$$

From the references to the quadrant used in the observations, we note that it was made of copper, for it was explicitly described as such (fol. 31r), and was in all likelihood graduated for every minute. The few times where the readings were given to seconds, the value of the seconds would be given as one half, which was probably an estimated value between two minutes. Among the instruments described by Mu'ayyad al-Din al-ᶜUrdi, the engineer referred to above who was in charge of building the observatory complex, there is a description of such a quadrant, made of copper, but mounted on a wooden base, which, in turn, was anchored in a brick wall six cubits long by six cubits high.[15] In fact, this instrument was the first one to be described by ᶜUrdi after his description of the method of determining the meridian line. Moreover, ᶜUrdi's description of this mural quadrant further confirms that it was indeed graduated to minute values.

But since ᶜUrdi's treatise on the Maraghah instruments was written sometime after 1262,[16] and because the first observation by Maghribi in this observatory was taken on 8 March 1262,[17] one has to conclude that at least this mural quadrant was operational by the beginning of 1262. The complaint raised by the observatory patron Hulagu in 1264, when he visited the observatory, about the work not being finished,[18] should be understood to mean the actual observations rather than the instruments themselves. This does not mean, however, that the instruments were all built at once, or that the building project did not extend over several years.

The Solar Eccentricity and Apogee

To determine the solar eccentricity, Maghribi draws Figure 1, where the points *A, B, G,* designate the positions of the Sun during the three positions observed. We note that the third observation *G* was chosen at such a time as to be almost in perfect opposition with the first observation *A*. In fact, the true value of the longitude at point *G* differs from true opposition by less than half a degree (actually, 0;34,5°). This small quantity is added to δ_2 to obtain straight line *ADG*, and was deemed by Maghribi to be too small to affect the results. Point *D* was taken to be the centre of the ecliptic.

At this point, Maghribi uses the above-mentioned observations to compute two sets of values δ_1, δ_2 and $\bar{\delta}_1$, $\bar{\delta}_2$ where δ is the true difference in longitude between two consecutive observations, and $\bar{\delta}$ the difference in mean longitude during the same time. These values are then used to determine the angles of triangle *ABD*:

angle $A = \frac{1}{2}\,\bar{\delta}_2$,
angle $B = \delta_2 - \frac{1}{2}\,\bar{\delta}_2$, and obviously,
angle $D = 180 - \delta_2$.

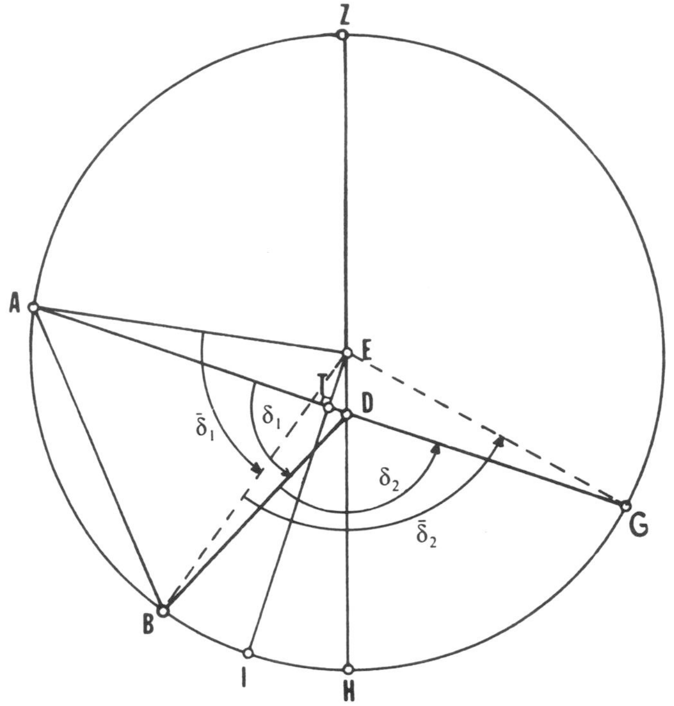

FIG. 1.

In the same triangle Chord $AB = 2 \text{ Sin} \dfrac{AEB}{2}$

$$= 2 \text{ Sin} \frac{\bar{\delta}_1}{2},$$

measured in the same units that make the diameter of the eccentre 120 parts.

Now using the Sine Law, Maghribi gets:

$$\frac{AB}{AD} = \frac{\text{Sin } ADB}{\text{Sin } ABD},$$

that is $AD \doteq [\text{Sin } (\delta_2 - \tfrac{1}{2}\bar{\delta}_2) / \text{ Sin } (180 - \delta_2)] \times AB.$

Knowing arc $ABG = \bar{\delta}_1 + \bar{\delta}_2$, it was easy to compute the chord AG from

$$\text{Chord } AG = 2\text{Sin} \left(\frac{\bar{\delta}_1 + \bar{\delta}_2}{2} \right),$$

and line $DG = AG - AD$ was known.

But once chord AG was noted to be less than 120 parts, the centre of the circle was then taken to be at E in the sector of the circle opposite to sector ABG.

Now using Euclid, III, 35, it was easy to show that:

$$ZD \times DH = AD \times DG,$$

and that

$$\overline{EH}^2 - \overline{ED}^2 = AD \times DG.$$

Thus,

$$ED = \sqrt{(\overline{EH}^2 - AD \times DG)}, \text{ where } EH = 60 \text{ parts.}$$

Therefore ED, the eccentricity, was known in the same units that make the radius 60 parts. The value obtained by Maghribi was 2;5,59^p which was significantly different from Ptolemy's value, 2;30^p.

After computing this value, Maghribi offered another method of computation that was obviously developed during Islamic times for it requires the application of the Sine Law, which was not available to Hellenistic astronomers. The method required that a perpendicular be dropped from E on line AG. Let that perpendicular be line ETI, which will bisect chord AG at T. Since AG was computed before from Chord $AG = 2 \text{ Sin } (\frac{\bar{\delta}_1 + \bar{\delta}_2}{2})$, then

$$AT = \text{Sin } (\frac{\bar{\delta}_1 + \bar{\delta}_2}{2}).$$

Now TD can simply be computed as $TD = AD - AT$, where AD was computed in the first method.

Moreover, arc

$$AI = \tfrac{1}{2} (\bar{\delta}_1 + \bar{\delta}_2),$$

and thus, angle $EAD = 90 - \tfrac{1}{2} (\bar{\delta}_1 + \bar{\delta}_2)$.

Therefore, line $ET = \text{Sin } (EAD)$, and the eccentricity ED is:

$ED = \sqrt{(\overline{TD}^2 + \overline{ET}^2)}$, which yields an eccentricity of 2;5,57^p.

Maghribi then states that its variation from the first value that he computed was indeed negligible.

Once the eccentricity ED was determined from triangle EDT, it was easy to determine angle TED by using the Sine Law again:

$$\frac{ED}{DT} = \frac{\text{Sin } (90)}{\text{Sin } (TED)}.$$

Thus,

$$\text{angle } TED = \text{Sin}^{-1} \frac{DT \times \text{Sin } (90)}{ED},$$

which determines arc HI, and

angle $ZDA = 90 - TED$, which, in turn, gives the position of the apogee Z with respect to the position of the first observation.

In Maghribi's computation, the solar apogee was at Gemini 28;50,21°, which was also at variance with the Ptolemaic value of Gemini 5;30°. Since the value for precession, as computed by Maghribi, was about 1°/66 years, and since that would have produced a variation slightly more than 17° from Ptolemy's time, it is therefore certain that Maghribi's value for the solar apogee, rather than being computed, was indeed a result of a direct use of the Maraghah observatory.

REFERENCES

1. Aydin Sayili, *The observatory in Islam and its place in the general history of the observatory* (Ankara, 1960).
2. *Ibid.*, 189-223.
3. *Ibid.*, 190.
4. *Ibid.*, 211.
5. P. Vardjavand, "La découverte archéologique du complexe scientifique de l'observatoire de Maraqé," in M. Dizer (ed), *International Symposium on the Observatories in Islam, 19-23 September, 1977* (Istanbul, 1980), 143-63.
6. Sayili, *The observatory*, 204; E. S. Kennedy, "A survey of Islamic astronomical tables", *Transactions of the American Philosophical Society*, xlvi, part 2 (1956), p. 125, no. 6.
7. Kennedy, *Survey*, p. 162, nos. 10, 20; Sayili, *The observatory*, 214.
8. Sayili, *The observatory*, 204, 212, 214, 219, *et passim*.
9. G. Saliba, "An observational notebook of a thirteenth-century astronomer", *Isis*, lxxiv (1983), 388-401.
10. Kennedy, *Survey*, p. 137, no. 108.
11. G. Saliba, "The determination of new planetary parameters at the Maraghah observatory", *Colloque Mathematiques Mediterranéennes, Luminy, April 16-21, 1984* (to appear).
12. O. Neugebauer, "Thabit ben Qurra 'On the Solar Year' and 'On the Motion of the Eighth Sphere'", *Proceedings of the American Philosophical Society*, cvi, no. 3 (1962), 264-99, esp. p. 274f.
13. O. Neugebauer, *The exact sciences in Antiquity* (Providence, 1957), 209-14.
14. An edition of this treatise and an English translation are currently being prepared by the present author for publication.
15. H. J. Seemann, "Die Instrumente der Sternwarte zu Maragha nach den Mitteilungen von al-ʿUrdi", *Sitzungsberichte der Phys.-Med. Sozietät zu Erlangen*, lx (1928), 15-126, esp. pp. 28-32.
16. *Ibid.*, 27.
17. Saliba, *Notebook*, 396 (fol. 69r).
18. Sayili, *The observatory*, 196.

TRANSLATION OF THE TEXT ON SOLAR ECCENTRICITY AND APOGEE

[fol. 58v] Chapter Five: On the determination of the distance between the centre of the universe and that of the eccentric sphere, and the position of the solar apogee **[fol. 59r]** on the ecliptic, by the observations along the Meridian that are used for that (purpose).

We say: We have measured the maximum height of the Sun on the meridian quadrant that was erected at the blessed Ilkhanid observatory in the suburb of the city of Maraghah on Monday, 3, Adarmah, 633 Y.E. (= Yezdigird Era) [JD 2182985 = 8 September, A.D. 1264], and found it with utmost precision to be 55;29°. This is in excess of the complement of the (terrestrial) latitude (of the city of Maraghah) by 2;49,30°, which is (also) the declination of the Sun[1] as it is descending from the north. We sought its arc in a table of declensions, and found it to be in Virgo at 22;53,59°,[2] which is the position of the Sun at noon of that day [λ = 172;53,59°].

We also measured the maximum (solar) height along the meridian on Sunday 21, Dimah [JD 2183033 = 26 October, A.D. 1264], and found it to be 37;35°. This is less than the complement of the (terrestrial) latitude by 15;4,30°, which is the declination of the Sun as it descends in the south. Its arc is (therefore) 10;42,44° in Scorpio[3] [λ = 220;42,44°].

We measured again the maximum height at noon of Thursday 26, Ardabhast, 634 Y.E. [JD 2183163 = 5 March, A.D. 1265), and found it to be 49;36,30°. This is less than the complement of the (terrestrial) latitude by 3;3,0°, which is the declination of the Sun as it ascends from the south. Its arc is (therefore) 22;19,54° in Pisces[4] [λ = 352;19,54], which is short of opposition with the first observation by 0;34,5°.[5] When measured in equal hours, that will be 13;47,11 hours.[6]

But the time between the first and the second observation was 48 days. In this time the mean motion of the Sun was 47;18,40°,[7] and its true (text: *mukhtalifah* = variable) motion was 47;48,45°.[8]

The time between the second and the third observations was 130 days 13;47,11 [hours]. In this time the mean motion of the Sun was 128;42,1°,[9] while its true motion was 132;11,15°.[10]

Now, after these preliminaries, let the eccentre [see Figure 1] be *ABG*, with *A* being the position of the Sun during the first observation, *B* its position during the second, and *G* its position during the third. We join *AG, AB*. We know that the centre of the universe was along line *AG*, for the first observation was in opposition with the third, and let that (centre) be (point) *D*. Join *DB*.

Since arc *BG* is 128;42,1°, its half, I mean angle *A*, is 64;21,0,30°. Angle *BDG* is 132;11,15°, and thus the (interior) angle *B* is 67;50,14,30°. Therefore, the angles of triangle *ABD* are known, and its side *AB* is known. Moreover, the ratio (of line *AB* to line)[11] **[fol. 59v]** *AD* is equal to the ratio of the sine of angle *D* to the sine of angle *B*.[12] Therefore, *AD* is known.

Its computation is thus: Sine angle *D* is equal to 44;27,25,40,40,[13] and Sine angle *B* is 55;34,1,24,11.[14] But arc *AB* = 47;18,40.[15] Its chord, I mean line *AB*, is 48;8,54,38,34,[16] in the same units that make the diameter 120 parts. We multiply it by the sine of angle *B*, to obtain 44,35;28,15,52,19,25.[17] When that is divided by the sine of angle *D*, the quotient would be 60;10,51,18,22, which is line *AD* in the same parts that make the diameter 120 parts.

Moreover, since arc *ABG* is 176;0,41,[18] its half is 88;0,20,30, and its Sine is 59;57,49,6,11.[19] Twice the Sine, i.e. line *AG*, is 119;55,38,12,22. We subtract from it line *AD*, to obtain the remainder *DG* as 59;44,46,54. The product of the two[20] is 59,55;35,27,11,13,23,24.[21]

Again, since the section *ABG* is less than a semi-circle, the centre (of the circle) must then be within the other section. Let it be at (point) *E*. We join *DE* and produce it in both directions to *Z* and *H* such that point *Z* will be the apogee and *H* the perigee.[22]

Now, since the rectangle[23] contained by $AD \times DG$ is equal to the rectangle contained by $ZD \times DH$, and since the first rectangle is known, then the second one is known too. Moreover, the rectangle contained by $ZD \times DH$ is, together with the square of *ED*, equal to the square of *EH*.[24] Therefore, *ED* is known.

Its computation is thus: We subtract the said rectangle from the square of the radius, which is 3600 parts,[25] to obtain 4;24,32,48,40,[26] whose square root, i.e. line *ED* – the distance between the two centres, is 2;5,59 in the same units that make the radius of the eccentre 60 parts.

In another method, we drop the perpendicular *ETI* to bisect line *AG* at point *T*, and arc (*AG*) at *I*. Since line *AT* = 59;57,49,6,11[27] and line *AD* = 60;10,51,18,22, then *TD* = 0;13,2,12,11, and $\overline{TD}^2$ = 0;2,49,57,21,37.[28] Moreover, arc *AI* = 88;0,20,30, whose complement is 1;59,39,30. The Sine (of the complement), i.e. line *ET*, is 2;5,15,52,13,[29] and its square is 4;21,31,11,46. The sum of the two squares[30] is 4;24,21,9,7,39. The square root (of the sum) is 2;5,57, and that is line

FIG. 2. Folios 58v–59r of Leiden Orientalis 110 (courtesy Leiden University Library).

ED – i.e. the distance between the two centres that is different from the first (value) by a negligible amount.

Determination of the Position of the Apogee

We say: Since the sides of triangle *EDT* are known, and the ratio of *ED* to *DT* is equal to the ratio of the sine of the right-angle *T* to the sine of angle *E*, then (*E*), **[fol. 60r]** i.e. arc *HI*, will be known.

Its computation is thus: We divide 0;13,2,12,11 (by) 2;5,59 reduced,[31] to obtain 6;12,31,37 whose arc is 5;56,22, which is equal to angle *E* – i.e. arc *HI*. Therefore, the remaining angle *EDT* is 84;3,38. But since point *D* was assumed to be the centre of the universe, and line *AD* (was found to be) passing through Virgo 22;53,59°, then line *DZ* should pass through Gemini 28;50,21°, which is the position of the solar apogee at the time of observation.

NOTES TO THE TRANSLATION

1. This is true, for $\bar{\varphi}$ of any locality is the height of the equator over the local horizon.
2. The actual computation yields:
   $\delta = 2;49,30$, and from $\sin\delta = \sin\varepsilon \times \sin\lambda$, and
   $\varepsilon = 23,30$,

$$\lambda = \sin^{-1}\frac{\sin(2;49,30)}{\sin(23;30)} = 7;5,59,47.$$

FIG. 3. Folios 59v–60r of Leiden Orientalis 110 (courtesy Leiden University Library).

Thus the Sun is at Virgo 22;54,0,13°.

3. The actual computation yields:

$$\lambda = \sin^{-1} \frac{\sin (15;4,30)}{\sin (23;30)} = 40;42,40.$$

Hence the Sun is at Scorpio 10;42,40°.

4. The computed value is:

$$\lambda = \sin^{-1} \frac{\sin (3;3)}{\sin (23;30)} = 7;40,5,26.$$

Hence the Sun is at Pisces 22;19,54,34°.

5. The actual value is 7;40,5,26 − 7;5,59,47 = 0;34,5,39°.
6. The exact value for 0;34,5° is 13;37,59 hours.
7. Using the solar mean motion given on folio 58v: 0;59,8,20,8,4,36,38°/day, we get in 48 days 47;18,40,6,27,41,18,24°.
8. This is indeed the difference between Scorpio 10;42,44° and Virgo 22;53,59°.
9. Here Maghribi computes the difference as if the third observation was in true opposition to the first. That meant that he had to add 13;47,11 hours to the number of days before multiplying by the solar mean motion. But 13;47,11 hours = 13;47,11 / 24 = 0;34,27,57,30 days, and 130;34,27,57,30 × 0.59,8,20,8,4,36,38 = 128;42,1,54,20,6,54,54,26,12,25°, which means that Maghribi may have truncated at the second sexagesimal fraction.
10. Pisces 22;19,54 + 0;34,5 − Scorpio 10;42,44 = 132;11,15°.
11. Written on the margin of the text.
12. I.e. by applying the sine law $AB / AD = \sin D / \sin B$.
13. The medieval sine function, designated by capital 'S', is related to the modern by $\text{Sin}\, x = 60 \sin x$. The more precise value for $\text{Sin}\, D = \text{Sin}\,(47;48,45) = 44;27,25,26,34$.

14. The more precise value is 55;34,1,13,18.
15. See note 7.
16. Using the equation Chord $x = 2$ Sin$(x/2)$, we get:
    Chord (47;18,40) = 2 Sin (23;39,20)
    = 48;8,54,32,45.
17. The more precise value is 44,35;28,15,52,19,24,0,40,14.
18. This is the sum of the two mean motions between observations 1,2 and 2,3, i.e. 47;18,40 + 128;42,1 = 176;0,41.
19. Modern value is 0;59,57,49,10.
20. Text has the surface bound by both lines.
21. The more precise number is 59,55;35,27,10,12,23,23,48.
22. The text uses the farthest distance and the closest distances respectively.
23. The text has *musattah* = surface. See Euclid, III, 35.
24. $ZD \times DH = (R + ED)(R - ED) = \overline{R}^2 - \overline{ED}^2 = \overline{EH}^2 - \overline{ED}^2$.
25. Since $EH = R$, then $\overline{EH}^2 - ZD \times DH = \overline{ED}^2$.
26. The correct value is 4;24,32,49,47,36,36,12.
27. See note 19 above.
28. The more complete value is 0;2,49,57,21,37,12,26,1.
29. The modern value is 0;2,5,16,50,12,22.
30. I.e. $\overline{TD}^2 + \overline{ET}^2$.
31. The text has *munhattan*, i.e. itself divided by 60, for if the required angle is x, then $\sin x / 60 = TD / ED$, and $\sin x = TD / (ED/60)$.

THE DETERMINATION OF THE SOLAR ECCENTRICITY AND APOGEE ACCORDING TO MU'AYYAD AL-DĪN AL-'URḌĪ (d. 1266 A.D.)

George Saliba

Introduction

The problem of determining the solar eccentricity and apogee was solved by Ptolemy in *Almagest* III,4; the eccentricity was then found to be 2;29,30 parts of the same parts that make the radius of the deferent 60, while the apogee was found to be fixed at 24;30 degrees before the summer solstice (i.e. at Gemini 5;30) [Pedersen 146f, *HAMA* 57f].[1] These parameters were redetermined several times during the ninth century and thereafter, and were found to be erroneous [*Thābit*, 274f]. Consequently, various criticisms of Ptolemy's work were initiated, and new observations and methods were devised specifically to resolve this problem.

Of the methods proposed during the ninth century, the one known as the *fuṣūl* method was in response to the difficulty of measuring accurately the solar declination at the solstices, where it indeed varies very little. The *fuṣūl* method required that the solar declination be observed during the middle of the seasons instead, and the parameters be then computed in exactly the same way Ptolemy calculated his. This meant that the distances between the observations had to be ninety degrees.

By the end of the tenth century, the problem of the solar apogee and eccentricity was realized as being a special case of the general problem used by Ptolemy himself to determine the eccentricities of the moon and the other planets, and their apogees [e.g. *Almagest* IV, 6, and X, 7].[2] We know, for example, that at least one astro-

[1] References enclosed in square brackets are to the bibliography at the end.

[2] For the trigonometry involved in the solution of this problem see O.

nomer of the tenth century, Abū Naṣr Manṣūr Ibn ʿIrāq (fl. 1000 A.D.), had "found out" that "the solution of the preceding problem," required "the determination of three points of the ecliptic, chosen *ad libitum*, and an accurate knowledge of the length of the solar year" [*Thābit, loc. cit.*, Bīrūnī, p. 167]. Bīrūnī goes on to say that in his *Kitāb al-Istishhād bi-ikhtilāf al-arṣād*, he had "shown that this method is as much superior to that of the modern astronomers [i.e. the *fuṣūl* method] as the method of the latter is superior to that of the ancient astronomers" [*ibid.*]. As far as I know neither Ibn ʿIrāq's method nor Bīrūnī's exposition of it has survived, and hence we are in the dark as to the details of its application.

The present author encountered another reference to the same method, without attribution to Ibn ʿIrāq, in the work of Mu'ayyad al-Dīn al-ʿUrḍī, *Kitāb al-Hay'ah*[3] [Chapter 18 of the edition]. But there the problem was solved without reference to a diagram, and the discussion quickly reverted to an analysis of the Ptolemaic method itself. During a recent visit to the *Institut für Geschichte der Arabisch-Islamischen Wissenschaften*, I noted in the microfilm collection of that institute two separate microfilms containing treatises by Mu'ayyad al-Dīn al-ʿUrḍī. It was through the courtesy of the Director, Prof. Dr. Sezgin, that I was allowed to investigate these microfilms, which contained, among other things, a short treatise by ʿUrḍī on the same subject of solar eccentricity and apogee. Other applications of this method were also noted by the present author in the works of Yaḥyā b. Abī al-Shukr al-Maghribī (d. 1283 A.D.) [Saliba 1].

The rest of this paper is devoted to an edition of this treatise based on the manuscripts available in the above-mentioned microfilms, and to an English translation, accompanied by explanatory notes to the texts and a commentary.

Neugebauer, *Exact Sciences in Antiquity*, 2nd ed. Brown University Press, Providence, 1957, pp. 209–214.

[3] This text is now edited by the present author, and is in the process of being translated into English with a commentary.

The Edition

The manuscripts are

1. Saib (Ankara), MS 5092, ff. 69r–70v, referred to in the notes to the text as Arabic *sīn*, and

2. Nuruosmaniye (Istanbul), MS 2971, ff. 94r–95v, referred to as Arabic *nūn*.

In the translation and in the Arabic text, paragraph numbers have been inserted between square brackets to facilitate reference to the text in the commentary.

ن ٢٩٧١ ٩٤و
[١] هذه رسالة لمولانا الإمام الأَفضل، ملك المهندسين، رئيس أَرباب التعاليم، مؤيِّد الملة والدين العرضي الدمشقي، في استخراج ما بين مركزي الشمس وموضع أَوجها. س ٥٠٩٢ ٦٩و

[٢] قال: نريد أَن نبيّن موضع أَوج الشمس وبعد مركز حاملها عن مركز العالم بالوجه الذي استخرجها المحدثون. وهو أَن تُرصد الشمس كيف اتفق – وعام واحد أَولى – وليكن رصدها في ثلثة مواضع من البروج على أَيّ الأَبعاد كانت الأَرصاد، وأَن تكون حركتها في الميل نقية واضحة في المواضع الثلاثة لئلاّ يخفى[١] انتقالها.

[٣] وقالوا إنّ من السهولة في العمل أَن يكون بين رصدين من الثلثة نصف[٢] وبين الآخر وأَحدهما كيف اتفق.

ن ٢٩٧١ ٩٤ظ
[٤] ويحتاج من أَراد أَن يعمل على هذا / الطريق – بل وعلى طريق الأَوائل – إلى دقيقة نافعة لم يذكرها أَحد من الفريقين. وهو أَن يُقاس الزمان الذي بين الرصدين المتقاطرين بزمان نصف السنة الشمسية ليعلم مقدار القوس التي تقطعها الشمس بالحركة الوسطى من الحامل الواقعة في هذا النصف من البروج. وبمقتضى هذه القوس يُعرف اختلاف أَوضاع الشكل الذي من قِبله يُستخرج المطلوب.

[٥] فنقول إنّ هذا الزمان إما أَن يكون نصف سنة شمسيّة أَو أَكثر أَو أَقلّ. فإنْ كان نصف سنة شمسية كان القطر الذي عند طرفيه كان الرصدان يقطع الحامل بنصفين فيمرّ بمركزه وببعديه الأَبعد والأَقرب، لأَنّه لا يوجد قطر ينصّف فلكي البروج والخارجَ غيره. ولهذه الحالة وضع خاصّ. ويكون موضعا الأَوج

[١] يخفى: يختفي في س دون النقط.
[٢] نصف: نصفي في ن.

Translation

[1] This is a treatise by our master, the venerable Imām, king of the engineers, chief of the mathematicians, Mu'ayyad al-Dīn al-'Urḍī of Damascus on the determination of the eccentricity of the sun and the position of its apogee.

[2] He said: We wish to determine the position of the solar apogee, and the distance between the center of the solar deferent and that of the universe using the method that was employed by the modern (astronomers). That is done by observing the sun in general – better that (the observations) be during the same year – and let those observations be at three positions on the ecliptic at whatever longitudes they may occur. Let the (solar) motion in inclination be clear and obvious at those three points lest its shift in position be concealed.

[3] They stated that the work could be simplified if two of the three observations were taken at half a circle apart [i.e. separated by half a solar year, and thus they would fall on the ecliptic at two points that are diametrically opposite]. Let the third observation be at any distance from either of them.

[4] Anyone following this method – or indeed the method of the ancients (as well) – needs a useful subtlety that was not mentioned by either of the two parties; namely, one should measure the time between the two observations that are diametrically opposite in terms of half a solar year, in order that one could determine the arc of the deferent that the sun covers in its mean motion in that half of the ecliptic. From this arc one could determine the variations in the configuration that is used to determine the required (quantities).

[5] We then say: This time (between the two opposing observations) is either half a solar year or more or less. If it were half a solar year, then the diameter at whose extremities the two observations were taken will bisect the deferent and pass through its center, through the apogee, and through the perigee, for there is no diameter that bisects the deferent and the ecliptic other than it. This case is considered special; and the apogee and perigee will be the points at which the sun was observed. Let those (observations)

والحضيض هما موضعي الشمس في الرصدين. وليكونا الأَول[٣] والثالث. ويُحتاج إلى تعيين موضع الأَوج وبعد ما بين المركزين.

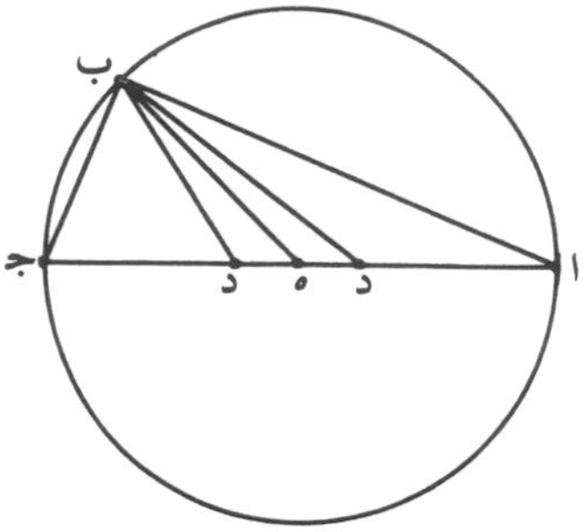

[٦] فنضع أنَّ الحامل ابج، على مركز ه. وليقطع قطرُ البروج الذي كان الرصدان على طرفيه الفلكَ الحامل[٤] على نقطتي ا، ج، وليكن مركزُ البروج عليه د. ويُخرج من نقطة د إلى موضع الرصد الثاني خطٌّ يقطع[٥] الحامل على نقطة ب. ونصل د ب، بج.

[٧] فأَقول: إنَّ مثلث بجد معلوم الأَضلاع بما به قطر اهج، قك جزءاً.

[٨] برهان ذلك أَنَّ القوسين من البروج اللتين فيما بين / الرصد الأَول والثاني وبين الثاني والثالث معلومتان. فتكون[٦] الزاويتان اللتان عند مركز البروج معلومتين – أعني زاويتي ا د ب، ب د ج. وإذا وُصل خط ا ب يكون كل واحد من مثلثي ب ج د، ا د ب معلوم الأَضلاع بما به قطر ا ج معلوم. وذلك أَنَّ كل واحد من قوسي ا ب، بج معلومة من قبل الزمانين اللذين بين الأَرصاد الثلثة. فكل واحد من وتري ا ب، بج معلوم بما به ا ج، قك، و ه ج، س. فتكون كل واحدة من زاويتي ا ج ب، ج ا ب معلومة عند محيط الحامل.

س ٥٠٩٢
٦٩ ظ

[٣] الأَول: الأُولى في ن.

[٤] الحامل: سقطت في ن.

[٥] يقطع: يقع في ن.

[٦] فتكون: فيكون في ن.

be the first and the third (observations). One will then need to determine the position of the apogee and the eccentricity.

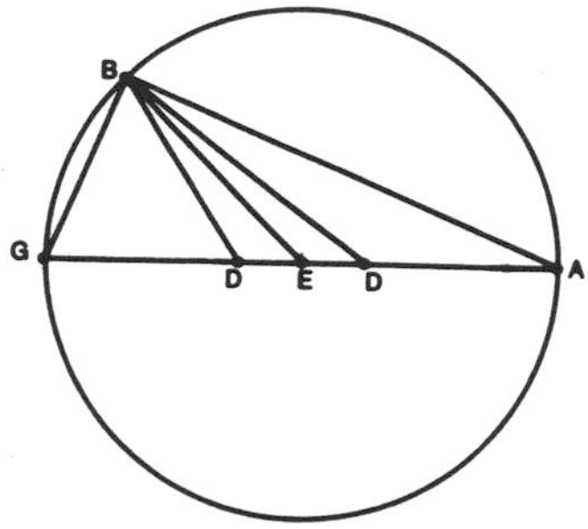

Figure 1

[6] We set the deferent to be *ABG*, on center *E* [Figure 1]. Let the ecliptic diameter, on whose extremities the two observations took place, intersect the deferent at *A*, *G* and let the center of the ecliptic *D* be on that (diameter). Let a line be issued from *D* to the point of the second observation and let it intersect the deferent at point *B*. Join *DB*, *BG*.

[7] Then I say: The sides of triangle *BGD* are known, in the same (units) that make diameter *AEG* 120 parts.

[8] The proof of that is that the ecliptic arcs between the first and the second observations, and between the second and the third are known. Thus the two angles at the center of the ecliptic are also known – i.e. the two angles *ADB*, *BDG*. Now, if line *AB* is drawn, the sides of both the triangles *BGD*, *ADB* will be known in the same (units) in which diameter *AG* is known. This is because the sides of each of the arcs *AB*, *BG* are known from the two time periods that separate the three observations.[4] Then each of the two chords *AB*, *BG* is known in the same (units) that make *AG* 120 parts, and *EG* 60. Then each of the two angles *AGB*, *GAB* are known at the circumference of the deferent.[5]

[4] By using the relationship $chord\ a = 2 sin \frac{a}{2}$, one could simply read the value of *chord AB* from a table of sines, or directly from a table of chords as the one in *Almagest* I, 11.

[5] This is simply an application of Euclid III, 20 where the angle at the circumference is half the angle at the center, and when the angle at the center E is now determined from, say, $chord\ AB = 2 sin \frac{AEB}{2}$.

[٩] وإذا أُضعفت كل واحدة من زاويتي د المركزية تبق كل واحدة من زاويتي ا بد، د ب ج معلومة. فأَضلاع مثلثي ا ب د، د بج معلومة. وذلك لأَنّا إذا أَدرنا على مثلثي د بج، ا ب د / دائرة كانت القسي التي توتّر الزوايا المعلومة معلومة. فأَوتارها تكون معلومة بما به قطر الدائرة المحيطة بالمثلث قك[٧]. فيكون كل واحد من ا ب، بج معلوماً[٨] بما به قطر الدائرة المحيطة بالمثلث قك[٩]. وكذلك كل واحد من[١٠] ضلعي اد، د ج. فلأَنَّ كل واحد من ا ب، ب ج[١١] معلوم بما به ا ج، قك جزءاً، فيكون[١٠] كل واحد من ا د، د ج معلوماً بما به ا ج قك[١٢] جزءاً. لأَنّه إذا ضربنا عدد أَجزاء خط د ج المعلومة بما به قطر الدائرة قك – أَعني المحيطة بمثلث بد ج – في عدد أَجزاء وتر ب ج المعلومة بما به قطر ا ج[١٣] – أَعني قطر الحامل – قك، وقسمنا الخارج من الضرب على عدد أَجزاء بج – أَعني التي كُنّا علمناها بما به قطر الدائرة المحيطة بمثلث بد ج، قك جزءاً[١٤] – خرج قدر د ج بما به ا ج، قك وخط ج ه، س. فالتفاضل بين خطي ج د، ج ه معلوم. فهد معلوم. وهو ما بين مركزي الحامل والبروج. فإن كان ج د أصغر من ج ه، فالأَوج نقطة ا والحضيض نقطة ج. وإنْ كان د ج أَعظم من ج ه فالأمر بالعكس. وكذلك يتبيّن لو عملنا[١٥] على هذا النحو في مثلث ا بد.

ن ٣٩٧١ / ٩٥ و

٧ قك: رك في ن.

٨ معلوماً: معلوم في ن وس.

٩ قك: رك في ن.

١٠ على هامش ن.

١١ ا ب، ب ج: ا ب ا في ن.

١٢ قك: رك في ن.

١٣ ا ج: اد في ن.

١٤ جزءاً: ج ا في ن.

١٥ عملنا: علمنا في ن وس.

[9] If each were subtracted [text has *uḍʿifat* = were doubled, but read *usqiṭat*] from the two central angles *D*, then each of the angles *ABD* and *DBG* will be known, and thus the sides of triangles *ABD*, *DBG* will also be known.[6] For if we draw the circumscribing circles about triangles *DBG*, *ABD*, then the arcs that measure the known angles will be known, and thus their chords will be known in the same units that measure the diameter of the circumscribed circle as 120 parts. Then each of *AB*, and *BG* would be known in the same units that measure the diameter of the circumscribed circles as 120 parts; and so will be the sides *AD*, *DG*. And since each of *AB*, *BG* is known, in the same (units) that make *AG* 120 parts, then each of *AD*, *DG* will be known in the same (units) that make *AG* 120 parts.[7] For if we multiply the number of known parts in line *DG*, in what makes the diameter of the circle 120 parts – i.e. the circle circumscribing triangle *BDG* – in the known parts of chord *BG*, in the same (units) that make *AG* – i.e. the diameter of the deferent – 120 parts, and then divide the product by the number of the parts of *BG* – I mean those which were known in the same units that make the diameter of the circle circumscribing triangle *BDG* 120 parts – then the quotient would be the value of *DG*, in the same (units) that make *AG* 120 parts, and *EG* 60. Then the difference between lines *GD* and *GE* is known. And thus *ED* is known, which is (the distance) between the center of the deferent and that of the ecliptic. Now, if *GD* is smaller than *GE*, then the apogee is at point *A* and the perigee at *G*, and the reverse is true if *DG* is greater than *GE*. The same (result) would have been reached had we applied this method to triangle *ABD*.

[6] By using Euclid I, 32, where the exterior angles are equal to the sum of the opposite interior ones.

[7] This and the following argument simply state that once *AB*, *BG* were found as functions of the same units that measure *AG*, they can then be recomputed as functions of the same units that measure the diameters of the circumscribed circles as 120 parts. Using *BG* as a parameter, one can then compute *DG* in the same units that make *AG* 120 parts.

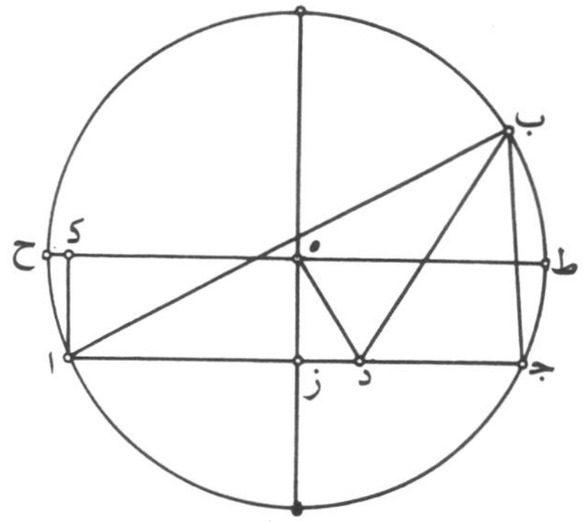

[١٠] وأمّا إذا كان الزمان الذي بين نقطتي الرصد الأول والثالث أعظم من نصف سنة شمسية أو أصغر، فإنّ خط اج يكون وتراً في حامل ابج. وهو معلوم من قبل مجموع قوسي اب، بج لأنّه وترهما. فنقسم اج / بنصفين على ز. ونصل ه ز، فيكون عموداً على اج. س ٥٠٩٢ / ٧٠و

[١١] ولمّا كان خط اج يمر بمركز البروج لكونه ينتهي إلى نقطتين متقابلتين منه، ودائرة ابج محيطة به، فهو على خط اج لا محاله. فقد يكون على نقطة ز وقد يكون على خط ز ج. وكل ذلك يتبيّن من جهة معرفة أضلاع مثلث ب د ج على الوجه الذي تقدم. فإن تبيّن أنّ ضلع ج د مثل ج ز، فأقول إنّ موضع الأوج وبعد المركز معلومان.

[١٢] برهانه أنّا نخرج من ه قطر ح ه ط موازٍ لخط اج، ونخرج جيب اك. فلأنّ فضل الزمان الذي بين الرصد الأوّل والثاني معلوم، فنصفه معلوم، والقوس من الحامل التي تقطعها الشمس في الزمان المعلوم معلومة. فقوس اج معلومة. فجيب اك معلوم. فخط ه ز المساوي له معلوم. وهو ما بين المركزين.

[١٣] وإذا أُنفذ عمود ز ه في الجهتين قسم القوسين اللتين فيما بين الرصد الأوّل

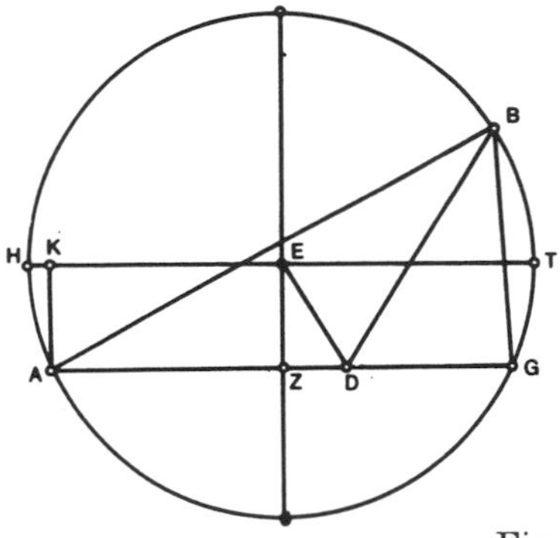

Figure 2

[10] But if the time between the first and the third observations were more or less than half a solar year, then line *AG* would be a chord in the deferent *ABG*, and it would be known since it is the chord of the sum of arcs *AB* and *BG*.[8] We bisect *AG* at point *Z* [Figure 2], and join *EZ*, which will be perpendicular to *AG*.

[11] Since line *AG* passes through the center of the ecliptic, because it connects two opposite points of it, and since (that center) is within circle *ABG*, then it must necessarily fall on line *AG*. It may coincide with point *Z*, or it may be on line *ZG*. All that may be determined once the sides of triangle *BDG* are determined by the above-mentioned method. If it were then found that side *GD* were equal to *GZ*, then I would say that the position of the apogee and the [amount of the] eccentricity would both be known.

[12] To prove that, we draw diameter *HET* through *E*, and parallel to *AG*. We also drop the perpendicular *AK* [text has the sine *AK*]. Now, since the difference in time between the first and the second observations [i.e. the one opposite to it on the ecliptic] is known, its half is also known, and the deferent arc that the sun covers during the known time is also known. Thus arc *AG* is known, and the sine *AK* is known. Therefore, line *EZ*, which is equal to it, is also known; and that is the eccentricity.

[13] If perpendicular *EZ* were extended in both directions, it

[8] Arcs *AB*, *BG* are known from the mean motion of the sun on the deferent, i.e. if we take $\bar{\theta}$ to be the mean angle, then it could be computed from $\dot{\lambda}(t_{B'}-t_{A'})$; where $\dot{\lambda}$ is the mean motion of the sun determined separately by equinoctial observations for example.

والثالث بنصفين نصفين في موضعين معلومين. فالأوج مما يلي نقطة ه والحضيض مقابله. فموضعاهما[١٦] معلومان.

ن ٢٩٧١ / ٩٥ظ [١٤] وأمّا أنّ قوسي / البروج منصّفين بعمود هز المخرج، فذلك بيّن من أجل أنّ[١٧] هز[١٨] عمود أُخرج من مركز البروج على قطر من أقطاره. فتفصل القسي بأرباعٍ متساوية.

[١٥] وأمّا إن وُجد ضلع جد أعظم أو أصغر من جز فنصل[١٩] ده فيحدث مثلث آخر، وهو مثلث دهز. فأقول إنّ أضلاع مثلث دهز[٢٠] وزواياه تكون معلومة.

[١٦] برهانه: أمّا ضلع هز فمساوٍ لجيب قوس اح المعلومة كما بيّنّاه قبل[٢١]. وأمّا ضلع زد فهو تفاضل ما بين زج وجد - أعني ضلع مثلث دبج - وقد تقدم كيفية معرفة ضلع جد بما به قطر الحامل معلوم. ونصف وتر اج به أيضاً معلوم. فدز، التفاضل بين جد، جز، معلوم. فمربعا هز، زد معلومان. فمربع ده المساوي لهما معلوم. فجذره معلوم - أعني خط ده - وهو ما بين المركزين.

[١٧] وإذا أدرنا على مثلث دهز دائرة كان كل واحد من هز، زد معلوماً، بما به يكون هد مائة وعشرين. / فالقوس التي وترها هز تصير معلومة. فزاوية هدز معلومة عند محيط الدائرة المحيطة بمثلث هدز. فزاوية هدز معلومة عند س ٥٠٩٢ / ٧٠ظ

١٦ فموضعاهما: طمست في س.
١٧ أجل أنّ: طمست في س.
١٨ هز: هج في ن.
١٩ فنصل: يتصل في ن دون النقط.
٢٠ دهز: ده في ن، طمست في س.
٢١ قبل: قبيل في س دون النقط.

would then bisect the two arcs that separate the first and the third observations in two known places. Then the apogee is in the direction of point *E*, and the perigee is opposite to that. Both of their places are known.

[14] As for the fact that the two arcs of the ecliptic are bisected by the extended perpendicular *EZ*, that is clear from the fact that *EZ* was issued from the center of the ecliptic to be perpendicular to one of its diameters. Thus it divides the arcs into equal quarters.

[15] But if *GD* were found to be greater or smaller than *GZ*, we then connect *DE*, thus forming another triangle, which is triangle *DEZ*. I then say that the sides of triangle *DEZ* and its angles would then be known.

[16] *The proof*: Side *EZ* is equal to the sine of arc *AH*, which is known, as we have shown above.[9] Side *ZD* is the difference between *ZG* and *GD* – i.e. the side of triangle *DBG* – and it was shown above how side *GD* could be determined in the units that make the diameter of the deferent known.[10] Then half of chord *AG* is also known. Therefore, *DZ*, the difference between *GD* and *GZ*, is known. And the two squares, of *EZ* and *ZD*, are known. Therefore, the square *DE*, which is equal to the sum, is also known; and its root – i.e. line *DE* – which is the eccentricity, is also known.

[17] If a circle is drawn so that it circumscribes triangle *DEZ*, then each of *EZ* and *ZD* would be known, in the same (units) that make *ED* 120 parts. Then the arc whose chord is *EZ* will also be known, and angle *EDZ*, at the circumference of the circle circumscribing triangle *EDZ*, will be known too. Then angle *EDZ*, at the

[9] Paragraph 12.

[10] What he means is that *GD* could be computed by using the same technique used above, i.e. finding the sides and the angle of triangle *BGD*. See the commentary for the actual computations.

مركز البروج بعد تنصيف قدرها عند المحيط. فالقوس من البروج الموترة لزاوية هدز معلومة. فبُعد نقطة الأَوج من إحدى نقطتي الرصد الأَول والثالث معلومة – وهي الموضع الذي ينتهي إليه خط ده إذا أُنفذ على الاستقامة إلى منطقة البروج.

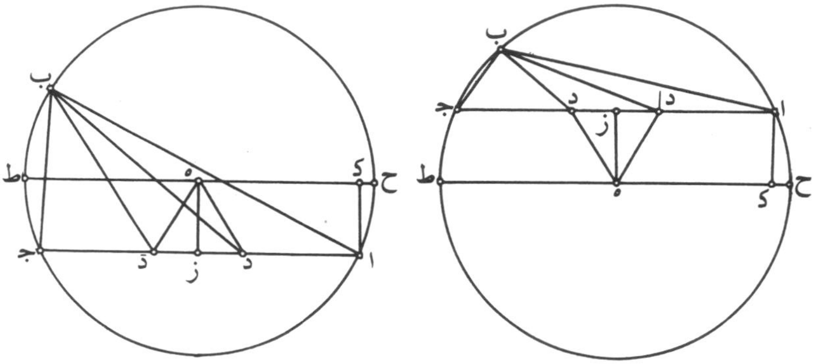

[١٨] هذه كلّها على أَنَّ الأَرصاد الثلاثة[٢٢] وقعت في زمان أَكثر من نصف سنة شمسيّة. فإن وقعت في زمان أَقلّ من نصف السنة فيكون التشكيل هكذا. واستخراج بُعد ما بين المركزين وموضع الأَوج يكون على الطريق الذي بيّـنّاه سهلاً على من يفطن لما تقدم، وسلك ذلك السبيل بعينه.

[١٩] فقد تمّ الكلام على اختلافات الأَوضاع لمعرفة هذين المطلبين. وذلك ما أَردناه.

٢٢ الثلاثة: الثلث في ن وس.

center of the ecliptic, will be known after halving its value at the circumference. Then the ecliptic arc that measures angle *EDZ* will be known, and the (angular) distance of the apogee from either of the two observations – the first or the third – will be known; and that is the point at the end of the extended line *DE* when it is extended straight to the ecliptic circle.

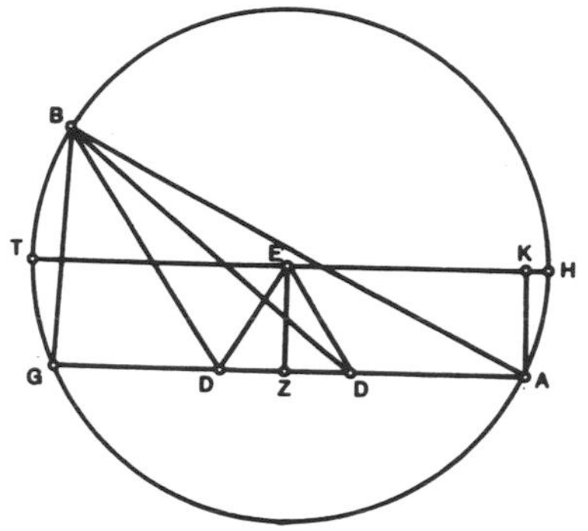

Figure 3a

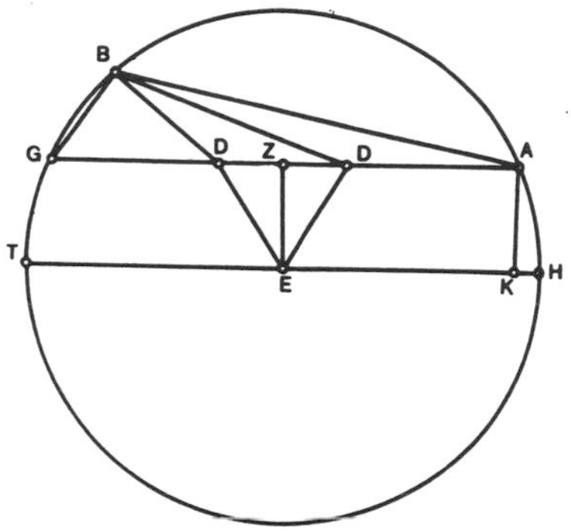

Figure 3b

[18] All of these assume that the three observations were taken in a period that exceeds half a solar year. If it were less than half a solar year then the configuration would be thus: [See Figure 3] The determination of the eccentricity and the position of the apogee would be easily determined by anyone who heeds the preceeding and follows the same method.

[19] Here ends the exposition of the various configurations that lead to the determination of the two requirements, and that was our desire.

Commentary

The problem of determining the solar eccentricity and the solar apogee is conceived by ʿUrḍī along the following lines:

In Figure 4, the observer is at point *D*, the center of the ecliptic *A'B'G'*. The sun is supposed to move along the deferent *ABG* with center *E*. In principle, the eccentricity *DE* could then be determined by any three observations taken at random around *D*. This, according to Bīrūnī, seems to have been the method followed by Ibn ʿIrāq, which is actually the same as the one used by Ptolemy to determine the eccentricity of the moon and the superior planets [See Introduction above].

Although there is a distinct advantage in observing the sun at positions other than the solstices – for at the solstices the variation in the solar declination is at its minimum, and thus difficult to observe – the difficulty of the resulting mathematical problem in the three-points method is not trivial, as can be easily ascertained from the treatment of the problem in *Almagest* IV, 6, and X, 7.

Ingenious solutions were devised to avoid the drawbacks of the solstice observations and the mathematical complexity of the three-point observations. One such solution employed the method known as the Method of Seasons (*fuṣūl*), which was apparently used as early as the time of Abū al-Wafāʾ al-Būzjānī (976 A.D.) [Hartner – Schramm, 209] if not earlier. In essence the method calls for observing the sun when the solar declination is changing rather fast, i.e. when the sun is in the middle of the season at Taurus 15, Leo 15, Scorpio 15, and Aquarius 15. This method is certainly easy to apply, and the resulting mathematical problem is identical to the one solved in *Almagest* III, 4, and thus easy to solve. But with this method, one still had to observe the sun at four different positions that have to be separated by 90 degrees from each other, and thus would require favorable observational conditions on specific days of the year, which is not always easy to obtain.

An alternative method, the one used by ʿUrḍī and his contemporary Yaḥyā b. Abī al-Shukr al-Maghribī [Saliba 1] seems to be a compromise between the two. It required that only two of the three observations be taken at times when two positions of the sun are 180 degrees apart (i.e. half a solar year apart). The third observation could be taken at any other time, thus allowing more freedom in the choice of good observational conditions.

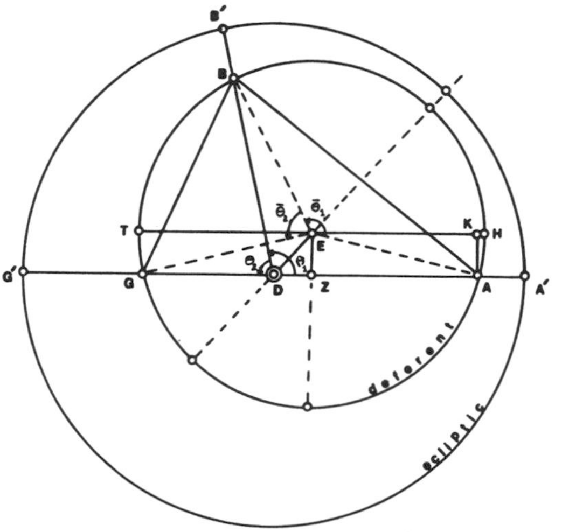

Figure 4

In Figure 4, the observer at point D has to observe the sun at times $t_{A'}$ when the sun is at A' on the ecliptic – A on the deferent – and when it is 180 degrees apart at G' – G at the deferent. The third observation at $t_{B'}$ could be taken at any convenient time. If in Figure 4, circle $A'B'G'$ is taken to be the ecliptic, with center D, and ABG the deferent with center E, then the problem is simply reduced to determining line DE.

But before reaching this general solution, ʿUrḍī starts by analysing the conditions of the problem (par. 1–4) and then solves the special case first, namely, when the sun is "accidentally" observed at the apogee and the perigee that are 180 degrees apart or separated by half a solar year. At that time the line of centers DE will join the two opposite observations (par. 5) and the resulting diagram is Figure 1, which shows the deferent and the ecliptic center D. The problem is then to determine the position of D along line AG.

In par. 6, the geometric conditions of the problem are laid out, and in par. 7–8, chords AB, BG are determined. ʿUrḍī does not spell out the exact relationship between the deferent chords AB, BG, measured by angles around center E, and the ecliptic arcs $A'B'$, $B'G'$ that are measured at center D. One has to assume that ʿUrḍī did not bother to explicitly compute arcs AB, BG, for it was obvious that they could be obtained by multiplying the mean motion of the sun by the time separating $t_{A'}$ from $t_{B'}$, and by the time separating $t_{G'}$ from $t_{B'}$. Once chords *AB BG* are known, then angles *AEB*, *BEG* would be simply deduced from:

$$chord\ A = 2 \sin \frac{A}{2}$$

a relationship which was definitely known to ʿUrḍī and probably judged to be too obvious to be explicitly mentioned here.

Par. 9 is then devoted to determining line *GD* as a side of triangle *BDG*, but to be measured in the same units that make diameter *AG* 120 parts. Once that is determined, *GD* is then compared with $GE = \frac{1}{2} AG$, which is also known. The difference between *GD* and *GE* is then the required eccentricity.

After this special case, ʿUrḍī goes on in par. 10 to solve the general case mentioned above in par. 3. Here the assumption is as in Figure 2, 4. The only restriction on the three observations is that *A′* be diametrically opposite to *G′* on the ecliptic.

In this case ʿUrḍī seems to know that in such configurations as Figure 2 and 4, the four quantities θ_1, θ_2 and $\bar{\theta}_1$, $\bar{\theta}_2$ are easily determinable by direct observation and by knowing the mean motion of the sun. More specifically θ_1, θ_2 are determined by direct observation as $\lambda_{B'}-\lambda_{A'}$ and $\lambda_{G'}-\lambda_{B'}$ respectively. And

$\bar{\theta}_1 = \dot{\lambda}(t_{B'}-t_{A'})$;

$\bar{\theta}_2 = \dot{\lambda}(t_{G'}-t_{B'})$, where $\dot{\lambda}$ is the mean angular velocity of the sun, a known parameter, *t* is the time of observation and λ the longitude of the sun.

Par. 11 only asserts that *D*, the center of the ecliptic, must fall on *AG* simply because *A′*, *G′* are separated by 180 degrees. The general condition is for *D* to be at any point on *AG*. But, as before, ʿUrḍī solves the special case first, namely, when *D* coincides with *Z*. If that were the case, then ʿUrḍī is right in concluding that the apogee's position would be known, for then it would be along line *ZE*.

ʿUrḍī proves in par. 12 that if *D* coincides with *Z* then *ZE* would be the required eccentricity, and that it would simply be equal to line *AK* which he determines as the sine of the angular difference between ½ arc *AG* and 90 degrees. ʿUrḍī does not explicitly say so, but simply remarks that *AK* can be determined from arc *AG* and its half. The position of the apogee as being along line *ZE* in the direction of *E* is then asserted in par. 13–14.

The general case, when *D* does not coincide with *Z*, i.e. $GD \neq GZ$ is taken up in par. 15f. ʿUrḍī draws triangle *DEZ*, par. 15, first, and then seeks to determine the three sides of this triangle. Line $EZ = AK$ was already determined in par. 12. Next the determination of side ZD is neither trivial nor obvious. ʿUrḍī correctly recognizes that ZD is only the difference between GZ – half the chord AG – and GD. One can argue that GZ could be easily determined as

$$GZ = \tfrac{1}{2}AG = \tfrac{1}{2}\left(2sin\frac{\bar{\theta}_1+\bar{\theta}_2}{2}\right)$$
$$= sin\frac{\bar{\theta}_1+\bar{\theta}_2}{2}$$

But he misleads the reader in allowing him to think that GD was determined before, presumably in the first special case in par. 9, for there the line passing through the center of the ecliptic did coincide with the line passing through the center of the deferent, and there was no resulting triangle DEZ. What he probably meant is that the strategy of the solution of the problem, i.e. determining GD from triangle BGD is the same as above, which is true.

The determination of GD, however, was not beyond ʿUrḍī nor his contemporaries. In fact Maghribī [Saliba 1] solves the same problem, and determines GD along similar lines:

$$chord\ BG = 2sin\frac{\bar{\theta}_2}{2}$$

$\sphericalangle BAG = \tfrac{1}{2}\bar{\theta}_2$, being at the circumference of arc GB.

Therefore, $\sphericalangle DBA = \theta_2 - \sphericalangle BAG$ is known, and

$$\begin{aligned}\sphericalangle DBG &= \sphericalangle ABG - \sphericalangle DBA\\ &= (\bar{\theta}_1 + \bar{\theta}_2) - \sphericalangle DBA\\ &= (\bar{\theta}_1 + \bar{\theta}_2) - (\theta_2 - \sphericalangle BAG)\\ &= (\bar{\theta}_1 + \bar{\theta}_2) - (\theta_2 - \tfrac{1}{2}\bar{\theta}_2) \text{ is also known.}\end{aligned}$$

Therefore, in triangle GBD

$\sphericalangle B = \sphericalangle DBG$ is known,

$\sphericalangle D = \theta_2$,

and $\sphericalangle G = 180 - (\theta_2 + \sphericalangle B)$,

and side BG is known in the same units that make $TH = 120$ parts, the diameter of the deferent.

Therefore, by using the sine theorem

$$\frac{GD}{BG} = \frac{B}{\theta_2} \text{ and } GD = \frac{BG \cdot B}{\theta_2}$$

ʿUrḍī does not carry out this computation, and one has to assume that the purpose of this treatise is only to sketch the main outline of the solution rather than to fill in the details.

Once *EZ* and *ZD* are determined then the eccentricity is simply the hypotenuse of triangle *DEZ*.

The only remaining problem is to determine the position of the apogee, which is in fact equivalent to the determination of any of the acute angles of triangle *DEZ*. ʿUrḍī could have done that by using the sine theorem, now that he knows all the sides of triangle *DEZ*. Instead, he chooses to follow the clumsy Ptolemaic method and solves for angle *EDZ* in par. 17 by circumscribing a circle around triangle *DEZ*.

The last case considered by ʿUrḍī is the one in which the difference between the two opposite observations is less than one half of a mean solar year. For that case, the resulting figures are as in Figure 3, with the case of 3a being essentially the same as Figure 2. ʿUrḍī dismisses all of these as obvious and does not go any further. In fact both cases are easy to prove and one could use for them the same technique used above in par. 16.

This brief text of ʿUrḍī seems to have been written while he was still a student, for the text seems to be heavily dependent still on the clumsy Ptolemaic trigonometric methods, which were definitely obsolete by ʿUrḍī's time. It seems as if he was still training himself to understand the Ptolemaic computational methods, and the problems that he would encounter as he read the *Almagest*. But he also was aware of the methodological improvements that were suggested by later Muslim astronomers as to the methods and the problems of the *Almagest*. The language of this treatise, however, and its conceptual approach have all the features of a beginner's attitude.

Bibliography

Bīrūnī: Abū al-Raiḥān al-Bīrūnī, *al-Āthār al-Bāqiyah*, tr. by E. Sachau as *The Chronology of Ancient Nations*, Allen & Co., London 1879.

HAMA: O. Neugebauer, *A History of Ancient Mathematical Astronomy*, Springer-Verlag, New York – Heidelberg – Berlin, 1975.

Hartner – Schramm: W. Hartner and M. Schramm, "Al-Bīrūnī and the Theory of the Solar Apogee: an example of originality in Arabic Science," in *Scientific Change*, ed. by A. C. Crombie, London, 1963.

Pedersen: O. Pedersen, *A Survey of the Almagest*, Odense University Press, 1974.

Saliba 1: G. Saliba, "Solar Observations at the Maraghah Observatory Before 1275: A New Set of Parameters," to appear in *Journal for the History of Astronomy*, 16 (1985) 113–122.

Saliba 2: G. Saliba, "An Observational Notebook of a Thirteenth Century Astronomer", *ISIS*, 74 (1983) 388–401.

Thābit: O. Neugebauer, "Thābit ben Qurra 'On the Solar Year' and 'On the Motion of the Eighth Sphere'," *Proceedings of the American Philosophical Society*, vol. 106 No. 3 (1962) 264–299.

The Determination of New Planetary Parameters at the Maragha Observatory

by

George Saliba

Introduction

In a recent issue of *Isis*[1] I devoted an article to a work of Yaḥyā b. Abī al-Shukr al-Maghribī (d. A.D. 1283), called *"talkhīṣ al-majisṭī"* (Compendium of the Almagest), preserved at Rijksuniversiteit Library, Leiden, as Orientalis 110.[2] In that article, I stated that Maghribī's work was, as far as I know, the first medieval text to come to light in which a thirteenth-century practising astronomer reports the results of his own observations, and then uses these results to draw up a *zīj* (astronomical handbook) that has also survived, but has not yet received detailed study.[3] The intention of the *Isis* article was only to give a general description of this unique work, and to report, without analysis, the observations and the results established by Maghribī.

In a more recent paper in the *Journal for the History of Astronomy*,[4] I analysed the observations related to the sun, and discussed in some detail the new parameters established there.

In this paper, I propose to investigate details of some further observations, which were employed by Maghribī to calculate the tables of his latest *zīj*. These concern a group of parameters related to the planetary eccentricities, which were established, as we shall see, along the same lines followed by Ptolemy in the *Almagest X*, 7, and repeated for each planet in detail. But due to limitations of space, I will select the iteration method used by Maghribī to determine the eccentricity of the planet Jupiter, only as an illustration of the method followed in exactly the same fashion for the other planets.

As was mentioned in the *Isis* article (p. 401), the section of the MS, which deals with Jupiter, covers folios 128r–132r, and constitutes the sixth chapter of the eighth treatise. With the exception of Figure *1a,* all the figures given here are found in the MS, and are redrawn only for publications purposes.

The Problem

By noting that none of the planets seems to an observer on the earth to be covering equal arcs in equal times, ancient astronomers correctly concluded that these planets must be moving uniformly around a center other than the earth (the center of the eccentric circle). Later Ptolemy displaced the center of uniform motion to a point even further removed from the earth (the equant point), viz. situated at twice the distance of the center of the eccentric. This was done in order to make theory agree with observations, and by a high degree of mathematical sophistication. Nevertheless, the fact that the motion on the eccentric circle thus became non-uniform with respect to this circle was later to be regarded as the most notorious soft spot in the Ptolemaic system, and a primary motivation for alternate geometric models that finally led to the Copernican models.

To Ptolemy, however, who did not seem to worry about the philosophical implications of this equant, nor about its physical reality, the problem was simply to determine as accurately as possible the distance and position of this equant with respect to the observer on the earth. And that he did with great mathematical ingenuity.

The Solution

I will draw up here the main outline of Ptolemy's solution of the problem which resulted in his determination of the eccentricities of the planets.[5] In this problem Ptolemy follows the same lines he had established in the case of the lunar model (*Almagest IV,* 6) and determined the planetary eccentricities by using three observations only.[6]

In Figure 1a, an observer at point *N* observes a planet in the direction of points *A, B,* and *G* respectively; when the planet is at opposi-

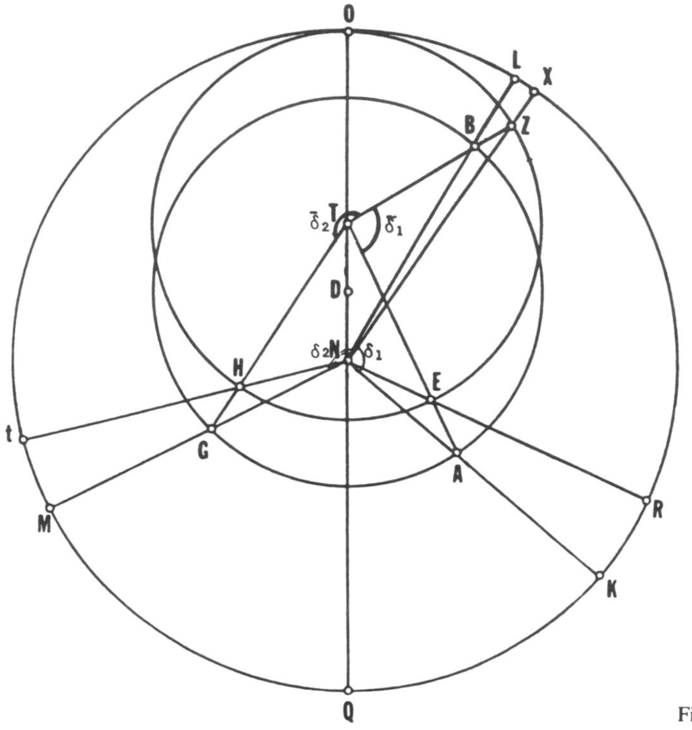

Figure 1a.

tion with the sun, and thus its true position is the same as that of the epicyclic center; and where the difference in position between A and B is denoted by δ_1, and that between B and G is denoted by δ_2. Now, since the times t_1, between observations (1) and (2), and t_2, between observations (2) and (3), can be determined, one can compute the distance a planet covers in its mean motion during these times. Since the mean motion parameters $\bar{\lambda}$ are determined independently of this model, the results $\bar{\delta}_1$, $\bar{\delta}_2$ are found to be different from the observed values δ_1, δ_2. The assumption then that the planet moves on an eccentric circle is inevitable, and the problem is reduced to determining the distance TN which will explain the variations between δ_1, δ_2 and $\bar{\delta}_1$, $\bar{\delta}_2$.

Once that is accepted, Ptolemy assumes first that the eccentric circle with center T is the same as the deferent circle that carries the epicycle, and then shows that this assumption cannot be true. This means that the center of the deferent and that of the equant should be different, and should both be eccentric to the center of the universe, the observer.

The method followed by Ptolemy is to take the analogy of the solar model (*Almagest III,* 4) and then determine the eccentricity *TN* for each of the planets. Knowing that there was a mistake generated by assuming the circle with center *T* to be overlapping with the deferent, one knows that the computation of *TN* itself will include a mistake generated by the overlapping of these two circles. The mistake can then be calculated, using the already determined eccentricity *TN*.

By assuming the mistake to be ε in Figures 4a, 4b, and 4c, one is also including in the computation of ε an approximation resulting from the fact that *TN* itself is an approximation. We could now use that ε to compute a new set of δ_1 and δ_2, say δ_1' and δ_2', the angles at which $\bar{\delta}_1$, and $\bar{\delta}_2$, are seen from the center of the ecliptic *N*, such that

$$\delta_1' = \delta_1 + \varepsilon_1 + \varepsilon_2, \text{ and}$$
$$\delta_2' = \delta_2 - \varepsilon_2 - \varepsilon_3.$$

With the refined values δ_1', and δ_2', one can compute a new eccentricity *TN*, and repeat the whole procedure from the beginning. I do not know if this iteration process will ever converge, but it can be shown that after the second trial the minute part of the eccentricity will no longer be affected.[7] That was probably realized by Ptolemy, for he computed two trials for Saturn and Jupiter and three for Mars.[8]

Maghribī's Derivation of Jupiter's Eccentricity

Since in the surviving portion of *talkhīṣ al-majisṭī,* Maghribī uses the same technique to compute the eccentricities of the planets Saturn, Jupiter and Mars, we reproduce his determination of Jupiter's eccentricity here as an example of the method followed, simply because the text is better preserved at this point.

1. Observational Data

The three Jupiter observations used by Maghribī are the following:

(1) On Sunday, 14 Dimah 633 Y.E. = **JD 2183026** = 19, October A.D. 1264, the planet was in true opposition at $\lambda_1 = 35;38,17°$ [Tuckerman[9] 35;11,2] at an absolute time[10] t_1 in Yezdigird years $632^a\ 284^d\ 8;5^h = [(632\times365)+284]^d\ 8;5^h = 230964^d\ 8;5^h$.

(2) On Tuesday, 24 Isfandarmah 635 Y.E. = **JD 2183826** = 28, December A.D. 1266, the planet was in true opposition at $\lambda_2 = 104;9,20°$ [Tuckerman 103;51,21] at an absolute time t_2 in Yezdigird years $634^a\ 354^d\ 8;3^h = 231764^d\ 8;3^h$.

(3) On Saturday, 8 Abanmah 643 Y.E. = **JD 2186610** = 12, August A.D. 1274, the planet was in true opposition at $\lambda_3 = 327;54,43$ [Tuckerman 327;10,12] at an absolute time t_3 in Yezdigird years $642^a\ 218^d\ 1^h = 234548^d\ 1^h$.

2. *Determination of the Angular Motion*

Once these observations were recorded, Maghribī, following Ptolemy, used them to determine the values of the observed angles:

$$\delta_1 = \lambda_2 - \lambda_1 = 104;9,20 - 35;38,17 = 68;31,3°$$

as in the text,

$$\delta_2^* = \lambda_3 - \lambda_2 = 327;54,43 - 104;9,20 = 223;45,23$$

as in the text, and the corresponding mean motion values:

$$\bar{\delta}_1 = (t_2 - t_1)\,\dot{\bar{\lambda}}^{11} = [(231764 + 8;3/24)-(230964 + 8;5/24)] \times 0;4,59,16,40,55,8 = 66;30,22 \text{ [text 66;30,14]},$$

and

$$\bar{\delta}_2^* = (t_3 - t_2)\,\dot{\bar{\lambda}} = [(234548\ 1/24)-(231764 + 8;3/24)] \times 0;4,59,16,40,55,8 = 231;25,02 \text{ [text 231;24,34]}.$$

To avoid working with angles greater than 180°, Maghribī sets up a new set of values as in Figure 1b (not to scale), which simply means working on a different side of the circle. Thus

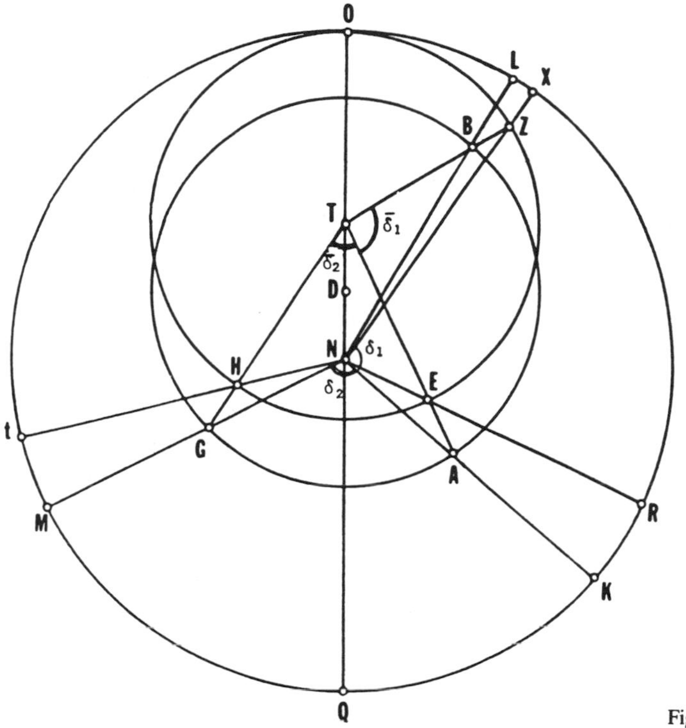

Figure 1b.

$$\delta_1 = 68;31,3,$$

and

$$\delta_1 + \delta_2 = 360 - \delta_2^* = 360-223;45,23 = 136;14,37,$$

and

$$\delta_2 = (\delta_1 + \delta_2) - \delta_1 = 136;14,37-68;31,3 = 67;43,34.$$

Similarly,

$$\bar{\delta}_1 = 66;30,14$$ [12]

$$\bar{\delta}_1 + \bar{\delta}_2 = 360 - \bar{\delta}_2^* = 360-231;24,34 = 128;35,26,$$

and

$$\bar{\delta}_2 = (\bar{\delta}_1 + \bar{\delta}_2) - \bar{\delta}_1 = 128;35,26 - 66;30,14 = 62;5,12.$$

Noting that there was an obvious difference[13] between the observed values of the arc $MK + KL = \delta_1 + \delta_2$, and the mean motion arc $\bar{\delta}_1 + \bar{\delta}_2$, Maghribī concluded, like Ptolemy, that the center of mean motion did not coincide with the center of the universe. With the eccentric model of the sun in mind, it was clear that the mean motion arc was seen from the center of the universe as being equal to arcs $tR + RL$ in Figure 1b. Arcs *tM, KR,* and *XL,* however, were still to be determined.

At this point, Ptolemy and after him Maghribī, identified the problem as being essentially the same as that of determining the eccentricity of the solar model – where the difference between an arc of motion and the actual observed value of that arc was sufficient to determine the eccentricity – only if one assumed as a first approximation that the solar model is sufficient in the sense that it did not require an equant circle. Hence, they both started with the false assumption that the equant center was identical to the deferent center. And by redrawing that deferent, Figure 2, the observer is now taken to be at point *D,* and the center of the deferent – assumed falsely to be the same as that of the equant – is to be found.

3. *First Determination of the Eccentricity*

(A) Determine the length of chord GE in Figure 2

Let points *G, A, B,* in Figure 2, be the positions on the deferent carrying the epicycle of the planet at observations (3), (1), and (2) respectively, as seen from the center of the universe *D.* By connecting *DG, DA, DB,* and extending *GD* to *E,* and by constructing *BR* perpendicular to *AE,* one can determine the length of chord *GE.* Here Maghribī's computation method differs slightly from that of Ptolemy. Maghribī started by determining:

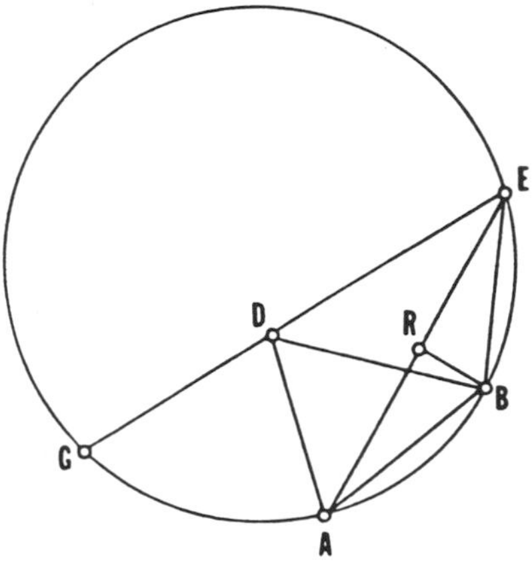

Figure 2.

(a) Chord BE

Since arc *GAB* = $\bar{\delta}_1 + \bar{\delta}_2$ = 360 – 231;24,34 = 128;35,26, is the arc of the deferent as seen from the center of the universe, then irrespective of the position of the center of that circle on which this arc is measured

angle *BEG* – 1/2 arc *GAB* – 1/2 (128;35,26) – 64;17,43,

since it is inscribed in the circle.

Angle *BDG,* as the observed angle, is $\delta_1 + \delta_2$ = 136;14,37. Now, using that as an exterior angle to triangle *BDE,* Maghribī computes angles *DBE* as 136;14,37 – 64;17,43 = 71;56,54, and *BDE* as 180 – 136;14,37 = 43;45,23. And to determine line *BE,* Maghribī applies the Sine Law – which was not available to Ptolemy – to triangle *BDE* to get:

(Sin *BDE*)/*BE* = (Sin *DBE*)/*DE*.[14]

Since these ratios in triangle *DBE* are as yet undetermed in absolute units, Maghribī sets *DE* = 60 units and computes *BE* = (Sin*BDE*/Sin*DBE*) × 60 in the same units that make *DE* = 60 units. That yields *BE* = (Sin 43;45,23/Sin 71;56,54) × 60 = 43;38,37,57 [text 43;38,42].

(b) Chord AE

Similarly, since arc $AB = \bar{\delta}_1 = 66;30,14$, then angle BEA can be determined $\bar{\delta}_1/2 = 66;30,14/2 = 33;15,7$, as an inscribed angle, and

$$\begin{aligned}\text{angle } AEG = \text{angle } BEG - \text{angle } BEA &= 64;17,43 - 33;15,7\\ &= 31;2,36.\end{aligned}$$

Moreover, since the observed angle $ADB = \delta_1$ is 68;31,2, then

$$\begin{aligned}\text{angle } ADG = \text{angle } BDG - \text{angle } ADB &= 136;14,37 - 68;31,3\\ &= 67;43,34 \text{ [text } 67;43,37].\end{aligned}$$

Since angle ADG is exterior to triangle DAE, therefore

$$\begin{aligned}\text{angle } DAE = \text{angle } ADG - \text{angle } AEG &= 67;43,37 - 31;2,36\\ &= 36;40,58.\end{aligned}$$

Now, in triangle ADE, using the Sine Law,

$$AE/(\text{Sin}ADE) = DE/(\text{Sin}DAE).$$

But angle ADE + angle $ADG = 180°$. Therefore,

$$\text{Sin}ADE = \text{Sin}ADG,$$

and

$$AE/(\text{Sin}ADG) = DE/(\text{Sin}DAE), \text{ with } DE = 60 \text{ units.}$$

Therefore,

$$\begin{aligned}AE &= (\text{Sin}ADG/\text{Sin}DAE) \times 60\\ &= (\text{Sin } 67;43,37/\text{Sin } 36;40,58) \times 60\\ &= 92;56,38,29 \text{ [text } 92;57,28].\end{aligned}$$

(c) Chord AB

Now, in triangle EBR, angle BER = angle $BEA = 33;15,7$, which was determined above, and angle $R = 90°$. Therefore, angle $EBR = 90 -$

33;15,7 = 56;44,53, and side *BR* can be determined in the same units that make *DE* = 60 units, i.e.

$$BR = 43;38,42 \times \text{Sin } 33;15,7 = 23;55,53,23 \text{ [text } 23;55,53].$$

And

$$\begin{aligned} ER = BE \text{ Sin} EBR &= 43;38,42 \times \text{Sin } 56;44,53 \\ &= 36;20,54,7 \text{ [text } 36;29,56]. \end{aligned}$$

Thus *AR* = *AE* − *ER* can now be determined, i.e. = 92;57,28 − 36;29,56 = 56;27,32.

Therefore,

$$AB = \sqrt{\overline{AR}^2 + \overline{BR}^2},$$

can be determined in the same units that make *DE* = 60 units, i.e.

$$\begin{aligned} AB &= \sqrt{(56;27,32)^2 + (23;55,53)^2} \\ &= 61;19,17,17 \text{ [text } 61;19,17,8]. \end{aligned}$$

(d) Determination of DE, *as part of GE, a chord in the deferent of diameter 120 parts*

Using the general identity, Chord α = 2 Sin(α/2), then Chord*AB* = 2 Sin*BER* = 2 Sin 33;15,7 = 65;47,54,56 [text 65;47,54,58], which gives the value of *AB* as a chord in a circle whose center is other than *D*, and whose diameter is 120 parts. Then noting the difference in value between side *AB* of triangle *ABR* – computed in units that make *DE* 60 – and chord *AB* in a circle of diameter 120 parts, Maghribī computes *DE* in units such that the diameter of the circle is 120, instead of continuing with the earlier assumption that it was 60 units. The ratio of *AB*, the chord, to the new value of *DE* must therefore be the same as the ratio of side *AB* to *DE* when both were measured in units that make *DE* = 60 units. Therefore,

$$\text{Chord}AB/DE = (\text{Side } AB)/60,$$

and

$$DE = 60 \times 65;47,54,58/61;19,17,8$$
$$= 64;22,50,30,26 \text{ [text } 64;22,50],$$

which gives a new value of *DE* as part of a chord in a circle of diameter 120 units.

(e) Determination of BE as a chord in a circle of diameter 120 parts

Since *BE* was determined above in units that make $DE = 60$ units, then it can now be determined in the units that make the diameter of the circle 120 parts. Therefore

$$BE = 43;38,37,57 \times (65;47,54,58/61;19,17,8)$$
$$= 46;49,49,23 \text{ [text } 46;49,52,29].$$

Now that *BE* can be measured in the circle of diameter 120 parts, Maghribī computes the angle it subtends at the center of that circle, by using the relationship:

$$\text{Chord } \alpha = 2 \text{ Sin } (\alpha/2),$$

and thus

$$\alpha = 2 \text{ Arcsin } (\text{Chord}BE/2)$$
$$= 2 \text{ Arcsin } [(46;49,52,29)/2] = 45;56,29 = \text{arc } BE.$$

(f) Determination of chord GE in a circle of diameter 120 parts

Now, adding arc α to arc $GAB = \bar{\delta}_1 + \bar{\delta}_2$, gives

$$\text{arc } GABE = 45;56,29 + 128;35,26 = 174;31,55,$$

and

$$\text{Chord } GE = 2 \text{ Sin } (\text{arc } GABE/2) = 2 \text{ Sin } 87;15,57,30$$
$$= 119;51,48,$$

in units that make the diameter of the circle 120.

Since this newly-found chord *GE* is less than the diameter, the center of the circle must therefore be in the major section above the chord *GE*. And since $GD = GE - DE$, therefore,

$$GD = 119;51,48 - 64;22,50 = 55;28,58.$$

And anticipating the next section, Maghribī computes the product $GD \times DE = 55;28,58 \times 64;22,50 = 59,32;0,43$ as in the text.

(B) Determination of the Eccentricity HD: First Approximation

Now that the center of the mean motion was shown to be within the major sector of the circle, Maghribī, following Ptolemy, draws Figure 3, where *HD* is assumed to be the required eccentricity, and the diameter is 120 parts. He then finds that

$$R^2 - GD \times DE = \overline{HD}^2$$
$$[\text{or } (R - HD)(R + HD) = GD \times DE, \text{ Euclid III, 35}]$$

where $R = 60$ is the radius of the standard circle in Figure 3.

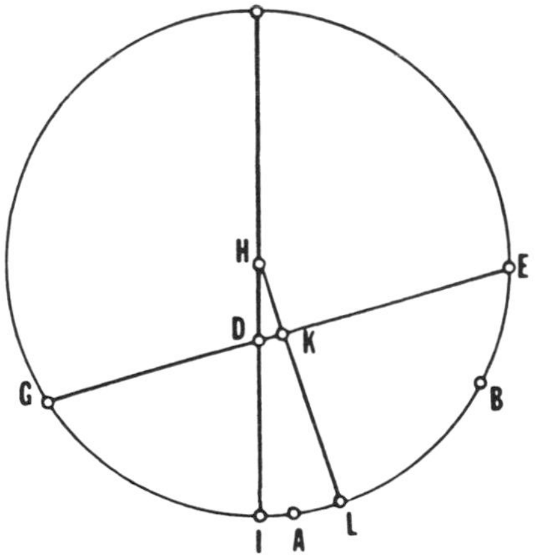

Figure 3.

Therefore,

$$HD = \sqrt{3600 - 59{,}32;0{,}43} = \sqrt{27;59{,}17} = 5;17{,}25.$$

And thus in the first attempt, Maghribī finds the required eccentricity to be:

$$2e = 5;17{,}25.$$

4. *Determination of the Position of the Apsidal Line*

(a) Compute GI

Since *DK* is known from

$$GE/2 - GD = (119;51{,}48/2) - 55;28{,}58 = 4;26{,}56 \text{ [text } 4;26{,}36],$$

then in the triangle *DHK,*

$$\mathrm{Sin}DHK = DK/HD,$$

and

$$DHK = \text{Arcsin } (4;26{,}36/5;17{,}25) = 57;10{,}2 \text{ [text } 57;14{,}28].$$ [15]

And since *GL* = 1/2 arc *GABE,* then,

GI = *GL* − *IL* (= angle *DHK,* since *H* is the center of the circle) = (174;31,55/2) − 57;14,28 = 30;1,29 as in the text. Therefore, the distance of observation (3) from the perigee is 30;1,29°.

(b) Compute AI

Since the inscribed angle *AEG* was determined above as being 31;2,36, then the central angle *GHA* = 2 (31;2,36) = 62;5,12, and arc *GA* = 62;5,12.

Therefore,

$$\text{arc } AI = GA - GI = 62;5{,}12 - 30;1{,}29 = 32;3{,}43$$

as in the text.

(c) Compute IB

Since angle BEA = 33;15,7, as an inscribed angle, was determined above, then the central angle AHB = 2 BEA = 66;30,14. And since arc $AB = \bar{\delta}_1$ = 66;30,14, then,

$$\text{arc } BI = AB + AI = 66;30,14 + 32;3,43 = 98;33,57$$

or

$$= 180 - 98;33,57 = 81;26,3$$

from the apogee as in the text.

This completes the computation of the eccentricity and the position of the apsidal line under the false assumption that the difference between the equant circle and that of the deferent is negligible.

5. *Determination of the Variation Between the Equant and the Deferent*

By redrawing Figure 1b, and separating the details in Figures 4a, 4b, 4c, the problem is then reduced to computing arcs *KR, XL, tM,* each designated by the angle ε, each representing the difference between the equant and the deferent as seen from the center of the universe.

In anticipation of computing $\varepsilon = \eta - \zeta$, the next step is to compute both η and ζ in each of the three cases.

Since, for the times of the observations, the distances of the positions from either the perigee or the apogee are known, then in Figures 4a, 4b, and 4c,

$$1 - \text{arc } AI = \text{angle } NTA = \alpha = 32;3,43$$
$$2 - \text{arc } BI = \text{angle } BNO = \beta = 81;26,3$$
$$3 - \text{arc } GI = \text{angle } GTN = \gamma = 30;1,29.$$

And since $TD = DN = TN/2$ = (5;17,25)/2, then in the three cases, sides *DC, TC, NS,* and *TS* can be determined. For that purpose, Maghribī computes

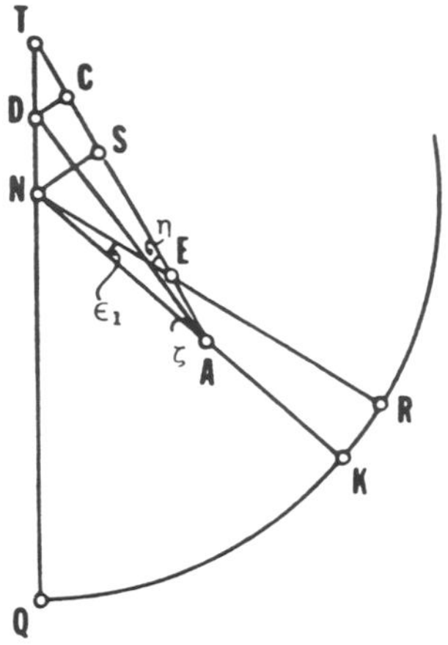

Figure 4a.

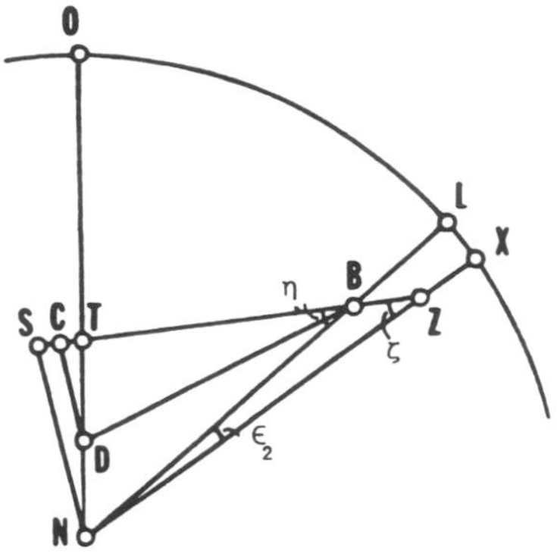

Figure 4b.

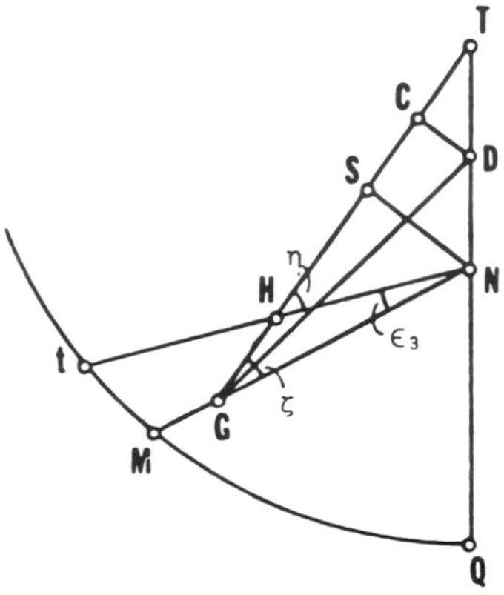

Figure 4c.

$$\text{Sin } \alpha = 31;51,50 \text{ [text } 31;50,0]$$
$$\text{Cos } \alpha = 50;50,54,31 \text{ [text } 50;50,55]$$

in Figure 4a,

$$\text{Sin } \beta = 59;19,50,36 \text{ [text } 59;19,51]$$
$$\text{Cos } \beta = 8;56,12,16 \text{ [text } 9;26,12]$$

in Figure 4b,

$$\text{Sin}\ \gamma = 30;1,20,42\ [\text{text } 30;1,21]$$
$$\text{Cos}\ \gamma = 51;56,54,52\ [\text{text } 51;56,55]$$

in Figure 4c.

And by using the value $TD = (5;17,25)/2 = 2;38,42$, determined above, it is easy to compute:

$$\begin{aligned}
DC, \text{ in Fig. 4a, as } TD \text{ Sin } \alpha &= 2;38,42 \times 0;31,50 \\
&= 1;24,11,56\ [\text{text } 1;24,12] \\
DC, \text{ in Fig. 4b, as } TD \text{ Sin } \beta &= 2;38,42 \times 0;59,19,51 \\
&= 2;36,55,48\ [\text{text } 2;36,56], \text{ and} \\
DC, \text{ in Fig. 4c, as } TD \text{ Sin } \gamma &= 2;38,42 \times 0;30,1,21 \\
&= 1;19,24,34\ [\text{text } 1;19,25]
\end{aligned}$$

Similarly,

$$\begin{aligned}
&\text{in Fig. 4a, } TC = TD \text{ Cos } \alpha = 2;14,27\ [\text{text } 2;13,30] \\
&\text{in Fig. 4b, } TC = TD \text{ Cos } \beta = 0;24,57,35\ [\text{text } 0;24,58], \text{ and} \\
&\text{in Fig. 4c, } TC = TD \text{ Cos } \gamma = 2;17,24 \text{ as in the text.}
\end{aligned}$$

Also, since $NS = 2DC$, then it can also be determined in all three cases, namely

$$\left.\begin{aligned}
&\text{in Fig. 4a, } NS = 2 \times 1;24,12 = 2;48,24 \\
&\text{in Fig. 4b, } NS = 2 \times 2;36,56 = 5;13,52 \\
&\text{in Fig. 4c, } NS = 2 \times 1;19,25 = 2;38,50
\end{aligned}\right\}\text{ as in the text.}$$

And since $TS = 2TC$, then it can also be determined for the three cases as well, namely

$$\left.\begin{aligned}
&\text{in Fig. 4a, } TS = 2 \times 2;13,30 = 4;27 \\
&\text{in Fig. 4b, } TS = 2 \times 0;24,58 = 0;49,56
\end{aligned}\right\}\text{ as in the text.}$$
$$\text{in Fig. 4c, } TS = 2 \times 2;17,24 = 4;34,48\ [\text{text } 4;38,48].$$

Therefore,

$$\left.\begin{aligned}
SE &= 60 - TS = 60 - 4;27 = 55;33 \\
ZS &= 60 + TS = 60 + 0;49,56 = 60;49,56 \\
HS &= 60 - TS = 60 - 4;34,48 = 55;25,12
\end{aligned}\right\}\text{ as in the text.}$$

But if DC in triangle ADC were seen as an arc on a circle whose center is at D, then, with $AD = 60$, in Figure 4a,

$$\begin{aligned} \mathrm{Sin}CAD &= DC/AD, \text{ and} \\ \text{angle } CAD &= \mathrm{Arcsin}(DC/60) = \mathrm{Arcsin}\ (0;1,24,12) \\ &= 1;20,24,44 \text{ [text } 1;20,25]. \end{aligned}$$

Similarly,

$$\begin{aligned} \text{in Fig. 4b, angle } DBC &= \mathrm{Arcsin}\ (DC/60) \\ &= \mathrm{Arcsin}\ (0;2,36,56) \\ &= 2;29,54 \text{ [text } 2;30,0] \end{aligned}$$

and

$$\begin{aligned} \text{in Fig. 4c, angle } DGC &= \mathrm{Arcsin}\ (DC/60) \\ &= \mathrm{Arcsin}\ (0;1,19,25) \\ &= 1;15,50,36 \text{ [text } 1;15,51]. \end{aligned}$$

Therefore, the remaining angles, are

$$\left.\begin{aligned} \text{in Fig. 4a, } ADC &= 90 - CAD = 88;39,35 \\ \text{in Fig. 4b, } BDC &= 90 - DBC = 87;30 \\ \text{in Fig. 4c, } GDC &= 90 - DGC = 88;44,9 \end{aligned}\right\} \text{as in the text.}$$

This yields,

in Fig. 4a, side $AC = AD \times \mathrm{Sin}ADC = 59;59,0,54$ [text 59;59,1]

in Fig. 4b, side $BC = BD \times \mathrm{Sin}BDC = 59;56,34,24$ [text 59;56,34]

in Fig. 4c, side $GC = GD \times \mathrm{Sin}GDC = 59;59,7,25$ [text 59;59,7].

Therefore,

$$\begin{aligned} \text{in Fig. 4a, } AS &= AC - CS, \text{ where } CS = TC \\ &= 59;59,1 - 2;13,30 = 57;45,31, \text{ as in the text,} \\ \text{and in Fig. 4b, } BC &= BC + CS, \text{ where } CS = TC, \\ &= 59;56,34 + 0;24,58 = 60;24,32, \text{ as in the text} \\ \text{and in Fig. 4c, } GS &= GC - CS, \text{ where } CS = TC \\ &= 59;59,7 - 2;17,24 = 57;41,43, \text{ as in the text.} \end{aligned}$$

Now, since *NS, SE, SA,* could be determined from triangles *NSE,* and *NSA,* then,

$$\begin{aligned}\text{in Fig. 4a, Tan } \eta &= NS/SE \\ &= (2;48,24/55;33) \times 60 \\ &= 3;1,53, \text{ as in the text, and} \\ \eta &= \text{Arctan } (3;1,53) = 2;53,32 \text{ as in the text.}\end{aligned}$$

Similarly,

$$\begin{aligned}\text{Since Tan } \zeta &= NS/SA, \\ &= (2;48,24/57;45,31) \times 60 \\ &= 2;54,56, \text{ as in the text, then} \\ \zeta &= \text{Arctan } (2;54,56) = 2;46,55 \text{ as in the text.}\end{aligned}$$

Therefore,

$$\begin{aligned}\varepsilon_1 &= \text{angle } ANE = \eta - \zeta \\ &= 2;53,32 - 2;46,55 = 0;6,37 = \text{arc } KR,\end{aligned}$$

which is now known.
Similarly,

$$\begin{aligned}\text{in Fig. 4b, Tan } \eta &= (NS/BS) \\ &= [(5;13,52)/(60;21,32)] \times 60 \\ &= 5;12,0,1 \text{ [text } 5;12,1].\end{aligned}$$

Thus

$$\eta = \text{Arctan } (5;12,1) = 4;57,12, \text{ as in the text,}$$

and

$$\begin{aligned}\text{Tan } \zeta &= (NS/ZS) \\ &= [(5;13,52)/(60;49,56)] \times 60 \\ &= 5;9,34 \text{ as in the text.}\end{aligned}$$

Thus

$$\zeta = \text{Arctan } (5;9,34) = 4;54,53 \text{ as in the text.}$$

Therefore,

$$\begin{aligned}\varepsilon_2 &= \text{arc } XL = \eta - \zeta \\ &= 4;57,12 - 4;54,53 = 0;2,19 \text{ as in the text.}\end{aligned}$$

Finally,

$$\begin{aligned}\text{in Fig. 4c, Tan } \eta &= (NS/SH) \\ &= [(2;38,50)/(55;25,12)] \times 60 \\ &= 2;51,57 \text{ as in the text.}\end{aligned}$$

Thus

$$\eta = \text{Arctan } (2;51,57) = 2;44,4,31 \text{ [text } 2;44,5].$$

And

$$\begin{aligned}\text{Tan } \zeta &= (NS/GS) \\ &= [(2;38,50)/(57;41,43)] \times 60 \\ &= 2;45,10 \text{ as in the text.}\end{aligned}$$

Thus

$$\zeta = \text{Arctan } (2;45,10) = 2;37,36 \text{ [text } 2;34,36].$$

Therefore,

$$\begin{aligned}\varepsilon_3 &= \text{arc } tM = \eta - \zeta \\ &= 2;44,5 - 2;37,36 = 0;6,29 \text{ as in the text.}\end{aligned}$$ [16]

6. *Iteration Procedure*

Now, reconsidering Figure *1b,* the value for δ_1 can now be improved to produce

$$\begin{aligned}\delta_1' &= \delta_1 - (KR + XL) = \delta_1 - (\varepsilon_1 + \varepsilon_2), \\ &= 68;31,30 - [(0;6,37)+(0;2,19)] = 68;22,7 \text{ as in the text.}\end{aligned}$$

And

$$\delta_2' = \delta_2 + (KR + tM) = \delta_2 + (\varepsilon_2 + \varepsilon_3),$$
$$= 67;43,34 + [(0;6,37)+(0;6,29)] = 67;56,40 \text{ as in the text.}$$

Substituting these values δ_1', δ_2' back in Figure 1b, and retaining the arcs *HE, EZ,* repeat the whole process from the very beginning to determine a new eccentricity $2e'$ and a new set of ε'.

Maghribī says that he has repeated this procedure [fol. 131r], and computed

$$2e' = 5;30,25, \text{ which yielded a new set of}$$
$$\delta_1'' = 68;21,41, \text{ and}$$
$$\delta_2'' = 67;57,46.$$

On a third trial, Maghribī says that he got the following values:

$$2e'' = 5;30,48$$
$$\delta_1''' = 68;20,44$$
$$\delta_2''' = 67;57,8.$$

And in a final fourth trial, Maghribī computed the following value for the eccentricity:

$$2e''' = 5;30,39,$$

which shows clearly that the variation seems to be restricted only to the seconds. Maghribī then accepts the eccentricity value as determined up to the minutes to be $2e = 5;30$, which incidentally is the same as the one accepted by Ptolemy.

7. *The Use of a Clock in the Maragha Observatory*

On a different subject, we note here that, as far as it can be established, Maghribī seems to be the first medieval astronomer to use a rather sophisticated clock to time the observations. The standard reference to this clock in the text is: "We release (or let loose, *aṭlaqnā*) the clock (*minkām*) when the sun (or a star) was at *x* degrees high, and the clock lasted (*khadama*) *y* revolutions (or a turn, *qalbat*[un]) and *z* minutes of revolutions till the planet reached the meridian". In the computation of the planetary positions such expressions as *dā'ir al-minkām* (the part that had revolved of the clock), and *dāra al-minkām* (the clock revolved) [fol. 113r], are used very frequently, and give the impression that we are dealing with some sort of a graduated disk or the like that is capable of revolving, once it is driven by water or sand or anything that can be released (*yuṭlaq*).

Although I am not sure at this point how this clock functioned exactly, I am convinced that it had two different kind of calibrations: one for the full revolutions, defined as being 15;24,44,26, and another one for the minutes of the revolutions, defined as 0;15,2,11. Since the minute calibration is not simply one sixtieth of the full revolutions, I suspect that the graduated plate was probably larger in size and was definitely capable of being operated alone as we shall see. We also know that the clock was breakable, for during one observation Maghribī had to give a new calibration for a new clock "for the old one was broken", (*al-minkām al-awwal qad inkasar*) [fol. 113r]. The new calibrations were given for the revolution as 15;45,12, and for the minutes as 0;15,37,23. Could one suggest a mechanical breakable device?

In another instance [fol. 132v], Maghribī clearly states that he used the minutes part of the clock only; as if to say that there were two containers (or mechanisms): one for the complete revolutions with its own calibrations to measure long periods of time, and a separate one for the minutes with a different calibration, and probably with much finer divisions or larger scale to measure shorter periods. From the context, it is definite that each of these two parts could be set in motion independently.

In one ambiguous situation, Maghribī says that he had used one half of the clock (*niṣf al-minkām*), but it is not clear how he used that portion of the clock, nor how he established the calibration then – for it must have varied – nor how he could get half the clock to work.

It is unfortunate that no other information about this *minkām* can be gleaned from this text in its present state, and one can only be certain that some kind of a clock was definitely used in the observations, without being able to tell precisely how the clock operated.

Conclusion

With the recovery of Maghribī's text, it has become clear that the work at the Maragha observatory between the years A.D. 1259 – the year when it was founded – and A.D. 1274 – the last year quoted in the text of Maghribī, and the year in which the director of the observatory, Naṣīr al-Dīn al-Ṭūsī died – was of a very sophisticated nature where a serious program of updating the Ptolemaic parameters was undertaken. We know of no other similar activity before the Copernican observations. And as such, Maghribī remains to be the only medieval astronomer that we know of who understood the full power of the observational basis of the Ptolemaic equant, and the full implications of Ptolemy's iteration method for determining the planetary eccentricities.

On the observational side, we also note that we clearly have, probably for the first time in a medieval source, an explicit reference to the use of a sophisticated clock in connection with astronomical observations. Moreover, one can not but admire the skill and the precision with which Maghribī conducted these observations, and his ability to determine planetary positions to within one degree of their true position as far as it can be ascertained from modern computations. Finally, although he stays as close as possible to the Ptolemaic method, he still felt free to use new techniques, such as in the case of the solar eccentricity, and felt that he needed, in the case of the planets, to repeat the iteration procedure four times, instead of Ptolemy's two times, for he did not seem to know whether the method converged or not.

As for the new parameters, including those for the sun, and those for mean motion, we note that they were indeed employed to compute the tables for the latest of Maghribī's *zījes,* and as a result, this last *zīj* contains the unique parameters that are definitely determined by observation and not copied from earlier sources as is the case with many other *zījes.*

NOTES AND REFERENCES

1. G. Saliba, "An Observational Notebook of a Thirteenth-Century Astronomer", *Isis* 74 (1983) 388–401.

2. The author wishes to thank the librarian of Rijksuniversiteit for allowing him to use a microfilm of the said manuscript.
3. This *zīj,* called *Adwār al-anwār madā al-Duhūr wa-l Akwār,* composed in 1275 A.D., just after the program of observations seems to have been completed, survives, e.g. in a copy at the Meshhed Shrine Library, MS 103, and is definitely different from Maghribī's earlier *zīj, Tāj al-azyāj* (Crown of Zījes), Escorial MS, Arabe, 932, which was composed in Damascus in 1257. For more details on both of these *zījes,* see E. S. Kennedy, "A Survey of Islamic Astronomical Tables", *Transactions of the American Philosophical Society,* 46 (1956), No. 41, 108.
4. G. Saliba, "Solar Observations at the Maraghah Observatory Before 1275: A New Set of Parameters", *Journal for the History of Astronomy,* 16 (1985) 113–122.
5. For an excellent, easy to follow, analysis of the Ptolemaic method, see O. Neugebauer, *A History of Ancient Mathematical Astronomy* (hereafter *HAMA*), New York, 1975, pp. 172–179.
6. The general problem is discussed by O. Neugebauer, *Exact Sciences in Antiquity,* 2nd. ed., Providence 1957, pp. 209–214.
7. *HAMA, op. cit.* (note 5), p. 178.
8. *Ibid.* p. 177.
9. B. Tuckerman, *Planetary, Lunar and Solar Positions A.D. 2 to A.D. 1649 at Five-day and Ten-day Intervals,* Memoirs, American Philosophical Society, 59, Philadelphia, 1964.
10. To simplify the comparison between observations, Maghribī uses a mathematical calendar where the first year of the Yezdigird Era is given the value 0 Y.E., and the first month is 0^m.
11. We use here the mean motion determined by Maghribī himself Fol. 132r.
12. From here on I use the values given in the text, rather than the computed values, in order to check the text.
13. I.e. the difference between the observed value of 136;14,37 and the mean motion value of 128;35,26.
14. We use the medieval form of the trigonometric functions, designated by capital letters, at this point and in the following. These are related to the modern functions by the assumption of a circle of radius 60 units instead of one unit. For example, $\text{Sin}\, x = 60 \sin x$, or, in general $\text{Sin} = R\sin$.
15. The mistake in the text is due to a computational error committed in the first step, namely $[(4;26,36)/5;17,25)] \times 60 = 50;24,55,34$, and not 50;27,26,25 as in the text. Arcsin (50;27,26,25), however, is indeed 57;14,28 as given in the text.
16. This means that the textual variant 2;34,36 for ζ is a scribal error.

IV. Theory and Observation

THEORY AND OBSERVATION IN ISLAMIC ASTRONOMY: THE WORK OF IBN AL-SHĀṬIR OF DAMASCUS

GEORGE SALIBA, Columbia University

Introduction

I am aware of only one study that is especially devoted to the relationship between theory and astronomical observations in medieval times, namely an article of Bernard Goldstein, which discusses mainly the works of Levi Ben Gerson (1288-1344).[1] Of the other medieval astronomers, especially those writing in Arabic, only a few have been studied; and that was done specifically in terms of their reaction to Ptolemaic astronomy. Furthermore, the study of the works of these astronomers has centred around the models for planetary motions that these astronomers proposed as alternatives to the Ptolemaic models, and has not, as far as I know, been concerned with the relationship between the models and the observations on which those models may have been based. The following paper attempts to fill this gap by concentrating on the works of the Damascene astronomer Ibn al-Shāṭir (d. 1375).

The Observational Activities of Ibn al-Shāṭir

Of all the surviving works of Ibn al-Shāṭir, the only one useful for our discussion is the one he published under the title *Nihāyat al-Sūl fī Taṣḥīḥ al-Uṣūl* (The Final Quest Concerning the Rectification of Principles).[2] In this book, Ibn al-Shāṭir laid down the details of what he considered to be a true theoretical formulation of a set of planetary models describing planetary motions, and actually intended as alternatives to the Ptolemaic models. The observational data for these models were supposed to have been discussed in Ibn al-Shāṭir's *Taᶜlīq al-Arṣād* (Discourse on Observations), no copy of which has as yet been found, and hence is presumed to be lost.

But despite the loss of the *Taᶜlīq*, there are enough indications in the extant *Nihāya* to give us a glimpse of the attitude of Ibn al-Shāṭir to the relationship between theory and observation in astronomy. The fact that he had conducted his own astronomical observations is quite clear from his statements in the *Nihāya* (referred to below), his later *Zīj* (Astronomical Handbook), and from the parameters that he finally adopted for the dimensions of his models and for the computations of the planetary tables in his *Zīj*.[3]

In the introductory chapter of the *Nihāya*, while discussing the general principles of Ptolemaic astronomy, he says: "Some of the verifiers of this science have enunciated some theoretical [*yaqīnīya*] doubts concerning those principles [i.e. Ptolemy's], while we enunciated other doubts that we based on observations [*waqafnā ᶜalaihā bi-l-raṣd*] and the like" (fol. lv).[4] The contrast is clearly between those astronomers who have raised doubts against the Ptolemaic principles using philosophical arguments, which Ibn al-Shāṭir refers to as *yaqīnīya* (which could also mean 'certain' in the sense that they are demonstrable from accepted premises), and Ibn al-Shāṭir who claims to have used the results of his observations for that purpose, with observation being accepted as a principle with the same validity as the other theoretical principles.

In the chapter devoted to the objections and doubts that Ibn al-Shāṭir himself had concerning the accepted astronomy (i.e. Ptolemaic astronomy), he says: "As for the Sun having an epicycle, that is acceptable. But that did not match with accurate observations as you will see below in the configuration [i.e. the model *hay'a*] of the Sun, for we have found the solar anomaly [literally 'variation', *ikhtilāf*], which is the equation, not in agreement with accurate observations at the midpoints of the zodiacal belt" (fol. 3r). This is a crucial passage for two main reasons. First, it establishes beyond doubt that Ibn al-Shāṭir had no philosophical objection to the epicyclic solar model of Ptolemy. This is an important statement, for it will explain later why the solar model of Ibn al-Shāṭir should not be understood as a philosophical refinement of the Ptolemaic model, but should rather be considered as being necessitated by observation. Second, this statement also confirms Ibn al-Shāṭir's use of the so-called *fuṣūl* method for solar observations. This method of observing the Sun at the midpoints of the seasons, i.e. at Taurus 15, Leo 15, Scorpio 15, and Aquarius 15,[5] where the solar declination would markedly change from one day to the next, was probably first devised sometime during the ninth century in direct response to the inaccurate method used by Ptolemy to observe the Sun at the solstices where, for a few days, the variation of the solar declination is minimal.[6] The main results derived from these observations, however, were the solar eccentricity (and thus the maximum equation of the Sun), and the position of the solar apogee.

Although we have no further details of Ibn al-Shāṭir's use of this method, we can be certain that he actually used it, for we know from the text of the *Nihāya* that he used a new parameter for the maximum equation of the Sun, namely 2;2,6°[7] (obviously derived from observations because it is different from the values given by Ptolemy and other later astronomers), and maintained that according to his observations the solar apogee moved at a different rate from precession.[8] The latter result is also derived from observation for it is not only contrary to Ptolemaic theory where the solar apogee is fixed at Gemini 5;30°, but also contrary to the theories of Ibn al-Shāṭir's own contemporaries who thought that the solar apogee moved at the same speed as precession.

If the parameters for the solar model were only the eccentricity and the position of the solar apogee, then Ibn al-Shāṭir would have been satisfied by adopting the Ptolemaic model (after correcting both values by his new observations). But, as we will see below, the theory of lunar eclipses seems to have given him an observable value for the apparent size of the solar disk, which Ptolemy takes to be 0;31,20° and invariable at all geocentric distances of the Sun. Therefore, a viable model for the Sun should consider the apparent diameter of the Sun, especially in that it is later to be compared to the apparent diameter of the Moon at its various geocentric distances, and consequently to the apparent radius of the shadow cast by the Earth during eclipses. A problem related to that has to do with the relative distances of the two luminaries, and consequently the relative distances of the other planets.[9]

Moreover, if the motion of the solar apogee is to be attributed to a specific sphere, and since it was found to be different from the precessional motion of the fixed stars in the eighth sphere, then the solar model must also include a special sphere that will move the whole configuration of the Sun by an amount equal to the motion of the apogee. As we will see below, Ibn al-Shāṭir called this sphere *the encompassing orb*. The fact that he had to do that specifically to meet the requirements of observation is clear from his statement: "The repeated accurate observations have confirmed that the motion of the apogee is faster than the motion of the eighth [sphere]. It was therefore necessary to add another orb which would move the apogee with the observed motion" (fol. 10r).

But this additional orb was still insufficient to account for the observational results that Ibn al-Shāṭir had reached. At that point, and just before he proposes his new model for the Sun, he says: "If it were assumed that the Sun had a parecliptic, an epicycle, and another orb to move the apogee, still the computation according to this principle [*aṣl*] would not match with the accurate observations, because we had observed [at] the midpoints of the quarters of the zodiacal signs [i.e. the mid-seasons] again and found that [i.e. the result] to be different from the computations carried out according to this principle. We demonstrated that in *Taᶜlīq al-arṣād*. We therefore needed a simple configuration [*aṣl*] that would match the observations, and God, may He be gratefully acknowledged, has granted us success in [finding] a configuration that would meet the requirement as you shall see, God willing" (fol. 10r). What this means is that the Ptolemaic model for the Sun, together with the modifications for the eccentricity and the solar apogee, were found wanting, and Ibn al-Shāṭir was obliged to devise a new model that would meet the new requirements. The critical observation that may have discouraged him from adopting a modified Ptolemaic model must have been the apparent size of the Sun, a parameter that was apparently determined from lunar eclipse observations.

The fact that Ibn al-Shāṭir took his observations seriously is further confirmed by his judgement of the theory of trepidation (a theory proposing that the equinoxes oscillate back and forth along the ecliptic and which could therefore account for the variation between the rate of precession inherited from Antiquity and that found in medieval times). The various mechanisms that were proposed in medieval times, and which could account for trepidation, do not concern us here. Rather, we emphasize the revealing attitude of Ibn al-Shāṭir who would have had no difficulty with the complexities of these mechanisms had they matched the observations. In a short remark, in the introductory section of the *Nihāya*, he says: "The motion of trepidation [*ḥarakat al-iqbāl wa-l-idbār*] is not sound, because it contradicts what was found to be true in ancient and modern observations. In addition, it is a false conception [*taṣawwur kādhib*]; this despite the fact that it would have been possible to imagine [*taṣawwur*] a setting of spheres that would produce this motion, provided it existed in reality [*kāna lahā ḥaqīqa*]" (fol. 3v). It is interesting to note that Ibn al-Shāṭir considers the observations to be, at least in this case, the arbiters of truth (*ḥaqīqa*).

In another context, in the discussion of the lunar model, one can further illustrate Ibn al-Shāṭir's regard for observations by referring to a short passage in his *Nihāya* which, as far as I know, has not been studied by modern writers. The ingenious lunar model of Ibn al-Shāṭir, described about two decades ago by Victor Roberts,[10] has been used to justify reference to Ibn al-Shāṭir as "a pre-Copernican Copernicus", merely because the Copernican lunar model was essentially identical to that of Ibn al-Shāṭir. But the crucial importance of Ibn al-Shāṭir's new model to our discussion of theory and observation has not been, as far as I know, duly analysed. In doing so, we assume the reader is familiar with the Ptolemaic lunar model.[11]

The empirical observation that would have shaken the Ptolemaic model for the Moon, would have been the obvious naked-eye observation of the Moon at quadrature, because, according to Ptolemy's model for the Moon, the Moon should then appear to be almost twice as large as when it is full or when it is in conjunction with the Sun. Anyone considering the apparent size of the Moon at quadrature and at opposition, could easily note the defect of the Ptolemaic model, for the Moon does not seem to change its size by any appreciable amount between these two positions, namely quadrature and opposition. The silence of most medieval astronomers about this discrepancy, especially the so-called Maraghah School astronomers who were proposing alternative models to those of Ptolemy, has led to the now-prevailing opinion that all these alternative models were actually motivated by philosophical considerations only. Even Ibn al-Shāṭir's model itself, which corrects the grossly overestimated distance in the Ptolemaic model at quadrature, has never been seen in that light, as far as I know, and it was assumed to be another philosophically motivated model like the other Maraghah School models.

The passage in the *Nihāya* that confirms Ibn al-Shāṭir's attention to observations and specifically to this discrepancy in the Ptolemaic lunar model is contained in the part of the text where Ibn al-Shāṭir is simply listing the mistakes of his predecessors, including Ptolemy. In his own words: "The alignment of the diameter of the epicycle with a centre other than that of its deferent is impossible [*muḥāl*], for on account of it the motion of the epicycle would be non-uniform, and it would then have two motions: one uniform, and one non-uniform. The non-uniform would not complete the revolution, and that is [also] impossible. It [i.e. the model of Ptolemy] [also] requires that the diameter of the Moon should be twice as large at quadrature than at the beginning, which is impossible, because it was not *seen* as such [*lam yura kadhālika*]" (fol. 3r, emphasis mine).

There is no doubt therefore that Ibn al-Shāṭir considered the problem of the apparent size of the Moon as one of the defects of the Ptolemaic model. Furthermore, his new alternative model not only solved the problem of the motion of the spheres that produce the motion of the Moon in longitude and latitude, without violating the accepted principles of uniform motion, but also corrected for the discrepancy in the apparent size of the Moon at quadrature. Only a cynic could still argue that, despite the explicit criticism of the Ptolemaic model on the issue of the apparent size of the Moon at quadrature, Ibn al-Shāṭir's model corrected for that discrepancy only incidentally, and was motivated not by that observational consideration but rather by the philosophical debate that seems to have motivated the other astronomers, especially those of the Maraghah School.

The decisive text that should have answered the cynics long ago is actually the curious solar model of Ibn al-Shāṭir,[12] because in the case of the Sun, the Ptolemaic model was acceptable to all medieval astronomers, including the Maraghah astronomers, since neither of its two principles – as the eccentric or the epicyclic alternative models described in the *Almagest* would have been referred to – violated uniform motion. The question is then, why would Ibn al-Shāṭir alone propose a new model for the Sun?

Ibn al-Shāṭir's Solar Model

We have seen above that Ibn al-Shāṭir used his own observations to determine a new eccentricity for the solar model (thus yielding a new maximum equation of 2;2,6°), and a new rate of motion for the solar apogee, which he found to be different from precession. We also saw that both of these new findings could have been satisfied by adopting a modified Ptolemaic model that had the new eccentricity and an additional encompassing sphere to move the solar apogee. That would not have required any epicycles additional to the one already proposed in the *Almagest*. We also remarked above that, according to Ibn al-Shāṭir, the solar model must include the apparent size of the solar disk as an additional observational parameter. In what follows, I will describe what I believe Ibn al-Shāṭir had in mind when he constructed his solar model. The observational variables that had to be accounted for, and which I believe Ibn al-Shāṭir verified, were simply: the solar eccentricity, the position and motion of the solar apogee (both determinable from repeated observations of the Sun using the *fuṣūl* method), and the apparent size of the solar disk.

We have also seen above that Ptolemy had assumed the apparent size of the solar disk to be invariable at all geocentric distances of the Sun, namely 0;31,20°. In addition to this approximation, there were also the faulty numbers associated with Ptolemy's grossly underestimated real geocentric distance of the Sun. As a result of that, at least two medieval astronomers, namely Jābir Ibn Aflaḥ (fl. 1150) and ᶜUrḍī (d. 1266), argued against Ptolemy's order of the planets and, by using Ptolemy's own figures, defended an order in which Venus was to be placed above the Sun. Without going into great detail at this point, we simply note that Ptolemy's estimate for the apparent size of the solar disk, and his computation of the actual geocentric distance of the two luminaries, were both crucial for the solution of other problems and were themselves unsatisfactory, and thus had to be redetermined from new observations.

Ibn al-Shāṭir must have seen the significance of this new program of research, and must have tried to correct the Ptolemaic values. In his *Nihāya*, he says: "Its [i.e. the Sun's] diameter, at mean distance is, according to Hipparchus 0;32,45 [degrees], the Indians 0;32,33, the moderns 0;32,35, while according to Ptolemy, at all its distances, it is 0;31,20. What I have verified by observation [*al-ladhī taḥarrara ᶜindī bi-l-raṣd*] is 0;32,32" (fol. 12v). In another place, while discussing the related problem of the apparent lunar diameter and the diameter of the Earth's shadow, he says:

> The shadow's diameter is, according to Ptolemy, two and three-fifths times the size of the lunar diameter [at mean distance]. But, by using

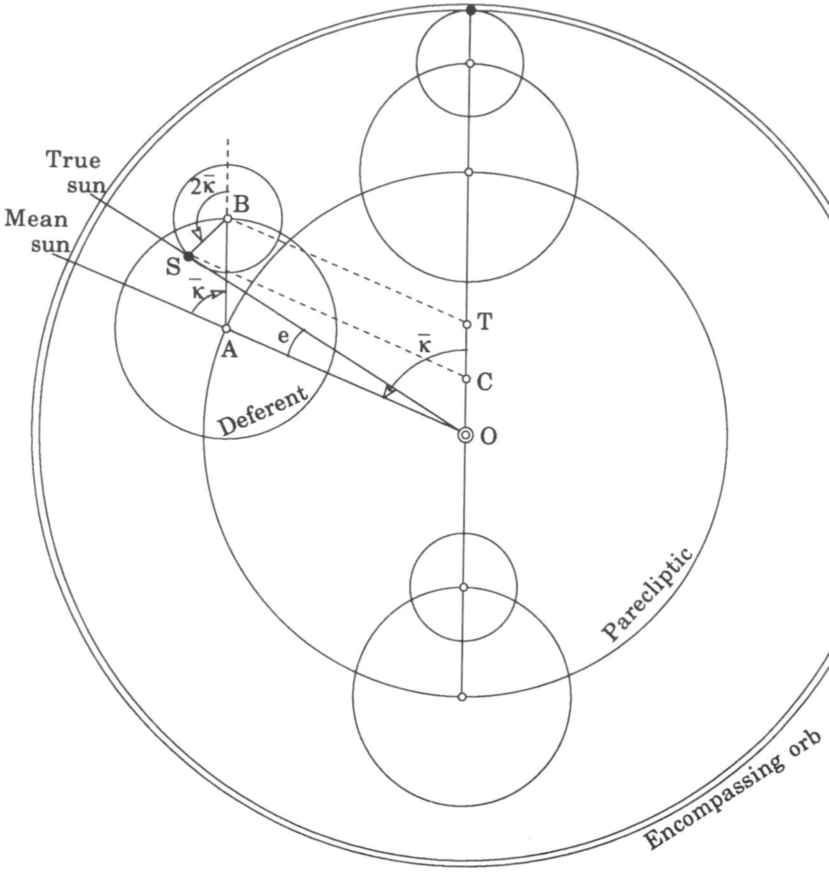

FIG 1.

several old and recent eclipse observations, I found it to be two and a half and one fifth [times the size of the lunar diameter], if we compute with the assumption that the maximum latitude of the Moon is five degrees. But if we compute with the assumption that it is four and two-thirds and one fourth of a degree [i.e. 4;55°], then it would be two and two-thirds times the size of the lunar diameter. [And that is] because we found the duration of eclipses to be more than what would be required by computation, if it were assumed [as Ptolemy did] that the diameter of the shadow was equal to two and three-fifths times the size of the lunar diameter (fol. 17v).

These statements indicate that Ibn al-Shāṭir may have tested the Ptolemaic value for the apparent size of the solar disk by using lunar eclipse observations. Unfortunately, Ibn al-Shāṭir must have recorded these observations, and the derivation of the final parameters necessitated by them, in his non-extant work the *Taᶜlīq*. In the *Nihāya*, and in at least two places (fols 12v, 41r), he gave only the final results for the apparent size of the solar diameter:

at apogee	0;29,5°
at mean distance	0;32,32°
at perigee	0;36,55°.

In a separate study, the present author discusses the methods used in the computations of these parameters and their effects on the theory of planetary distances.[13] For our present purposes, we assume that Ibn al-Shāṭir must have convinced himself that he had reached much finer observational results than those of Ptolemy, and thus had to construct a solar model that accommodated these results. At this point, it becomes clear why the Ptolemaic solar model, even with minor adjustments, could not account for all the observations, and in particular could not accommodate the greater observed variations in the apparent size of the solar diameter, which in turn entailed greater variations in the geocentric distances of the Sun.

According to Ibn al-Shāṭir's observations, the implications for the geocentric distances of the Sun are such that the ratio of the distance at perigee to that at apogee should be the same as

$$(0;29,5) \,/\, (0;36,55) = 0.78781,$$

which is quite different from the result predicted by the Ptolemaic model, 57;30 / 62;30 = 0.92 (and taken by Ptolemy to be close enough to unity, and thus negligible in terms of its effects on the apparent solar diameter).

Ibn al-Shāṭir had therefore to devise a solar model that would retain the valid property of the Ptolemaic model (i.e., predict the longitude of the Sun reasonably well), but at the same time would accommodate the new observational variations in the apparent size of the solar diameter, and the new maximum solar equation which he says was 2;2,6° (fol. llr). To do that, he assumed (see Figure 1) the following orbs for the solar model: (1) An orb of radius 60 parts, which he called *the parecliptic*, concentric with the observer at point *O*, the centre of the world, and moving in the direction of the signs at the same speed as the daily mean motion of the Sun, namely 0;59,8,9,51,46,57,32,3° per day; this parecliptic orb carries another smaller one (2), called *the deferent*, of radius 4;37 parts in the units that make the radius of the first orb 60 parts. The second orb moves on its own centre at the same speed as the first, but in the opposite direction, thus keeping line *AB* always parallel to *OCT* and having the same effect as transferring the eccentricity *OT* to an epicycle with centre *A* (as in Figure 1). (3) The third orb, called *the director*, of radius 2;30, is carried by the deferent in a direction opposite to that of the signs, but moves on its own centre in the opposite direction at twice the speed of the first orb. That last orb carries the body of the Sun *S*, which now seems, according to ᶜUrḍī's lemma,[14] to be moving at uniform speed around point *C*. Finally, all of these orbs are embedded within a final orb (4) called *the encompassing one* (*al-Shāmil*), that moves at the same speed as the solar apogee, in the direction of the signs, which was found to be 1°/60 Persian years.

The effect of this model is to allow the Sun *S* to move uniformly around point *C*, i.e. eccentricity *OC* = 4;37 − 2;30 = 2;7 which is close to the Ptolemaic eccentricity of 2;30, and thus predicts longitudes very close to those predicted by the Ptolemaic model (to be corrected later by the different solar equation of Ibn al-Shāṭir). As was already noted by Neugebauer[15] this model allows the Sun to have its own equant *C*, so to speak, by fixing the model so that the Sun would look as if it is describing uniform motion around point *C*, which is neither the position of the observer nor the centre of the deferent. But unlike the Ptolemaic model, that of Ibn al-Shāṭir allows for a variation in the apparent size of the solar disk of magnitude

$$52;53 \; / \; 67;7 = 0.7879,$$

which is very close to the value predicted by the observations of the apparent size of the solar diameter. Ibn al-Shāṭir adds that his model possesses a further advantage in that the mean motion (in this case that of the parecliptic orb) is around the observer *O*, and not around the centre of the eccentric as would have been required by the Ptolemaic model.

Conclusion

This solar model of Ibn al-Shāṭir seems to have been the only one of the models devised by the Maraghah astronomers that can be shown to have been motivated by a genuine concern for observational data, and that seems to have been constructed specifically for that purpose. Otherwise, the Ptolemaic model, in its simple eccentric or epicyclic form, would not have been philosophically objectionable to Ibn al-Shāṭir, as it was not objectionable to his predecessors from Ibn al-Haytham to Quṭb al-Dīn al-Shīrāzī. If that concern for observations is genuine, and there is every reason to believe so for otherwise the motivation for the solar model is inexplicable, then we should conclude that Ibn al-Shāṭir's observation concerning the defect of the Ptolemaic lunar model, in regard to the apparent size of the lunar diameter at quadrature, was similarly motivated, and was instrumental in his construction of the model that he finally adopted where such an empirical absurdity as the lunar size at quadrature is corrected.

REFERENCES

1. Bernard Goldstein, "Theory and observation in medieval astronomy", *Isis*, lxiii (1972), 39-47.
2. The present author has completed a working edition of this book based on all the manuscripts known to be extant, and is currently engaged in preparing a critical edition to be sent to the press soon.
3. For a synopsis of the contents of this *Zīj*, and the parameters underlying its tables, refer to E. S. Kennedy, "A survey of Islamic astronomical tables", *Transactions of the American Philosophical Society*, xlvi (1956), 162-4.
4. The manuscript quoted here for reference is Arabic Marsh 139 of the Bodleian Library, Oxford. The author wishes to thank the Keeper of Oriental Books at this library, and all other librarians who have supplied the microfilms necessary for this study.
5. For a discussion of this method, and its possible early use, see O. Neugebauer, "Thabit ben Qurra 'On the solar year' and 'On the motion of the eighth sphere' ", *Proceedings of the American Philosophical Society*, cvi (1962), 264-99.
6. Medieval astronomers devised other methods as well, such as the one using only three solar observations, two of them in opposition, at points on the zodiac where the solar declination varies sensibly from one day to the next. See G. Saliba, "Solar observations at the Maraghah Observatory before 1275: A new set of parameters", *Journal for the history of astronomy*, xvi (1985), 113-22, and *idem*, "The determination of the solar eccentricity and

apogee according to Mu'ayyad al-Dīn al- ʿUrḍī (d. 1266)", *Zeitschrift für Geschichte der Arabisch-Islamischen Wissenschaften*, ii (1986), 47-67.

7. Sexagesimal fractions written in this form mean (here, for example) $2 + 2/60 + 6/60^2$.
8. *Cf.* fols 6r and 8v for precession value being 1°/70 Persian years, where he says *ḥaqqaqt*[u] *dhālika bi-l-raṣd*, and fol. 10v for the motion of the apogee as being 1°/60 Persian years.
9. We cannot discuss this very complicated problem here, nor could we survey the medieval literature that this problem had given rise to. The reader should consult N. Swerdlow, "Ptolemy's theory of the distances and sizes of the planets: A study of the scientific foundations of medieval cosmology" (unpublished Ph.D. diss., Yale University, 1968), and B. Goldstein and N. Swerdlow, "Planetary distances and sizes in an anonymous Arabic treatise preserved in Bodleian Ms Marsh 621", *Centaurus*, xv (1970-71), 135-70.
10. Victor Roberts, "The solar and lunar theory of Ibn al-Shāṭir: A pre-Copernican Copernican model", *Isis*, xlvii (1957), 428-32.
11. For a brief description of the model, *cf.* O. Neugebauer, *The exact sciences in Antiquity* (Providence, R.I., 1957), 193-7.
12. Roberts, *op. cit.*
13. This study will include an analysis of the numerical methods given in Ibn al-Shāṭir's astronomical handbook (Bodleian Seld., A. 30, fols 83r-84r), and their effect on the determination of planetary sizes and distances.
14. In general terms, a paraphrase of ʿUrḍī's Lemma states: If two equal lines are erected on the same side of a straight line, such that they produce two equal angles with the straight line, be they corresponding or interior, then the line connecting the extremities of the two equal lines will be parallel to the first straight line (*Kitāb al-Hay'a*, Bodleian Library, Ms. Arabic Marsh 621, fol. 158r). In Figure 2 line *GD* is always parallel to *AB*, if *AG* and *BD* are equal

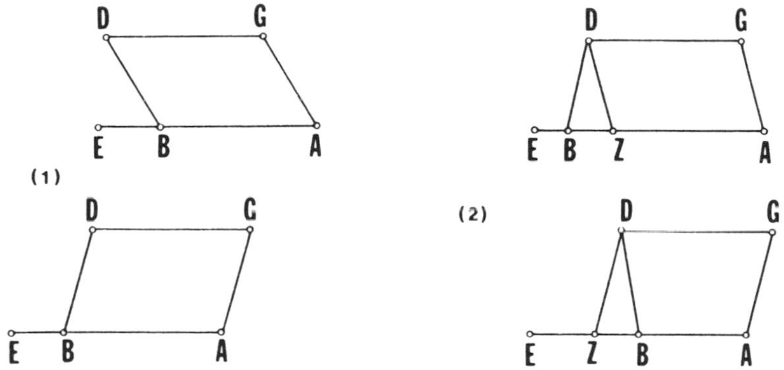

FIG 2.

and describe equal angles with respect to line *AB*. The proof is straightforward; both when the corresponding angles *DBE* and *GAB*, or the interior angles *DBA* and *GAB* are equal, since with the construction of line *DZ* parallel to *AG*, both cases become identical and require only *Elements* I, 27-33 to be proved.

15. O. Neugebauer, "On the planetary theory of Copernicus", *Vistas in astronomy*, x (1968), 89-103, esp. pp. 95-96, and p. 96 n.1.

V. Arabic Astronomy and Copernicus

THE RÔLE OF MARAGHA IN THE DEVELOPMENT OF ISLAMIC ASTRONOMY : A SCIENTIFIC REVOLUTION BEFORE THE RENAISSANCE

INTRODUCTION

Research conducted in the History of Arabic astronomy, within the last three decades, has brought to light a group of texts, that were hitherto unknown, and which radically altered our conception of the originality and scope of Arabic astronomy. The works of astronomers such as Mu'ayyad al-Dīn al-ʿUrḍī (d. 1266), Naṣīr al-Dīn al-Ṭūsī (d. 1274), Quṭb al-Dīn al-Shīrāzī (d. 1311), and Ibn al-Shāṭir (d. 1375), to name only a few, were barely known in the nineteenth century or in the early part of the present century. Only Ṭūsī was mentioned in nineteenth-century literature, although his contribution was not even recognized. In 1893, Bernard Carra de Vaux wrote in an appendix (vi), to Paul Tannery's *Recherches*[1], in regard to Ṭūsī, that while Arabic astronomy did not hold Ptolemy's work with much regard, it did not on its own have enough « *génie* » to transform astronomy altogether. Subsequent research has shown that de Vaux, armed with his own prearranged concepts of

1. Paul TANNERY, *Recherches sur l'histoire de l'astronomie ancienne*, Paris, Gauthier, 1893, p. 337-361. The only text of ʿUrḍī that was known in the early part of this century was the one that he wrote on the instruments which he built at Maragha as the engineer of that observatory. See, e.g. Hugo J. SEEMAN, « Die Instrumente der Sternwarte zu *Maragha* nach den Mitteilungen von al-ʿUrḍī », *Sitzungsberichte der Physikalisch—Medizinischen Sozietät zu Erlangen, 60,* 1928, p. 15-126.

periodization of science, could not see the originality in what later came to be known as the most original chapter of Ṭūsī's astronomy, despite the fact that de Vaux had actually taken the trouble to translate it. In this chapter, for example, Ṭūsī proved a very ingenious theorem, namely that simple harmonic motion could be obtained as a result of allowing two circles — the radius of one of them being twice the size of that of the other — to move one inside the other with the inner circle moving at twice the angular velocity of the outer one and in the opposite direction. These two circles, which were called by Edward S. Kennedy the « Ṭūsī Couple »[2], were used by most astronomers who came after Ṭūsī up to and including Copernicus.

An assessment similar to that of de Vaux was offered a few years later when François Nau translated the major astronomical work of Bar Hebraeus[3], and completely misunderstood the significance of two sections in that work, namely sections 6 of chapters three and four of part I[4], simply because, he too, was under a frame of mind that did not expect to find anything original in those medieval works, which were in no way comparable to the works of the Renaissance. While de Vaux had concluded that Arabic science could not develop any further than it did simply because of its « *faiblesse* », and « *mesquinerie* », Nau, on the other hand, had the following to say when evaluating the work of Bar Hebraeus and his Arab colleagues of the thirteenth century :

> « Au XIIe [*sic,* read XIII, A. D. 1279] siècle, à l'époque où écrivait Bar-Hebraeus, les Arabes s'occupaient d'astronomie depuis près de quatre siècles et notre auteur cite un certain nombre de leurs résultats ; mais ces résultats semblent peu importants ; les auteurs arabes que nous connaissons furent surtout des commentateurs et des astrologues amateurs, on ne les a admirés que faute de connaître les œuvres grecques, leurs modèles. On peut donc considérer le présent *Cours d'astronomie* comme un résumé des œuvres de Ptolémée (avec quelques *adjuncta* dus aux Arabes)... »[5].

This general underestimation of the rôle of Arabic astronomy also colored the thinking of J. L. E. Dreyer, who wrote towards the beginning

---

2. See Edward S. KENNEDY, « Late Medieval Planetary Theory », *Isis, 57,* 1966, p. 365-378, esp. p. 370.

3. François NAU, *Le Livre de l'ascension de l'esprit*, Paris, Bouillon, 1899.

4. *Ibid.* : in these chapters, Bar Hebraeus discussed the contradictions in the Ptolemaic system pertaining to the model of the Moon and the equant of the upper planets. It is true that he did not elaborate his criticism enough, nor did he offer new models as alternatives to the Ptolemaic ones, but he was reporting on the status of these problems as he understood them from the Maragha astronomers. In a forthcoming article, the present author plans to discuss the relationship between these sections in Bar Hebraeus's work and the works of the Maragha astronomers.

5. *Ibid.*, p. xiv.

of this century. The same prejudices and preconceptions prevented Dreyer from appreciating the real significance of the material that was known to him, despite the fact that he showed a great ingenuity in pulling this material together and in bringing some coherence to ideas that were scattered among various obscure publications [6].

The model that explained the development of Arabic astronomy and which prevailed until the middle of the present century was essentially that of an astronomy that was only a translation of Greek astronomical works, and, at best, did not go beyond the mere summarizing of Greek works. Therefore one studied this tradition expressly to recapture the Greek texts, which were indeed the object of the admiration that Nau had so clearly expressed. Viewed from this perspective Arabic astronomy was perceived as an intermediary that had translated the Greek works between the ninth and the eleventh century, which had preserved this Greek tradition, in order to pass it on to Europe during the twelfth and thirteenth centuries, when Europe was ready to develop its own medieval science. The assumption then, was that once this tradition was handed over to Europe, Arabic astronomy receded from center stage to pass into oblivion, while the real developments were left to take place in Europe, thus leading to one revolution after another independent of any outside agent.

The prevailing periodization could then be summarized along the following stages : (1) the translation stage, when Greek astronomy passed into Arabic, and that seems to have been understood as *just* a translation stage ; (2) a stage of additional minor commentaries of a type that Nau called *adjuncta* to Greek astronomy ; and finally (3) a stage of general decline in Arabic scientific creativity, which must have started sometime during the twelfth century just as Europe was in the process of acquiring the Greek heritage, especially the astronomical and mathematical one, through the translations from Arabic into Latin. From then on, there was no longer any need to pay attention to the Arabic tradition, for Europe was developing science on its own.

This essay will attempt to establish that the prevalent model, which is used to explain the development of Arabic astronomy is essentially ahistorical because it neglects or misunderstands three major facts. (1) It fails to understand the nature of the translation period that took place in stage one. (2) This model totally misrepresents the real developments within the Arabic astronomical tradition itself because it neglects the creative

6. John Louis Emil DREYER. *History of the Planetary Systems from Thales to Kepler*, Cambridge, 1906 (repr. N. Y., Dover, 1953 as *A History of Astronomy from Thales to Kepler*).

productivity that had begun as early as the ninth century, concomitantly with the translation activity, and which continued to develop, as far as astronomy is concerned, until well beyond the fifteenth century. (3) It fails to acknowledge the actual extent of the contact between European and Arabic astronomical works which has only been brought to light by the research of the last three decades or so. Once these facts are recognized and studied, the claim can then be made that we need a new periodization in Arabic astronomy, which could explain in a more coherent manner the historical circumstances of the most important transmission phase that determined the parameters of the contact between European and Arabic astronomy.

TRANSLATION PERIOD

Although we do not know yet the full significance of the early translation period when Greek scientific works were translated into Arabic due to a lack of studies devoted to such translated works as Euclid's *Elements*, or Ptolemy's *Almagest,* we still know enough to assert that this period was by no means a simple transfer of texts from one language into the other. Despite the fact that we know very little about the group of translators who worked during this period, and the conditions under which they worked, we possess enough information about two of them, namely Ḥunain Ibn Isḥāq (d. 873) and Thābit Ibn Qurra (d. 901) to assess the kind of work that these translators performed.

In the case of Ḥunain, he left a treatise in which he described his method of translation, as well as the conditions under which he worked [7]. From that treatise we learn that he sought manuscripts from a wide geographical area that covered the entire ancient Near East. Ḥunain collated the original Greek texts, i.c. edited them, before he embarked upon translating them. We also know from another source that Ḥunain would first read the sentence in an original Greek text, and then render it in Arabic in his own words as he saw fit [8]. This implies that he must have had an excellent command of the contents of such texts so well, first to understand them, and then to develop the appropriate technical terms in the target language to translate them. Work such as this could not have been developed by a translator who only commanded two languages. In fact, we also know, from Ḥunain's biography, that he had

7. See Gotthelf BERGSTRÄSSER, « Ḥunain b. Isḥāq, "Über die Syrischen und Arabischen Galenübersetzungen" », *Abhandlungen für die Kunde des Morgenlandes, 17,* 1925, II, p. 4f, n° 3.

8. AL-SAFADI, Khalil b. AYBAK, *Al-Ghaith al-musajjam,* Cairo, 1305 H., I, p. 46, transl. by Franz ROSENTHAL, *The Classical Heritage in Islam,* Berkeley, U. C. Press, 1975, p. 17.

started his career by studying medicine in Baghdad, that is, before he began translating [9]. If this information is accurate, then we must assume that there was sufficient medical knowledge available at this time, first for Ḥunain to study medicine in order to appreciate someone like Galen — for the translation of whose works be devoted nearly his entire life — and second, for there to have been enough technical knowledge in Arabic so that Ḥunain dit not have to coin new technical terms. Finally, the extant works of Ḥunain, such as his works on ophthalmology, do indeed support the thesis that translators like Ḥunain were producing original works at the same time that they were translating.

Similarly, a close study of Thābit Ibn Qurra's career reveals that he too was producing original works, such as his text on the amicable numbers, the sundials, the crescent visibility, etc., while he was correcting Isḥāq Ibn Ḥunain's translations of Euclid's *Elements*, and Ptolemy's *Almagest*.

Scientists active during the same period, who do not seem to have depended on these translation activities, further confirm the character of the creativity that was taking place at this time. The work of someone like al-Khwārizmī (c. 800-847), or Ḥabash al-Ḥāsib (c. 850), or else the Ma'mūn astronomers who produced a new set of astronomical tables correcting and updating the Ptolemaic parameters, definitely bespeak of a very active scientific environment that was yielding new results while the translations from Greek were underway. This claim can be made of scientific fields other than astronomy. Moreover, it should be remembered that this period witnessed the birth of a totally new mathematical discipline, namely *Algebra*, at the hands of Muḥammad b. Mūsā al-Khwārizmī.

During this translation period therefore, astronomy witnessed as much original creative work, as it did translated work. And if we were to assign a name to this stage of Arabic astronomy we would have to call it a period of innovation, or an upsurge in activities, during which Greek works were rendered in Arabic as they were needed, but by mature scientists who knew what they wanted from the Greek heritage. It should be born in mind that this same Greek heritage was neglected in Greek-speaking Byzantium and would have remained so if it were not resuscitated by those concerned scientists working in ninth-century Baghdad.

For our general periodization paradigm, we have to designate this stage as the background phase for what we will later refer to as a genuine revolution in astronomical activity.

---

9. See, for example, QIFṬĪ, *Ta'rīkh al-ḥukamā'*, ed. by Julius LIPPERT, Leipzig, Dieterich'sche Verlagsbuchhandlung, 1903, p. 174.

THE MARAGHA SCHOOL REVOLUTION

In order to understand the results achieved by a group of astronomers who lived after the first half of the thirteenth century, and who are now known as the « Maragha School » [10], one must review the activities that were initiated sometime during the eleventh century, if not earlier. All of these activities seem to have begun with a factual criticism of Ptolemy's *Almagest*, in which Arabic-writing astronomers managed to isolate the few parameters that were simply erroneous in the Ptolemaic text. The values for the obliquity of the ecliptic, and the precession of the fixed stars, for example, were the two glaring mistakes that were quickly rectified as early as the ninth century. Similarly, the solar apogee of the sun, which was assumed to have been fixed by Ptolemy, was also found to be tied up to precession and hence had moved by about twelve degrees. But most importantly, this early period also witnessed a critical attack on Ptolemy's methodology, as in the case of determining the length of the solar year by using the Method of Seasons [11].

To understand the new perceptions that led to the Maragha Revolution, the reader should be reminded that Ptolemy himself had described the movements of the planets, including the Sun and the Moon, as moving on epicyclic spheres which were in turn carried within the thickness of other spheres that he called deferents. In the *Almagest*, these spheres were represented by circles, and were described as though they were mathematical curves, without any attempt to coordinate their motion with the motion of physical bodies having the same shape. In the *Planetary Hypothesis*, however, Ptolemy described these spheres as physical bodies, and he made no attempt there as well to match these spheres with the mathematical circles that were supposed to describe the universe in the *Almagest*.

It was these kinds of considerations that were noted by Arabic-writing astronomers, sometime during the eleventh century, and perhaps earlier, and which led Ibn al-Haytham of Baṣra and Egypt (d. c. 1048) and the Persian Abū ᶜUbayd al-Jūzjānī (d. c. 1070) to write texts objecting specifically to that feature of Ptolemy's astronomy. According to Ibn al-Haytham, one could not assume within a physical universe that there can be a sphere that would move uniformly around an axis, which does not pass through its center. The Ptolemaic equant was therefore in direct vio-

10. The term was first introduced by Victor ROBERTS, « The Planetary Theory of Ibn al-Shāṭir », *Isis, 57,* 1966, p. 210, and was later codified by E. KENNEDY, *art. cit. supra* n. 2, p. 365.

11. Otto NEUGEBAUER, « Thābit ben Qurra "On the Solar Year" and "On The Motion of the Eighth Sphere" », *Proceedings of the American Philosophical Society,* vol. 106, 1962, p. 264-299.

lation of this rule, and that implied that the models described with great ingenuity in the *Almagest* could not be describing the real physical universe, and thus should be abandoned in favor of a better set of models, which could meet that requirement. Ibn al-Haytham reported these results in his seminal work, which became a landmark in medieval Arabic astronomy. He called his book *al-Shukūk ᶜalā Baṭlamyūs (Dubitationes in Ptolemaeum)* [12], in which he surveyed all the works of Ptolemy, and gathered together what seemed to him to be unforgivable contradictions.

The work of Abū ᶜUbayd, on the other hand, took up one specific problem in Ptolemy's astronomy, and attempted to find an alternative

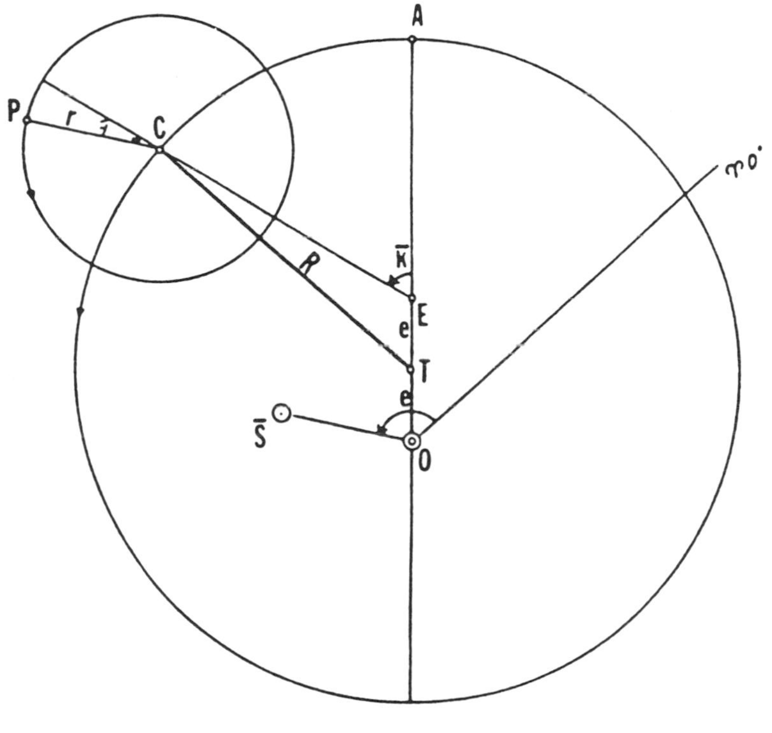

Figure 1
Ptolemy's model for the superior planets Saturn, Jupiter, and Mars, and for the inferior planet Venus. Point *C*, the center of the epicycle, moves on a deferent with center *T*, but measures equal arcs in equal times around the equant point *E* instead of the deferent center *T*.

12. See ABD AL-ḤAMĪD SABRA, Nabīl SHEHABY, *Al-Shukūk ᶜalā Baṭlamyūs (Dubitationes in Ptolemaeum)*, Cairo, National Library Press, 1971.

solution for it [13]. The problem chosen was the one that was later called the problem of the *equant*, which was an integral part of Ptolemy's model for the upper planets Saturn, Jupiter and Mars, and the lower planet Venus. In brief, the *equant* in the model required that a sphere, the deferent sphere, should move at a uniform speed around a point, which was not its center. For a physical sphere, this was an absurdity (see *Fig.* 1).

With the works of Ibn al-Haytham and Abū ᶜUbayd, the research had begun in earnest, namely on the theoretical level, by objecting to what Ptolemy had postulated, and on the practical level by attempting to offer alternative models to the Ptolemaic ones.

In the following two centuries, the center of these activities shifted to the western part of the Islamic Empire, to Andalusian Spain [14]. The names of al-Biṭrūjī (Alpetragius, c. 1200), Ibn Rushd (Averroes, 1126-1198), and Jābir Ibn Aflaḥ (Geber, c. 1200) have all been mentioned in connection with one reform of Ptolemaic astronomy or another [15]. But the most significant results, from technical and mathematical perspectives were still to be reached in the eastern part of the Empire, and sometime during the thirteenth century and thereafter.

THE THIRTEENTH CENTURY

If one were to seek a specific century that could be called the Golden Age of Arabic astronomy, one would have to chose the period stretching from the middle of the thirteenth to the middle of the fourteenth. In this century, we know of at least four attempts to resolve the Ptolemaic difficulties, that we have referred to above [16]. The alternative models for the upper planets have been conveniently summarized in one diagram, which was published by Kennedy in 1966 [17]. The only emendation to be made in that diagram is in the vector connection designated as that of Quṭb al-Dīn, for there it should be added that that vector connection was originally invented by Mu'ayyad al-Dīn al-ᶜUrḍī some forty years before Quṭb al-Dīn (see *Fig.* 2).

13. George SALIBA, « Ibn Sīnā and Abū ᶜUbayd al-Jūzjānī : The Problem of the Ptolemaic Equant », *Journal for the History of Arabic Science, 4,* 1980, p. 376-404.

14. Léon GAUTHIER, « Une réforme du système astronomique de Ptolémée », *Journal asiatique,* 10ᵉ Sér., *14,* 1909, p. 483-510.

15. Bernard GOLDSTEIN, *Al-Biṭrūjī : On The Principles of Astronomy,* New Haven, Yale, 1971.

16. For a brief review of the Ptolemaic System, see O. NEUGEBAUER, *The Exact Sciences in Antiquity,* Providence, Brown University Press, 1957, p. 191-207. For a much more detailed analysis of this system, see ID., *A History of Ancient Mathematical Astronomy,* New York, Springer, 1975, p. 21-256.

17. See E. S. KENNEDY, *art. cit. supra* n. 2, p. 367, and *Figure* 2.

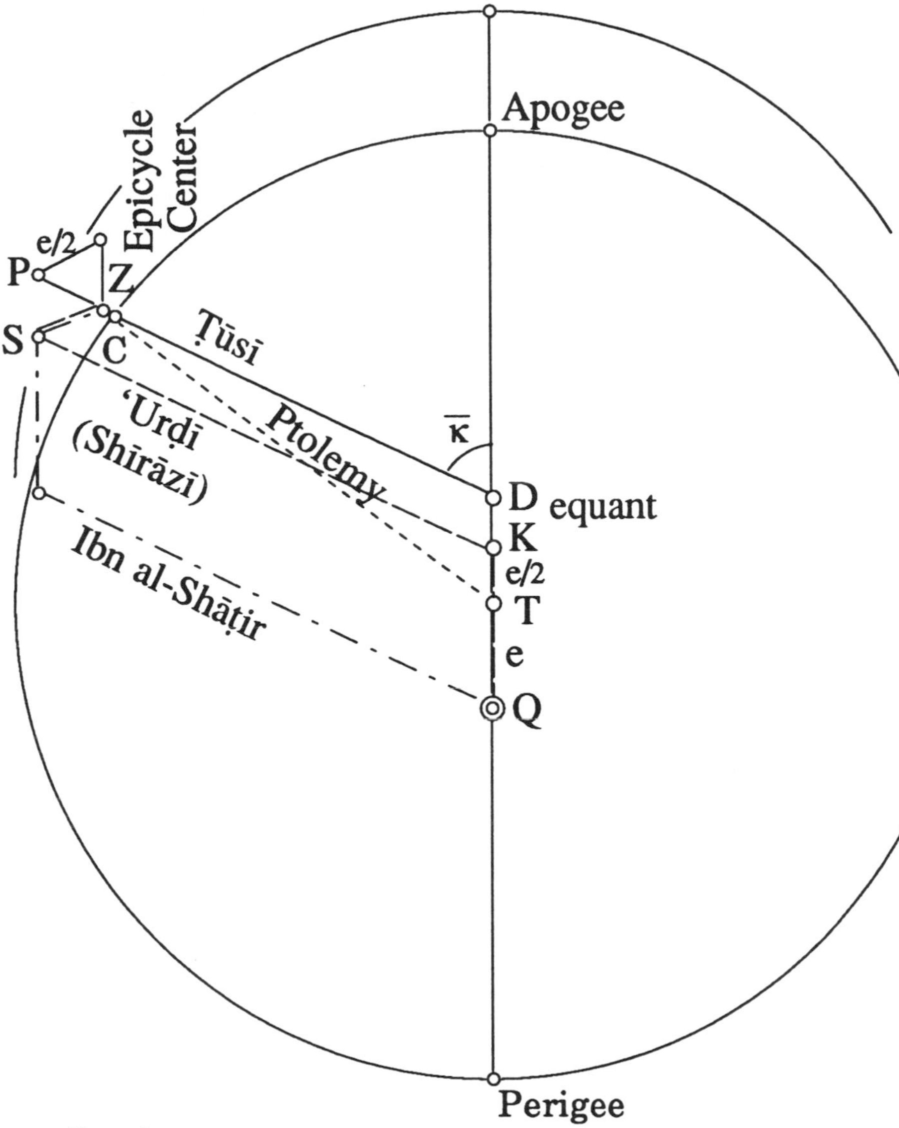

Figure 2

A summary of the models proposed by ʿUrḍī, Ṭūsī, and Ibn al-Shāṭir, all superimposed over that of Ptolemy. Note that they all produce the motion of point *Z*, the center of the epicycle, as being uniform around point *D*, the *equant*. Note also that point *Z* is very close to point *C*, Ptolemy's center of the epicycle, with a difference exaggerated simply to state that they are not identical. The earlier version of this diagram, which was published by E. S. Kennedy, *Isis, 57,* 1966, p. 367, had the vector *KS* ascribed to Quṭb al-Dīn al-Shīrāzī, and that was later shown to have been invented by ʿUrḍī some forty years earlier.

In all of the works of these astronomers, we note that the Ptolemaic observational requirements could still be maintained. At the same time, however, the motion of the planets could then be described in mathematical models that were consistent with the physical bodies, which they were supposed to represent. Most of the recent research in Arabic Planetary theories have been devoted to the works of these astronomers, designated in Kennedy's diagram. And most of the important results have been reported in the same publications quoted so far, with the exception of the results established by the present author, specifically referring to the works of ᶜUrḍī [18], and the work of a student of Ulugh Beg (c. 1450) who thus far remains unknown [19].

THE MARAGHA SCHOOL AND COPERNICUS

Beginning with an article written by Victor Roberts (*Isis*, 1957), and several others that have followed since then [20], our understanding of the rôle of Arabic astronomy has changed drastically. In 1957, Roberts showed that the lunar model of Ibn al-Shāṭir (d. 1375) was essentially identical to that of Copernicus (1473-1543), thus raising the specter of indebtedness and transmission. Since then there has been a series of articles dealing with this possible link between the works of Copernicus and what came to be known as the works of the « Maragha School » [21]. The last work to deal with Copernican astronomy, for example, concluded

18. See G. SALIBA, « The Original Source of Qūṭb al-Dīn al-Shīrazī's Planetary Model », *Journal for the History of Arabic Science, 3,* 1979, p. 3-18.

19. See ID., « Arabic Astronomy and the Critique of Ptolemy », delivered at the Wellcome Institute, Dec. 14, 1984 (forthcoming).

20. Now conveniently gathered in several places, namely, in Edward S. KENNEDY, Imad GHANEM, *The Life and Works of Ibn Al-Shāṭir,* Aleppo, Aleppo University, 1976 ; E. S. KENNEDY *et al., Studies in the Islamic Exact Sciences,* Beirut, American University of Beirut, 1983, p. 50-107. Add to that the works listed in Noel M. SWERDLOW, Otto NEUGEBAUER, *Mathematical Astronomy in Copernicus's De Revolutionibus,* New York, Springer, 1984, p. 46, n. 7, and the most recent work of the present author, « Arabic Astronomy and Copernicus », *Zeitschrift für Geschichte der Arabisch-Islamischen Wissenschaft,* vol. 1, 1985, p. 225-229.

21. See, for example, the works of E. S. Kennedy, F. Abbud, V. Roberts, now gathered in E. S. KENNEDY *et al, Studies, op. cit. supra,* p. 50-107 ; N. M. SWERDLOW, « The Derivation and First Draft of Copernicus's Planetary Theory : A Translation of the Commentariolus with Commentary », *Proceedings of the American Philosophical Society, 117,* 1973, p. 423-512 ; Willy HARTNER, « Nāṣīr al-Dīn al-Ṭūsī's Lunar Theory », *Physis, 11,* 1969, p. 287-304 ; ID., « Ptolemy, Azarquiel, Ibn al-Shāṭir, and Copernicus's Mercury Models : An Accuracy Test », *Archives internationales d'histoire des sciences, 24,* 1974, p. 5-25 ; G. SALIBA, *art. cit. supra* n. 18 ; ID., « The First Non-Ptolemaic Astronomy at the Maragha School », *Isis, 70,* 1979, p. 571-576 ; ID., *art. cit. supra* n. 13 ; ID., *art. cit. supra* n. 19.

by saying : « The question therefore is not whether, but when, where, and in what form he [i.e. Copernicus] learned of Marāgha theory » ; and : « In a very real sense, Copernicus can be looked upon as, if not the last, surely the most noted follower of the "Marāgha School" » [22].

Such, briefly, are the results reached thus far. Namely, there seems to be a dramatic similarity between the technical results reached by Copernicus, and those reached by the Maragha astronomers some two to three

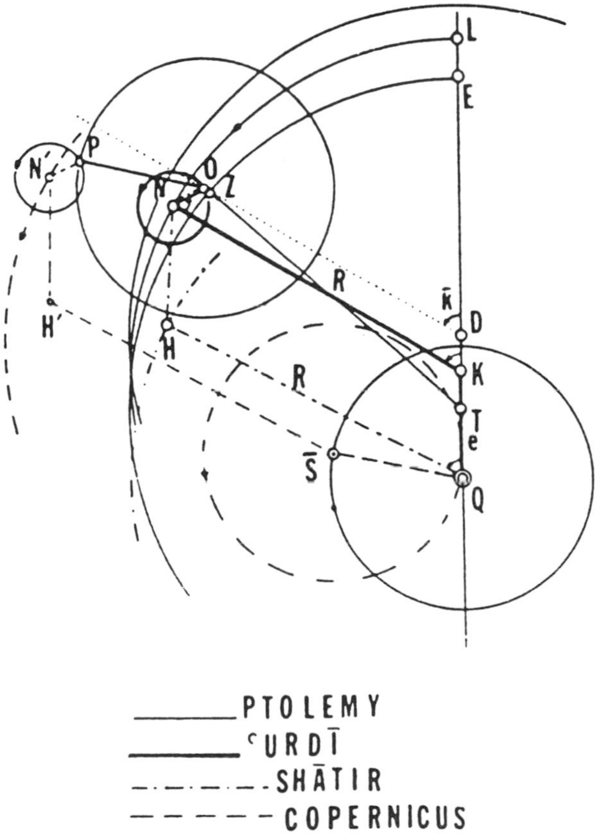

Figure 3

The four models superimposed here give the same position for planet *P* along equal and parallel vectors. The feature of dividing the Ptolemaic eccentricity $e = DT = TQ$ at point *K* was first proposed by ʿUrḍī, as far as we can now tell, and was obviously used by Copernicus as vector *NP*.

22. See N. M. Swerdlow, O. Neugebauer, *op. cit. supra* n. 20, p. 47, 295.

centuries earlier. The only distinction, of course, is the heliocentric theory of Copernicus, versus the geocentric one of the Maragha astronomers. But, mathematically speaking, and to put it in modern terminology, this reversal of the direction of the vector that connects the earth to the sun was so well known to Copernicus as to have been of no real mathematical significance. The realization that Copernicus's models are identical with those of the earlier Maragha astronomers, and the relationship of all these models to that of Ptolemy was illustrated by the present author in a separate article [23], where it was shown that for an observer on the earth *Q*, all these projected models of Ptolemy, ᶜUrḍī, Ibn al-Shāṭir, and Copernicus predicted the same position for the planet at point *P*. Note also that the adoption of the heliocentric theory, merely translates all positions into new ones along equal and parallel lines in the same direction (see *Fig*. 3).

CONCLUSION

In contrast to the results reached in the nineteenth century, modern research has shown that even Copernican astronomy cannot be very well understood, on the mathematical and technical levels, without a careful study of the achievements of the earlier Maragha astronomers. In another place, I have argued that these developments in Arabic astronomy can be viewed as a continuous tradition only among Arabic-writing astronomers, and not among Copernicus's predecessors [24]. But the real revolution in the work of the « Maragha School » astronomers lies in the philosophical dimension that was equal in importance to the mathematical and astronomical dimensions if not more so, and which was in the realization that astronomy ought to describe the behaviour of physical bodies in mathematical language, and should not remain a mathematical hypothesis, which would only save the phenomena. Most importantly, this tradition, which was not fully appreciated by de Vaux, Nau and Dreyer, did indeed face the realization that the Aristotelian division of motion in the universe as being only circular or linear was not altogether true, for one could very well produce linear motion by applying circular motion only, as in the case of the « Ṭūsī Couple » that was mentioned above.

23. See G. SALIBA, « Arabic Astronomy and Copernicus », *art. cit. supra* n. 20, p. 215-229, esp. p. 228.
24. *Ibid.*

To recast the chronological periodization of Islamic astronomy, one would have to expand the stages of original production to include the span from the ninth to the fifteenth century. This period had several peaks of various heights ; the most important was the one that took place during the thirteenth and the fourteenth centuries, and which we have described as the Maragha Revolution.

Within the general scope of the history of astronomy, the Maragha Revolution is on the one hand a natural climax to the activities that took place between the ninth and the twelfth century, but, on the other hand, an essential link to Copernican astronomy without which Copernican astronomy will be hard to explain.

George SALIBA,
Columbia University.

THE ASTRONOMICAL TRADITION OF MARAGHA: A HISTORICAL SURVEY AND PROSPECTS FOR FUTURE RESEARCH

GEORGE SALIBA

To: 2;31 ≠ e

INTRODUCTION

Ever since the discovery in 1957 of *Nihāyat al-Sūl fī Taṣḥīh al-Uṣūl*[1] of Ibn al-Shāṭir of Damascus (d. 1375), the most remarkable aspect of Arabic atronomy has been the one dealing with the recovery of the revolutionary astronomical results reached by a group of medieval astronomers commonly referred to as the Maragha School.

The crucial issue with regard to the identity and background of the Maragha School members was already raised by Ibn al-Shāṭir in his introduction to the *Nihāyat al-Sūl*, just mentioned. The names of al-Majrīṭī (d. 1007), Jābir Ibn Aflaḥ (12th cent.), Mu'ayyad al-Din al-'Urḍī (d. 1266), Naṣīr al-Dīn al-Ṭūsī (d. 1274), and Quṭb al-Dīn al-Shīrāzī (d. 1311) were all mentioned by Ibn al-Shāṭir as having produced astronomical models that were different from the standard Greek Ptolemaic models. Other astronomers such as Ibn al-Haytham (d. *c.* 1040), al-Walīd al-Maghribī (i.e. Abū al-Walīd ibn Rushd?) (d. 1195), and Yaḥyā Ibn Abī al-Shukr al-Maghribī (d. 1283) were also noted in the introduction of another of Ibn al-Shāṭir's later astronomical works *al-Zīj al-Jadīd* (The New Astronomical Handbook) as having criticized the Ptolemaic models. Some of the works of these forerunners of Ibn al-Shāṭir have been identified and partially studied, while others have yet to be located and discussed. As far as I know, works of astronomers who were similarly critical of Ptolemy and were either contemporary or posterior to Ibn al-Shāṭir have thus far received very little attention, if any.

[1] The *Ultimate Quest regarding the Rectification of [Astronomical] Principles.* A critical edition of this text using all the extant manuscripts is now completed by the present author. There exists an English translation based on one manuscript, completed by Victor Roberts more than twenty years ago but never published. A new comprehensive translation of the critically edited text and a commentary on the whole work are now in preparation by the present author.

I would like to describe here the status of our knowledge regarding the Maragha School astronomers, outline the most important results recovered so far, and then suggest a course of future research. I hope to demonstrate that the most important statement that can be made at this time about this revolutionary development in Arabic astronomy is that it was neither limited to Maragha, in northwestern Iran, from which the school takes its name, nor confined to the thirteenth and the fourteenth centuries, but that it was the main feature of Arabic astronomical research stretching at least from the eleventh to the sixteenth century.

THE MARAGHA SCHOOL STUDIES

In what follows, I describe in some detail the present status of research on the Maragha School astronomers. To start with, I should mention that it was Otto Neugebauer who first drew attention to the importance of the Maragha result.[2] But, quite independently, legend has it that Ibn al-Shāṭir's most important work, the *Nihāyat al-Sūl*, was stumbled upon by Edward Kennedy, while he was at the Bodleian Library waiting for Ibn al-Shāṭir's *Zīj*. What seems to be certain, however, is that it was the convergence of Kennedy's accidental discovery and Neugebauer's on-going research which gave the initial impetus to the Maragha studies. Furthermore, since the real significance of the Maragha School astronomy is usually seen in terms of its relationship to Copernican astronomy, the beginnings of serious research on the Maragha School could then be dated to 1957 when both Neugebauer and Victor Roberts published their respective works: the former the appendix to his second edition of the *Exact Sciences in Antiquity*, and the latter his first article in *ISIS* (48: 428–432) devoted to the solar and lunar models of Ibn al-Shāṭir. In Roberts' article, which was inspired by Edward Kennedy, Ibn al-Shāṭir's model was referred to as a "Pre-Copernican Copernican model." Roberts duly credited the discovery of the Copernican connection to Neugebauer in

[2] O. Neugebauer, *Exact Sciences in Antiquity* (Providence, RI, 1957), Appendix, pp. 197, 203–204. Neugebauer was already working on the Maragha results from a French translation of a text by Naṣīr al-Dīn al-Ṭūsī (d. 1274) describing the "Ṭūsī Device" and Ṭūsī lunar model. It was Baron Carra De Vaux who first made that text available in French as Appendix VI to P. Tannery's *Recherche sur l'histoire de l'astronomie ancienne* (Paris, 1893), pp. 337–361.

the second footnote of the same article. At the same time, Neugebauer had by then already noted other similarities between the works of Copernicus and another member of the Maragha School, namely Naṣīr al-Dīn al-Ṭūsī.[3]

In the years that followed, Victor Rcberts, Edward Kennedy, and Fuad Abbud, either independently or jointly managed to publish notices about Ibn al-Shāṭir's remaining models and about the possible connection with Copernicus.[4] Abbud went as far as to compare the numerical parameters of Ibn al-Shāṭir's *Zīj* and Copernicus's *De Revolutionibus*, and concluded that although the tables of Ibn al-Shāṭir were similar to those of Copernicus, the latter's were not a direct copy of the first, despite the fact that they both deviated in the same direction from Ptolemy's tables.

In 1966, while summarizing the results achieved up to that date, Kennedy coined the term "Maragha School," and identified the models of two more astronomers of that school, namely, Ṭūsī,[5] and Quṭb al-Dīn al-Shīrāzī. It was later shown that Shīrāzī's model for the upper planets, as described in Kennedy's article, was indeed composed by Mu'ayyad al-Dīn al-'Urḍī, the third member of the Maragha School,[6] (figs. 1 and 2). Since then, a critical edition of 'Urḍī's work, together with a translation and a commentary on the whole text, have been prepared for publication by the present author and are now in press.[7]

As a result of these studies, the works of the Maragha School astronomers which were actually subjected to some analysis are:

[3] Neugebauer, O., *Exact Sciences*, note 2.

[4] All these articles are now gathered together in E.S. Kennedy *et al.*, *Studies in the Islamic Exact Sciences* (American University of Beirut, Beirut, 1983), pp. 50–107.

[5] The important chapter in Ṭūsī's work, where the description of his lunar model is to be found, was already published in translation by Carra De Vaux, see note 2 above.

[6] See, for example, G. Saliba, "The Original Source of Quṭb al-Dīn al-Shīrāzī's Planetary Model," *Journal for the History of Arabic Science* (1979) 3: 3–18.

[7] Urḍī's text, *Kitāb al-Hay'a*, was first used by Noel Swerdlow in his unpublished Ph.D. dissertation, "Ptolemy's Theory of the Distances and Sizes of the Planets: A Study of the Scientific Foundation of Medieval Cosmology" (Yale, 1968), and identified simply as the "Anonymous Astronomical Treatise in Bodleian Arabic Ms March 621." Later, the same manuscript was used by B. Goldstein and N. Swerdlow in "Planetary Distances and Sizes in an Anonymous Arabic Treatise Preserved in Bodleian Ms March 621," *Centaurus* (1970–1971) 15: 135–170. The present author finally identified this Bodleian MS as being the work of 'Urḍī in "The First non-Ptolemaic Astronomy at the Maragha School," *ISIS* (1979) 70: 571–576.

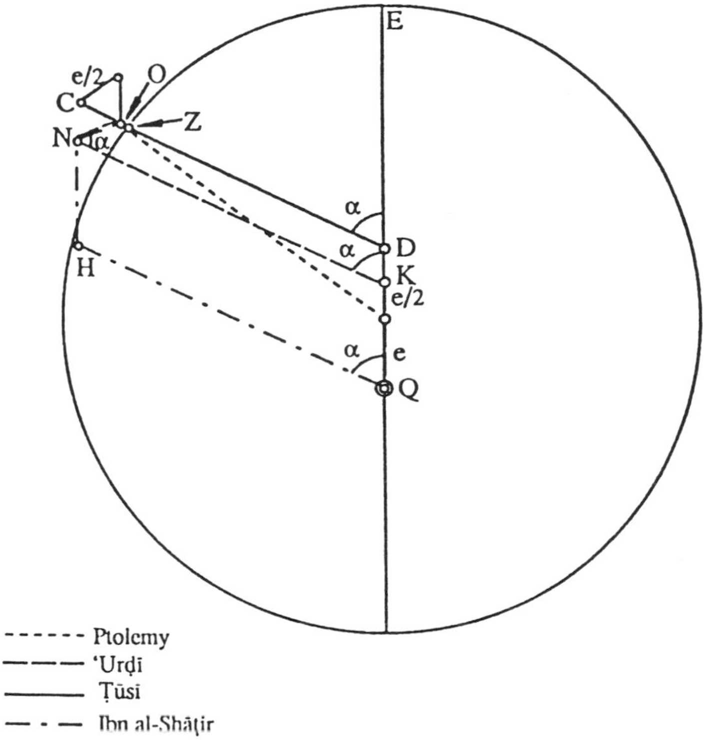

Fig. 1. A revised summary of the models of the upper planets as interpreted by Kennedy in the 1966 publication. The model designated as that of 'Urḍī here was ascribed to Shīrāzī by Kennedy.

i) Ibn al-Shāṭir's *Nihāya*, the main source, and through it all the planetary models of Ibn al-Shāṭir, was studied between the years 1957 and 1966.

ii) The lunar model of Ṭūsī[8] as well as his model for the upper planets were studied by Carra De Vaux in 1893, and by Kennedy in 1966 (fig. 3).

iii) The models of Quṭb al-Dīn al-Shīrāzī (d. 1311) were also studied by Kennedy in 1966. With the exception of the model for the upper planets, just mentioned, Shīrāzī's other models, namely, the lunar and the Mercury models (figs. 4 and 5) are up till now considered to be his own genuine models. But a

[8] In reality it was Carra De Vaux who first published Ṭūsī's lunar model, see note 2 above.

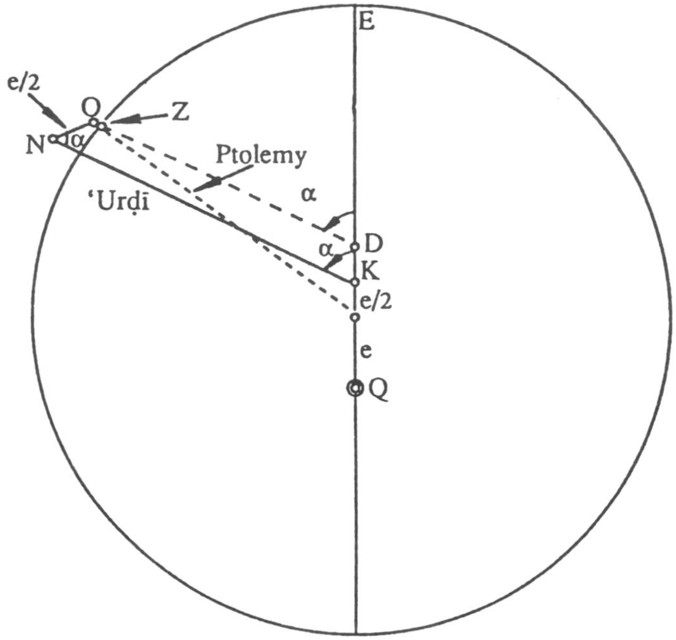

Fig. 2. Urḍī's Model superimposed over that of Ptolemy.

close reading of Kennedy's article, where he admits that he had great difficulty in disentangling the genuine work of Shīrāzī, as well as a reading of the two most important surviving works of Shīrāzī, namely the *Nihāyat al-Idrāk* (The Ultimate Understanding) and the *al-Tuḥfa al-Shāhīya* (The Shāhī Precious [Gift]), lead me to believe that future studies may very well change the picture that we now have of Shīrāzī's contributions to the Maragha Studies.

iv) 'Urḍī's models for the upper planets and the moon (figs. 2 and 6) were published by the present author in 1979[9] and 1989[10] respectively.

Of all the studies so far mentioned, the only one that included a working edition of the original text was the article describing 'Urḍī's model for the upper planets. The other texts remain unpublished, in any form, up to this very day. Besides the critical edition of the work of 'Urḍī, just mentioned, and its

[9] See note 6.

[10] G. Saliba, "A Medieval Arabic Reform of the Ptolemaic Lunar Model," *Journal for the History of Astronomy* (1989) 20: 157–164.

English translation, I have recently completed a critical edition of the *Nihāya* of Ibn al-Shāṭir. Other than that, I am only aware of a work in progress on an edition of Ṭūsī's *Tadhkira* (Memento), but cannot at this point say anything about its status.[11] This is more or less the sum total of our knowledge of the texts of the Maragha School so far.

The works of earlier astronomers, which are related to the Maragha School, and have come to light within the last two decades are:

i) Ibn al-Haytham's criticism of Ptolemy. The text of this extremely significant work has been published in a working edition by 'Abd al-Ḥamīd Sabra and Nabīl Shehaby,[12] but has not yet been formally translated into any language, nor has it really been fully studied. I am aware of one translation of this text which was presented as a Ph.D. dissertation at the University of Chicago, but it is hard to assess the quality of this translation at this time, or to say whether it will ever be published.

All we can say at this point is that Ibn al-Haytham's text has raised, among other things, the question of the importance of the Arabic translations of the Ptolemaic texts, namely the texts of the *Almagest* and the *Planetary Hypothesis*. Since Ibn al-Haytham's criticism of Ptolemy depends in great part on the nuances of the Ptolemaic texts, and since Ibn al-Haytham knew these texts in their Arabic translations, it is only reasonable to say that a real appreciation of the exact nature of Ibn al-Haytham's criticism can only be fully understood after a detailed analysis of the Arabic translations of the Ptolemaic texts. Unfortunately, none of these texts are as yet edited in any critical fashion.[13]

ii) Another text, which is related to the activities of the Maragha School in that it also represents a criticism of

[11] Parts of the *Tadhkira* were edited, translated into English, and supplied with a commentary by F. Jamil Ragep as a Ph.D. dissertation at Harvard University, 1982. Since then, I understand that the same author has undertaken to edit the whole work and to translate it into English and comment upon it.

[12] See Ibn al-Haytham, *Al-Shukūk 'alā Baṭlamyūs*, edited by A. Sabra and N. Shehaby (Dubitationes in Ptolemæum) (Cairo, 1971).

[13] The present author is aware of the facsimile edition produced by B. Goldstein, "The Arabic Version of Ptolemy's Planetary Hypothesis," *Transactions of the American Philosophical Society* (1967) 57, and of an on-going project, conducted by Régis Morelon, the aim of which is to produce a critical edition of the *Planetary Hypothesis*.

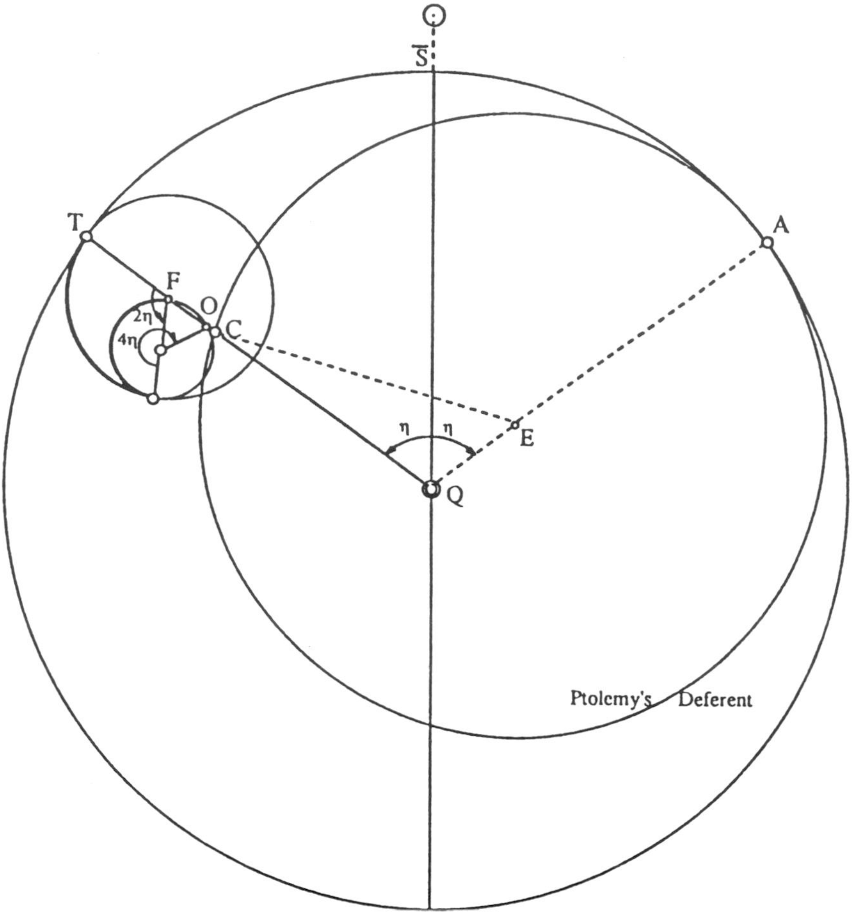

Fig. 3. Ṭūsī's lunar model using the Ṭūsī's Couple. Note that the trajectory of point O generated by the Couple comes very close to point C on the Ptolemaic deferent.

Ptolemaic astronomy, is that of al-Biṭrūjī.[14] But that text came from Islamic Spain and therefore was part of a slightly different tradition of criticism. It was published in a facsimile edition, supplied with a translation, and still awaits to be critically edited.

[14] B. Goldstein, *Al-Biṭrūjī: On the Principles of Astronomy* (New Haven and London, 1971).

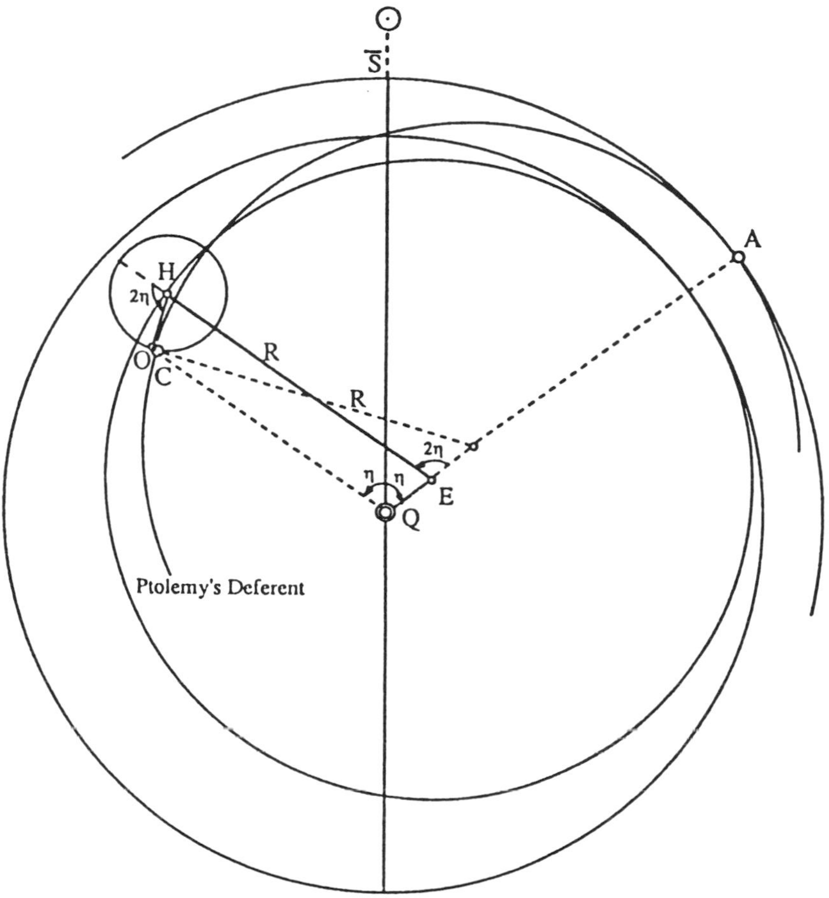

Fig. 4. Shīrāzī's Lunar model superimposed over that of Ptolemy. Note that it uses 'Urḍī's lemma which makes line QO always parallel to line EH. Also note that the difference between points O and the Ptolemaic point C is intentionally exaggerated, otherwise they are very close.

THE MARAGHA SCHOOL AND COPERNICUS

First, the Maragha results were, from the very beginning, deemed extremely important on account of their relationship to the works of Copernicus. But one should say immediately that this relationship did not touch upon the Copernican notion

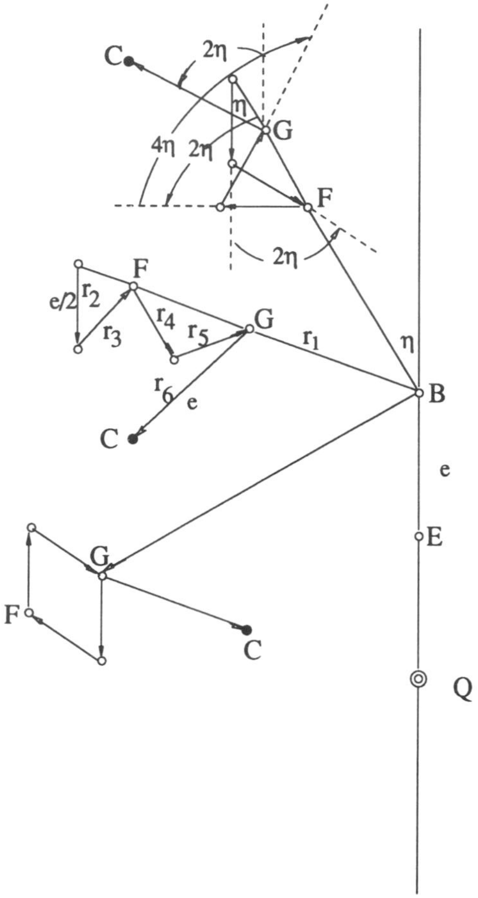

Fig. 5. Shīrāzī's model for Mercury as described by Kennedy. Note the use of the two Ṭūsī Couples which allow the point C to oscillate back and forth with respect to the center of the deferent B. The use of 'Urḍī's Lemma is implied by taking the radius of the large sphere of the Ṭūsī Couple to be equal to the eccentricity *e*. The effect is that CE will always be parallel to r_1.

of heliocentricity. That feature of Copernican astronomy entails the transformation of geocentric mathematical models to heliocentric ones by the reversal of the vector connecting the sun to the earth, while leaving the rest of the mathematical models intact. It is rather the similarity of the Copernican geocentric

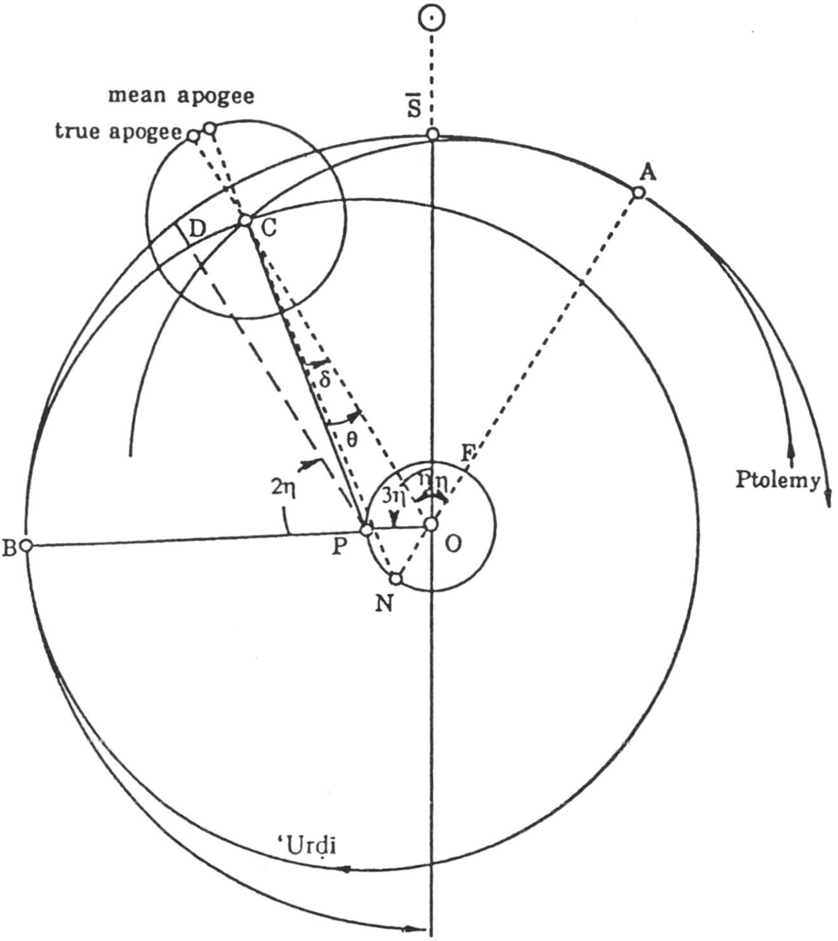

Fig. 6. 'Urḍī's Lunar model superimposed over that of Ptolemy. Note that the difference between 'Urḍī's equation θ, and Ptolemy's δ is so small that it "could be missed even by a skillful observer."

versions of those models to those of the Maragha astronomers that invited curiosity.

Second, the often held claim that the "glory of Copernican astronomy was that it abandoned the equant," as Koyré put it, was demonstrated by Neugebauer to be neither true, nor was the concern with the equant original to Copernicus, as the research on the Maragha astronomers can now show.[15] In fact, Swerdlow and Neugebauer have recently referred to Copernicus as the "most noted follower of the Maragha School," specifically because he, like the Maragha astronomers before him, was concerned with developing models that *preserved* the effect of the equant, and was not attempting to abandon it.[16]

Finally, the formal statement concerning the actual relationship between Copernicus and the Maragha astronomers was made by Neugebauer in a technical article devoted to the astronomy of Copernicus in 1968. In that article, Neugebauer spoke of the "Islamic antecedents of the Copernican methods," and went as far as to assert that "the basic identity of the Copernican methods with the Islamic ones needs no special emphasis in each individual case."[17]

Within the five years that followed, Willy Hartner and Noel Swerdlow each pursued that relationship further, and devoted at least five major works to Copernicus and the Maragha School.[18] Hartner went so far as to assert that there was an actual textual transmission at least in regard to the specific mathematical theorem called the aṭ-Ṭūsī Device by Neugebauer, and later the "Ṭūsī Couple."[19] In 1973, Hartner devoted an article to the representational diagrams of the "Couple" and attempted to show that both Ṭūsī and Copernicus had used the same alphabetic references to refer to identical geometric points

[15] Koyré's statement, in R. Taton, *Histoire générale des sciences*, vol. 2, p. 64, was also quoted in O. Neugebauer, "On the Planetary Theory of Copernicus," *Vistas in Astronomy* (1968) vol. 10, p. 89, reprinted in O. Neugebauer, *Astronomy and History: Selected Essays* (New York, Berlin, Heidelberg, Tokyo, 1983), pp. 491–505. See also *infra*.

[16] N. Swerdlow and O. Neugebauer, *Mathematical Astronomy in Copernicus's De Revolutionibus* (New York, Berlin, Heidelberg, Tokyo, 1984), p. 295.

[17] O. Neugebauer, "On the Planetary Theory of Copernicus," p. 90, note 15.

[18] See, for example, W. Hartner, "Naṣīr al-Dīn al-Ṭūsī's Lunar Theory," *Physis* (1969) 11: 287–304; "La science dans le monde de l'Islam après la chute du califat," *Studia Islamica* (1970) 31: 135–151; "Copernicus, the Man, the Work, and its History," *Proceedings of the American Philosophical Society* (1973) 117: 413–422; "The Islamic Astronomical Background to Nicholas Copernicus," Ossolineum 1975, *Colloquia Copernica III*, Nadbitka, 7–16 [all now reprinted in W. Hartner, *Oriens-Occidens II* (1984)]; N. Swerdlow, "The Derivation and First Draft of Copernicus's Planetary Theory: A Translation of the Commentariolus with Commentary," *Proceedings of the American Philosophical Society* (1973) 117: 423–512.

[19] See, W. Hartner, "Copernicus, the Man," note 18.

on their respective diagrams.[20] In the same year, and in the same issue of the *Proceedings of the American Philosophical Society*, Swerdlow articulated the most daring conclusion regarding the relationship between Copernicus and the Maragha School thus far. In the context of a detailed commentary on the *Commentariolus* of Copernicus, Swerdlow noted that the extent of indebtedness between Copernicus and the earlier Maragha astronomers could not be attributed to coincidence.[21]

Technically, this relationship depended on two basic mathematical theorems, namely the Ṭūsī Couple, and the lemma that I have elsewhere referred to as the 'Urḍī Lemma (figs. 7 and 8).[22] The importance of these theorems cannot be overemphasized, for the first allows for the transformation of circular motion into linear motion, and the second is a developed form of the Apollonius theorem which allows for the transformation of eccentric models to epicyclic ones. The real Copernican indebtedness to the Maragha astronomers not only lies in the fact that he uses these same theorems to build his own models, but that he also uses them at the identical points in the models where they were used earlier by the Maragha astronomers. The question is whether it was possible for Copernicus to know of these two theorems, and if so, through which channels?

The only concrete evidence for the actual transmission of the Maragha School works to the Latin west was once more first uncovered by Neugebauer. In his monumental work, *A History of Ancient Mathematical Astronomy*, Neugebauer published the photographs of a page from a Byzantine Greek manuscript, which eventually entered the Vatican Collection sometime after the fall of Constantinople in 1453.[23] On that

[20] Hartner continued to explore this connection between Copernicus and the Maragha astronomers till the last years of his life. Just before he died, he published, for example, "Ptolemaische Astronomie im Islam und zur Zeit des Regiomontanus," *Regiomontanus-Studien*, Österreichische Akademie der Wissenschaften, Philosophisch-Historische Klasse, Sitzungberichte, 364. Band (1980), Heraugegeben von Günther Hamann, 109–124.

[21] N. Swerdlow, "Derivation," note 18.

[22] For a detailed analysis of the use of 'Urḍī's Lemma by the Maragha astronomers and its eventual use by Copernicus, see G. Saliba "Arabic Astronomy and Copernicus," *Zeitschrift für Geschichte der Arabisch-Islamischen Wissenschaften* (1984) 1: 73–87, esp. pp. 78–79.

[23] See *A History of Ancient Mathematical Astronomy* (New York, Heidelberg, Berlin, 1975), p. 1456 for plate IX of *Vat. Graœc.* 211, fol. 116r.

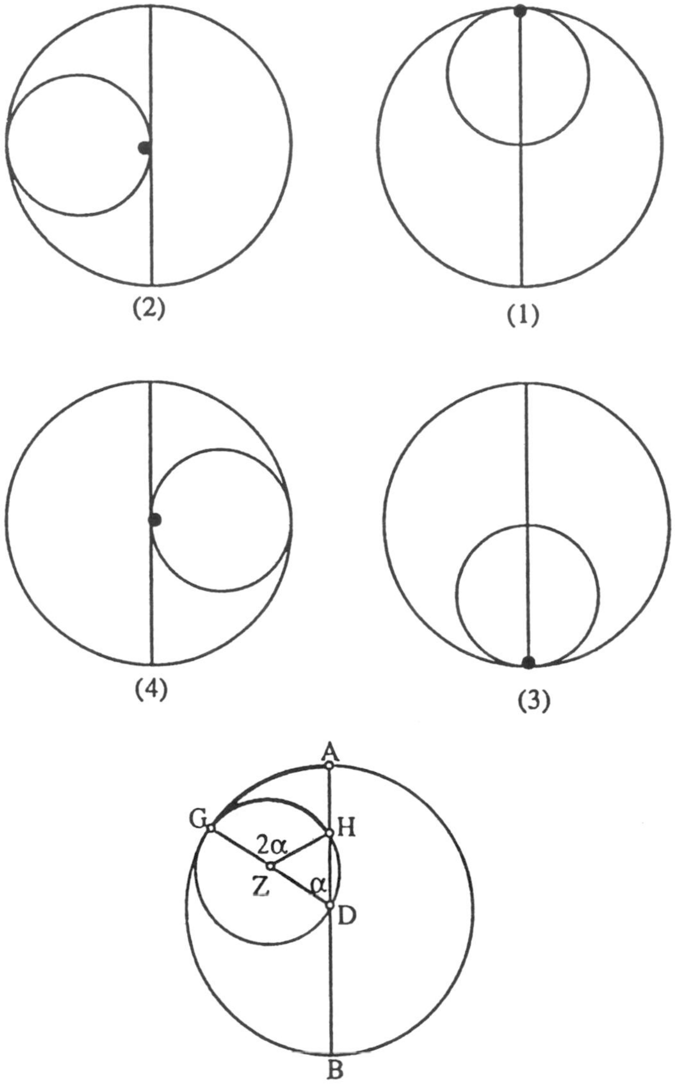

Fig. 7. The Ṭūsī Couple. As the big sphere moves by an angle α, and the small sphere moves in the opposite direction by an angle 2α, the common point H will oscillate back and forth along diameter AB. Hartner drew attention to the similarities between the lettering used by Copernicus and that used by Ṭūsī to prove the same theorem.

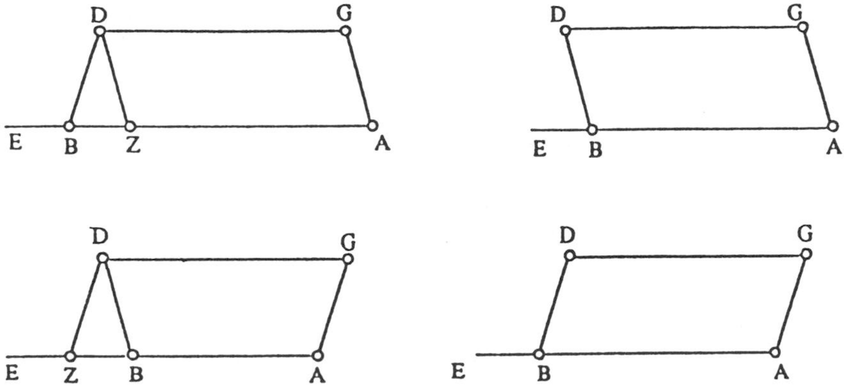

Fig. 8. ʻUrḍī's Lemma. If any two equal lines AG, BD, describe equal angles with respect to line AB, whether internally or externally, then line GD, which joins the extremeties of the two said lines will always be parallel to line AB.

page, Neugebauer noted the clear representation of the Ṭūsī Couple, and used that diagram to point to the possible route of the textual transmission which brought the results of the Maragha astronomers to Europe. He did not point, however, to the diagram on the upper part of the same page, which seems to be a poor rendering of Ibn al-Shāṭir's lunar model as seen in solid spheres. The real significance of Neugebauer's discovery, however, lies in the fact that these results, which finally reached Italy – a country where Copernicus took residence for a few years – could have been made available to Copernicus at the various stages of their transmission, since they were written in Greek, a language that Copernicus could read. It remains to show that Copernicus, at one time or another, saw this specific Greek manuscript, or discussed its contents with someone who had studied it.

Neugebauer continued to trace this line of transmission in his publication, ten years later, of another page of the same Greek manuscript in which it became clear that the Greek manuscript also contained the lunar model of Ṭūsī, as well as a diagram demonstrating the transformation of the Ṭūsī Couple to a configuration of solid bodies.[24] Of course, no serious discussion regarding the role of this manuscript can be launched until a critical edition of the entire Greek text is produced. I

[24] Noel Swerdlow and Otto Neugebauer, note 16, figs. 5 and 6.

understand that the edition is currently being completed by David Pingree of Brown University.

THE MARAGHA SCHOOL AND ARABIC ASTRONOMY

The texts of Ibn al-Shāṭir raised more questions than they answered. It was quickly learned from those texts that the crucial work, which was completed by Ibn al-Shāṭir before he wrote the *Nihāya* (i.e. the work that he called *Taᶜlīq al-Arṣād* (Record of Observations) was not available for investigation, and as of now is assumed to be lost. We now have an excellent idea of the subject matter of that text, for we have several references to it in Ibn al-Shāṭir's other works. But we still lack a full-fledged treatment of the relationship between observation and theory which was apparently discussed in great detail in this text.

We also learned from the texts of Ibn al-Shāṭir that the history of the criticism of Ptolemy was an old one in Arabic astronomy, and that several astronomers were already engaged in that debate in one way or another for several centuries before the time of Ibn al-Shāṭir. The picture that comes out is not that of a maverick Ibn al-Shāṭir dreaming up models of his own without any tradition to refer to.

Other aspects of Arabic astronomy were also brought into focus by the on-going Maragha studies. The issue of the chronology of the works of the individual astronomers, whenever that constituted a problem, became very important because it was needed for the demonstration of the logical progress of the mathematical theorems and the step by step development of the models themselves. In the final analysis this chronology was also crucial to determining the real reason that triggered the criticism of Ptolemy. From this perspective, it is important to note that the "Ṭūsī Couple," for example, was first invented to attend to the desperately flawed Ptolemaic theory of planetary latitudes and was not intended to solve the problem of the equant in the other planetary models themselves, as it later did.[25]

The implications of the Maragha School research for the

[25] See, for example, G. Saliba, "The Role of the *Almagest* Commentaries in Medieval Arabic Astronomy," *Archives Internationales d'Histoire des Sciences* (1987) 37: 3–20.

general history of Arabic astronomy, however, have not always been correctly perceived.

First, we note that although the Maragha studies were conducted with the best of intentions, they nevertheless had their own share in legends and false interpretations which have now unfortunately reached the secondary and tertiary literature.[26] One such legend concerns the goal of the Maragha astronomers and by implication the purpose of the whole Arabic tradition to which they belonged. The most common interpretation in this regard is to state that all this activity of model building was motivated only by the desire to preserve the uniform motion of the Aristotelian homocentric spheres, i.e. by philosophical considerations, and not by the empirically oriented activity of observation.

Although one could argue that most of the new models that were being proposed to replace the Ptolemaic models were essentially motivated by the need to preserve uniform circular motion, which was so well entrenched in the classical Greek philosophical tradition, one cannot (1) argue that *all* the models were so motivated, nor (2) that the real purpose was to attend only to the problem of uniform circular motion, which was so blatantly violated by Ptolemy. In a recent article, I have argued that Ibn al-Shāṭir, for example, had explicitly stated that he had no objection against the solar model of Ptolemy, and yet he felt he had to replace it with a new model (fig. 9), simply to account for the observations.[27] Ptolemy's statements regarding the apparent size of the solar disk – as being 0;31,20° – that it remains constant at all its distances, and remains equal to the apparent size of the lunar disk when the moon is at its farthest distance from the earth, are not philosophical statements, and could be easily countered by one example of an annular eclipse. Although the issue of the annular eclipse was not raised at all, the whole solar model of Ibn al-Shāṭir was specifically constructed to account for the variation in the apparent size of the solar disk.

[26] Most of these interpretations are now grouped together for the reader's convenience in one article by Owen Gingerich, "Islamic Astronomy," *Scientific American* (1986) 254: 74–83. This article was later translated into Arabic with many gross mistakes in the Arabic and published in the Arabic version of the Scientific American *Majallat al-'Ulūm*, 1.1: 8–19.

[27] G. Saliba, "Theory and Observation in Islamic Astronomy: The Work of Ibn al-Shāṭir of Damascus (d. 1375)," *Journal for the History of Astronomy* (1987) 18: 35–43.

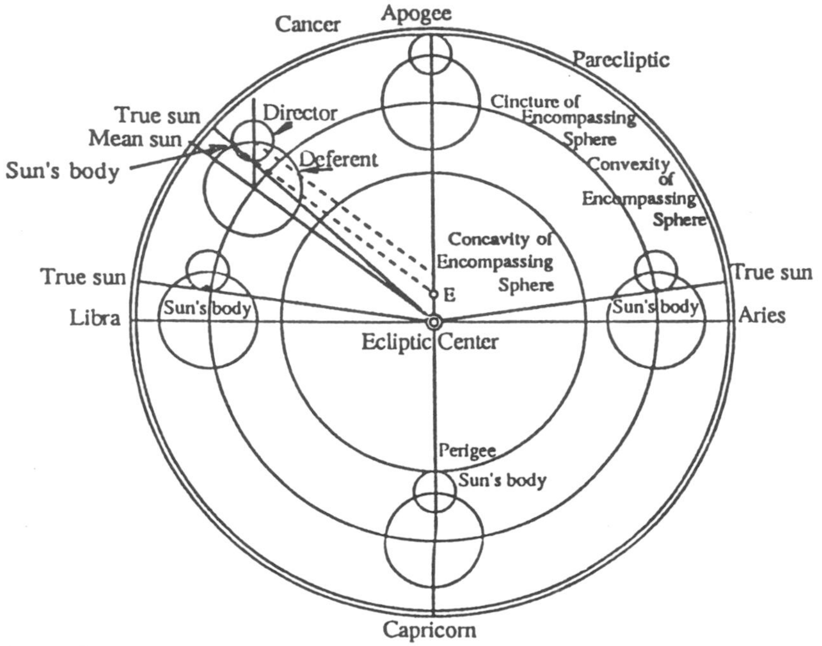

Fig. 9. The solar model of Ibn al-Shāṭir. By using 'Urḍī's Lemma note that the sun will look as if it is moving around point E rather than around the ecliptic center. This allows for the eccentricity of the sun. At the same time it also allows for a considerable variation in the solar disk for an observer at the center of the world.

In the same article, I also drew attention to the fact that Ibn al-Shāṭir was equally aware of the observational problems connected with the Ptolemaic lunar model, where, according to that model, the moon at quadrature is supposed to look almost twice as large as the full moon. Ibn al-Shāṭir objected to that specific feature of the Ptolemaic model by saying that the moon "was not seen to be so" (*lam yurā kadhālika*). And in his own model he resolved this contradiction with observation.

In another article, I have also demonstrated that Ṭūsī's Couple was first proposed in the *Taḥrīr* (Reduction) in order to solve the kinematic problems in Ptolemy's latitude theory, and was not then used for model building.[28] This is not philosophy!

The second interpretation has to do with the relationship between this new activity of model building and the parameters

[28] Saliba, "The Role of the *Almagest* Commentaries," note 25.

used by the astronomers in question in their respective astronomical handbooks (*Zījes*). One finds modern historians of Arabic astronomy lamenting the fact that although a specific astronomer produced a new set of models, the arrangement of the tables in his *Zīj*, or sometimes even the parameters used in these tables, exhibit only very slight variations from the parameters of Ptolemy or the arrangement of Ptolemy's *Handy Tables* as they were known in Theon's version.[29] In consequence, this interpretation led to the conclusion that all this activity had no tangible implications in practice.

Now to succumb to this interpretation, and to say that the model builders intended to translate their models into tabular forms so that they could incorporate them in practical *Zījes*, is to miss the whole purpose of the activity of model building. In fact, there were some astronomers, such as Mu'ayyad al-Dīn al-'Urḍī, who did not even write a *Zīj*, and yet produced one of the more extensive reformulations of Greek astronomy, and a drastic modifications of the Greek models, as I have shown in 'Urḍī's lunar model mentioned above.[30]

To understand Why 'Urḍī was doing this, one has to examine the details of the criticism of Ptolemy. No one of the Maragha School astronomers that I know of ever complained about the inaccuracy of the Ptolemaic models in terms of their ability to predict the positions of the planets concerned. Whatever criticism they had in that regard was restricted to minor observational details such as the inclination of the ecliptic, the precession value, or the mobility of the solar apogee, which are passed over very quickly. In fact, most of these minor criticisms were already raised and answered as early as the ninth century, some four to five hundred years before the time of the Maragha astronomers. Hence, on that ground alone, there was no need to reformulate the Ptolemaic models.

The more dramatic criticism to which the Ptolemaic models were subjected had to do with a much more serious problem inherent in Ptolemaic astronomy. Ptolemy had accepted at the beginning of the *Almagest* uniform circular motion as the only motion which was befitting to the celestial bodies, and then went ahead to describe that motion in a mathematical language (i.e. by using mathematical models) that did not allow for this

[29] See Roberts, note 4.

[30] See note 10.

uniform circular motion. The problem was therefore a problem in consistency. And it is immaterial whether one believed the universe to be made of spherical shells, as was propounded by Ptolemy in the *Planetary Hypothesis*, or of complete spheres which was the general belief of most astronomers of antiquity and medieval times. The problem was to be able to represent whichever system one believed in a mathematical language that could possibly account for the motion of that system. One could not accept a set of principles regarding the spheres that constitute the universe, as Ptolemy did, and then produce models like the Ptolemaic models that force these spheres to move uniformly on axes that do not pass through their centers.

To say that such a requirement of rigorous consistency is only a philosophical requirement, and has nothing to do with the science of astronomy *per se*, is to trivialize the distinction between philosophical issues and the methodological consistency required in any scientific discipline. A careful analysis of the works of the Maragha astronomers readily reveals that their concern was not restricted to preliminary philosophical doctrines relating to the nature of the universe and its appropriate motions. It went beyond that to include the development of a mathematical methodology that could describe, in a mathematical language, whatever philosophical doctrine one held. In a very real sense, this concern with the consistent mathematical formulation to describe empirical observations is different from the philosophical concern with the nature of the universe and its appropriate motion.

Therefore, the Maragha astronomers were holding themselves to a rigorous requirement of consistency, and were attempting to produce models that would solve the Ptolemaic contradictions. In essence, they required a consistent mathematics that accounted for the observable physical world, irrespective of the doctrines regarding the nature of the world. Hence their criticism was not directed at the predictability aspect of the Ptolemaic system, which for all practical purposes was quite satisfactory.

As a result, the Maragha astronomers were willing to accept the observational accurracy of Ptolemy, use machinery similar to Ptolemaic machinery, or slightly improve it, but they all questioned the veracity of the Ptolemaic models in regard to their consistency with the Ptolemaic presuppositions themselves. Someone like ʿUrḍī would explicitly state that he had no objections to the Ptolemaic observations *per se*, but that he had considerable objections to the methods used by Ptolemy to describe the motions of the spheres that he had already posited. He would even go as far as saying that the observations themselves can be accounted for by various mathematical models; those posited by Ptolemy were inadequate for the purpose.

Once the consistency issue mentioned above is properly understood, one would not require the Maragha astronomers to translate their models to tables that would differ in form or even content from the Ptolemaic tables. One could simply say: let the planets be at the critical points cited by Ptolemy, at exactly the points where Ptolemy says they were (for they were not too far off the true positions), the question remains how does one produce a mathematical model that allows the planets to be at those points, and accommodate the new observations that were different from those of Ptolemy, without falling into inconsistencies.

As an example, we can refer to Victor Roberts who published an early version of the solar model of Ibn al-Shāṭir and had this to say about it: "Ibn al-Shāṭir gives no motivation for his adoption of two epicycles, and it is difficult to see how this model constitutes an improvement over the Ptolemaic one."[31] Since the need for the two epicycles was not perceived by Roberts, one has to assume that he thought the purpose of the model was to improve the predictability in the solar longitude, i.e. improve the table for the solar equation in the *Zīj*. Ibn al-Shāṭir's model did not do that for there was no marked difference between the observations and the solar longitudinal positions predicted by the Ptolemaic models. The model did in fact improve the value for the solar eccentricity, just so slightly, thus also modifying the maximum solar equation, but in a marginal way. The main concern of Ibn al-Shāṭir's model, however, was to explain the variation in the apparent size of the solar disk, and was purposely supposed to retain the longitudinal predictions of the Ptolemaic model. The fact that these features have no major direct implications for the form of the tables of the solar equations in the *Zījes*, was totally missed by Roberts and those who followed him.

[31] Victor Roberts, note 4, p. 430.

IMPORTANCE OF THE MARAGHA STUDIES

Despite all that, the following results have been established so far:

a) Arabic astronomy can no longer be perceived as being merely a storehouse for Greek astronomy. Even those who do not believe in the validity of the Ptolemaic criticism have to admit that these criticisms were pervasive, and at times extremely original.

b) Arabic astronomy, after the Maragha Studies, can no longer be considered marginal to Medieval or Renaissance astronomy. The theoretical connection with Copernicus not only forces us to reconsider our traditional channels of contacts between Europe and the East, but it also forces us to reconsider the periods of contacts as well as the modes of these contacts. Such contacts did not apparently stop with the end of the thirteenth century, nor was the mode of transmission only through the translations of Arabic texts into Latin.

c) By the same token, the whole issue of periodization of Arabic astronomy, traditionally accepted to constitute periods of translation, assimilation, creativity, and decline, had to be abandoned, for most of the original results of the Maragha School fell well within the traditional period of decline.[32]

d) Once the periodization paradigm is abandoned, one could look at the so-called age of decline and expect to find original results. In fact, a preliminary study of the period of "decline" has already yielded many interesting findings: the most important of these is that it can now be asserted that Ibn al-Shāṭir's criticism from Damascus was contemporary with another criticism issuing from the city of Bukhara in Central Asia. The author of this criticism, the religious scholar and linguist Tāj al-Sharīʿa (d. 1347), was himself continuing the tradition already started by ʿUrḍī, Ṭūsī and Shīrāzī, and was building models of his own.[33] The equally important works of later astronomers will be discussed below.

[32] For a more detailed treatment of the problem of periodization in Arabic astronomy, see G. Saliba, "The Role of Maragha in the Development of Islamic Astronomy: A Scientific Revolution Before the Renaissance," *Revue de Synthèse* (1987) 3.4: 361–373.

[33] For a short survey of Tāj al-Sharīᶜa's models, see G. Saliba, "Islamic Planetary Theories After the Eleventh Century," to appear in a book devoted to the history of Arabic science edited by R. Rashed. See also the edition, translation, and commentary on Tāj al-Sharīᶜa's works in the Ph.D. dissertation of Aḥmad al-Dallāl, Department of Middle East Languages and Cultures, Columbia University (1990).

FUTURE RESEARCH

Beginnings of Ptolemaic Criticism

This activity stretches back to the beginning of Arabic astronomy. One may not have enough sources to trace it to the times before the ninth century. But some systematic effort has to be exerted in order to explain the methodological criticism that led, beginning with the ninth century, to the correction of the Ptolemaic precession, solar eccentricity, and solar apogee during that century.

In the eleventh century, criticism of Ptolemy seems to have become more systematized, and full-length books were apparently written on that subject. We have already hinted at the extant work of Ibn al-Haytham in that regard. But no effort should be spared to locate two similarly important books: one by an anonymous Spanish author, and the other by the famous Bīrūnī. In the case of the Spanish author, we have some idea of the contents of his book *al-Istidrāk 'alā Baṭlamyūs* (Recapitulation in Regard to Ptolemy), and if that is ever found it will illuminate the Arabic astronomical literature immensely, for it will shed light on the critical activity itself and its early motivation, as well as shed some very important light on the origins of the Spanish school of criticism.[34]

The title and description of Bīrūnī's work, on the other hand, has just come to light, but has not yet been located. All we know so far comes from a relatively unknown text by Shīrāzī, called *Fa'altu Fa-lā Talum* (I Have Done [what I did] so Don't Blame Me). While discussing the Ptolemaic theory of planetary latitudes, Shīrāzī refers to Bīrūnī in these words: "For that reason Ustādh Abū al-Rayḥān has stated in the book of *Ibṭāl al-Buhtān bi-Īrād al-Burhān* (Disqualifying Falshood by Expounding Proof), the following: 'As for the motions of the five epicyclic apogees in inclination, as it is commonly known (*al-mashhūr*), and is mentioned in the *Almagest*, that would require motions that are appropriate for the mechanical devices of Banū Mūsā, and do not belong to the principles of Astronomy (*uṣūl al-hay'a*).' "[35]

[34] The only reference we have to this book comes from an elementary treatise called *Kitāb al-Hay'a* (A Book on Astronomy), by the same anonymous Spanish author, now preserved at the Osmania University Library, Hyderabad, MS N° 520RH.

[35] Cf. Arabic manuscript Aḥmad III 3338, fol. 4v, in the Topkapı Library, Istanbul.

This stray remark, ambiguous as it is, leaves no doubt regarding the identity of the author or the purpose of his book. We do not know of this book from any other source. But it is not unlikely that Bīrūnī would have devoted a book to the difficult latitude theory of Ptolemy. Since we have a list of Bīrūnī's works, written by Bīrūnī himself, one has to assume that this work, in which Bīrūnī seems to criticize the Ptolemaic theory, was probably composed towards the end of his life.

As was stated above, we still have to explore the extant work of Ibn al-Haytham, which comes from the same century. The text should be properly edited, translated, commented upon, and fully integrated into our body of knowledge on Arabic astronomy.

We noted already that a work of Majrīṭī, which was already mentioned in the introduction of Ibn al-Shāṭir's *Nihāya*, was also critical of Ptolemaic astronomy. That work, which obviously belongs to the end of the tenth century or the beginning of the eleventh, needs to be identified and studied.

We also mentioned the work of Biṭrūjī from the next century, and pointed to the historical significance of that work in connection with the Spanish School of criticism. In general, the Spanish school deserves much more than the very few cursory studies it has received so far,[36] and Biṭrūjī's work deserves to be integrated within that school. Similarly, the work of his contemporary Jābir Ibn Aflaḥ, extant in Arabic and Latin, needs to be fully incorporated with that school.[37]

All of these works are indeed precursors to the works of the Maragha astronomers, and it would be highly presumptuous to think that we can formulate a coherent statement regarding the purposes of the Maragha astronomers without giving full credit to the works of these earlier authors.

The Remaining Works of the Maragha Astronomers

I have noted above that most of the Maragha studies which have appeared so far were based on the analysis of the extant

[36] The latest of these studies is A.I. Sabra, "The Andalusian Revolt against Ptolemaic Astronomy," in *Transformation and Tradition in the Sciences*, edited by Everett Mendelsohn (Cambridge, 1984).

[37] The last study of N. Swerdlow, "Jābir Ibn Aflaḥ's Interesting Method for Finding Eccentricities and Direction of the Apsidal Line of a Superior Planet," in *From Deferent to Equant*, edited by D. King and G. Saliba, *Annals*, New York Academy of Sciences (1987) 500: 501–512, explains the methodological sophistication of Jābir, but does not touch directly upon the issues raised here.

texts of Ibn al-Shāṭir, Ṭūsī, and Shīrāzī. In addition, I noted that the work of 'Urḍī is now in press and that the critical edition of Ibn al-Shāṭir's text, the *Nihāya*, is also completed and awaits publication. Furthermore, I have hinted at the work in progress devoted to Ṭūsī's *Tadhkira*.

This, in effect, is all that has been done on that group of revolutionary texts. One immediately notices the inadequacy of the coverage and the difficulty one faces when assessing the total impact of those works. To start with, we do not even have all the extant works of the Maragha astronomers themselves in published form in order that we can all share in their discussion. In addition, very important texts of these astronomers are still waiting to be located.

For example, we definitely need to have critical editions of Ṭūsī's earlier works, especially the *Taḥrīr* of the *Almagest*, and his Persian treatise, *Ḥall-i Ishkāl-i Mu'īnīya* (Solution of the Mu'īnīya Problem), for both of these texts bear heavily on the very issue of the purpose of the Maragha astronomers.[38]

Of Shīrāzī's works, none has been published so far, and none is contemplated for the near future, as far as I am aware. The difficulty lies in the amount of labor it will take anyone to complete an edition of the voluminous works left by Shīrāzī. Each of Shīrāzī's major works is more than two hundred densely written folios. And to use Kennedy's words, when he tried to describe Shīrāzī's planetary models, each folio is "exasperating" by itself. After reading Shīrāzī's third work, namely his *Fa'altu Fa-lā Talum*, which is not yet studied in any depth, we know why. He himself admits that he had constructed "nine models to solve the problem of Mercury's equant, only the ninth is the correct one. The remaining eight, each has some fault." Shīrāzī goes on to say that he "exposed the faults of six of them in the *Tuḥfa* [another one of his works] and intentionally left the faults of the seventh and the eighth in order to test whether those with intelligence will ever discover them."[39] The work is sufficiently difficult as it is without the author intentionally playing tricks with it.

But no matter how difficult the work is, the actual contribution of Shīrāzī to the Maragha School has to be determined,

[38] I have noted the importance of these texts and their interrelationship in the preliminary survey of the *Taḥrīr*. See G. Saliba, "The Role of the *Almagest* Commentaries," note 25.

[39] Cf. Shīrāzī's text, Majlis Shūra-i Milli MS 3944, Teheran, fol. 7r.

and to do so these texts have to be studied at some point or other. More urgently, since I have noted above that I have determined quite some time ago that the model for the motion of the upper planets, which was attributed to Shīrāzī by Kennedy, was indeed that of ʻUrḍī, one is left with the problem of determining the actual model of Shīrāzī. That in itself is an enormous task.

Ideally, one would like to have critical editions of the three extant works of Shīrāzī, namely the *Nihāya*, the *Tuḥfa*, and *Faʻaltu*, translations of them, with commentaries upon all the three works, and a full analysis of the nature of the mathematical models for all the planets. This has to be done in order to understand the full originality of Ibn al-Shāṭir's work itself. But before we reach that final stage of analyzing the texts belonging to the Maragha tradition, much more work needs to be done on the present manuscripts themselves.

Finally, the last member of the Maragha School, who was mentioned by Ibn al-Shāṭir as having contributed some models of his own, is Yaḥyā Ibn Abī al-Shukr al-Maghribī (d. 1283). The works intended by Ibn al-Shāṭir's remark have not yet been identified. The study which I have recently devoted to Maghribī's *Talkhīṣ al-Majisṭī* (Summary of the *Almagest*) revealed that this work does not contain the kind of models mentioned by Ibn al-Shāṭir.[40]

Post Ibn al-Shāṭir Period

I have noted above that the works of astronomers who were either contemporaries with Ibn al-Shāṭir, or came after him, have so far received very little attention. In addition, once we re-orient ourselves to cease to think of the centuries after Ibn al-Shāṭir as centuries of decline, the study of the works of the astronomers of this period may produce novel results. In fact, just a cursory survey of these particular works, which I have conducted in a few of the manuscript collections of Istanbul during two months of the summer of 1989, has already revealed the following important works which need to be located and studied:

1) Among the works attributed to ʻAlī al-Qushjī (d. 1474) there are two treatises that are of particular importance to our

[40] Se *ISIS* (1983) 74: 388–401 and *Centaurus* (1986) 29: 249–271.

discussion. The first is a treatise dealing with the solution of the problems of the Ptolemaic lunar model, apparently called "*Ḥall Ishkāl al-Qamar*" (The Solution of the Lunar Problem).[41] Nothing was said about the contents of this treatise, except that Ulugh Beg himself, who was originally sceptical about its importance, finally praised it when he heard it read to him by the author. There is a very good chance that manuscripts of this treatise will soon be recovered from among the immense collections of Arabic manuscripts still in the Middle East.

The second treatise is extant in many copies, and deals with the solution of Mercury's model.[42] In a forthcoming article, the present author intends to publish a critical edition of this treatise with translation and commentary.

Finally, there is the general introductory work of Qushjī, called *al-Risāla al-Fatḥīya fī-l-Hay'a* (The Fatḥīya Treatise on Astronomy), composed for Muhammad al-Fātiḥ (1451–1481) on the occasion of his conquest (*fatḥ*) of Iraq, which contains no radical criticism of the Ptolemaic models of the kind discussed here, but which gave rise to such criticism as we shall soon see.

2) Maḥmūd b. Muḥammad b. Qāḍīzādeh al-Rūmī, also known as Mīrem Çelebī (d. 1524)[43] was the grandson of Qushjī, on his mother's side, and of Qāḍīzādeh Rūmī, on his father's. Besides Çelebī's commentary on Ulugh Beg's *zīj*,[44] he had also written a commentary on *al-Fatḥīya*, the elementary treatise just mentioned of his grandfather Qushjī, which he apparently called *Dhayl al-Fatḥīya* (Appendix to the *Fatḥīya*). The text of this *Dhayl* has not yet been located. But its subject matter clearly belongs to the group of texts under discussion. In the only copy of Çelebī's commentary on the *Fatḥīya* consulted by the present author so far,[45] the following remark is made in connection with the problems of Mercury's model: "That which was added

[41] This treatise was mentioned by the biographer Taşköprü Zādeh (d. 1561), *al-Shaqā'iq al-Nu'mānīya fī al-Dawla al-'Uthmānīya*, edited by Aḥmad S. Furāt, Istanbul Üniversitesi Edebiyat Fakültesi Yayinlari N°: 3353 (Istanbul 1985), p. 159.

[42] The existence of this treatise was first brought to my attention, in 1981, by A.I. Sabra, of Harvard University, who has kindly sent me a copy of his own hand-written selections from it. I gladly acknowledge his kind gesture.

[43] See H. Suter, *Die Mathematiker und Astronomen Der Araber und Ihre Werke* (Leipzig, 1900), p. 188.

[44] See L.P.E.A. Sédillot, *Prolégomènes des Tables Astronomiques d'Ouloug-Beg* (Paris, 1853).

[45] Süleymaniye, Hüsrev Paşa MS 246.

by the moderns, may God look favorably upon their attempts, in regard to the spheres of the wandering planets and the moon, cannot be mentioned in this compendium. But my intention, if I am spared by death and granted good fortune by God almighty, is to mention all of them in the promised treatise, the *Dhayl*, if God grants mercy and success..."[46] A similar remark is made in connection with the reforms of the lunar model.[47] Therefore, the recovery of Çelebī's treatise, the *Dhayl*, promises to yield some positive results regarding his own work on the subject as well as the works of his predecessors and contemporaries.

3) In the same century, and in the Persian city of Shīrāz, there flourished an encyclopedic scholar whose works may be of great interest to our subject. The scholar is a relatively obscure person by the name of Ghiyāth al-Dīn Manṣūr b. Muḥammad al-Ḥusainī (al-Dashtāghī?) al-Shīrāzī (d. 1542/3).[48] In a collection of texts, preserved at the Topkapı Seray, Istanbul,[49] this author attempted to encompass science (*'ilm*), religious doctrines (*'aqā'id*), as well as speculative theology (*kalām*). In this collection, the author includes a short treatise (fols. 85v-98v) with the title *al-Safīr fī 'Ilm al-Hay'a* (The Ambassador: On the Science of Astronomy). The treatise in itself is an elementary introduction to Ptolemaic astronomy. But during the discussion of this astronomy, Ghiyāth al-Dīn has occasion to comment on the faults of such an astronomy, thereby leading us to other works of his which are more relevant to our discussion here. While discussing the motions of the lunar spheres, for example, he says: "The (fact that the) motion is uniform around the center of the world, rather than around its own center [meaning the motion of the deferent], that is one of the problems (*ishkālāt*) in this discipline. The ancients had nothing to say about it. Its solution, according to the opinion of the inquirer (*muḥaqqiq*) Ṭūsī, is by (using) the principle (*aṣl*) of the Large (sphere) [*al-kabīra*, a reference to Ṭūsī's large and small spheres of the Ṭūsī Couple], and according to the opinion of the author of the *Tuḥfah* [i.e. Quṭb al-Dīn al-Shīrāzī], by the principle of the Encompassing (sphere) [*al-muḥīṭa*, a reference to 'Urḍī's Lemma, as this theorem is called in the *Tuḥfah* and

[46] *Ibid.*, fol. 46v.

[47] *Ibid.*, fol. 50v.

[48] See, for example, Suter, *Die Mathematiker und Astronomen*, p. 189, note 43 and C. Brockelman, *Geschichte der Arabischen Literatur* (Berlin, 1902), II, p. 414.

[49] MS Arabic Revan 1996.

the *Nihāya*]. I have various other excellent methods (for solving it), which I have explained in (the book) *al-Hay'a al-Manṣūrīya* (The Manṣūrī Astronomy), and I have also referred to (still) other marvellous methods in (the book) *al-Lawāmi' wa-l-Ma'ārij* (The Sparkles and the Ascensions)."[50]

At another point, while discussing the problem of prosneusis, he also says: "This prosneusis is also among the problems (*ishkālāt*). The famous solutions [proposed up till now] for it are impossible. People made many statements about it which are all fantasies and delusions. The truth (concerning it) is what I have established in *al-Hay'a al-Manṣūrīya*, which shines with the *Lawāmi'* (Sparkles) of lights."[51]

Later on, while discussing the problem of the equant, he also says: "This too is among the problems (*ishkālāt*), which *al-Hay'a al-Manṣūrīya* (The Manṣūrīya Astronomy) is capable of solving. The inquirer [i.e. Ṭūsī] had used the principle of the Large (sphere) in order to solve it, while the author of the *Tuḥfah* used the principle of the Encompassing (sphere)."[52]

In a commentary on 'Āmilī's astronomy, discussed below, we also note the statement of the marginal commentator, who must have lived at least one century after Ghiyāth al-Dīn, when he says, regarding the problems of Ptolemaic astronomy: "Anyone requiring the solutions of these problems (*ishkālāt*) should seek them in the *Ma'ārij* [part] of the *Lawāmi'* of *al-Manṣūrīya*."[53]

Therefore, there is no doubt that this Ghiyāth al-Dīn had composed two separate books specifically dealing with the reform of Ptolemaic astronomy, which have yet to be located and studied. The first book is called *al-Hay'a al-Manṣūrīya*, and the other is called *al-Lawāmi' wa-l-Ma'ārij*.

4) From the same century, a noteworthy book was composed by the Syrian astronomer Ghars al-Dīn Aḥmad b. Khalīl al-Ḥalabī (d. 1563),[54] apparently from the city of Aleppo. The book, of which the present author had not yet had a microfilm copy to study, is titled *Tanbīh al-Nuqqād 'alā mā fī al-Hay'a al-*

[50] *Ibid.*, fol. 90r.

[51] *Ibid.*

[52] *Ibid.*, fol. 92v.

[53] Istanbul University MS Arabçe 2466.

[54] See, Suter, *Die Mathematiker und Astronomen*, p. 190, note 43, where he gives a variant of the name as Chalīl b. Aḥmed el-Naqīb, Ġars ed-dīn Ḥalebī, but does not mention the work discussed here.

Mashhūra min al-Fasād (Warning the Critics in Regard to the Faults of the Generally Accepted Astronomy). As far as I can tell, a unique copy of this book is kept together with a collection of astronomical manuscripts at the Süleymaniye Library, Istanbul.[55] According to the present author's notes, the author says in this text: "Since the generally accepted astronomy is not free of doubts (*shukūk*), especially those regarding the eccentrics, I have confronted them in this treatise, not in order to belittle the principles of this craft (*ṣinā'a*), but (to point to) slips where the intention did not match (the results), and to have that as a proof for what we have written in *Taḥrīr al-Wuṣūl ilā Nihāyat al-Sūl* (The Redaction of the Ascent to the Ultimate Request). I have composed (this treatise) in five chapters."[56] Chapter four of this treatise, subdivided into several sections, is devoted to the doubts (*shukūk*) regarding the spheres of the moon. The treatise itself is dated A.H. 958 (= 1551 A.D.).

Although the text of Ghars al-Dīn, the *Tanbīh*, may be of great importance by itself, simply because it seems to deal with the problem of the eccentrics, it is also important because it comes from such a late date and from Syria. Its importance is further enhanced by the reference it makes to Ibn al-Shāṭir's *Nihāyat al-Sūl*, for it is clear that Ghars al-Dīn must have written a commentary on Ibn al-Shāṭir's *Nihāya*. The contents of this commentary, if they can ever be determined, may be extremely important, not only because this commentary seems to deal with the problem of the eccentrics, a problem mainly raised in Spanish Arabic astronomy as far as we know, but because it must also concern the study of Ibn al-Shāṭir's work and his possible influence on later generations of Syrian astronomers.

5) The astronomical work of Muḥammad b. al-Ḥusain Bahā' al-Dīn al-'Āmilī (d. 1622), called *Tashrīḥ al-aflāk* (Anatomy of the Spheres),[57] is indeed an elementary treatise on Ptolemaic astronomy. But at this late period the so-called problems (*ishkālāt*) of Ptolemaic astronomy were so well known that it was difficult for any astronomer, no matter how elementary was his work, not to mention them. While 'Āmilī's own work may not have included a detailed discussion of the reform to

[55] MS Arabçe Yeni Cami 1181.

[56] *Ibid.*, fol. 174v.

[57] More on this author in Suter, *Die Mathematiker und Astronomen*, p. 194, note 43.

Ptolemaic astronomy, his commentators did indeed fill that gap. There is some evidence, however, that he himself may have after all discussed such issues in his book, *Sharḥ al-Ḥadīqa al-Hilālīya min Ḥadā'iq al-Ṣāliḥīn* (A Commentary on al-Ḥadīqa al-Hilālīya [part] of Ḥadā'iq al-Ṣāliḥīn), now kept in a collection together with a number of other mathematical and astronomical manuscripts.[58] In addition, this treatise of 'Āmilī does contain, among other things, a defense of the science of astronomy.

But the more promising field of research is in the works of the commentators who wrote marginal notes to al-'Āmilī's *Tashrīḥ*. The names of two such commentators, 'Abdallah Fakhrī and Muḥammad Bāqir, are mentioned on the flyleaf of one of the copies of al-'Āmilī's work.[59] And although it is difficult to tell with certainty which commentator is saying what, it is important to note that at least one of them did comment on the faults of Ptolemaic astronomy.

When al-'Āmilī mentions the motions of the lunar spheres, for example, he highlights the Ptolemaic description of that motion by saying that "the motion of each sphere is uniform with respect to its center except the sphere of the lunar deferent, which is uniform with respect to the center of the world."[60] On that occasion one of the commentators says: "This problem (*ishkāl*) is one of those about whose solution nothing was said by the ancients, from the time of Adam, peace be upon him, till the time of the inquirer Ṭūsī. He [i.e. Ṭūsī] solved it by using the principle of the Large and the Small (spheres) [i.e. the Ṭūsī Couple], and his student after him, the author of *al-Tuḥfah*, solved it with the principle of the Encompassing (sphere). Credit, however, should go to the first one who preceded in opening this guiding door to those with intelligence." Although this comment is not historically accurate, it nevertheless demonstrates the interest in the subject at this later date.

Either the same commentator, or someone else, recapitulated a few lines later by saying:

> The first among the moderns who spoke about the solution of the insoluble (problems) was al-Waḥīd al-Jurjānī, the student of al-Ra'īs Abū 'Alī Ibn Sīnā

[58] Süleymaniye Library, Istanbul, Laleli Arabic MS 2126, fols. 64r–116v.

[59] Istanbul University, MS Arabçe 2466.

[60] *Ibid.*, fol. 6v.

[*sic.*, meaning 'Abd al-Wāḥid al-Jūzjānī].[61] He wrote a treatise, which he called *Tarkīb al-Aflāk* (The Structure of the [Celestial] Spheres), and in which he mentioned the models with which these problems (*ishkālāt*) could be solved. After him came Abū 'Alī Ibn al-Haytham, then the inquirer Ṭūsī, and then the learned Shīrāzī, who collected from his contemporaries such as Muḥyī al-Dīn al-Maghribī – because the Principle of the Inclined (*al-mumayyila* or *al-mumīla*) is copied from him – and then the Excellent master Shams al-Dīn Muḥammad b. 'Alī b. Muḥammad al-Ḥammādī (?). You should note that the statements of Abū 'Ubayd are very weak, and nothing could be solved with Ibn al-Haytham's words, as it was already stated in the *Tadhkira* by the inquirer Ṭūsī. With the words of the inquirer (Ṭūsī) himself, as we have copied their gist, the problems of the prosneusis, Mercury's equant, and the latitudes of the cinctures (*manāṭiq*) of the epicycles and the deferents cannot be solved. As for the author of the *Tuḥfah*, he had elaborated too much. Master Muḥammad al-Munajjim al-Ḥammādī composed a treatise, in which he claimed that these problems (*ishkālāt*) could all be solved with one hundred and forty spheres. He indeed established three principles, which are, in reality, erroneous. Anyone requiring (more information about) them he should seek them in *al-Ma'ārij* [part] of the *Lawāmi'* of *al-Manṣūrīya*.[62]

Besides the interesting titbits that this comment brings to light, it attempts a more accurate historical picture than the previous one. In addition it sheds some light, although faintly, on the intriguing personality of al-Ḥammādī(?) who was in turn mentioned in Shīrāzī's text *Fa'altu*. It also tells us more about the importance of the just mentioned work of Ghiyāth al-Dīn. And finally, it does demonstrate the general awareness regarding the history of these problems, and gives some form of an adumbrated bibliography for the student seeking more information about them.

6) Another commentator on 'Āmilī's text, *al-Tashrīḥ*, is Muḥammad Ṣadr al-Dīn b. Ṣādiq al-Ḥusainī, otherwise unknown but who must have lived after 1622 A.D. In contradistinction to the other commentators, who were mainly recorders of the histories of the Ptolemaic problems, this one was a participant in the solutions. He does explicitly state at one point: "I have two respectable methods for the solution of the problems of the Moon and Mercury. If they [i.e. these two methods] are not better than those offered by other people, they are not worse than them. I have recorded them in a separate treatise."[63] The

[61] See, G. Saliba, "Ibn Sīnā and Abū 'Ubayd al-Jūzjānī: The Problem of the Ptolemaic Equant," *Journal for the History of Arabic Science* (1980) 4: 376–403.

[62] Istanbul University, MS Arabçe 2466, fol. 6v.

[63] *Ibid.*, fol. 7r.

recovery of such a treatise may carry this discussion beyond the middle of the seventeenth century.

In summary, with the scanty and scattered evidence which has been collected so far, one can postively state that the future research regarding the reform of Ptolemaic astronomy promises to uncover still wider areas of interest than the ones presently identified. The conclusion that can be drawn at this point is that the Maragha School results did indeed reach a very wide circle of astronomers, and managed, in the later centuries, to reach even the less sophisticated astronomers and commentators. One could safely state that after the fourteenth century no professional astronomer could afford to remain ignorant of the results of the Maragha School. In a different context, I intend to show that this wide-spread consciousness of the problems afflicting Ptolemaic astronomy, while it urged good astronomers to continue their research and to find new answers, may also have given ammunition to some religious scholars who saw in this continuous revision of astronomy enough reasons to doubt the validity of the discipline altogether.[64]

The Copernican Connection

Finally, the trail left by Neugebauer regarding the connection between Copernicus and the Maragha astronomers – now a much larger group than we originally thought – needs to be deepened and followed more systematically. One awaits, with great anticipation, the complete publication of the works of Gregory Chioniades (end of the thirteenth–beginning of the fourteenth century) by David Pingree of Brown University, for the Byzantine manuscript, which contains the diagrams of the Ṭūsī Couple and the lunar model that were published by Neugebauer, also contains most of the works of Chioniades; one of these works in particular is devoted to theoretical astronomy and preserves the models referred to in the diagrams.

This does not mean that we should abandon the search for other channels of contact between Renaissance Europe and the East, nor should we always think of the contacts as taking place along textual lines, or think that the historical significance of

[64] In this context I am thinking of the work of the Ḥanbalite theologian Ibn Taymīya al-Ḥarrānī (d. 1328) who did make such statements in his *Dar' al-Ta'āruḍ Bayn al-'Aql wa-l-Naql*, but this is the subject of another article.

this tradition should be seen only in terms of its European repercussions.

ARABIC ASTRONOMY AND COPERNICUS

George Saliba

Introduction

In 1968, O. Neugebauer first analyzed Copernicus's planetary system in terms of its relationship to the system propounded in Ptolemy's *Almagest* [Neugebauer, 1968]. In that article, he also noted: "The basic identity of the Copernican methods with the Islamic ones needs no special emphasis in each individual case. The mathematical logic of these methods is such that the purely historical problem of contact or transmission, as opposed to independent discovery, becomes a rather minor one". [*Ibid*, p. 90.]

Five years later, in 1973, in a now-classic study of Copernicus's *Commentariolus*, N. Swerdlow had the following to say in connection with the analysis of Copernicus's model for the upper planets: "Neither in the *Commentariolus*, where admittedly it would not be expected, nor in *De Revolutionibus*, where it would, does Copernicus present any analysis of this sort. One may seriously wonder whether he understood the fundamental properties of his model for the first anomaly, and this of course bears strongly on the important question of whether the model was his own invention or something he learned of from a still undiscovered transmission to the west of a description of Ibn al-Shāṭir's planetary theory." [Swerdlow, 1973, p. 469.]

In this paper, I will assume that there is some relationship between the works of Copernicus and those of Ibn al-Shāṭir, and without attempting to decide whether this relationship was one of dependence, I will investigate the genesis of Ibn al-Shāṭir's planetary model itself. The attempt is to formulate a more comprehensive idea of the interaction among the Muslim astronomers themselves, that led to Ibn al-Shāṭir's planetary model, and, only as a biproduct, shed some light on the Copernican model, for it is technically equivalent to that of Ibn al-Shāṭir.

Statement of the Problem

Ptolemy describes the motion of the upper planets, i. e. Saturn, Jupiter, Mars and the lower planet Venus, with one model which he states very briefly in Book IX, Chapter 6, of the *Almagest* [Figure 1]. In that simplified model, the motion of the planet P in longitude takes place when that planet moves uniformly around center C of the epicycle which is itself carried by a deferent sphere with center T. At this stage, Ptolemy states without any proof that the deferent sphere only carries the epicycle center C, while its uniform motion is measured from yet another point E, which in later times came to be called the *equant*. He only set here, again without proof, that OT = TE = e.

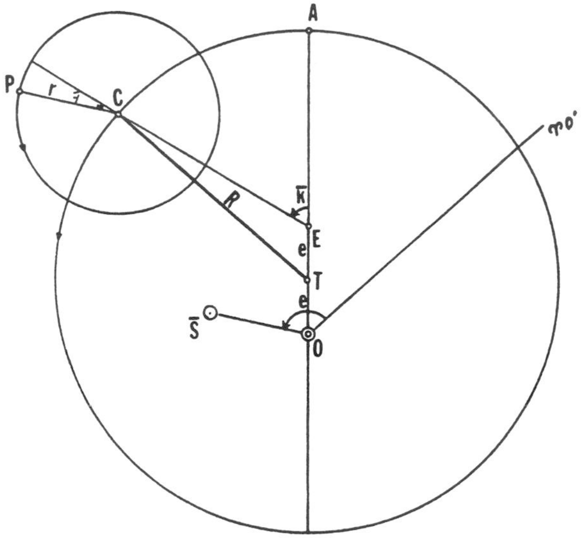

Figure 1: The Ptolemaic Model for the Upper Planets

In Book X, Ptolemy took up the problem of determining the eccentricities of the individual planets by relying totally on observational data. Here he showed great ingenuity in developing very sophisticated mathematical methods that allowed him to establish the eccentricity e for each planet from a set of only three observations. But the general model, already established in IX, 6, was never questioned again.

As it stands therefore, Ptolemy's model for the upper planets forced the sphere of the deferent to move uniformly around a center E, later called the *equant*, which is not its own center. Had the deferent been only a mathematical imaginary circle, there would have been no harm done, and the model could save the phenomena as closely as medieval observational precision could allow. But neither Ptolemy, nor any medieval astronomer for that matter, really believed that the observed motions of the planets were really produced by merely imaginary mathematical circles.

The problem is then reduced to having to force a physical sphere to move uniformly around an axis which does not pass through its center, a true physical absurdity.

Objections to Ptolemy's Model

Recent research has uncovered several criticisms of Ptolemaic astronomy, some more sophisticated than others, by Muslim astronomers who felt that Ptolemy's theoretical astronomy was defective in various respects, especially at the point just raised in connection with the model for the upper planets. Some of those criticisms have been edited and published, while others still await to be fully identified, edited and made available to the general historians of science. At this point, I will refrain from giving a comprehensive list of these criticisms of Ptolemy, and limit myself to those criticisms that were cast in the form of alternative models that are related to the model that was finally adopted by Ibn al-Shāṭir and Copernicus[1].

a – Abū ʿUbayd al-Jūzjānī (d.c. 1070)

The first astronomer-philosopher that we know of who has left us a treatise that purports to reform Ptolemy's astronomy, namely to solve the problem of the *equant*, is Abū ʿUbayd al-Jūzjānī, the

[1] Only some of the works criticising Ptolemy have been so far uncovered. And future research still promises to be very fruitful in that regard, as is evident from the introduction of Quṭb al-Dīn al-Shīrāzī-s *Nihāyat al-idrāk*. Of the published works, see Ibn al-Haytham, Jūzjānī, Biṭrūjī, and the individual studies in the periodical literature that were devoted to the works of Ibn al-Shāṭir, Naṣīr al-Dīn al-Ṭūsī, and Quṭb al-Dīn al-Shīrāzī, now conveniently collected in Kennedy-Ghanem.

student and collaborator of Avicenna. [Saliba, 1980.] In it he tells us that Avicenna had also made the incredible claim that he too had solved the same problem, but he was not going to tell his student about it, for he wanted him to work it out for himself. In a mixture of cynicism and wit, Abū ʿUbayd continues to say: "I suspect that I was the first to achieve these results." [*Ibid*, p. 380.]

A summary of Abū ʿUbayd's solution is given in Figure 2. He clearly thought that he could replace the Ptolemaic deferent by the

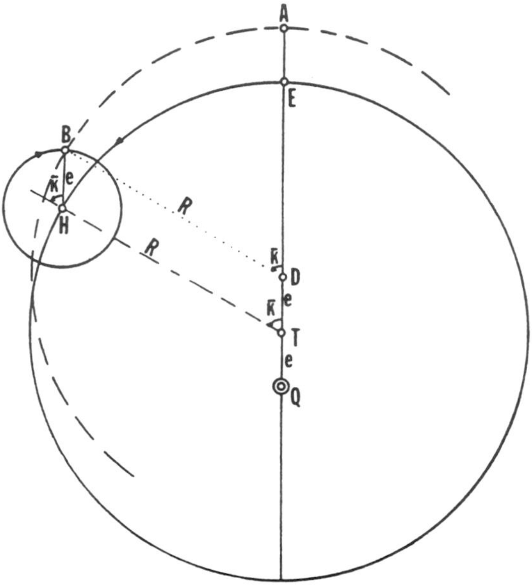

Figure 2: The Model Proposed by Jūzjānī
using the Apollonius equivalence

equant sphere itself – shown here in dotted lines – and thus transfer the motion of the epicycle from point H on the deferent to point B, now carried on a secondary epicycle of radius e. The advantage of such a model would obviously be that B, the epicycle center, would now move uniformly around H, while H itself also moves uniformly around T. Moreover, if the secondary epicycle, with center H, is made to move at the same speed as the deferent, but in the opposite direction, then point B, the planet's epicyclic center, will look as if it is moving uniformly around D, the *equant*, as required by observation. As such the new model seems to satisfy both uniform motion and observation.

All this would have been acceptable if the distance of point B, the planet's epicyclic center, from the observer at Q, were not also determined by observation, and thus can not be easily replaced. The laborious and lengthy computations in Book X of the *Almagest* were specifically carried out to determine the relative dimensions of the model of each planet in such a way as to satisfy the observational data that Ptolemy was trying hard to save.

Moreover, if Abū ʿUbayd's model were to work, Ptolemy would have been the first to adopt it, for it only seems to replace an eccentric sphere, the deferent, by a concentric one and a secondary epicycle. This equation was very well known to Ptolemy who further attributed it to Apollonius in Book XII, 1 of the *Almagest*, and efficiently used it in Books III, 3 and IV,6 [Neugebauer, 1959]. It would be naive therefore, to assume with Abū ʿUbayd that the observational problem of the *equant* could be solved simply by replacing the eccentric hypothesis by the epicyclic hypothesis as Ptolemy would have called this transformation.

The problem therefore, was still to find a model that preserves both, the Ptolemaic deferent, the effect of the *equant*, and still be the result of the motion of spheres that move uniformly around their own centers.

b – Muʾayyad al-Dīn al-ʿUrḍī (d. 1266)[2]

Taking advantage of the fact that one could transfer motion on an eccentric circle to a motion along a concentric with an epicycle – the Apollonius equation referred to above - ʿUrḍī's problem was to devise such a motion so that point B [Figure 3] in Jūzjānī's model could be brought closer to Ptolemy's deferent, if possible to coincide with Z. This does not necessarily mean that ʿUrḍī was trying to emend Jūzjānī's model directly, for he does not mention Jūzjānī at all, and he could have been working directly with the Apollonius equation. But it was a strike of genius to realize that one does not have to transfer the whole eccentricity TD = BH to the secondary epicycle, but accept a compromise and transfer only half of that eccentricity KD = NB. To do so, and approximate Ptolemy's deferent as close as possible, ʿUrḍī found out that the epicyclet BOH

[2] For a full edition and translation of ʿUrḍī's planetary model, cf. Saliba, 1979.

must revolve in the same direction and by the same amount as the new deferent with center K that he just introduced. Only then the combined motion of the deferent with center K and the epicyclet with center N will produce a resultant path marked by point O which hugs very closely the Ptolemaic deferent EZH. Once that technique was discovered by ʿUrḍī, it was used by every astronomer that came after him in one way or another to adjust the Ptolemaic model.

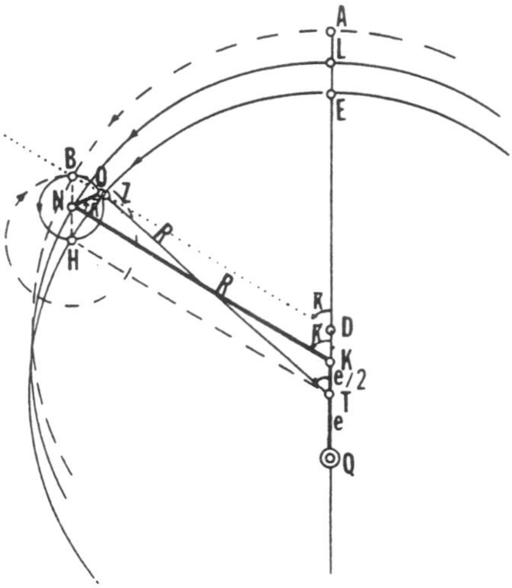

Figure 3: The Three Models of Ptolemy (continuous lines) Jūzjānī (dashes), and ʿUrḍī (boldface)

But to preserve the effect of the *equant* as well, ʿUrḍī had to show that the resultant motion of point O had to look as if it is itself uniform with respect to point D, the *equant*. This is tantamount to proving that under the stated conditions – namely, the epicyclet moving by the same angle $\bar{k}$ as the proposed deferent and in the same direction – the lines OD and NK will always be parallel.

To do so, ʿUrḍī stated the problem in the form of a general lemma, namely: "Every straight line upon which we erect two equal lines on the same side so that they make two equal angles with the (first) line, be they corresponding or interior, if their edges are connected, the resulting line will be parallel to the line upon which they were erected." [Saliba, 1979, p. 7.] Figure 3a is taken from ʿUrḍī's text in which he shows that line GD is always parallel to AB in all the cases where AG and BD describe equal angles with line AB. It is also assumed that AG = BD. The proof is then straightforward; both when the corresponding angles DBE and GAB, or the interior angles DBA = GAB are equal, for with the construction of line DZ parallel to AG, both cases become identical and require only *Elements* I, 27–33, to be proved.

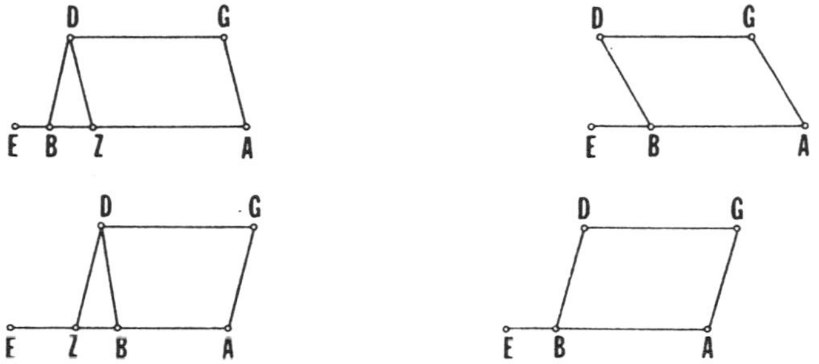

Figure 3a: ʿUrḍī's lemma

Now that line OD [Figure 4] was shown to be always parallel to NK, point O could then be taken as the center of the planet's epicycle and the Ptolemaic conditions would be very closely approximated. ʿUrḍī was quite aware of the fact that the path resulting from the motion of O coincides exactly with the Ptolemaic deferent only at the apogee E and the opposite perigee. To quote ʿUrḍī in full on this point, he says: "As for the center of the epicycle, i. e. the point of tangency mentioned above [O in Figure 4], it looks as though it were carried along the circle whose center is closer to the point of sight [T in Figure 4], on account of the fact that the center of the epicycle will be on this circle at its two distances, i. e. its farthest distance from the eye and its closest distance to it. And since it is very close to its circumference at the remaining portions of its revolution, that has led Ptolemy to believe that the center of the epicycle is coincident with its circumference, and describes it with its motion." [*Ibid*, p. 9.]

Instead of calculating the variation between the resulting path of the model and the Ptolemaic deferent, which is very small indeed

[Swerdlow, 1973, p. 469], ʿUrḍī assumes confidently that his model was the true one and that the burden of proof should be required of Ptolemy for it was Ptolemy who was confused about the true path when he assumed that it was along a circular deferent. This is exactly the same sentiment expressed by Maestlin some three centuries later when he explained this same point in Copernicus's astronomy to his student Kepler: "For Copernicus shows (V,4) that the path is not perfectly circular . . . [and] that Ptolemy thought that this path of the planet . . . was truly circular." [Grafton, 1973, p. 526.] It is also interesting to note that Maestlin also proves a specific case of the introductory lemma stated and proved by ʿUrḍī, without stating it in general terms. [*Ibid*, p. 528.]

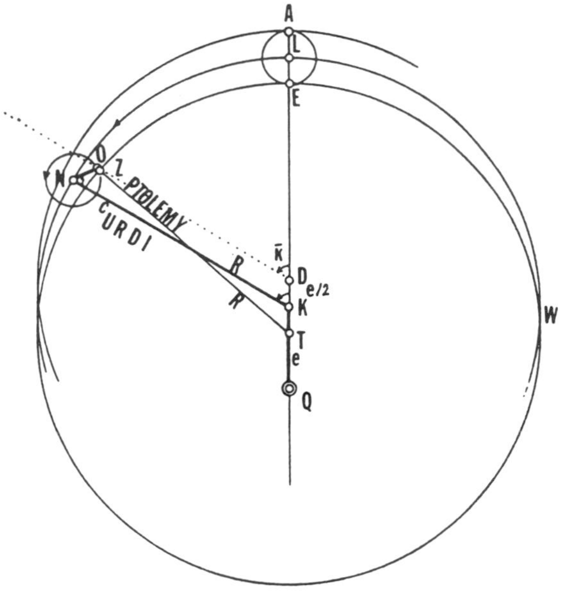

Figure 4: ʿUrḍī's Model Superimposed over that of Ptolemy

In the words of Copernicus himself [V,4], the same argument is made thus: "Hence it will also be demonstrated that by this composite movement the planet does not describe a perfect circle in accordance with the theory of the ancient mathematicians but a curve differing imperceptibly from one." [*De Revolutionibus* p. 743.]

Therefore, both ʿUrḍī and Copernicus were satisfied with this new technique of bisecting the Ptolemaic eccentricity for it allowed them to preserve Ptolemy's deferent, the effect of the *equant*, and still allow them to describe all the motions in their respective models as uniform motions of spheres that revolve on their own centers, thus avoiding the apparent contradictions in Ptolemy's model. But to understand the possible relationship between the Copernican model for the upper planets and that of ʿUrḍī, we need to investigate an intermediary model described by Ibn al-Shāṭir of Damascus (d. 1375).

c – Ibn al-Shāṭir

Because of the historical importance of Ibn al-Shāṭir's model, and its possible relationship to the works of Copernicus, a full English translation of the short section in which Ibn al-Shāṭir describes his model for Saturn will be given here. The text comes from Ibn al-Shāṭir's *Nihāyat al-Sūl* in an unpublished edition of the present author, and varies from the text that describes the models of Jupiter, Mars and Venus only with respect to the actual dimensions. The general relationships that are applicable to the model of all the upper planets are summarized in Figure 5.

Chapter twelve of Ibn al-Shāṭir's *Nihāyat al-Sūl* begins thus: "Concerning the Configuration of the Spheres of Saturn according to the Correct Manner.

Of the spheres of Saturn, let there be a sphere that is represented (*mumaththal*) by the sphere of the zodiacal signs, occupying the same surface and having the same center and the same poles [not represented in Figure 5 for simplicity].

One then imagines that there would be another sphere [represented by radius QH in Figure 5], inclined with respect to the first, at a fixed inclination of 2;30 parts, intersecting it at two opposite points: one (of the points) is called the head and the other the tail.

Then let there be a third sphere [represented by the circle with center H in Figure 5] whose center is on the periphery of the inclined, and whose radius is equal to 5 $^1/_8$ parts, being in the same units that measure the radius of the inclined [R in Figure 5] as 60 parts. Let (this sphere) be called the deferent (*al-ḥāmil*).

A fourth sphere is imagined to have its center on the periphery of the deferent [circle with center N in Figure 5], and whose radius is 1;42,30 parts. Let it be called the director (*al-mudīr*).

A fifth sphere is imagined, with its center on the periphery of the director [circle with center O in Figure 7], and whose radius is 6;30 of the same parts; it is called the sphere of the epicycle [omitted in Figure 5].

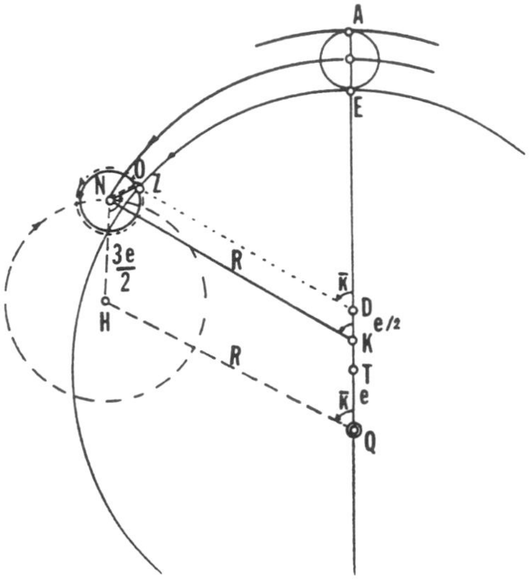

Figure 5: A Comparison between the Models of Ibn al-Shāṭir (dashes) and ʿUrḍī (continuous lines)

The center of the body of Saturn is fixed to one point on the belt (*minṭaqah*) of the epicycle."

From the dimensions given, we can verify the following relationships as applicable for all the other upper planets:

$HN = 3e/2$, and
$NO = e/2$, where e is the same as the Ptolemaic eccentricity.

In the case of Saturn, $HN = 5^1/_8 = 5;7,30$ is indeed equal to $3NO = 3 \times 1;42,30$, and $HN + NO = 2e = 6;50$ which is exactly twice the Ptolemaic eccentricity of 3;25 parts.

The directions of the motions of the spheres in Figure 5 are surmised from the following set of values as given by Ibn al-Shāṭir:

Sphere (1) moves at 0;0,0,9,52°/day, in the direction of the signs. Not represented.

Sphere (2) moves at 0;2,0,26,17 in the direction of the signs. Radius QH.

Sphere (3) moves at 0;2,0,26,17 opposite to the direction of the signs. Radius HN.

Sphere (4) moves at 0;4,0,52,34 in the direction of the signs, twice (2). Radius NO.

Sphere (5) moves at 0;57,7,43,34,22 in the direction of the signs. Not represented.

From these relationships, which are applicable to the other upper planets as well, it is clear that what Ibn al-Shāṭir calls the deferent, circle with center H, moves at the same speed as the inclined sphere, represented by radius QH, but in the opposite direction. This, in effect, transfers the portion of the eccentricity QK from the center to the periphery, using the same technique referred to above and used by Ptolemy in the *Almagest*, III, 3. This allowed Ibn al-Shāṭir to make his model actually geocentric, for now the radius HQ revolves around the center of the earth itself.

To adjust for the remaining portion of the eccentricity, and to retain the Ptolemaic deferent EZ, Ibn al-Shāṭir makes the epicyclet with center N revolve in the opposite direction to the deferent with center H, and thus making angle HNO = 2 $\bar{k}$. Since NH is parallel and equal to QK, lines NK and QH are also equal and parallel. Therefore, angle KNH is equal to $\bar{k}$ = angle KNO.

But it was ʿUrḍī who proved earlier the general lemma [Figure 3a] that if DK = NO and both lines describe the same angle with respect to KN, then OD, the line that connects their extremities, will be parallel to KN, and point O will be brought very close to Z on the Ptolemaic deferent.

What Ibn al-Shāṭir seems to have done therefore, is to combine two results already available to him from previous research. First, he used the Apollonius equivalence to transfer the effect of QK to the periphery HN, and then used the result already reached by ʿUrḍī to draw point N back to O, by using ʿUrḍī's lemma. We do not need to speculate whether Ibn al-Shāṭir knew directly of the work of ʿUrḍī, for he explicitely tells us that he did, and he criticized ʿUrḍī specifically for retaining eccentric spheres.

The net result is an orbit very close to the Ptolemaic deferent, and a geocentric model that is strictly concentric and free from the Ptolemaic contradictions. Figure 6 shows the relationship between Ibn al-Shāṭir's model – the model drawn in dashes – and that of

Ptolemy – the continuous lines – with the dotted lines KN and DO as reminders of ʿUrḍī's model. I have intentionally exaggerated the distance between points O and Z just to make the point that they are not in general identical, but in no way to suggest that they could have been differentiated by any observational result. For Mars, the planet with the largest eccentricity, the value of OZ is in the order of 0.005 for a radius R taken to be 60 units. [Swerdlow, 1973, p. 469.]

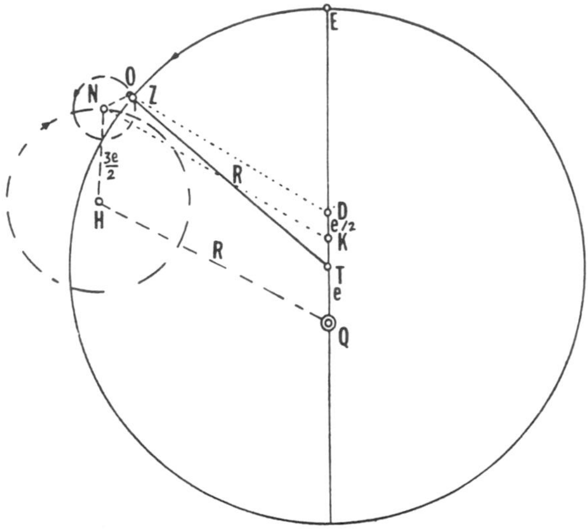

Figure 6: A Comparison between the Models of Ibn al-Shāṭir (dashes), Ptolemy (continuous lines), and ʿUrḍī (dotted)

Ibn al-Shāṭir and Copernicus

In Figure 7, I superimposed Ibn al-Shāṭir's model over that of Copernicus as described in the latter's works the *Commentariolus* [Swerdlow, 1973, 465f.] and *De Revolutionibus* [V,4]. To facilitate the transformation between the heliocentric Copernican model, the model in dashes, and the geocentric model of Ibn al-Shāṭir, in continuous lines, I have held the mean sun $\bar{S}$ in Ibn al-Shāṭir's model as fixed and allowed the other relationships and motions to remain the same. Once $\bar{S}$ was held fixed, Ibn al-Shāṭir's model, with all its dimensions, was translated to the model adopted by Copernicus. Since we now know that the addition of vectors is commutative, it is not surprising to find that both models predict the same position for planet P, irrespective of whether the earth or the mean sun is taken to be fixed.

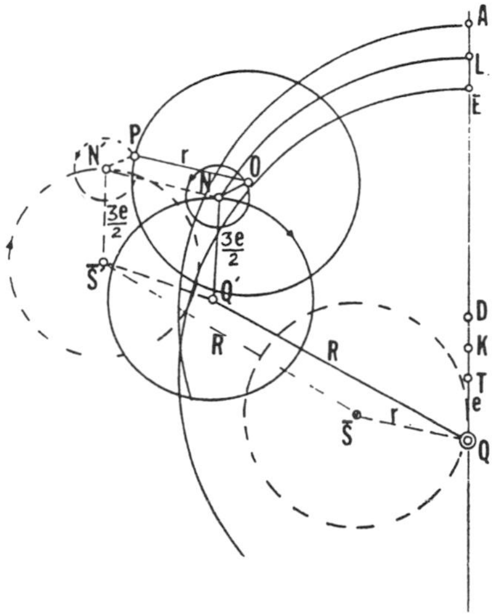

Figure 7: A Comparison between the Models of Copernicus (dashes) and Ibn al-Shāṭir (continuous lines).
Note that both models predict the same positions for planet P

Conclusion

In Figure 8, all the four models discussed above, namely those of Ptolemy, ʿUrḍī, Ibn al-Shāṭir and Copernicus, are superimposed on the same Ptolemaic deferent. Jūzjānī's model was disregarded for obvious reasons. The equivalence of the remaining models, however, is best illustrated here by the fact that they all predict the position of planet P, without having to accept the Ptolemaic contradictions. The historical relationship between ʿUrḍī and Ptolemy may have gone through the first attempt of Abū ʿUbayd, but may very well be a direct modification of the Apollonius equivalence, with the elegant and successful bisection of the Ptolemaic eccentricity. Once that result was achieved, Ibn al-Shāṭir, realizing its full significance, simply combined it with the Apollonius equivalence to produce his own model. We noted that Ibn al-Shāṭir knew of the works of ʿUrḍī, and took issue with him for retaining the eccentrics in his model. Then it is understandable that he did not feel obliged to prove the parallelism of OD and NK [Figure 8], for it was already proved by ʿUrḍī with the general lemma [Figure 3a]. Similarly, Copernicus did not prove that parallelism either, and it was Maestlin who explicitely proved it again in his letter to Kepler. [Grafton, 1973, p. 528f.]

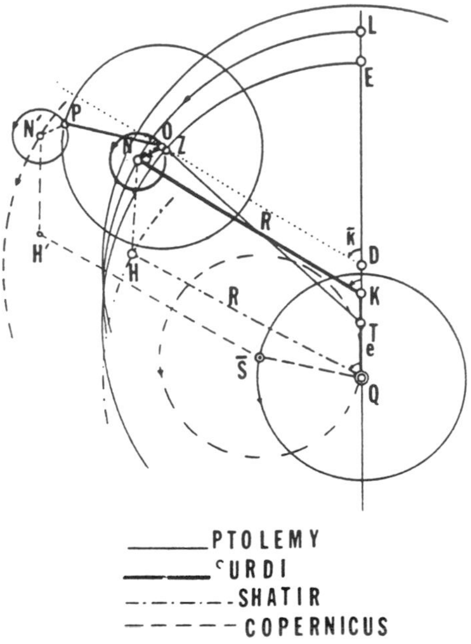

Figure 8: A Comparison between all the models

The question of the explicit relationship between Copernicus and Ibn al-Shāṭir remains open, and further research will have to be done before it can be decisively established one way or the other. What is clear, however, is that the equivalent model of Ibn al-Shāṭir seems to have a well established history within the results reached by earlier Muslim astronomers, and could therefore be historically explained as a natural and gradual development that had started some three centuries earlier. The same could not be said of the Copernican model. But some more research has to be done on the Islamic sources themselves, before their inner relationships can be fully understood and exploited.

Bibliography

Biṭrūjī *Kitāb fī al-Hay'ah*, translated by B. Goldstein, *Al-Biṭrūjī: On the Principles of Astronomy*, Yale, New Haven, 2 vols., 1971.

De Revolutionibus Copernicus, *Revolutions of Heavenly Spheres*, Great Books, University of Chicago, 1952.

Grafton A. Grafton, "Michael Maestlin's Account of Copernican Planetary Theory", *Proceedings of the American Philosophical Society*, 117 (1973) 523–550.

Ibn al-Haytham Ibn al-Haytham, *al-Shukūk ʿalā Baṭlamyūs*, ed. A. Sabra and N. Shehabi, Dār al-Kutub, Cairo, 1971.

Jūzjānī, Abū ʿUbayd G. Saliba, "Ibn Sīnā and Abū ʿUbayd al-Jūzjānī: The Problem of the Ptolemaic Equant", *Journal for the History of Arabic Science* 4 (1980) 376–403.

Kennedy-Ghanem E. S. Kennedy and I. Ghanem, *The Life and Work of Ibn al-Shāṭir*, Aleppo, 1976.

Neugebauer, 1959 O. Neugebauer, "The Equivalence of Eccentric and Epicyclic Motion According to Apollonius", *Scripta Mathematica*, 24 (1959) 5–21.

Neugebauer, 1968 O. Neugebauer, "On the Planetary Theory of Copernicus", *Vistas in Astronomy* 10 (1968) 89–103.

Saliba, 1979 G. Saliba, "The Original Source of Quṭb al-Dīn al-Shīrāzī's Planetary Model", *Journal for the History of Arabic Science* 3 (1979) 3–18.

Saliba, 1980 See Jūzjānī.

Swerdlow, 1973 N. Swerdlow, "The Derivation and First Draft of Copernicus's Planetary Theory: A Translation of the Commentariolus with Commentary", *Proceedings of the American Philosophical Society*, 117 (1973) 423–512.

Bibliography

Aaboe, A. "On the Babylonian Origin of Some Hipparchian Parameters," *Centaurus* 4.1955-56.122-25.

Abbud, Fuad. "The Planetary Theory of Ibn al-Shāṭir: Reduction of the Geometric Models to Numerical Tables," *Isis* 53.1962. 492-99.

Abel, A. "La place des sciences occultes dans la décadence." In R. Brunchwig and G. E. von Grunebaum (eds.) *Classicisme et declin culturel dans l'histoire de l'Islam*. Paris, 1957, pp. 291-318.

Abū Ma'shar. *Kitāb al-madkhal ilā 'ilm al-nujūm*. Carullah Ms. 1508.

Alhazen. *See* Ibn al-Haytham.

Averroes. *See* Ibn Rushd.

Avicenna. *See* Ibn Sīnā.

al-Baghdādī, al-Khaṭīb. *Risāla fī 'ilm al-nujūm*. Asir Ms. 190.

Banū Mūsā (Muḥammad b. Mūsā) (pseudo). *Kitāb ḥarakat al-falak*. Ẓāhirīya Ms., Falak 4489.

Bāqillānī. *Kitāb al-tamhīd*. Ed. by J. McCarthy. Beirut, 1957.

Bar Hebraeus. *Ta'rīkh mukhtaṣar al-duwal*. Ed. by A. Ṣālḥānī. Beirut, 1890.

Bergstrasser, Gotheil. "*Ḥunain b. Isḥāq, "Über die Syrischen und Arabischen Galenübersetzungen"*." Abhandlungen für die Kunde des Morgenlandes. Leipzig, 1925.

Bīrūnī, Abū al-Raiḥān. *Chronology of Ancient Nations*. Tr. by E. Sachau. London, 1879.

_____. *Al-Āthār al-bāqiya (Chronologie Orientalischer Völker-von Alberuni)*. Ed. by E. Sachau. Leipzig, 1923.

Bīrūnī, Abū al-Raiḥān. *Kitāb al-tafhīm li-awā'il ṣinā'at al-tanjīm (Elements of Astrology).* Tr. by R. Wright. London, 1934.

_____. *The Coordinates of Cities.* Tr. by J. 'Alī. Beirut, 1967.

_____. *The Exhaustive Treatise on Shadows.* Tr. by E. S. Kennedy. Aleppo, 1976.

_____. *Al-Qānūn al-mas'ūdī.* Hyderabad, 1954-56.

al-Biṭrūjī. *On The Principles of Astronomy.* Tr. by B. Goldstein. New Haven, 1971.

Boyle, J. "The Longer Introduction to the Zīj-i Īlkhānī of Naṣīr-ad-Dīn Ṭūsī," *Journal of Semitic Studies* 8.1963.244-54.

Brockelmann, C. *Geschichte der Arabischen Literature.* Leiden, 1937-1949.

Būnī. *Shams al-ma'ārif al-kubrā.* Beirut, (n.d.).

Carra de Vaux, Bernard. "Les sphères célestes selon Nasîr-Eddîn Attûsî." In Paul Tannery. *Recherches sur l'histoire de l'astronomie ancienne.* Paris, 1893. Appendice VI, 337-61.

_____. "L'Almageste d'Abu-lwefa albuzjani," *Journal Asiatique*, 8e ser. 19.1892.408-71.

Cheikho, Louis. "*Risālat al-Khujandī fī al-mayl wa-'arḍ al-balad,*" *Mashriq* 11.1908.60-69.

Chelkowski, Peter. (ed.) *The Scholar and the Saint.* New York, 1975.

Copernicus. *De Revolutionibus.* Tr. by Charles Glenn Wallis. Chicago, 1952.

al-Damīrī. *Ḥayāt al-ḥayawān al-kubrā.* Cairo, 1963.

Delambre, M. *Histoire de l'astronomie du Moyen Âge.* Paris, 1819.

Dorotheus of Sidon. *Carmen Astrologicum.* Ed. by D. Pingree. Leipzig, 1976.

Druart, T. A. "Astronomie et Astrologie selon Al-Fārābī," *Bulletin de Philosophie Médiévale* 20.1978.43-47.

Dryer, J. L. E. *A History of Astronomy From Thales to Kepler.* New York, 1953.

Fārābī. *Iḥṣā' al-'ulūm* (Census of the Sciences). Ed. by Osman Amine. Cairo, 1968.

_____. *Nukat Abī Naṣr al-Fārābī fīmā Yaṣuḥḥu wa-mā lā Yaṣuḥḥu min aḥkām al-nujūm.* Hrsg. by Fr. Dietrich in *al-Fārābī's Philosophische Abhandlungen.* Leiden, 1890.

al-Farghānī, Muḥammad Ibn Kathīr. *Elementa astronomica.* Tr. by J. Golius. Amsterdam, 1669.

Fleischer, H. O. *Catalogus Codicum Manuscriptorum Orientalium: Bibliothecæ Regiæ Dresdensis.* Leipzig, 1831.

Gauthier, Léon. "Une Reforme du Système Astronomique de Ptolemée tentée par les Philosophes Arabes du XIIe Siècle," *Journal Asiatique*, 10e ser. 14.1909.483-510.

Ghazzālī, Abū Ḥāmid al-. *Al-Munqidh min al-ḍalāl.* Cairo, 1964.

_____. *Iḥyā' 'ulūm al-dīn.* Cairo, (n.d.).

Gingerich, Owen. "Islamic Astronomy," *Scientific American*, 254.1986.74-83.

Goldstein, Bernard. "The Arabic Version of Ptolemy's *Planetary Hypotheses.*" *Transactions of the American Philosophical Society* 57.1967.1-55.

_____. "Some Medieval Reports of Venus and Mercury Transits," *Centaurus* 14.1969.49-59.

_____. "Theory and Observation in Medieval Astronomy," *Isis* 63.1972.39-47.

Goldstein, Bernard, and Noel Swerdlow. "Planetary Distances and Sizes in an Anonymous Arabic Treatise Preserved in Bodleian MS Marsh 621," *Centaurus* 15.1970.135-70.

Goldziher, I. "Stellung der Alten Islamischen Orthodoxie zu den Antiken Wissenschaften," *Abhandlungen der Königlich Preussischen Akademie der Wissenschaften* 8.1916.3-46.

Grafton, A. "Michael Maestlin's Account of Copernican Planetary Theory," *Proceedings of the American Philosophical Society* 117.1973.523-50.

Gregory of Nyssa (Pseudo). *Kitāb ṭabī'at al-insān.* Ẓāhirīya Library, Ms. 4871, fols. 57r-60r.

Ḥājjī Khalīfa (Kātib Chelebī). *Kashf al-Ẓunūn.* Ed. by Sharaf al-Dīn Yaletqaya. Istanbul, 1941.

Hartner, W. "Naṣīr al-Dīn al-Ṭūsī's Lunar Theory," *Physis* 11.1969.287-304.

_____. "La science dans le monde de l'Islam après la chute du califat," *Studia Islamica* 31.1970.135-51.

_____. "Copernicus, the Man, the Work, and its History," *Proceedings of the American Philosophical Society* 117.1973.413-22.

_____. "Ptolemy, Azarquiel, Ibn al-Shāṭir, and Copernicus's Mercury Models: An Accuracy Test," *Archives internationales d'histoire des sciences* 24.1974.5-25.

Hartner, W. "The Islamic Astronomical Background to Nicholas Copernicus." In *Colloquia Copernicana III*. Ossolineum, 1975. Nadbitka 7-16.

_____. "Ptolemaische Astronomie im Islam und zur Zeit des Regiomontanus," *Regiomontanus Studien. Österreichische Akademie der Wissenschaften, Philosophisch-Historische Klasse, Sitzungerichte* 364.1980.109-24.

Hartner, W., and M. Schramm. "Al-Bīrūnī and the Theory of the Solar Apogee: an Example of Originality in Arabic Science." In A. C. Crombie (ed.) *Scientific Change*. London, 1963.

Heinen, Anton. *Islamic Cosmology: A Study of As-Suyūṭī's al-Hay'a as-sanīya fī l-hay'a as-sunnīya*. Beirut, 1982.

Ibn Al-Akfānī, Shams al-Dīn Muḥammad b. Ibrāhīm b. Ṣā'id al-Sinjārī al-Miṣrī. *Irshād al-qāṣid ilā asnā al-maqāṣid*. Ed. by A. Sprenger. In *Bibliotheca Indica*, Fascicule 1, vol. VI, No. 21, 1849.

Ibn al-Fuwaṭī. *Talkhīṣ mu'jam al-alqāb*. In *Oriental College Magazine*. Lahore, 1939-1945.

Ibn al-Haytham. *Al-Shukūk 'alā Baṭlamyūs* (*Dubitationes in Ptolemaeum*). Ed. by A.I. Sabra and Nabil Shehaby. Cairo, 1971.

Ibn Ḥazm. *Marātib al-'ulūm*. Ed. by Iḥsān 'Abbās. Cairo, (n.d.).

_____. *Al-Faṣl fī al-milal wa-l-niḥal*. Cairo, 1903.

Ibn Khaldun. *al-Muqaddima*. Tr. by F. Rosenthal. Princeton, N. J., 1958.

Ibn Qayyim al-Jawzīya. *Miftāḥ dār al-sa'āda*. Cairo, 1939.

Ibn Rushd (Averroes). *Tahāfut al-tahāfut*. Tr. by Simon Van den Bergh. London, 1969.

Ibn al-Shāṭir. *Nihāyat al-sūl fī taṣḥīḥ al-uṣūl* (*The Final Quest Regarding the Rectification of [Astronomical] Principles*). Ed. by George Saliba (forthcoming).

Ibn Ṭāwūs, 'Alī Ibn Mūsā. *Faraj al-mahmūm fī ta'rīkh 'ulamā' al-nujūm*. Najaf, 1949.

Ibn Taymīya, Abū 'Abbās Taqī al-Dīn Aḥmad b. 'Abd al-Ḥalīm. *Dar' ta'āruḍ al-'aql wa-l-naql*. Ed. by Muhammad Rashad Salim. Jedda, 1979-1981.

Ibn al-Ukhuwwa, Muḥammad b. Muḥammad b. Aḥmad al-Qurashī. *Ma'ālim al-qurba fī 'aḥkām al-ḥisba*. Ed. by Reuben Levy. London, 1938.

Jābir Ibn Aflaḥ. *See* Lorch, R. P., in *Dictionary of Scientific Biography*, vol. 7, New York, 1973, pp. 37-39.

Jourdain, Amable, "Mémoire sur les instruments employés à l'observatoire de Maragha," *Magasin encyclopédique au journal des sciences, des lettres et des arts* 6.1809.43f.

Kasravī, Aḥmad. *Zandegānī man*. Tehran, 1323 =1945.

Kāshī, Ghiyāth al-Dīn al-. *Ghiyâth al-Dîn al-Kâshî's Letter on Ulugh Bey and the Scientific Activity in Samarqand*. Ed. and tr. by Aydın Sayılı. Ankara, 1985.

Kataye, S. *Les manuscrits medicaux et pharmaceutiques dans les bibliotheques publiques d'Alep*. Aleppo, 1976.

Kennedy, E.S. "Survey of Islamic Astronomical Tables," *Transactions of the American Philosophical Society*, new series 46.2.1956.123-77.

_____. "A Letter of Jamshīd al-Kāshī to His Father: Scientific Research at a Fifteenth Century Court," *Orientalia* 29.1960.191-213.

_____. *The Planetary Equatorium of Jamshīd Ibn Ghiyāth al-Dīn al-Kāshī*. Princeton, N. J., 1960.

_____. "Ramifications of the World Year Concept in Islamic Astrology." In *Proceedings of the 10th International Congress of the History of Science,* Paris, 1964, pp. 23-43.

_____. "Late Medieval Planetary Theory," *Isis* 57.1966.365-78.

_____. "The Lunar Visibility Theory of Ya'qūb Ibn Ṭāriq," *Journal of Near Eastern Studies* 27.1968.126-32.

_____. "Al-Bīrūnī on the Muslim Times of Prayers." In Chelkowski, P. (ed.) *The Scholar and the Saint* New York, 1975, pp. 83-94.

_____. "Two Persian Treatises by Naṣīr al-Dīn al-Ṭūsī," *Centaurus* 27.1984.109-20.

Kennedy, E. S, and M. L. Davidian. "Al-Qāyinī on the Duration of Dawn and Twilight," *Journal of Near Eastern Studies* 20.1961.145-53.

Kennedy, E. S., and I. Ghanim. *The Life and Work of Ibn al-Shāṭir*. Aleppo, 1976.

Kennedy, E. S., and H. Krikorian-Preisler. "The Astrological Doctrine of Projecting the Rays," *Al-Abḥāth* 25.1972.3-15.

Kennedy, E. S., and Victor Roberts. "The Planetary Theory of Ibn al-Shāṭir," *Isis* 50.1959.227-235.

Kennedy, E. S. et al. *Studies in the Islamic Exact Sciences*. Ed. by D. King and M. H. Kennedy. Beirut, 1983.

Khwārizmī, Muḥammad Ibn Aḥmad Ibn Yūsuf, Abū 'Adallāh al-. *Mafātīḥ al-'ulūm*. Ed. by G. Van Vloten. Leiden, 1895.

King, David. "An Analog Computer for Solving Problems of Spherical Astronomy," *Archives internationales d'histoire de sciences* 24.1974.219-42.

_____. "Universal Solutions in Islamic Astronomy." In J. L. Berggren and B. R. Goldstein (eds.) *From Ancient Omens to Statistical Mechanics: Essays on the Exact Sciences Presented to Asger Aaboe*, Acta Historica Scientiarum Naturalium et Medicinalium, edidit Bibliotheca Universitatis Hauniensis, Vol. 39. Copenhagen, 1987, pp. 121-132.

_____. "Universal Solutions to Problems of Spherical Astronomy from Mamluk Egypt and Syria." In *A Way Prepared: Essays on Islamic Culture in Honor of Richard Bayly Winder*. New York, 1988, pp.153-84.

Kunitzsch, P. *Arabische Sternnamen in Europa*. Wiesbaden, 1959.

_____. *Untersuchungen zur Sternnomenklatur der Araber*. Wiesbaden, 1961.

_____. *Die Syntaxis Mathematica des Claudius Ptolemaeus in Arabisch-Lateinischer Überlieferung*. Wiesbaden, 1974.

_____. *Ibn al-Ṣalāḥ, zur kritik der koordinatüberlieferung im Sternkatalog des Almagest*. Gottingen, 1975.

_____. "Über einige Spuren der Syrischen Almagestübersetzung" In *Prismata: Festschrift für Willy Hartner*. Wiesbaden, 1977.

_____. *Der Sternkatalog des Almagest: Die arabisch-mittelalterliche Tradition*. Wiesbaden, 1990.

Livingston, John. "Naṣīr al-Dīn al-Ṭūsī's *al-Tadhkirah*: A Category of Islamic Astronomical Literature," *Centaurus* 17.1972-73.260-75.

Mehren, M. A. F. "Vue d'Avicenne sur l'astrologie et sur le rapport de la responsabilité humaine," *Museon* 3.1884.383-403.

Minorsky, V. *Tadhkirat al-Mulūk: A Manual of Ṣafavid Administration*. London, 1943.

Morelon, Régis. *Thābit Ibn Qurra, Œuvres d'astronomie*. Paris, 1987.

Muḥaqqiq, Mahdi. *Al-Rāzī, fīlusūf-i Rayy*. Teheran, 1974.

al- Nadīm, Abū al-Faraj Muḥammad Ibn Abī Ya'qūb Isḥāq. *Al-Fihrist*. Ed. by R. Tajaddud. Teheran, 1971.

Nallino, C. A. *'Ilm al-falak : ta'rīkhuhu 'inda al-'Arab fī al-qurūn al-wusṭā*. Rome, 1911.

Nau, François. *Livre de l'ascension de l'esprit*. Paris, 1899.

Neugebauer, Otto. *The Exact Sciences in Antiquity*. 2nd. ed. Providence, R. I., 1957.

_____. "The Equivalence of Eccentric and Epicyclic Motion According to Apollonius," *Scripta Mathematica* 24.1959.5-21.

_____. "Thabet Ibn Qurra 'On the Solar Year' and 'On the Motion of the Eighth Sphere'," *Proceedings of the American Philosophical Society* 106.1962.264-99.

_____. "On the Planetary Theory of Copernicus," *Vistas in Astronomy* 10.1968.89-103.

_____. *A History of Ancient Mathematical Astronomy*. New York, 1975.

Niẓāmī, 'Arūḍī. *Chehar Maqāla*. Tr. by Edward G. Browne. London, 1978.

Paulus Alexandrinus. *Eisagogeka*. Ed. by E. Boer. Leipzig, 1958.

Pedersen, Olaf. *A Survey of the Almagest*. Odense, 1974.

Pines, Shlomo. "al-Rāzī." In *Dictionary of Scientific Biography*. New York, 1975.

_____. "The Semantic Distinction between the Terms *Astronomy* and *Astrology* according to Al-Bīrūnī," *Isis* 55.1964.343-49.

Pingree, David. "The Fragments of the Works of Ya'qūb b. Ṭāriq," *Journal of Near Eastern Studies* 27.1968.97-125.

_____. "The Fragments of the Works of Fazzārī," *Journal of Near Eastern Studies* 29.1970.103-23.

_____. "The Greek Influence on Early Islamic Mathematical Astronomy," *Journal of the American Oriental Society* 93.1973.32-43

Ptolemy, Claudius. *Tetrabiblos*. Ed. and tr. by F.E. Robins. Cambridge Mass., 1971.

Qabīṣī (Alchabitius). *Fī imtiḥān al-munajjimīn*. Ẓāhirīya Ms. 4871.

Rajab, F. J. *Cosmography in the Tadhkira of Naṣīr al-Dīn al-Ṭūsī*. Unpublished dissertation. Harvard, 1982.

Rashīd al-Dīn. *Jāmi' al-tawārīkh*. Ed. by Bahman Karīmī. Teheran, 1960.

Rizavi, Muḥammad Mudarris. *Aḥvāl va-āsār qudwat al-muḥaqqiqīn ... Naṣīr al-Dīn*. Teheran, 1976.

Roberts, Victor. "The Solar and Lunar Theory of Ibn al-Shāṭir: A pre-Copernican Copernican Model," *Isis* 48.1957.428-32.

Roberts, Victor. "The Planetary Theory of Ibn al-Shāṭir: Latitudes of the Planets," *Isis* 57.1966.208-19.

Rosenthal, Franz. *The Classical Heritage in Islam*. Berkeley, 1975.

Sabra, A. I. "The Andalusian revolt against Ptolemaic Astronomy." Chapter seven in Everett Mendelsohn (ed.) *Transformation and Tradition in the Sciences*. Cambridge, 1984, pp. 133-53.

_____. "The Scientific Enterprise." In B. Lewis (ed.) *Islam and the Arab World*. London, 1976, pp.181-200.

Sabra, A., and Nabil Shehaby. *Ibn al-Haytham al-Shukūk 'Alā Baṭlamyūs (Dubitationes in Ptolemaeum)*. Cairo, 1971.

Sachau, Edward. *Inedita Syriaca*. Hildesheim, 1968.

Ṣafadī, Khalīl Ibn Aybak al-. *Nakt al-humyān fī nukat al-'umyān*. Cairo, 1900, repr. Baghdad, 1963.

_____. *Al-Ghayth al-musajjam*. Cairo, 1887.

Saidan, A.S. *The Arithmetic of Uqlīdisī*. Boston, 1978.

Sakhkhāwī, Shams al-Dīn Muḥammad b. 'Abd al-Raḥmān. *Al-Ḍaw' al-lāmi' li-ahl al-qarn al-tāsi'*. Cairo, 1935.

Saliba, George. "The Planetary Tables of Cyriacus," *Journal for the History of Arabic Science* 2.1978.53 -65.

_____. "The Original Source of Quṭb al-Dīn al-Shīrāzī's Planetary Model," *Journal for the History of Arabic Science* 3.1979.3-18.

_____. "The First Non-Ptolemaic Astronomy at the Marāgha School," *Isis* 70.1979.571-576.

_____. "A Damascene Astronomer Proposes a non-Ptolemaic Astronomy," (Arabic with English Summary), *Journal for the History of Arabic Science* 4.1980.3-17.

_____. "Ibn Sīnā and Abū 'Ubayd al-Jūzjānī: The Problem of the Ptolemaic Equant," *Journal for the History of Arabic Science* 4.1980.376-403.

_____. "Astrology/Astronomy, Islamic." In Joseph R. Strayer (ed.) *Dictionary of the Middle Ages*. Vol. 1. New York, 1982, pp. 616-24.

_____. "An Observational Notebook of a Thirteenth Century Astronomer," *Isis* 74.1983.388-401.

_____. "Solar Observations at the Marāghah Observatory Before 1275: A New Set of Parameters," *Journal for the History of Astronomy* 16.1985.113-122.

_____. "Arabic Astronomy and Copernicus," *Zeitschrift für Geschichte der Arabisch-Islamischen Wissenschaften* 1.1984.73-87.

_____. "The Determination of Solar Eccentricity and Apogee According to Mu'ayyad al-Dīn al-'Urḍī (d. 1266)," *Zeitschrift für Geschichte der Arabisch-Islamischen Wissenschaften* 2.1986.47-67.

_____. "The Role of the *Almagest* Commentaries in Medieval Arabic Astronomy: A Preliminary Survey of Ṭūsī's Redaction of Ptolemy's *Almagest*," *Archives internationales d'histoire des sciences* 37.1987.3-20.

_____. "The Role of Maragha in the Development of Islamic Astronomy: A Scientific Revolution Before the Renaissance," *Revue de synthèse* 108.1987.361-373.

_____. "Theory and Observation in Islamic Astronomy: The Work of Ibn al-Shāṭir of Damascus (d.1375)," *Journal for the History of Astronomy* 18.1987.35-43.

_____. "A Medieval Arabic Reform of the Ptolemaic Lunar Model," *Journal for the History of Astronomy* 20.1989.157-64.

_____. "The Astronomical Tradition of Maragha: A Historical Survey and Prospects for Future Research," *Arabic Sciences and Philosophy* 1.1991.67-99.

_____. "The Role of the Astrologer in Medieval Islamic Society," *Bulletin d'Études Orientales* 44.1992.45-68.

_____. "Early Criticism of Ptolemaic Astronomy: The Andalusian School" (forthcoming).

_____. "Persian Scientists in the Islamic World: Astronomy from Maragha to Samarqand." (forthcoming).

al-Samau'al al-Maghribī. *Kashf 'uwār al-munajjimīn wa-ghalaṭihim fī akthar al-a'māl wa-l-aḥkām*. Leiden, Ms. Or. 98.

Sayılı, Aydın. *The Observatory in Islam and Its Place in the General History of the Observatory*. Ankara, 1960.

_____. *Ghiyâth al-Dîn al-Kâshî's Letter on Ulugh Bey and the Scientific Activity in Samarqand*. Ankara, 1985.

Schoy, C. "*Gnomonik der Araber*." In *Die Geschichte der Zeitmessung und der Uhren*. Berlin, 1923.

_____. *Beiträge zur Arabisch-Islamischen Mathematik und Astronomie*. Frankfurt, 1988.

Seeman, Hugo J. "Die Instrumente der Sternwarte zu *Maragha* nach den Mitteilungen von *al-'Urḍī*," *Sitzungberichte der physikalisch-medizinischen Sozietät zu Erlangen* 60.1928.15-126.

Sezgin, F. *Geschichte des Arabischen Schrifttums*, vols. 6 and 7. Leiden, 1978-79.

Suter, Heinrich. *Die Mathematiker und Astronomen der Araber und Ihre Werke*. Leipzig, 1900.

Swerdlow, Noel. *Ptolemy's Theory of the Distances and the Sizes of the Planets: A Study of the Scientific Foundation of Medieval Cosmology*. Unpublished dissertation. Yale University, 1968.

_____. "The Derivation and First Draft of Copernicus's Planetary Theory: A Translation of the Commentariolus with Commentary," *Proceedings of the American Philosophical Society* 117.1973.423-512.

_____. "Jābir Ibn Aflaḥ's Interesting Method for Finding the Eccentricities and Direction of the Apsidal Line of a Superior Planet." In D. King and G. Saliba (eds.) *From Deferent to Equant: A Volume of Studies in the History of Science in the Ancient and Medieval Near East in Honor of E. S. Kennedy*. New York Academy of Sciences, Annals 500.1987.501-12.

Swerdlow, Noel, and Otto Neugebauer. *Mathematical Astronomy in Copernicus's De Revolutionibus*. New York, 1984.

Tannery, Paul. *Recherches sur l'histoire de l'astronomie ancienne*. Paris, 1893.

Tannūkhī. *Nushwār al-muḥāḍara*. Beirut, 1973.

Taqīzādeh, Hasan. *Yādnāmeh*. Tehran, 1349 =1971.

Taşk̲öprülü-zādeh. *al-Shaqā'iq al-nu'mānīya fī al-dawla al-'Ūthmānīya*. Ed. by A. Furāt. Istanbul, 1985.

Taton, R. *Histoire générale des sciences*. Paris, 1957.

Toomer, G. J. "The Solar Theory of Az-Zarqāl: An Epilogue." In D. King and G. Saliba (eds.) *From Deferent to Equant: A Volume of Studies in the History of Science in the Ancient and Medieval Near East in Honor of E. S. Kennedy*. New York Academy of Sciences. Annals 500.1987.513-19.

_____. *Ptolemy's Almagest*. New York, 1984.

Tuckerman, B. *Planetary, Lunar and Solar Positions A.D. 2 to A.D. 1649 at Five-day and Ten-day Intervals*. Philadelphia, 1964.

Ukta'ī. *Fihrist ... Quds Rizavī*. Meshhed, 1926.

Ullmann, M. *Die Natur und Geheimwissenschaften im Islam*. Leiden, 1972.

'Urḍī, Mu'ayyad al-Dīn al-. *Kitāb al-hay'a: The Astronomical Works of Mu'ayyad al-Dīn al-'Urḍī.* Ed. by G. Saliba. Beirut, 1990.

Uri, Joanne. *Bibliotheca Bodleinae Codicum Manuscriptorum Orientalium.* Oxford, 1787.

Vadet, Jean Claude. "Une defence de l'astrologie dans le madḫal d'Abū Ma'shar al-Balḫī," *Annales Islamologiques* 5.1963.131-80.

Vaglieri, L. V., and G. Celentano. "Trois Épîtres d'Al-Kindī," *Annali, Insitituto Orientale di Napoli* 34.1974.523-62.

Vardjavand, P. "La découverte archéologique du complexe scientifique de l'observatoire de Maragé." In M. Dizer (ed.) *International Symposium on the Observatories in Islam.* Istanbul, 1980.

Welch, C. *Imperial Moghul Paintings.* New York, 1978.

Wiedemann, E., and Th. W. Juynbol. "Avicennas Schrift über ein von ihm ersonnenes Beobachtunginstrument," *Acta Orientalia* 11.1926.81-167.

Williams, L. P., and H. J. Steffens. *The History of Science in Western Civilization.* Washington, 1977.

Yāqūt al-Ḥamwī. *Mu'jam al-udabā'*. Cairo, 1936-38.

_____. *Mu'jam al-buldān.* Beirut, 1979.

Index

Sun (*continued*)
236; apparent disk at mean distance according to Indians, 236; apparent disk at mean distance according to Ptolemy, 236; apparent disk at mean distance according to Ibn al-Shāṭir 236,238; apparent disk at mean distance according to moderns 236; declination of, observed, 187; diameter of, computed, 173; dimension of model Maghribī, 178; distance of from earth, 173; eccentricity modified, 235; eccentricity of according to 'Urḍī, 188; eccentric model of, 171; eccentricity and apogee (Maghribī text translated), 182; eccentricity and apogee determined by 'Urḍī, 187-207; eccentricity determined by Maghribī, 178, 179-86; eccentricity determined, 171; eccentricity of, 234, 236; eccentricity of, Ptolemaic, 279; equant of, 240; equation of, 14, 18, 171, 240; equation of, Ptolemaic, 24; geocentric distance of, 239; Ibn al-Shāṭir's model of, 277; maximum equation Ibn al-Shāṭir, 234; maximum height, 178; mean motion, in Maghribī, 169; model of Ibn al-Shāṭir, 236; motion of apogee, 236, 239; observation of, 10; observation of, at Marāgha, 177-86; observations cited by Maghribī, 178; position of apogee, 206; Ptolemaic model of, 5, 10, 25, 235; spheres of, 91; year determined by verified observation, 171
sundial theory, 61, 78; of Thābit, 249
Suter, 77, 114; on Leiden (Ms. Or. 110), 164, 166; on Maghribī, 165
Ṣuwar al-kawākib (of Ṣūfī), 78
Ṣuyūṭī, 42n. 23
Swerdlow, 28, 29, 41n. 13, 43nn. 31, 35, 44n. 39, 64, 113, 113n. 3, 114, 114nn. 6, 9, 119n. 2, 121; on *commentariolus*, 269, 291; on Copernicus as follower of Marāgha, 268; on planetary distances, 241n. 9
Syria, 3
Syriac, manuscript (BN 346), 67; text, 42n. 22; tradition, 17; language, 51, 67

Tabriz, 118
al-Tabṣira fī al-hay'a (of Kharaqī), 37
al-Tadhkira fī 'ilm al-hay'a (of Ṭūsī), 34, 37, 38, 45n. 48, 47n. 54, 64n. 49, 118, 147, 154, 155, 263, 281, 288; commentary on, 34, (Khafri), 47n. 54, (Nīsābūrī), 45n. 51; in school curriculum, 34
Tadhkirat al-Mulūk, 47n. 60
ta'dīl al-nahār (equation of half daylight), 170
Taḥrīr al-majisṭī (Redaction of the Almagest) (of Ṭūsī), 74, 145, 147, 151, 274, 281; (composed in 1247), 155; contents of, 147-55
Taḥrīr al-wuṣūl ilā nihāyat al-sūl (of Ghars al-Dīn), 286
taḥwīl al-sana (defined), 71
Tāj al-azyāj (of Maghribī), 167, 230
Tāj al-Sharī'a (d. 1347), 278
takht (dustboard), 58
Ta'līq al-arṣād (Discourse on Observations, of Ibn al-Shāṭir), 10, 77, 233, 235, 239, 272

About the Author

George A. Saliba is Chairman of the Department of Middle East and Asian Languages and Cultures at Columbia University in the city of New York, and Professor of Arabic and Islamic Science at the same institution. He works mainly on the history of Arabic astronomy, with a special interest in the development of planetary theories. He has won many grants and awards from various organizations including the National Science Foundation and the National Endowment for the Humanities. His current research involves the extension of the survey presented in this book to include the centuries before the eleventh and after the fifteenth.